Access to Justice for Persons with Psychosocial Disabilities

Taking Kenya as a case study, this book examines the application of criminal procedure in the context of persons with psychosocial disabilities. It discusses how the right to participation of persons with psychosocial disabilities who have been declared unfit can be best protected during and after the criminal process in Africa and at the international level. In doing so, it hypothesises that the social model of disability is inadequate to respond to violations against the right to participation of persons with psychosocial disabilities in the criminal justice system and thus the need for other normative frameworks such as Foucauldian and decolonial theories. It recommends that legislative enactment and reform are imperative not only to promote participation in access to justice but also to remove the barriers inhibiting the legal capacity of persons with psychosocial disabilities. The study will encourage intercontinental dialogue on disability, unfitness declarations, and participation policy analysis, while also contributing to theory and legal development. The book will be of interest to academics, researchers, and policy-makers working in the areas of criminal procedure, disability studies, and international human rights law.

Paul Ochieng Juma is Lecturer in Law and Director, Center for Legal Aid and Clinical Legal Education, Kabarak University, Kenya.

Routledge Contemporary Issues in Criminal Justice and Procedure

Series Editor Ed Johnston

Associate Professor of Criminal Justice and Procedure at the University of Northampton, UK

Contemporary Challenges in the Jury System
A Comparative Perspective
Nicola Monaghan

Implementation of Rights for Crime Victims in Theory and Practice
Lessons from India
Anupama Sharma

Justifying Punishment
Perspectives from Post-Communist Europe
Edited by Jakub Drápal

International Perspectives of Neuroscience in the Youth Justice Courtroom
Edited by Hannah Wishart and Ray Arthur

Poor Defence Lawyering in Criminal Proceedings
A Comparative View
Edited by Ashlee Beazley, Michele Panzavolta and Andrew Sanders

The Digital Courtroom
Participation, Attendance, Engagement and Consumption
Lisa Flower

Justice Denied: Exploring Inequities in the Legal System
Edited by Ed Johnston and Claire-Michelle Smyth

Access to Justice for Persons with Psychosocial Disabilities
A Comparative Analysis of Participation in the Kenyan Criminal Justice System
Paul Ochieng Juma

See more at https://www.routledge.com/Routledge-Research-in-Legal-History/book-series/CONTEMPCJP

Access to Justice for Persons with Psychosocial Disabilities

A Comparative Analysis of Participation in the Kenyan Criminal Justice System

Paul Ochieng Juma

Routledge
Taylor & Francis Group
LONDON AND NEW YORK

First published 2026
by Routledge
4 Park Square, Milton Park, Abingdon, Oxon OX14 4RN

and by Routledge
605 Third Avenue, New York, NY 10158

Routledge is an imprint of the Taylor & Francis Group, an informa business

British Library Cataloguing-in-Publication Data
A catalogue record for this book is available from the British Library

Library of Congress Cataloging-in-Publication Data
Names: Juma, Paul Ochieng author
Title: Access to justice for persons with psychosocial disabilities : a comparative analysis of participation in the Kenyan criminal justice system / Paul Ochieng Juma.
Description: Abingdon, Oxon [UK] ; New York, NY : Routledge, 2025. | Series: Routledge contemporary issues in criminal justice and procedure | Includes bibliographical references and index.
Identifiers: LCCN 2025039666 (print) | LCCN 2025039667 (ebook) | ISBN 9781041088165 hardback | ISBN 9781041088196 paperback | ISBN 9781003647102 ebook
Subjects: LCSH: Offenders with mental disabilities—Legal status, laws, etc.—Kenya | Mentally ill offenders—Services for—Kenya | Insanity (Law)—Kenya | Mental health laws—Kenya. | Defense (Criminal procedure)—Kenya | Criminal justice, Administration of—Kenya | Legal assistance to people with disabilities—Kenya | People with disabilities—Legal status, laws, etc.—Kenya | International law and human rights—Kenya | LCGFT: Law materials
Classification: LCC KSK518 .J86 2025 (print) | LCC KSK518 (ebook) | DDC 362.2096762—dc23/eng/20250825
LC record available at https://lccn.loc.gov/2025039666
LC ebook record available at https://lccn.loc.gov/2025039667

ISBN: 978-1-041-08816-5 (hbk)
ISBN: 978-1-041-08819-6 (pbk)
ISBN: 978-1-003-64710-2 (ebk)

DOI: 10.4324/9781003647102

Typeset in Galliard
by Apex CoVantage, LLC

Data availability statement: The participants of this study did not give written consent for their data to be shared publicly, so due to the sensitive nature of the research, supporting data is not available.

This book is dedicated to all those who hope to awaken and strengthen an understanding of the human rights of persons with disabilities in Africa. You must win! Continue working, continue saving, continue sacrificing, continue enduring, continue fighting cheerfully and do your utmost as if the issue of the whole struggle depends on you alone.

Contents

Preface

This book appraises the adequacy of the social model of disability in responding to violations of declarations of unfitness during plea and proceedings (unfitness declarations) against persons with psychosocial disabilities in Kenya's criminal justice system. The volume hypothesises that the social model of disability is inadequate to respond to violations against the right to participation of persons with psychosocial disabilities in Kenya's criminal justice system.

The study argues that unfitness declarations violate the right of persons with psychosocial disabilities to participate in access to justice. It explores the legal framework of the declarations, the effects or consequences of unfitness declarations, possible causal factors of unfitness declarations, intervention strategies, and the different ways in which they can be reformed. These themes cannot be addressed solely by the social model of disability because it leaves many gaps in the holistic understanding of disability and society. I argue that the social model of disability is limited because it does not adequately address mental disabilities.

Taking into account the limitations of the social model of disability, this book draws from a syncretic archive of knowledge and normative frameworks such as the Foucauldian and decolonial theories of disability. The theories are employed because they focus more on the body thus shaping the discourse on mental impairment by seeking new ways and more progressive forms of action in the realisation of disabled persons' rights. The Foucauldian theory is a useful discourse for reforming the law on unfitness declarations in Kenya by improving the agency and visibility of persons with psychosocial disabilities. Decolonial theory serves to ensure that reforms of unfitness declarations are responsive to the legacy of colonial ideology and governance. The author also employed empirical research, to interrogate the factors that inhibit the participation of persons with psychosocial disabilities in Kenya's criminal justice system, which revealed that unfitness declarations are caused by attitudinal, social, and cultural factors. Accordingly, this book recommends that legislative enactment and reform are imperative not only to promote participation in access to justice but also to remove the barriers inhibiting the legal capacity of persons with psychosocial disabilities.

Acknowledgements

I would like to express my heartfelt gratitude to the late Professor Charles Ngwena and Professor Michael Ashley Stein for their brilliant intellectual guidance during the preparation of this book. Through their guidance, they have assisted me attain a foothold on the academic ladder as a disability rights academic.

Abbreviations and acronyms

AAMD	American Association on Mental Deficiency
AAMR	American Association on Mental Retardation
ACHR	American Convention on Human Rights
ADA	Americans with Disabilities Act
ADHD	Attention deficit hyperactivity disorder
ADR	Alternative Dispute Resolution
African Charter	African Charter on Human and Peoples' Rights
African Disability Protocol	Protocol to the African Charter on Human and Peoples' Rights on the Rights of Persons with Disabilities in Africa
ALRC	Australian Law Reform Commission
AU	African Union
AOT	Assisted Outpatient Treatment
APA	American Psychiatric Association
APCOF	African Policing Civilian Oversight Forum
CAT	United Nations Convention against Torture and Cruel, Inhuman and Degrading Treatment or Punishment
CCRP	Code of Criminal Procedure (Estonia)
CEDAW	United Nations Convention on the Elimination of all forms of Discrimination against Women
CERD	Convention on the Elimination of all forms of Racial Discrimination
CJRA	Criminal Justice Reform Act (Singapore)
CLA	Criminal Lunatics Act
CPA	Criminal Procedure Act (South Africa)
CRC	Convention on the Rights of the Child
CRPD	Convention on the Rights of Persons with Disabilities
DPO	Disabled Persons Organisations
DSM	Diagnostic Statistical Manuals
DTC	Drug Treatment Courts
European Convention	European Convention for the Protection of Human Rights and Fundamental Freedoms
ECtHR	European Court of Human Rights

FGD	Focus Group Discussion
First Protocol	Convention for the Protection of Human Rights and Fundamental Freedoms
GFCC	Federal Constitutional Court of Germany
HALT Act	Humane Alternatives to Long-Term Solitary Confinement Act (New York)
HRC	Human Rights Committee
ICCPR	International Covenant on Civil and Political Rights
ICD	International Classification of Disease
IIED	International Institute for Environment and Development
IQ	Intelligence Quotient
JCBB	Judiciary Criminal Procedure Bench Book
LSK	Law Society of Kenya
MHC	Mental Health Court
MI Principles	Principles for the Protection of Persons with Mental Illness and the Improvement of Mental Health Care
MMR	Mixed Method Research
NALEAP	National Legal Aid and Awareness Programme
NCAJ	National Council on Administration of Justice
NCCJR	National Council on Administration of Justice Committee on Criminal Justice Reform
NCPWD	National Council for Persons with Disabilities
NDFPWD	National Development Fund for Persons with Disabilities
NGEC	National Gender and Equality Commission
NGO	Non-governmental Organisations
NI Act	Mental Capacity Act (Northern Ireland)
OHCHR	Office of the High Commissioner for Human Rights
ODPP	Office of the Director of Public Prosecutions
TJ	Therapeutic Jurisprudence
UK	United Kingdom
UN	United Nations
Universal Declaration	Universal Declaration of Human Rights
UPIAS	Union of the Physically Impaired against Segregation
US	United States of America
VLRC	Victorian Law Reform Commission
WHO	World Health Organisation

Table of cases

Table of legislation

1 Introduction and background

1.0 Introduction

Declarations of unfitness during plea and proceedings (unfitness declarations) are a fundamental component of many criminal legal systems around the globe, including Kenya.[1] The administration of criminal justice involves the institutional architecture, the procedures and apparatus used to process, adjudicate and ultimately decide criminal cases.[2] Unfitness declarations are orders, which are issued as part of the criminal process to determine whether an accused person with a psychosocial disability has the capacity to proceed with a criminal trial.[3] It is a judicial determination on whether a person has the ability under law to carry out a specific act or series of acts.[4] They are the criteria used by clinicians in order to determine the ability of an accused person with a psychosocial disability to participate in courtroom proceedings.[5] This is different from non-criminally responsible based verdicts, which are issued when persons who have been charged with the commission of crimes are acquitted after being found not criminally responsible on account of mental disability.

This book focuses on psychosocial disability and not intellectual disability. However, the discourse has relevance to mental disability in general which encompasses both psychosocial and intellectual disability. Disability relates to people, their living settings, nature of their treatment, and personality traits that define how they live with barriers and not the disease with which they are suffering from.[6] Psychosocial disability is produced by the social environment

1 L Anker et al. 'Fitness to stand trial: a general principle of European criminal law?' (2011) 7 *Utrecht Law Review* 120.

2 G Hezel *Judging civil justice* (2010) 17–24.

3 As above.

4 D Miller 'Dementia and competency in United States courtrooms: a case law review' https://academicworks.cuny.edu/cgi/viewcontent.cgi?article=1157&context=jj_etds (accessed 10 September 2021) 13.

5 P Brown et al. 'Fitness to plead: development and validation of a standardised assessment instrument' (2018) 13(4) *PLoS One* 1.

6 N Sartorius 'Disability and mental illness are different entities and should be assessed separately' (2009) 8 *World Psychiatry* 1.

DOI: 10.4324/9781003647102-1

that presents barriers to the equality of persons with psychosocial disabilities with others.[7] Psychosocial disabilities affect a person's feelings and behaviour.[8] They are not permanent but maybe episodic or cyclical.[9] However, intellectual disability is a permanent learning deficit, which is present from birth and will be evident before adulthood.[10] It was previously referred to as 'mental retardation'.[11] Persons with intellectual disabilities are at risk of developing psychosocial disabilities.[12]

According to the Convention on the Rights of Persons with Disabilities (CRPD),[13] the existence of a disability alone is not a justification for the deprivation of legal capacity.[14] Legal capacity is not related to mental disability that results in the inability of persons to understand or direct their actions.[15] Article 12 of the CRPD recognises that disabled persons[16] are 'persons before the law' and have legal capacity on an equal basis with others.[17]

The law on unfitness declarations in Kenya's criminal justice system is based on the mental capacity of an accused person with psychosocial disability, which is used to determine legal capacity.[18] It is important to note the difference between legal capacity and mental capacity. Legal capacity means the ability of a person to hold rights and duties and to exercise those rights and duties within the framework of a legal system, while mental capacity denotes the ability to make decisions.[19] Legal capacity relates to the ability of persons not

7 As above.

8 Inclusion Europe & Mental Health Europe 'The differences between mental illness and intellectual disability' https://bapid.com/pdf/razliki_en.pdf (accessed 27 August 2021).

9 Government of Western Australia 'Operational instruction 10: prisoners with disabilities' https://www.correctiveservices.wa.gov.au/_files/prisons/adult-custodial-rules/operational-instructions/oi-10.pdf (accessed 27 August 2021) 1.

10 Inclusion Europe & Mental Health Europe (n 8).

11 R Lakhan 'The coexistence of psychiatric disorders and intellectual disability in children aged 3–18 years in the Barwani district, India' (2013) *International Scholarly Research Notices* 1.

12 National Mental Health Consumer & Carer Forum 'Issue: Intellectual/developmental disability (ID) and mental health' (2012) 1.

13 Convention on the Rights of Persons with Disabilities (CRPD) Adopted on 13 December 2006 UN Doc A/61/611 (entered into force on 3 May 2008).

14 European Union Agency for Fundamental Rights *Legal capacity of persons with intellectual disabilities and persons with mental health problems* European Union Agency for Fundamental Rights (2013) 7.

15 European Union Agency for Fundamental Rights (n 14) 14.

16 In this study the term 'disabled persons' is used in a specific sense to mean the socio-construction of the phenomenon of disability as opposed to the physical or mental impairments. It implies that disability is created by a socio-economic environment that does not accommodate physical or mental impairments.

17 European Union Agency for Fundamental Rights (n 14) 8.

18 A Wambulwa 'Explainer: What "fit to stand trial" means' 21 December 2019 https://www.the-star.co.ke/news/2019-12-21-explainer-what-fit-to-stand-trial-means/ (accessed 12 April 2021).

19 CRPD Committee General Comment 1: Article 12: Equal recognition before the law (2014) UN Doc CRPD/C/GC/1 dated 19 May 2014 par 12.

only to have, but also to act on the basis of their legally recognised rights and duties on an equal basis with others, while mental capacity is simply a person's putative psychological ability which varies from one individual to another.[20]

In Kenya, legal capacity is generally applied to persons who have attained the age of majority, which is pegged at 18 years.[21] However, this is not the position adopted for persons with psychosocial disabilities who are treated as objects of pity who cannot exercise their right to participate in the society, including in the criminal justice system.[22] Mental capacity determines whether accused persons with psychosocial disabilities will proceed with the trial, be granted an opportunity to defend themselves, and instruct an advocate.[23] All these determinations go to constrain the right of participation for persons with psychosocial disabilities, which is not only a recognised right under Kenya's domestic law, but also in international law.

The procedure on unfitness declarations violates the right of persons with psychosocial disabilities to participate in access to justice. Often, persons with psychosocial disabilities are not able to participate effectively in the criminal justice sector because of the procedural barriers following unfitness to plead declarations.[24] Unfitness declarations are criminal processes. Criminal procedural rules are instruments for the implementation of rights that are recognised and protected under substantive laws. According to Jeremy Bentham, evidence and judgements are connected by procedural rules.[25] Procedural rules, according to Robert Allen Sedler, are meant to guide judges in the application of substantive law, analysis of relevant evidence and when making determinations of law and facts.[26] Through procedural rules, the society is able to participate effectively in court. Therefore, effective access to justice requires that every individual who is engaged in criminal proceedings be accorded fair procedural rules.[27] Proper enforcement of substantive rights can only be guaranteed through fair procedural rules. Participation in access to justice of persons with psychosocial disabilities was alien to Kenya's legal system at the time of the promulgation of the Criminal Procedure Code in 1963.

Unfitness declarations are not designed with the needs and interests of persons with psychosocial disabilities in mind. They can be raised by any member

20 W Holness & S Rule 'Legal capacity of parties with intellectual, psycho-social and communication disabilities in traditional courts in KwaZulu-Natal' (2018) 6 *African Disability Rights Yearbook* 41.

21 Age of Majority Act Cap 33, Laws of Kenya, sec 2.

22 Kenya National Commission on Human Rights & the Open Society Initiative for Eastern Africa *How to implement article 12 of convention on the rights of persons with disabilities regarding legal capacity in Kenya: a briefing paper* KNHCR (2012) 16.

23 Wambulwa (n 18).

24 S Ortoleva 'Inaccessible justice: human rights, persons with disabilities and the legal system' (2011) 17 *ILSA Journal of International & Comparative Law* 282.

25 J Bentham in Hezel (n 2) 13.

26 RA Sedler *The Ethiopian civil procedure* (1986) 1.

27 Hezel (n 2) 17–24.

of the court when there is *bona fide* doubt as to the accused person's competency without due regard to their participation. Mental assessment reports are discriminatory as they only apply to persons with psychosocial disabilities.[28] Accused persons with psychosocial disabilities are not afforded an opportunity to participate during unfitness hearings. Unfitness declaration orders are made on the basis of documentary evidence, without hearing from the accused persons with disabilities thus, resulting into a breach of the principle of adversarial proceedings.[29]

The exclusion of persons with psychosocial disabilities from unfitness hearings makes it impossible for them either in person or through their representatives to challenge the experts' report recommending their unfitness status.[30] They are also precluded from scrutinising the allegations before the court due to their automatic indefinite detention in prisons and mental institutions following unfitness declarations without any procedural safeguards. Under Kenyan law, most accused persons with psychosocial disabilities are excluded from participating in the criminal process and instead are detained arbitrarily under sections 162 and 167 of the Criminal Procedure Code.[31] Their detention is solely based on the nature of their disability without considering any available alternatives and support mechanisms to ensure their legal capacity thus amounting to violations of their right to participation.[32]

Other than procedural barriers, persons with psychosocial disabilities also face attitudinal, social, and cultural barriers in Kenya's criminal justice process. These barriers relate to the attitude of judicial officers and lawyers towards persons with psychosocial disabilities. Judicial officers and lawyers in Kenya have a perception that persons with psychosocial disabilities are not capable of participating in criminal proceedings due to their impairment.[33] Social norms do not recognise persons with psychosocial disabilities as right holders because of the nature of their disabilities.[34] An accused person with a history of mental disability, will be subjected to several mental examinations before he or she can be declared fit or unfit to stand trial.[35] The condition of schizophrenia has led

28 Users & Survivors of Psychiatry in Kenya (USP-K) *Advancing the rights of persons with psychosocial disability in Kenya* USP-K (2017) 16.

29 *Shtukaturov v Russia* (2008) ECtHR, para 73.

30 *Salontaji-Drobnjak v Serbia* (2009) ECtHR, para 127.

31 Criminal Procedure Code, Cap 75 of 1930 (Laws of Kenya).

32 B McSherry et al. *Unfitness to plead and indefinite detention of persons with cognitive disabilities: addressing the legal barriers and creating appropriate alternative supports in the community* Melbourne: Melbourne Social Equity Institute, University of Melbourne (2017) 26.

33 Article 48 Initiative (A48), Arthur's Dream Autism Trust (ADAT) & Southern Africa Litigation Centre *An exploratory study of the interaction between the criminal justice system and persons with intellectual and psychosocial disabilities in Nairobi, Kenya* (September 2021) 75.

34 UNICEF *Breaking down barriers: equitable access to justice for children with disabilities* UNICEF (2020) 8.

35 *Republic v GKN* (2018) eKLR.

to an accused being denied his or her right to participate because the court formed an opinion that the accused was of unsound mind and thus unable to understand the proceedings.[36]

Unsoundness of mind automatically results in accused persons being stripped of their legal capacity to participate in criminal trials and declared incapable of giving their defence.[37] Shouting in court is perceived as a sign of mental instability and will lead to an accused person being subjected to a mental assessment.[38] An accused person who at the time of examination cannot tell the time and hears voices or hallucinates is unfit to stand trial.[39] These perceptions affect not only the legal capacity of persons with psychosocial disabilities, but also how they participate in Kenya's justice sector. Such stigmatising attitude is what leads to persons with psychosocial disabilities being excluded from Kenya's criminal justice system.[40] The label of unfitness diminishes the ability of persons with psychosocial disabilities to act on their own capacity and contributes to the risk of stereotyping, objectification, and other forms of exclusion, which people with psychosocial disabilities disproportionately face in Kenya's criminal justice system.[41]

Recognition of violations of unfitness declarations on the part of states around the globe is not new. The social model of disability regards unfitness declarations as a widespread and serious problem.[42] The construction of unfitness declarations involves a number of themes, including the framework of the declarations, the effects or consequences of unfitness declarations, possible causal factors, intervention strategies and the different ways in which they can be reformed. However, these themes cannot be addressed solely by the social model of disability. One of the limitations of the social model lies in its origins. It is not really a theory but an approach and a praxis that was championed by middle-class activists who were wheelchair users.[43] Its main proponents were members of the Union of the Physically Impaired against Segregation (UPIAS), which originated in 1972 in the United Kingdom.[44]

36 *Republic v GKN.*

37 *Charles Mwangi Muraya v Republic* (2001) eKLR.

38 *Nyawa Mwajowa v Republic* (2016) eKLR.

39 *Charles Mwangi Muraya v Republic.*

40 G Barbaresch et al. '"When they see a wheelchair, they've not even seen me" – factors shaping the experience of disability stigma and discrimination in Kenya' (2021) 18 *International Journal of Environmental Research & Public Health* 1.

41 Council of Europe *Who gets to decide? Right to legal capacity for persons with intellectual and psychosocial disabilities* Council of Europe Publishing (2012) 12.

42 J Beqiraj et al. *Access to justice for persons with disabilities: From international principles to practice* International Bar Association (2017) 32.

43 C Ngwena 'Developing juridical method for overcoming status subordination in disablism: the place of transformative epistemologies' (2014) 30 *South African Journal of Human Rights* 283.

44 M Berghs et al. 'Do disabled people need a stronger social model: a social model of human rights?' (2019) 34 *Disability & Society* 1034.

Original members of UPIAS were Mike Oliver, Paul Hunt, Vic Finkelstein, and Ken and Maggie Davis who were all physically impaired.[45]

According to UPIAS, the foundation of the social model of disability is constituted by the binary distinction of disability and impairment/illness. On the one hand, impairment occurs when an individual lack either all, part, or has a defect on a limb, organ, or mechanism of the body. Disability on the other hand, was defined in terms of the society that takes little or no account of persons with physical impairments thus, creating an exclusive environment that constricts their ability to participate in mainstream social activities.[46] From this, it has been argued that the social model seeks only to interpret disability in materialistic terms without focusing on explanations regarding different bodily impairments and how they cause disability.[47] It was primarily developed to serve the environmental barriers experienced by persons with physical disabilities who can function like their enabled counterparts if the barriers are removed. When it was popularised, the model arrived divorced from its Marxist origins. In its beginnings, it had nothing to say about the body, especially the mental body. Also, it had nothing to say about the Global South and its colonial history. For these reasons, the social model leaves many gaps in the holistic understanding of disability and society. Therefore, there is need for drawing on other normative frameworks such as the Foucauldian[48] and decolonial[49] theories of disability.

1.1 Background

According to the common law tradition, no person should stand trial or be punished for an alleged offence unless they have the mental capacity to defend themselves and to commit the offence respectively.[50] One of the basis for this common law principle is the right to fair trial, which entitles all accused persons to participate in legal proceedings.[51]

The concept of unfitness declarations was transplanted to Kenya by force through colonisation.[52] Kenya was declared a Crown colony in 1920.[53] When

45 As above.

46 Union of the Physically Impaired Against Segregation *Fundamental principles of disability* (1976) 3.

47 Ngwena (n 43) 283.

48 H Baxter, 'Bringing Foucault into law and law into Foucault' (1996) 48 *Stanford Law Review* 449; J Nickolas 'Law and power: ten lessons from Foucault' (2018) 30 *Bond Law Review* 31.

49 H Meekosha 'Decolonising disability: thinking and acting globally' (2011) 26 *Disability & Society* 668; SA Nixon et al. 'Using postcolonial perspectives to consider rehabilitation with children with disabilities: the Bamenda-Toronto dialogue' (2015) 2 *Disability and the Global South* 571.

50 *Republic v GKN.*

51 Anker et al. (n 1) 120.

52 JF Sandra 'The evolution of the common law: legal developments in Kenya and India' (2006) 68 *Political Science Faculty Publications* 3.

53 As above.

the country attained independence in 1963, it inherited the colonial legal system, including the common law of England. Kenya's sources of law include the substance of the common law, the doctrines of equity and the statutes of general application in force in England on 12 August 1897, and the procedure and practice observed in courts of justice in England at that date.[54] Unfitness declarations are part of the common law of England and were being used as tools of domination against the indigenous Africans of Kenya.[55] Despite them being previously unknown and not representing the interest of the indigenous people, unfitness declarations were aimed at regulating their activities, denying them justice, and detaining them indefinitely in prisons.[56]

Article 2(5) of the Constitution of the Republic of Kenya 2010 (the Constitution) recognises international law as a source of law in Kenya. It provides that the 'general rules of international law shall form part of the law of Kenya'.[57] It means that Kenya has adopted the monist approach to international law. The monist approach regards international law and national law as part of a single legal order where international law is directly applicable in the national legal order without the need for any act of domestic incorporation.[58] However, legislative practice in Kenya suggests that domestic implementing legislation is nonetheless adopted in regards to specific treaties.[59] Kenya has adopted the Persons with Disabilities Act[60] in regards to domesticating the CRPD.

Historically, participation was mainly viewed from the perspective of political rights. Participation as popularly perceived was represented within the traditional notions of state sovereignty.[61] Prior to the Second World War, individuals were not viewed as subjects of rights and duties under international law.[62] Therefore, individuals were not allowed to vindicate their rights directly on the basis of a special international agreement.[63] After the Second World War, events such as the Nuremberg Trials, the founding of the United Nations (UN), and the passage of the Universal Declaration of Human Rights (Universal Declaration)[64] by the UN General Assembly in 1948 led to the recognition of individuals as subjects of rights and duties under international

54 Judicature Act 14 of 1977, sec 3.
55 Sandra (n 52) 3.
56 As above.
57 Constitution of the Republic of Kenya, 2010, art 2(5).
58 TP Van Reenen & H Combrinck 'The UN Convention on the Rights of Persons with Disabilities in Africa: progress after 5 years' (2011) 8 *International Journal on Human Rights* 145.
59 *David Njoroge Macharia v Republic* (2011) eKLR, para 45.
60 Persons with Disabilities Act (Act 14 of 2003), Laws of Kenya.
61 GH Fox 'The right to political participation in international law' (1992) 17 *Yale Journal of International Law* 544.
62 Fox (n 61) 545.
63 As above.
64 Universal Declaration of Human Rights (adopted 10 December 1948 UNGA Res 217 A(III) (UDHR), art 20.

law.[65] However, certain specific rights such as participatory rights emerged only after the development of the International Covenant on Civil and Political Rights (ICCPR) and with limitations.[66] Regrettably, even with the development of the right to participation, disabled persons were not listed among the groups explicitly protected against discrimination in the ICCPR and other later post-war human rights instruments that make up the International Bill of Rights.[67]

The right to participation in the context of access to justice is a fundamental human right guaranteed under international human rights law. It is protected under international and regional human rights instruments, including the Universal Declaration, the ICCPR, the Convention on the Rights of the Child (CRC),[68] the CRPD, the European Convention on Human Rights (European Convention),[69] the African Charter on Human and Peoples' Rights (African Charter),[70] and Protocol to the African Charter on Human and Peoples' Rights on the Rights of Persons with Disabilities in Africa (African Disability Protocol).[71] According to article 25 of the ICCPR, the right to participation is not an absolute right. It allows for limitation of the right to participation based on 'reasonable and objective' criteria. In fact, while it is considered unreasonable to restrict participation rights of persons with physical disabilities, General Comment 25 to the ICCPR permits restrictions based on 'established mental incapacity'.[72] Kenya acceded to the ICCPR in 1972.

The ICCPR contrasts with the CRPD which does not foresee any limitation to participation rights. The CRPD serves as an acknowledgement that the broad protections of the Universal Declaration and ICCPR were not designed to address needs and barriers of disabled persons thus, their limited utility in ensuring participation in access to justice.[73] It calls on states parties to not only protect disabled persons from discrimination, through 'negative rights',

65 Fox (n 61) 545.

66 International Covenant on Civil and Political Rights (adopted 16 December 1966, entered into force 23 March 1976) 999 UNTS 171 (ICCPR), art 21.

67 L Series 'The development of disability rights under international law: from charity to human rights' (2015) 30 *Disability & Society* 158.

68 Convention on the Rights of the Child, 20 November 1989 1577 UNTS. 3; 28 I.L.M 1456 (1989), art 15.

69 Convention for the Protection of Human Rights and Fundamental Freedoms (European Convention on Human Rights, as amended) ETS. No. 5, art 11.

70 African Charter on Human and Peoples' Rights (adopted 27 June 1981, entered into force 21 October 1986) (1982) 21 ILM 58 (African Charter), art 11.

71 Protocol to the African Charter on Human and Peoples' Rights on the Rights of Persons with Disabilities in Africa (African Disability Protocol), adopted on 29 January 2018, entered into force on 5 May 2024.

72 UN Human Rights Committee (HRC) General Comment 25: The right to participate in public affairs, voting rights and the right of equal access to public service (Art. 25) 12/07/96 CCPR/C/21/Rev.1/Add.7, para 4.

73 A Raub et al. 'Constitutional rights of persons with disabilities: an analysis of 193 national constitutions' (2016) 29 *Harvard Human Rights Journal* 237.

but to also take positive measures to ensure their rights to live, work, and engage with their societies on equal terms as their non-disabled peers.[74] For example, article 29 guarantees the right of every disabled person to political participation, including persons with psychosocial disabilities. There is neither limitation nor restriction provided for under article 29. Therefore, apart from affirming the right to participation for persons with psychosocial disabilities, the CRPD recognises their freedom to be involved in all aspects of life, including certain specific areas of state action besides politics, such as access to justice. International courts have started to give recognition to the participation of persons with psychosocial disabilities in court proceedings.

In *Shtukaturov v Russia* the appellant was stripped of his legal capacity in domestic judicial proceedings without his participation. The European Court of Human Rights (ECtHR) held that persons with mental disabilities must have access to a court and the opportunity to be heard in person or through any form of legal representation.[75] Similarly, in the case of *Zagidulina v Russia*[76] the court made an order for the applicant to be hospitalised in her absence. However, in attendance were the prosecutor, a psychiatrist, and a representative of a psychiatric hospital. The ECtHR emphasised the need to ensure the applicant's right to be heard.[77] In *Proshkin v Russia*[78] the ECtHR stated that

> although not having an absolute character, the right of being heard enjoys such a prominent place in a democratic society and has such a fundamental value for the protection of an individual against arbitrariness on the part of public authorities, that the mere fact of the individual suffering from a mental illness, as well as his being declared legally incapacitated, cannot automatically lead to the exclusion of the exercise of that right altogether. It is the very weakness of a mentally ill defendant which should enhance the need for supporting his rights. In this context, authorities must show requisite diligence in ensuring the accused's right to be present in an effective manner and must act particularly carefully when infringing upon that right, so as not to place the mentally ill at a disadvantage when compared with other defendants who do enjoy such a right.[79]

In *Proshkin*, the applicant had been detained in a psychiatric hospital solely on the basis of the doctor's examination. The ECtHR ruled that the participation of the applicant is key and that even the presence of the applicant's defence counsel and mother cannot compensate for the applicant's inability to present

74 As above.
75 *Shtukaturov v Russia*, para 73.
76 *Zagidulina v Russia* (2013) ECtHR.
77 *Zagidulina v Russia*, para 62.
78 *Proshkin v Russia* (2012) ECtHR.
79 *Proshkin v Russia*, para 102.

his own arguments in court.[80] In *Romanov v Russia*,[81] the applicant after being declared incompetent, was excluded from participating in court proceedings because under the law, the Russian remand centre was not obligated to bring him to court. Moreover, the testimony of a person who had been declared incompetent was not admissible. The ECtHR faulted state authorities for failing to take any steps to secure the applicant's attendance at the hearings.[82] What these cases establish is that mental disability cannot be used to automatically deny a person the right to participate in a trial.[83]

On 19 May 2008, Kenya ratified the CRPD.[84] The CRPD has partly adopted a social model of disability that regards the state and societal practices and attitudes as the disabler rather than a person's disability.[85] It highlights the need to actively remove obstacles to, and to promote, the full and equal enjoyment of human rights by persons with psychosocial disabilities.[86] The CRPD obliges states parties to provide the appropriate enabling environment so that disabled persons can fully enjoy their rights on an equal basis with others.[87]

Therefore, the objective of the principle of participation is to engage disabled persons in the wider society when making decisions that will affect them.[88] Under the CRPD, the right to participation in the context of access to justice rights is contained in article 13. States parties are obliged to safeguard and promote the realisation of the right of access to justice, including for those who are found unfit to plead, by taking a range of steps listed in article 13. The steps include provision of procedural and age-appropriate accommodations in order to facilitate their effective role as direct and indirect participants in access to justice. State parties are also required to provide training to those working in the administration of justice in order to help ensure effective access to justice for disabled people.[89] In essence, article 13 is an extension of the principles stated in previous UN human rights conventions such as the ICCPR.

80 *Proshkin v Russia*, para 104.

81 *Romanov v Russia* (2005) ECtHR.

82 *Romanov v Russia*, para 109.

83 Y Vasyl et al. 'Mental health of a person as a criterion of personal participation in the trial during criminal proceedings' (2020) LXXIII *Wiadomości Lekarskie* 2739.

84 Office of the High Commissioner for Human Rights 'Ratification status for CRPD' http://tbinter net.ohchr.org/_layouts/TreatyBodyExternal/Treaty.aspx?Treaty=CRPD&Lang=en (accessed 17 June 2021).

85 J Stavert 'Paradigm shift or paradigm paralysis? National mental health and capacity law and implementing the CRPD in Scotland' (2018) 7 *Laws* 2.

86 As above.

87 United Nations 'Chapter 2: the convention in detail – the rights and principles enumerated in the Convention' https://www.un.org/development/desa/disabilities/resources/handbook-for-parliamentarians-on-the-convention-on-the-rights-of-persons-with-disabilities/chapter-two-the-convention-in-detail–3.html (accessed 12 April 2021).

88 As above.

89 As above.

Other than being guaranteed in the CRPD and the abovementioned instruments, the right of participation in access to justice is also provided for in a majority of national constitutions, including the Constitution of Kenya. Article 48 provides that 'the State shall ensure access to justice for all persons and, if any fee is required, it shall be reasonable and shall not impede access to justice'.[90] The phrase 'all persons' includes disabled persons. It signifies that everyone, including disabled persons, are entitled to the rights and freedoms recognised under article 48 of the Constitution.

The obligation of the state to ensure that disabled persons participate at the same level stems from article 27(1) of the Constitution, which provides that every citizen is equal before the law and has the right to equal protection and equal benefit of the law.[91] Article 54 of the Constitution emphasises the participation of disabled persons as follows:

> A person with any disability is entitled-a) to be treated with dignity and respect and to be addressed and referred to in a manner that is not demeaning. b) to access educational institutions and facilities for persons with disabilities that are integrated into society to the extent compatible with the interests of the person; c) to reasonable access to all places, public transport, and information; d) to use sign language, Braille, or other appropriate means of communication; e) to access material and devices to overcome constraints arising from the person's disability.

From the language of the Constitution, participation rights of disabled persons are guaranteed rights and not aspirational rights. Aspirational rights are either phrased in non-authoritative language, listed as non-enforceable goals for example when the enforcement of the right is subject to the state's abilities or resources, or when the Constitution contains an article that states that particular rights are non-enforceable.[92] Terms used in this category include 'promote', 'endeavours to', or 'directs its policy towards'. Guaranteed rights are phrased unambiguously or imposes duties or obligations on the part of the state.[93] In the case of the Constitution, the use of the term 'entitled' in the participation of disabled persons implies that the right is guaranteed. Therefore, disabled persons have a right on an equal basis with others, to effective access to justice at all phases of the administration of justice, and to be direct and indirect participants, including being witnesses to receive procedural and age-appropriate accommodations to facilitate access to justice.[94]

90 Constitution of the Republic of Kenya 2010, art 48.

91 Constitution of the Republic of Kenya 2010, art 27(1).

92 Raub et al. (n 73) 213.

93 As above.

94 A Roomaney 'Assessing the right to physical access to justice, for persons with disabilities' LLM Dissertation, University of the Western Cape, 2014, 16.

The principle of participation is an essential component of democracy and a vehicle for the exercise of many other civil, cultural, economic, political, and social rights. In discharging its legal obligation, the state must ensure that the right to participate for disabled persons is taken into account. This is because it is the custodian of the people's rights, including the right to participation. The Constitution's preamble affirms this by providing that: We, the people of Kenya – recognising the aspirations of all Kenyans for a government based on the essential values of human rights, equality, freedom, democracy, social justice, and the rule of law.[95]

However, in spite of its importance, the actual exercise of the right to participation by persons with psychosocial disabilities in the context of the right of access to justice in Kenya exist only on paper and not 'in vivo', in realistic environments and with support.[96] Failure of the state to fulfil its obligations defeats the purpose of article 13 of the CRPD. Disability is a human rights issue.[97] In Kenya, unfitness declarations are among the disabling legal barriers.[98] They hinder persons with psychosocial disabilities from participating in the criminal justice system.[99]

The social model of disability assumes that disability is caused by the society and that it can be solved by the removal of societal and environmental barriers. However, such assumption neglects the body and the shifting power dynamics among disabled persons and between disabled persons and the state. The social model of disability is a useful political tool for the mobilisation of a movement. However, this materialistic-based framework is inadequate and unless it is supplemented, political action will continue to be based on an incomplete picture of disability. Central to this argument is the social model's refusal to engage with the body and its ignorance of how power relations among disabled persons and between them and the government can influence disability within the society. This runs the danger of continuing to exclude the participation of various groups such as persons with psychosocial disabilities. Therefore, the power dynamics among persons with psychosocial disabilities and between persons with psychosocial disabilities and the state should be investigated so as to determine whether persons with psychosocial disabilities who are generally classified as powerless fit this description or if there were some who were more powerful than others and, if so, in what ways. Understanding and addressing injustices and powerlessness can go a long way in

95 Constitution of the Republic of Kenya 2010, preamble.

96 As above.

97 L Waddington 'Disability: a human rights issue' (1994) 1 *Maastricht Journal of European & Comparative Law* 334.

98 E Flynn *Disabled justice? Access to justice and the UN Convention on the Rights of Persons with Disabilities* (2016) 11.

99 L Series & A Nilson 'Article 12 CRPD: equal recognition before the law' in I Bantekas et al. (eds) *The UN Convention on the Rights of Persons with Disabilities, a commentary* (2018) 357.

enhancing the participation of persons with psychosocial disabilities in Kenya's criminal justice system.[100]

Apart from the social model, the CRPD has also adopted a human rights approach to disability. According to Stein, the human rights approach extends human rights to individuals, such as persons with psychosocial disabilities who were previously excluded by the social model.[101] However, human rights instruments such as the CRPD are expressed with a high degree of abstraction thus lacking concrete content to adequately deal with specific issues such as unfitness declarations.[102] To bridge this gap, this book has employed Foucault and decolonial theories of power and coloniality respectively because they provide a cogent space for understanding the scope of the rights of persons with psychosocial disabilities under the CRPD vis-à-vis unfitness declaration laws. The theories also offer a rich and normative platform for appraising psychosocial disabilities in relation to the concept of unfitness. Therefore, the provisions of the CRPD combined with Foucault and decolonial theories have the potential of bringing about holistic reforms of unfitness declaration laws and empowerment of persons with psychosocial disability in Kenya's criminal justice system as discussed throughout this book.

However, based on the conventional understanding of the social model of disability, governments are seen to be reacting to fixed and identifiable barriers while ignoring legal framework reforms that should be used to ensure the participation of persons with psychosocial disabilities in Kenya's criminal justice system. The social model of disability not only constrains, but also enables the non-participation of persons with psychosocial disabilities in Kenya's criminal justice system. It theorises away the body thus resulting in a failure to interrogate disabled people's differences. Therefore, drawing upon the CRPD's provisions, Foucault's work, and the decolonial theory, this book engages in discursive analysis of unfitness declarations in Kenya's criminal justice system. Its objective is to interrogate the limitations of the social model of disability in understanding as well as remedying the human rights violations arising from unfitness declarations against persons with psychosocial disabilities in Kenya's criminal justice system.

1.2 Aims and objectives of this book

The main aim of this book is to interrogate the limitations of the social model of disability in responding to violations of unfitness declarations against persons with psychosocial disabilities in Kenya's criminal justice system. In order to develop more socially responsive normative standards for combating ableism

100 EL Nuwagaba & PN Rule 'Power dynamics among PWDs during adult learning processes: motivator or demotivator?' (2015) 3 *Rwandan Journal of Education* 53.

101 MA Stein 'Disability human rights' (2007) 95 *California Law Review* 62.

102 Stein (n 101) 30.

and realising the right to participation of persons with psychosocial disabilities in access to justice, it is necessary to go beyond the social model of disability so as to also include the Foucauldian and decolonial theories. The Foucauldian and decolonial theories are used to strengthen the social model of disability in order to fully and effectively guarantee the participation rights of persons with psychosocial disabilities in access to justice. In the purview of critical exploration, unfitness declarations are discussed in relation to social construction of psychosocial disability, human rights jurisprudence, and pertinent domestic legislation.

The volume examines the concept of psychosocial disability with a view of deconstructing the ideologies inherent in Kenya's unfitness declaration laws. It also offers insights into the historical underpinnings of psychosocial disability in Kenya. A pervasive, if not dominant, methodological approach in this study is the treatment of all norms, including psychosocial disability norms as socially constituted. Social norms are the producers of unfitness declaration knowledge. The incipient danger with socially embedded unfitness knowledge in post-colonial Kenya is that the society can instinctively claim it as its own in the absence of critical reflection. Without an attempt to critically appraise the germaneness of psychosocial disability norms, there will be contradictions in the quest for transformative goals.

The author supports the view that it is not possible to treat psychosocial disability as objective phenomena. The book does not in any way assume that psychosocial disability norms exists as a monolith, but, instead, concedes that they exist in a plural form and are always open to contestation. Different paradigms of thinking about psychosocial disability, each with its own implications for participation have emerged over time. The book proceeds on the premise that to enhance the participation of persons with psychosocial disability under the Constitution, and under legislation, it is essential to begin with an understanding about how society and the stratifications within society understand psychosocial disability.

The writer contends throughout the study that unfitness declaration laws do not carry inherently neutral values and certainly have no neutral centre. Ultimately, it is the social construction of psychosocial disability that holds the key to interrogating unfitness declaration norms in a serious manner and not merely restating what the legislature and the judiciary proclaim about the participation of persons with psychosocial disabilities. Against this backdrop, the book aligns itself with the Foucauldian and decolonial theories. It captures how shifting power dynamics in Kenya's criminal justice system can operate to support the participation of persons with psychosocial disabilities in Kenya's criminal justice system.

International human rights jurisprudence is also an integral part of this work to the extent that it can both illuminate as well as inform domestic norms on the participation of persons with psychosocial disabilities. The earlier discussion on the advent of the CRPD, sought, inter alia, to capture a paradigm shift in the participation in access to justice of persons with psychosocial disabilities.

The Kenyan Constitution is receptive to international human rights. Kenyan constitutional jurisprudence domesticates international human rights norms in various ways by complementing, concretising, and even substantively expanding upon fundamental rights that are guaranteed in international human rights treaties. The aim of employing international human rights law in this study is to examine the legality of unfitness declarations under international human rights law and how the right to participation in access to justice of persons with psychosocial disabilities can be realised in Kenya. International human rights is also used to interrogate the normative content and the extent of the duty of states to accommodate persons with psychosocial disabilities in access to justice.

Legislation is often the immediate vehicle for implementing the Constitution. Without legislative and policy reforms, which unequivocally guarantees the participation of persons with psychosocial disabilities in access to justice, discrimination of persons with psychosocial disabilities through unfitness declarations will remain unchecked. Under Kenyan law, the Criminal Procedure Code is the main legislative instrument for protecting and promoting the participation of persons with psychosocial disabilities in the criminal justice system. Thus, the study aims to unpack the concept of participation in access to justice in Kenya's criminal laws.

Further, the book examined through empirical research, how legal, social, economic, and cultural factors prevent the participation of persons with psychosocial disabilities in Kenya's justice sector. The study aims to assess respondents' views on the participation of persons with psychosocial disabilities in terms of unfitness declarations and access to justice for persons with psychosocial disabilities. Ultimately, the book aims to make recommendations especially in terms of mechanisms apart from unfitness declarations, to empower persons with psychosocial disabilities in order to ensure their effective participation in Kenya's criminal justice sector.

1.3 Methodology

This work utilises the mixed methods methodology, which employ desk research as well as empirical research comprising qualitative research methods. As part of the desk-based research, primary sources, including constitutions, laws, cases, and parliamentary hansards have been critically analysed. In order to understand Kenya's existing obligations, key global and regional human rights instruments have been gathered and analysed. This data sources are primarily from the UN, African Union (AU), European Union, and foreign case law. There is also an examination of national laws, including the Constitution of Kenya, the Criminal Procedure Code, the Evidence Act, and the Penal Code. A broad range of secondary publications have also been extensively examined. These include reports from various institutions, scholarly works, academic books, journal articles, newspapers, and other media materials. However, the fact that there is little or no data on the factors of the unfitness declarations laws that lead to the limitation of persons with psychosocial disabilities' right to participation in the context of Kenya's criminal justice system necessitates the need for empirical research.

The empirical component of this study was carried out in Kenya. In order to address the issue of factors of the unfitness declarations laws that inhibit the participation of persons with psychosocial disabilities in the context of Kenya's criminal justice system, key research participants were magistrates, prosecutors, defence counsels, NGOs dealing with psychosocial disabilities, and doctors. The empirical research method involved the use of focus group interviews and discussions and the distribution of a semi-structured questionnaire.

The rights of respondents of the empirical component of this work were taken into account. Approval for the empirical research was sought from the Ethics Committee, Faculty of Law, University of Pretoria in accordance with the University of Pretoria's Ethics Policy. Approvals were also obtained from the relevant agencies and boards and ethics committees to enable the investigator conduct research in the designated state and non-state agencies. The empirical study is premised on complying with research ethics, including obtaining informed consent and assuring confidentiality.

1.4 Theories of disability participation

Whereas this book draws its arguments from a syncretic archive of knowledge and theory, in conceptualising how we think about psychosocial disability, the work of Michel Foucault is the main influence. Foucault's theory is relevant because it seeks to reform the law on unfitness declarations in Kenya, which is hampered by centuries of common law theology, which holds that it is unfair and improper to subject persons with psychosocial disabilities to a criminal trial.[103] Moreover, Foucault and decolonial theories that underpin this research were conceptualised in order to complement the limitations of the social model of disability, which demands closer attention to social causes of disability as opposed to physical bodies. Since the theoretical background is discussed in further details in Chapter 2, this section provides a brief review of relevant research theories in the area of unfitness declarations.

The methodical analysis of disabled persons' rights in the larger disability studies owes much of its intellectual roots to the social model of disability. According to the social model of disability, disability is construed as a social construct as opposed to an inevitable consequence of a disease or dysfunction of the body.[104] The focus on impairment is the view of the medical model which, instead of removing social and legal barriers that restrict the participation

103 R Burt & N Morris 'A proposal for the abolition of the incompetency plea' (1972–1973) 66 *Chicago Law Review* 75.

104 J Sztobryn-Giercuszkiewicz 'Critical disability theory as a theoretical framework for disability studies' (2017) https://www.researchgate.net/publication/326353943 (accessed 1 April 2021).

of persons with disabilities in mainstream activities, relies mostly on interventions by health professionals in normalising deficits in the body so that it can conform with desirable 'natural' standards.[105]

The social model shifts the concept of disability from focusing on the impairment to focusing on the social processes and policies that constrict disabled people's lives. It is premised on the adage that disabled persons are excluded by the society rather than by their bodies.[106] The social model refers to the interrelationships between a dysfunction, an individual response to this dysfunction, and the environment.[107] Ultimately, the social model of disability explains that disabilities are caused by the physical and institutional environment as well as by the attitudes in this environment towards disabled people who do not meet the social expectation of 'normality'.[108]

As seen above, the social model of disability is related to the human rights model, which informs both the CRPD and the African Disability Protocol. However, despite the close affinity between the human rights and social model of disability, it has been argued that the former avoids the shortcomings of the latter.[109] According to Stein, while the social model of disability focuses on the underlying social factors that shape our understanding of disability, the human rights model expands this notion by emphasising the human dignity of disabled persons.[110] The human rights model of disability incorporates both first and second generation human rights, in the sense that 'it encompasses both sets of human rights, civil and political as well as economic, social, and cultural rights'.[111]

Moreover, while the social model has been criticised for failing to appreciate the reality of pain and suffering in the lives of some disabled people, the human rights model respects the fact that some disabled persons are indeed confronted by such challenging life situations and argues that such factors should be taken into account in the development of relevant social justice theories.[112] A further difference relates to the importance of identity politics. On the one hand, the social model has been criticised for failing to pay adequate attention to the importance of identity politics. On the other hand, the human rights model has been hailed because of its ability to offer 'room for minority and cultural identification'. Also, the social model is mostly critical of public health policies that advocate the prevention of impairment, however,

105 As above.
106 J Beaudry 'Welcoming monsters: disability as a liminal legal concept' (2018) 29 *Yale Journal of Law & the Humanities* 316.
107 A Twardowski 'Controversies around the social model of disability' (2019) 2/16 *Culture – Society – Education* 10.
108 Sztobryn-Giercuszkiewicz (n 105).
109 Stein (n 101) 24.
110 Stein (n 101) 22.
111 As above.
112 M Retief & R Letšosa 'Models of disability: a brief overview' (2018) 74 *HTS Teologiese Studies/Theological Studies* 5.

human rights model promotes the adoption of properly formulated prevention policies which may be regarded as instances of human rights protection for disabled persons. Another difference between the social model and the human rights model is that while the former helpfully explains why so many disabled people are living in poverty, the latter offers constructive proposals for improving the life situation of disabled people.[113]

The Foucauldian theory is relevant because it aims at explaining the incorporation of unfitness declarations in our colonially-inherited laws using the power and knowledge paradigm. It is the main influence of this research because it enriches the social model of disability in the legal landscape by focusing more on the impairment as opposed to the social phenomenon. Like the social model, the Foucauldian theory's aim is to integrate disabled persons as talented social participants.[114] However, it goes a step further to provide the disability community with a language of resistance.[115] Disabled persons groups are urged to reject the subordinate place that the legal order, such as unfitness declarations and traditional liberal theories of justice give to disabled persons.[116]

The body plays a central role in the Foucauldian theory of disability thus shaping the discourse on psychosocial disability. It offers ways of understanding the creation of mental impairment in the society. The Foucauldian discourse supports the idea that there is a social hierarchy of health, whereby non-disabled bodies are privileged over disabled bodies and functions as a layer of social class. Foucauldian theory bases itself on Foucault's notion of modern power. Foucault defines power as 'a set of actions upon other actions', an individual exercises power through actions upon another individual and their responding actions.[117] Foucault explains that to understand power, is to see it as a form of governing, in which one individual (or power structure built by society) dictates how another should act in a particular situation.[118] This power is created and reinforced in disability and Foucault argues that scientific knowledge is the *par excellence* of such power.[119] Therefore, the notion of biopower is linked to control or governmentality.[120] It forms the basis for the medicalisation, classification, management, and measuring of people in terms

113 As above.
114 Beaudry (n 106) 319.
115 Beaudry (n 106) 320.
116 As above.
117 M Foucault 'The subject and power' in P Rabinow (ed) *Power: essential works of Foucault 1954–1984* (1994) 340.
118 S Wendy et al. 'From criminalisation to individual choice: policy responses to changing constructions of intellectual disability in Western Australia' (2019) 21 *Scandinavian Journal of Disability Research* 102.
119 A Anders 'Foucault and "the right to life": from technologies of normalization to societies of control' https://dsq-sds.org/article/view/3340/3268 (accessed 17 April 2021).
120 Wendy et al. (n 118) 102.

of their variance from the 'norm'.[121] It has also informed the normalisation and legitimisation of certain procedures and practices in institutions.[122]

The legacy of power as popularly perceived is the one represented by the sovereign as law and prohibition.[123] However, Foucault posits that power is not a preserve of one class whose object is to maintain it, while another class struggles to win it.[124] In fact, power relations extend far beyond the confines of the state. According to him power has no essence, it is everywhere.[125] Social relationships between groups or individuals create power.[126] Therefore, disabled persons also can exercise power over other groups or individuals like any other able-bodied groups.

The Foucauldian theory is a transformative theory which can be used to reform the law on unfitness declarations in Kenya. This work seeks to argue that Kenya's unfitness declarations are used to regulate and discipline persons with psychosocial disabilities so as to conform with the criminal justice system of power. Foucauldian scholars examine the ways in which bodies and lives are constituted, regulated, governed, and violated. They seek not only to defy the practices and expectations of the abled body but also endeavour to highlight non-normativity as exposing alternative ways of living and being in the world. Foucauldian theory is both a political and methodological tool that exposes and critiques oppressive normative regimes and common *topoi* such as those governing the interactions of disabled persons and the criminal justice system. The latter is still permeated by policies based on ableism and disablism.

Decolonial theory was selected because it helps trace the historical underpinnings of unfitness declarations in Kenya's laws. Mental disability is the new colonialism. Decolonial theory can be used to examine unfitness declarations as part of colonial governance and ideology. Therefore, the researcher used the theory to critically assess the influence of colonialism in constraining the participation of persons with psychosocial disabilities in Kenya's criminal justice system following unfitness declarations.

The experience of colonisation, colonialism, and neo-colonial power have resulted in the disablement of vast numbers of people in the Global South.[127] Decolonial theory situates disability in a global context and makes a distinction between experiences of the Global North and Global South.[128] The North/South distinction was coined in the 1960s as reference to the complex inequalities and dependencies between industrialised versus raw material

121 As above.
122 As above.
123 F Branfield 'Not quite human: an exploration of power resistance and disability' PhD Thesis, University of York, 158.
124 Branfield (n 123) 157.
125 Branfield (n 123) 158.
126 As above.
127 Meekosha (n 49) 668.
128 Meekosha (n 49) 667.

producing countries, rich versus poor, those with military power versus those without, and high technology versus low technology.[129] Southern countries are those that were historically conquered or controlled by modern imperial powers thus leaving a continuing legacy of poverty, economic exploitation, and dependence.[130] Therefore, in political, economic, and social terms, this world is, 'the west and the rest of us'.[131] Kenya is part of the Global South.

The emergence of the decolonial theory as a critical disability theory was inspired by the tendency of the West to universalise disability discourses without regard to the experience and views of the Global South which is caught in social and economic marginalisation.[132] With survival being the major goal of the Global South, debates around disability and impairment, independent living, care and human rights often take a backseat.[133] As regards penal colonies, the decolonial movement is concerned not only with the detention of criminal classes, the poor, petty thieves and homeless, but also people with psychosocial disability.[134] In colonial Kenya, persons with psychosocial disabilities who were in conflict with the law were institutionalised in prisons and mental institutions.[135] This practice subsisted and was adopted in the period after colonialism.

1.5 The structure of this volume

This book is divided into nine chapters. Chapter 1 is this introduction which lays down the background for the study. It identifies the issues that will be investigated or considered, suggests the significance of the study, and describes the methodology used. The chapter also clarifies some of the relevant concepts and contexts. It also sets out the limitations of the study and ends by setting out the structure of the study.

Chapter 2 discusses the theoretical framework that guide the study. In this chapter, the Foucauldian and decolonial theories have been used to interrogate the legality of unfitness to plead declarations. These theoretical approaches have been selected because they are able to explore the difficult area of disability regulation in access to justice and complement the limitations of the social model of disability. Chapter 2 provides a constructive fusion of the Foucauldian and decolonial theories in order to complement the limitations of the social model of disability which demands closer attention to social causes of

129 Meekosha (n 49) 669.

130 As above.

131 S Zondi 'A decolonial turn in diplomatic theory: unmasking epistemic injustice' (2016) 41 *Journal for Contemporary History* 22.

132 Meekosha (n 49) 670.

133 As above.

134 Meekosha (n 49) 672.

135 R Keller 'Madness and colonization: psychiatry in the British and French empires, 1800–1962' (2001) 35 *Journal of Social History* 307.

disability as opposed to physical bodies. The two theories, through the principles of knowledge, power, and coloniality, leads to a rich analytical framework for realising disabled persons' right of access to justice in participation.

In Chapter 2, the book, mainly using the Foucauldian and decolonial theories provides a conceptual template for the cognition of psychosocial disabilities. The chapter presents the findings of a literature review of Foucauldian and decolonial theories, which includes not only a detailed description and development of the theoretical framework but also the principles that are applied during the critique of unfitness declarations. These theories are used as hermeneutics in subsequent chapters to advance the thesis that unfitness declarations in Kenya violate the right to participation in access to justice for persons with psychosocial disabilities.

Chapter 3 presents a conceptualisation of psychosocial disability. It examines how psychosocial disability has been constructed in Kenya from the pre-colonial era to the colonial and post-colonial eras. Issues surrounding the monopoly of the classification, eventual medicalisation and diagnosis of medical disabilities eminent in the social construction of psychosocial disabilities are discussed. It challenges the conceptualisation of psychosocial disability that is hard-wired in traditional customs, common law, and judicial decision-making process. The chapter is organised around interrogating representations of psychosocial disability and ultimately suggesting a philosophical way forward in the manner psychosocial disability is contested. It highlights that narratives which represent psychosocial disability should always be understood as being culturally and historically situated. They are representations constructed within the knowledge and power system(s) of a given polity at a particular historical time and location, together with a social and political dynamics for social stratification, domination, and status subordination. The chapter uses the representation of psychosocial disability in pre-colonial, colonial, and post-colonial discourses to point out the dominant discourses during different debates and shows how the influence of culture and other socio-legal frameworks underpinned the lack of textual standard on psychosocial disability. It proposes that judicial decision-making process must not be accommodative to negative public representations of persons with psychosocial disabilities.

Chapter 4 examines the concept of participation in access to justice and how it empowers persons with psychosocial disabilities. The chapter supports the role of the CRPD and other international and regional instruments for revolutionising the international law of participation for disabled persons, including persons with psychosocial disabilities. Chapter 4, also examines what participation entails for persons with psychosocial disabilities in Kenya's criminal justice system. It also discusses the extent of participation for persons with psychosocial disabilities in Kenya's criminal justice sector. The backdrop to Chapter 4, is the enhancement of disabled persons' participation in the criminal process. It analyses the extent to which Kenya's criminal justice laws have complied with international standards regarding the right to participation in access to justice. It regards as landmark provisions that facilitate disabled persons right to participation in access to justice, which casts them beyond their traditional role of unfit witnesses, in which role commentators allege objectification. The chapter develops a framework for recognising the right to participation of persons with psychosocial disabilities in ways that are informed by a transformative understanding of participation. The framework seeks to deconstruct scripted knowledge about participation in order to build an understanding that reveals the complexity, diversity, and ultimately political nature of participation. The author argues that recognising the right to participation in the realm of criminal procedure requires a radical epistemology that is capable of moving beyond the mere involvement or engagement of persons with psychosocial disabilities.

Chapter 5 examines the scope and limits of states parties' duty to provide reasonable accommodation in access to justice under the CRPD. I argue that the principle of reasonable accommodation is related to Foucault's notion of power. Accommodation rights ensure the agency of persons with psychosocial disabilities and therefore function as a tool of inclusion and participation in access to justice. The chapter examines the aspects of reasonable accommodation. Drawing from international human rights law, this chapter explores how courts across the globe have interpreted the right of reasonable accommodation and its implication to persons with psychosocial disabilities.

Chapter 6 contains a detailed description of the empirical research methodology. It captures the research approach, type of research, the research design, population and sample of the study, data collection methods, analysis of data, the trustworthiness of the study, and the ethical aspects pertaining to the study. Furthermore, it indicates the limitations of the study.

Chapter 7 analyses the findings of the empirical study. The chapter elaborates on the results garnered from the data obtained from the empirical aspect of this research. It uses the research questions of the study as themes and sub-themes for reviewing the results. Research findings are presented, analysed, and interpreted with reference to prosecutors, defence counsels, doctors, and NGOs working in Kenya's criminal justice system. A discussion on empirical findings where themes and sub-themes from the quantitative and qualitative studies, which have been identified, are also included.

Chapter 8 analyses the manner and extent to which states have undertaken comprehensive legislative reforms to their unfitness declaration regimes in order to decolonise and remedy potential or actual violations of the rights of accused persons with psychosocial disabilities under the CRPD. It examines the extent of compliance of national laws on unfitness to stand trial in selected jurisdictions across the globe, with the demands of the CRPD. Some countries have adopted a passive transformation approach to the CRPD which occurs by assessing the compliance of already existing domestic laws with the Convention in order to determine whether there is need for any adjustment. In others, the CRPD has been used to set new standards for the protection of persons with psychosocial disabilities thus, providing the impetus for further and ever deeper modifications to the regulation of active legal capacity. On the flipside, some states have specifically rejected the recommendation of the CRPD Committee to eliminate declarations that are based partly or exclusively on the disability of accused persons with psychosocial disabilities from criminal justice systems. It also problematises default positions such as the institutionalisation of persons with psychosocial disabilities following unfitness declarations.

Chapter 9 summarises the book's findings and provide key recommendations on what can be done to increase the space within which persons with psychosocial disabilities may be able to exercise their right of access to justice. The recommendations focuses on both legislative and institutional reforms aimed at preventing violations in the context of right to participation in access to justice.

1.6 Conclusion

Against the above background, this book hypothesises that the social model of disability is inadequate to respond to violations of unfitness declarations against the right to participation of persons with psychosocial disabilities in Kenya's criminal justice system. Under conventional international law, states are under an obligation to respect and ensure the participation of persons with psychosocial disabilities in the context of their right of access to justice. In order for participation of persons with psychosocial disabilities in the context of their right of access to justice to be realised, there is need for a legal framework that adequately protects its exercise. The phenomenon of unfit declarations and the resultant indefinite detention of persons with psychosocial disabilities should be removed. In its stead, the state should put in place safeguards to protect the liberty and participation of persons with psychosocial disabilities in the criminal justice process.

This work uses the Foucauldian and decolonial theories to explore the limitations of the social model of disability in ensuring the participation of persons with psychosocial disabilities within Kenya's criminal justice system. By examining unfitness declarations, this volume identifies common threads of discussion and how these threads illustrate values, attitudes, and beliefs surrounding psychosocial disability in Kenya. A deeper understanding of the perception of psychosocial disability will help improve on the social model theory, which considers disability in relation to the society, therefore ensuring the full participation of disabled persons in the criminal justice system. This book presents an account of a systematic investigation of how power can be used by the state through reforms of unfitness declarations in Kenya's criminal legal system to ensure the participation of persons with psychosocial disabilities. Deciding how to respond to unfitness declarations depends on a normative framework that cannot be supplied by the social model. The framework might be libertarian, utilitarian, egalitarian, some combination thereof, or something else. The social model itself, however, has essentially nothing to say about which framework to use.

As such, the book interrogates the limitations of the social model of disability in responding to violations of unfitness declarations against the rights of persons with psychosocial disabilities in Kenya's criminal justice system. It also identifies how violations of accused persons with psychosocial disabilities human rights in the context of unfitness declarations can be prevented and redressed in the particular context of Kenya. To do so, it analyses the national legal framework on unfitness declarations and non-participation of accused persons with psychosocial disabilities in Kenya's criminal justice system and assess their compatibility with international standards. The book also examines the legality of the exclusion and non-participation of accused persons with psychosocial disabilities following the unfitness declarations. In addition, it assesses measures to enhance the participation of persons with psychosocial disabilities in Kenya's criminal justice process.

References

African Charter on Human and Peoples' Rights (Adopted 27 June 1981, entered into force on 21 October 1986) '21 ILM 58' (1982).

Age of Majority Act Cap 33 'Laws of Kenya'.

Anders A 'Foucault and "the right to life": from technologies of normalization to societies of control' https://dsq-sds.org/article/view/3340/3268 (accessed 17 April, 2021).

Anker L et al. 'Fitness to stand trial: a general principle of European criminal law?' (2011) 7 *Utrecht Law Review* 120. https://doi.org/10.18352/ulr.174.

Article 48 Initiative (A48), Arthur's Dream Autism Trust (ADAT) and Southern Africa Litigation Centre 'An exploratory study of the interaction between the criminal justice system and persons with intellectual and psychosocial disabilities in Nairobi, Kenya' (September 2021) 75.

Barbaresch G et al. '"When they see a wheelchair, they've not even seen me" – factors shaping the experience of disability stigma and discrimination in Kenya' (2021) 18 *International Journal of Environmental Research & Public Health* 1. https://doi.org/10.3390/ijerph18084272.

Baxter H 'Bringing Foucault into law and law into Foucault' (1996) 48 *Stanford Law Review* 449.

Beaudry J 'Welcoming monsters: disability as a liminal legal concept' (2018) 29 *Yale Journal of Law & the Humanities* 316.

Beqiraj J et al. *Access to justice for persons with disabilities: from international principles to practice* International Bar Association (2017).

Berghs M et al. 'Do disabled people need a stronger social model: a social model of human rights?' (2019) 34 *Disability & Society* 1034. https://doi.org/10.1080/09687599.2019.1619239.

Branfield F 'Not quite human: an exploration of power resistance and disability' PhD Thesis, University of York, 1997.

Brown P et al. 'Fitness to plead: development and validation of a standardised assessment instrument' (2018) 13(4) *PLoS One* 1. https://doi.org/10.1371/journal.pone.0194332

Burt R & Morris N 'A proposal for the abolition of the incompetency plea' (1972–1973) 66 *Chicago Law Review* 75.

Charles Mwangi Muraya v Republic (2001) eKLR.

Constitution of the Republic of Kenya (2010).

Convention for the Protection of Human Rights and Fundamental Freedoms (European Convention on Human Rights, as amended) ETS. No. 5.
Convention on the Rights of Persons with Disabilities (CRPD) Adopted on 13 December 2006 UN Doc A/61/611 (entered into force on 3 May 2008).
Convention on the Rights of the Child, Nov 20, 1989 1577 UNTS. 3; 28 I.L.M 1456 (1989).
Council of Europe *Who gets to decide? Right to legal capacity for persons with intellectual and psychosocial disabilities* Council of Europe Publishing (2012).
Criminal Procedure Code, Cap 75 of 1930 (Laws of Kenya).
CRPD Committee General Comment 1: article 12: equal recognition before the law (2014) UN Doc CRPD/C/GC/1 (19 May, 2014).
David Njoroge Macharia v Republic (2011) eKLR.
European Union Agency for Fundamental Rights *Legal capacity of persons with intellectual disabilities and persons with mental health problems* European Union Agency for Fundamental Rights (2013).
Flynn E *Disabled justice? Access to justice and the UN Convention on the Rights of Persons with disabilities* (2016).
Foucault M 'The subject and power' in Rabinow P (ed) *Power: essential works of Foucault 1954–1984* (1994).
Fox GH 'The right to political participation in international law' (1992) 17 *Yale Journal of International Law* 544.
Government of Western Australia 'Operational instruction 10: prisoners with disabilities' https://www.correctiveservices.wa.gov.au/_files/prisons/adult-custodial-rules/operational-instructions/oi–10.pdf (accessed 27 August 2021).
Hezel G *Judging civil justice* (2010).
Holness W & Rule S 'Legal capacity of parties with intellectual, psycho-social and communication disabilities in traditional courts in KwaZulu-Natal' (2018) 6 *African Disability Rights Yearbook* 41.
Inclusion Europe and Mental Health Europe 'The differences between mental illness and intellectual disability' https://bapid.com/pdf/razliki_en.pdf (accessed 27 August 2021).
International Covenant on Civil and Political Rights (adopted 16 December 1966, entered into force on 23 March 1976) 999 UNTS 171 (ICCPR).
Keller R 'Madness and colonization: psychiatry in the British and French empires, 1800–1962' (2001) 35 *Journal of Social History* 307. https://doi.org/10.1353/jsh.2001.0126
Kenya National Commission on Human Rights & the Open Society Initiative for Eastern Africa *How to implement article 12 of convention on the rights of persons with disabilities regarding legal capacity in Kenya: a briefing paper* KNHCR (2012).
Lakhan R 'The coexistence of psychiatric disorders and intellectual disability in children aged 3–18 years in the Barwani district, India' (2013) *International Scholarly Research Notices* 1. https://doi.org/10.1155/2013/875873
McSherry B et al. *Unfitness to plead and indefinite detention of persons with cognitive disabilities: addressing the legal barriers and creating appropriate alternative supports in the community* Melbourne: Melbourne Social Equity Institute, University of Melbourne (2017).
Meekosha H 'Decolonising disability: thinking and acting globally' (2011) 26 *Disability and Society* 668. https://doi.org/10.1080/09687599.2011.602860.
Miller D 'Dementia and competency in United States courtrooms: a case law review' https://academicworks.cuny.edu/cgi/viewcontent.cgi?article=1157&context=jj_etds (accessed 10 September 2021).
National Mental Health Consumer and Carer Forum 'Issue: intellectual/developmental disability (ID) and mental health' (2012).

Ngwena C 'Developing juridical method for overcoming status subordination in disablism: the place of transformative epistemologies' (2014) 30 *South African Journal of Human Rights* 283.

Nickolas J 'Law and power: ten lessons from Foucault' (2018) 30 *Bond Law Review* 31. https://doi.org/10.53300/001c.5658.

Nixon SA et al. 'Using postcolonial perspectives to consider rehabilitation with children with disabilities: the Bamenda-Toronto dialogue' (2015) 2 *Disability and the Global South* 571.

Nuwagaba EL & Rule PN 'Power dynamics among PWDs during adult learning processes: motivator or demotivator?' (2015) 3 *Rwandan Journal of Education* 53.

Nyawa Mwajowa v Republic (2016) eKLR.

Office of the High Commissioner for Human Rights 'Ratification status for CRPD' http://tbinternet.ohchr.org/_layouts/TreatyBodyExternal/Treaty.aspx?Treaty=CRPD&Lang=en (accessed 17 June 2021).

Ortoleva S 'Inaccessible justice: human rights, persons with disabilities and the legal system' (2011) 17 *ILSA Journal of International & Comparative Law* 282.

Persons with Disabilities Act (Act 14 of 2003), Laws of Kenya.

Proshkin v Russia (2012) ECtHR.

Protocol to the African Charter on Human and Peoples' Rights on the Rights of Persons with Disabilities in Africa (African Disability Protocol) (29 January 2018).

Raub A et al. 'Constitutional rights of persons with disabilities: an analysis of 193 national constitutions' (2016) 29 *Harvard Human Rights Journal* 237.

Republic v GKN (2018) eKLR.

Retief M & Letšosa R 'Models of disability: a brief overview' (2018) 74 *HTS Teologiese Studies/Theological Studies* 5. https://doi.org/10.4102/hts.v74i1.4738.

Romanov v Russia (2005) ECtHR.

Roomaney A 'Assessing the right to physical access to justice, for persons with disabilities' LLM dissertation, University of the Western Cape, 2014.

Salontaji-Drobnjak v Serbia (2009) ECtHR.

Sandra JF 'The evolution of the common law: legal developments in Kenya and India' (2006) 68 *Political Science Faculty Publications* 3.

Sartorius N 'Disability and mental illness are different entities and should be assessed separately' (2009) 8 *World Psychiatry* 1. https://doi.org/10.1002/j.2051-5545.2009.tb00220.x.

Sedler RA *The Ethiopian civil procedure* (1986).

Series L 'The development of disability rights under international law: from charity to human rights' (2015) 30 *Disability and Society* 158. https://doi.org/10.1080/09687599.2015.1066975.

Series L & Nilson A 'Article 12 CRPD: equal recognition before the law' in Bantekas I et al. (eds) *The UN convention on the rights of persons with disabilities, a commentary* (2018).

Shtukaturov v Russia (2008) ECtHR.

Stavert J 'Paradigm shift or paradigm paralysis? National mental health and capacity law and implementing the CRPD in Scotland' (2018) 7 *Laws* 2. https://doi.org/10.3390/laws7030026.

Stein MA 'Disability human rights' (2007) 95 *California Law Review* 62.

Sztobryn-Giercuszkiewicz J 'Critical disability theory as a theoretical framework for disability studies' 2017 https://www.researchgate.net/publication/326353943 (accessed 1 April, 2021).

UN Human Rights Committee (HRC) 'General Comment 25: the right to participate in public affairs, voting rights and the right of equal access to public service (Art. 25) 12/07/96 CCPR/C/21/Rev.1/Add.7'.

UNICEF *Breaking down barriers: equitable access to justice for children with disabilities* UNICEF (2020).

Union of the Physically Impaired Against Segregation *Fundamental principles of disability* (1976).

United Nations 'Chapter two: the convention in detail – the rights and principles enumerated in the Convention' https://www.un.org/development/desa/disabilities/resources/handbook-for-parliamentarians-on-the-convention-on-the-rights-of-persons-with-disabilities/chapter-two-the-convention-in-detail-3.html (accessed 12 April, 2021).

Universal Declaration of Human Rights (adopted 10 December 1948 UNGA Res 217 A(III)).

Users and Survivors of Psychiatry in Kenya (USP-K) *Advancing the rights of persons with psychosocial disability in Kenya* USP-K (2017).

Van Reenen TP & Combrinck H 'The UN convention on the rights of persons with disabilities in Africa: progress after 5 years' (2011) 8 *International Journal on Human Rights* 145.

Vasyl Y et al. 'Mental health of a person as a criterion of personal participation in the trial during criminal proceedings' (2020) LXXIII *Wiadomości Lekarskie* 2739. https://doi.org/10.36740/WLek202012207.

Waddington L 'Disability: a human rights issue' (1994) 1 *Maastricht Journal of European and Comparative Law* 334.

Wambulwa A 'Explainer: what 'fit to stand trial' means' (21 December 2019) https://www.the-star.co.ke/news/2019-12-21-explainer-what-fit-to-stand-trial-means/ (accessed 12 April, 2021).

Wendy S et al. 'From criminalisation to individual choice: policy responses to changing constructions of intellectual disability in Western Australia' (2019) 21 *Scandinavian Journal of Disability Research* 102. https://doi.org/10.16993/sjdr.571.

Zagidulina v Russia (2013) ECtHR.

Zondi S 'A decolonial turn in diplomatic theory: unmasking epistemic injustice' (2016) 41 *Journal for Contemporary History* 22. https://doi.org/10.18820/24150509/jch.v41i1.2.

2 Theoretical framework

2.0 Introduction

This chapter discusses the theoretical framework of the study. The Foucauldian and decolonial theories are used to interrogate the legality of unfitness declarations in Kenya. The approaches draw on combined components of Foucauldian and decolonial theories with a view to developing a normative framework for realising disabled persons' right of access to justice in participation. To discuss the Foucauldian perspective, this chapter draws on works by Michel Foucault, including *Madness and civilization*, *The birth of the clinic*, *The order of things*, *Discipline and punish*, and *The history of sexuality*.[1] As for the decolonial theory, this book considers the works of Thomas Dirth, Glenn Adams, Achille Mbembe, Charles Ngwena, and Sabelo Ndlovu-Gatsheni.[2]

Foucault's theory is the main discourse in this work. However, it is not the sole theoretical framework because it focuses more on the body as opposed to the environment or society as the disabling factor. This means that, if adopted on its own, it will account only partially for the protection of the right of access to justice in participation for persons with psychosocial disabilities in Kenya's criminal justice system. This is why Foucault's works as a whole cannot account for the investigated aspects of the phenomenon of unfitness declarations on its own.

1 M Foucault *Madness and civilization: a history of insanity in the age of reason* (1965), M Foucault *The birth of the clinic: archaeology of medical perception* (1973), M Foucault *The order of things: an archaeology of the human sciences* (1970), M Foucault *Discipline and punish: the birth of the prison* (1991) and M Foucault *The history of sexuality: an introduction* trans R Hurley (1978) vol 1.

2 TP Dirth & GA Adams 'Decolonial theory and disability studies: on the modernity/coloniality of ability' (2019) 7 *Journal of Social and Political Psychology* 269; A Mbembe *Out of the dark night: essays on decolonisation* (2021); CG Ngwena *What is Africanness? Contesting nativism in race, culture and sexualities* (2018); C Ngwena 'Developing juridical method for overcoming status subordination in disablism: the place of transformative epistemologies' (2014) 30 *South African Journal of Human Rights* 283; and SJ Ndlovu-Gatsheni *Decolonization development and knowledge in Africa: turning on a new leaf* (2020).

DOI: 10.4324/9781003647102-2

This chapter is divided into four sections. Section one is an overview of Michel Foucault's work and its relevance for the present study, including his foundational concepts of power, knowledge, discipline, domination, and the counter-conduct ideology. Section two examines decolonial theory. It places an emphasis on the ideology of dominance and superiority over marginalised groups in order to promote dialogue about decolonisation and other critical perspectives on the rights of persons with psychosocial disabilities. Section three discusses the strengthening of the social model of disability through the Foucauldian and decolonial theories. Section four is the conclusion.

2.1 Foucauldian theory

The themes, which are discussed in this section are power, knowledge, discipline, and rights. This work reviews and applies Foucault's positions in Kenya's unfitness declaration laws. Foucault's theories on governmentality and the ethics of inclusion are used in this book to analyse the power of the state to conduct and govern the participation of persons with psychosocial disabilities in Kenya's criminal justice system.

2.1.1 Management of psychosocial disabilities through power

The management of psychosocial disability in Kenya's criminal justice system is profoundly bureaucratic and political. Through Foucault's notions of power, the state is able to intervene in the private lives of persons with psychosocial disabilities. According to Foucault, power is not a thing but a relation that ordinarily excludes, represses, censors, masks, conceals, or abstracts depending on the discourse.[3] He further stated in *Discipline and punish: The birth of the prison*, that power is capable of producing reality, domains of objects, and rituals of truth, including how individuals with psychosocial disabilities are perceived by the society.[4] Power relations are more pronounced and established in the study of unfitness and the criminal justice system.[5] It is power and not force that has subjected persons with psychosocial disabilities to the government of unfitness declarations.

The technology of unfitness declaration power clearly set persons with psychosocial disabilities apart from the mainstream society and facilitates the objectification of their bodies by state institutions. Unfitness declaration laws are strategies of power used by states and those with influence over the state's lawmaking processes to influence the thoughts, actions and, well-being of

3 M Foucault cited in NJ James 'Law and power: ten lessons from Foucault' (2018) 30/1 *Bond Law Review* 40.

4 M Foucault *Discipline and punish: the birth of the prison* (1991) 194.

5 'Chapter 1: the Foucauldean concept of power' https://www.lkouniv.ac.in/site/writereaddata/siteContent/202004021930365629saroj_dhal_socio_FOUCOULT.pdf (accessed 27 June 2021) 20.

persons with psychosocial disabilities.[6] Kenya's parliament and judicial institution are the state's key agencies used to produce unfitness declaration related laws. These state agencies create and apply laws that categorise human beings into fit and unfit categories.[7] That is so despite the fact that the consequences of such labels are to limit the ability of persons with psychosocial disabilities from being effective participants in the justice sector.[8] Once an unfitness is conceived by justice actors, there is always a corresponding norm that is defined.[9] In that case, it is always the fit person who has power over the unfit individual. For example, the psychologist tells about madmen, the physician about the patients, the criminologist talks about the criminals, but never the reverse.[10]

The accused person with psychosocial disability never escapes power relations but is rather constituted by them.[11] Of interest to this book are the practices of coercing accused persons with psychosocial disabilities to submit themselves to medical and judicial forms of scrutiny that require them to meet a set of unquestioned standards before they can access Kenya's criminal justice system. Such processes, which are inscribed within invisible power relationships, inherently limit the conceptual horizon of recourses available to both disabled persons and non-disabled persons.[12] The label that accused persons with psychosocial disabilities are unfit to stand trial is a process that is tied up with power relations that constitutes them into impaired subjects with limited legal options.[13]

However, relational power should not only be limited to humans as stated by Foucault.[14] Instead, relational power is dispersed throughout every relationship, including in nonhumans and environments. Such a relationality implies a radicalness that even Foucault did not acknowledge. In this sense, a more radical relational agency recognises that humans, nonhumans, and environments are all participants within relations of unfitness declarations power. They all contribute to the definition of the situation and identity formation that limit the participation of persons with psychosocial disabilities in access to justice.[15] What is needed is a holistic reform process that ensures the participation of persons with psychosocial disabilities in Kenya's justice sector.

6 N James 'Law and power: ten lessons from Foucault' (2018) 30 *Bond Law Review* 39.
7 As above.
8 J Beaudry 'Welcoming monsters: disability as a liminal legal concept' (2018) 29 *Yale Journal of Law & the Humanities* 306.
9 As above.
10 As above.
11 LE Zheng 'Colonial psychiatry in Africa: a distorted science? Practice, knowledge, and power' https://www.researchgate.net/publication/328051535 (accessed 30 June 2021).
12 J Beaudry 'The vanishing body of disability law: power and the making of the impaired subject' (2018) 31 *Canadian Journal of Family Law* 27.
13 As above.
14 PE Kezia 'A radical relational agency: Foucault, complexity theory and environmental resistances' PhD Thesis, University of Nottingham, 2010, 45.
15 D Bednarz 'Power, identity and social change as we enter degrowth' https://www.resilience.org/stories/2013-08-14/power-identity-and-social-change-as-we-enter-degrowth/ (accessed 19 July 2022).

A holistic reform process involves the use of humans, nonhumans, and the environment to ensure the participation in access to justice of persons with psychosocial disabilities.

2.1.2 *Unfitness declarations and societal norms*

Kenya's discourse on psychosocial disability is based on social norms and people's cultural beliefs, which in most cases is dehumanising and alienating as will be detailed in Chapters 3 and 7. Unfitness declarations are a result of societal norms that persons with psychosocial disabilities lack the necessary legal capacity required to participate in Kenya's criminal justice system. Unfitness laws are a response to what the society considers abnormal. However, societal norms should not be universalised. According to Foucault the society is not a coherent totality which can be analysed by means of general conceptions. Foucault argues that norms such as unfitness of persons with psychosocial disabilities develop first in a piecemeal fashion before spreading into 'vast, coherent ensembles'.[16]

Acting on societal norms, the state's interventionist arm of biopower governmentality consisted in enacting laws that further alienated persons with psychosocial disabilities through unfitness declaration systems aimed at limiting their rights and capacity. The government took away the right to participation in access to justice of persons with psychosocial disabilities and replaced it with unfitness declaration laws. The typical role of an accused person with psychosocial disability following unfitness declarations in Kenya is that of a 'dummy player' due to inability to participate in court proceedings.[17] Unfitness declaration laws present challenges to persons with psychosocial disabilities because they assume equality across the board. This approach is inherently flawed because it does not take account of differences.

2.1.3 *Scientific knowledge and unfitness declaration 'truths'*

According to Foucault, knowledge can be produced from power.[18] Unfitness declaration laws entered into new relations with scientific knowledge such as criminology, psychology, economics, and psychiatry in order to maximise their effectiveness in changing criminals with psychosocial disabilities into 'useful legal subjects'. Through a combination of law and psychiatry, perpetrators of a criminal act are judged on the 'soundness or unsoundness of mind' at the time of the act.[19]

16 D Lacombe 'Reforming Foucault: a critique of the social control thesis' (1996) 47 *The British Journal of Sociology* 338.

17 P Carlen *Magistrates' justice* (1976) 98.

18 'Chapter 1: the Foucauldean concept of power' https://www.lkouniv.ac.in/site/writereaddata/siteContent/202004021930365629saroj_dhal_socio_FOUCOULT.pdf (accessed 27 June 2021) 20.

19 As above.

The law is used to define the act while a combination of law and psychiatry determines the degree of responsibility of the perpetrator. The determination of whether an accused person is fit to stand trial is made by engaging with medical, welfare, or legal frameworks which are controlled by differently embodied people.[20] Judicial officers in Kenya are not bound by the opinions of psychiatrists, however, they rely on them when making a decision as to whether an accused person with psychosocial disability is fit or unfit. Foucault has criticised this reliance of psychiatrists by judicial officers in unfitness declarations.[21]

Using Foucault's theory, the author argues that the use of psychiatrists in unfitness declarations usurps the function of judicial officers as they are the ones who really determine whether an accused person with psychosocial disability is fit or unfit.[22] Persons with psychosocial disabilities are not viewed as criminals because they are not rational, wilful, and self-determined actors and consequently, judgement cannot be pronounced until they are examined for unfitness. Persons with psychosocial disabilities are treated and not punished and treatment depends on the degree of disability. The higher the degree of unfitness, the greater the danger posed by the perpetrator to the society thus the need for intensive treatment and limitation of the right to participation.[23]

Linked to the relationship between power and knowledge is the power and truth dyad. The justice system in Kenya has transformed certain misconceptions regarding psychosocial disabilities into legal truths. Justice system actors, through power and knowledge have produced truths about the unfitness of persons with psychosocial disabilities, which have been codified in the country's laws and regulations.[24] Unfitness declaration truths are also found in science which is of paramount importance in Kenya's criminal justice system thus the use of doctors in assessing the mental capacity of accused persons in unfitness declarations. Scientific institutions and scientists are the main conduits through which truths about psychosocial disabilities and unfitness declarations are disseminated thus the need for reform.[25]

One of the main criticisms of Foucault's ideas on knowledge and truth is that they are not empirical in terms of method and content.[26] Legal reform in Kenya should be based on objective and scientific observation of the effects of the unfitness declaration phenomena. As part of legal reform, it is important

20 Zheng (n 11).

21 M Foucault *Abnormal. Lectures at the Collège de France 1974–1975* (2003) 23.

22 As above.

23 As above.

24 M Dubois 'The governance of the third world: a Foucauldian perspective on power relations in development' (1991) 16 *Alternatives: Global, Local, Political* 7.

25 As above.

26 PJ Verovšek 'The reluctant postmodernism of Jürgen Habermas: reevaluating Habermas's debates with Foucault and Derrida' (2022) 84 *The Review of Politics* 26.

to identify and challenge misconceptions about the unfitness of persons with psychosocial disabilities in Kenya's criminal justice system. Apart from applying the Foucauldian theory, this research relies on empirical method in order to measure Foucault's ideas against the circumstances of persons with psychosocial disabilities in Kenya as will be discussed in Chapters 6 and 7.

2.1.4 Unfitness declarations as a disciplinary technique

The constitution of persons with psychosocial disabilities as legal persons is essential in access to justice.[27] Unfitness declarations disciplines people into two categories, 'persons of sound mind' and 'persons of unsound mind'. Persons of sound mind are considered to have capacity to act and are able to understand and participate effectively as opposed to persons of unsound mind. Persons of unsound mind are labelled so because of their failure to live up to some human standard, whether moral, psychological, or physical.[28] Unsound mind is synonymous to Foucault's 'monster', which is a socially engineered figure of a disabled person.[29] Foucault used the term 'monster' to denote an obstacle of the law.[30] Monsters can only be dealt with in extra-legal ways. The exclusion of persons with psychosocial disabilities from accessing justice is anchored on Foucault's theory of 'monstrous'.

In Kenya, persons with psychosocial disabilities are excluded from participating in the criminal process and subjected to control through disciplining techniques such as detention. The purpose of the detention is to regulate behaviour. Unfitness declarations against persons with psychosocial disabilities allows for their detention at the pleasure of the president because they do not have the cognitive capacity to understand their actions or the judicial process. Detention in prisons or medical institutions is a form of control aimed at normalising persons with psychosocial disabilities.[31] Powers to detain and discharge persons with psychosocial disabilities following unfitness declarations rests with the President of Kenya.[32] This power of control by the president is one that emanate from societal norms about disability.

The disciplinary regime of unfitness declarations in Kenya was inherited from the British colonial administrations. In post-colonial Kenya, the disciplinary power of unfitness declarations is produced through the state's policies and laws on individual normalisation under the Criminal Procedure Code. Unfitness declaration technology continues to control persons with

27 JC Suntrup 'Michel Foucault and the competing alethurgies of law' (2017) 37 *Oxford Journal of Legal Studies* 301.
28 Beaudry (n 8) 306.
29 Beaudry (n 8) 304
30 Beaudry (n 8) 306.
31 EJ Donaldson 'The corpus of the madwoman: toward a feminist disability studies theory of embodiment and mental illness' (2002) 14 *NWSA Journal* 100.
32 Criminal Procedure Code, secs 162 & 167.

psychosocial disabilities and deny them legal capacity. Courts use unfitness declarations as a way of disciplining and reducing persons with psychosocial disabilities, with the label of unsound mind into docile bodies, which meekly adopt their social roles. Those found to be of unsound mind are separated and detained in the relevant established institutions in order to educate the curable cases of idiocy and to shelter and supervise the incurable.[33] Therefore, I argue using Foucault's theory, that in order to resist the disciplinary regime of unfitness declaration, it is important to reform the concept of unfitness in the criminal justice system.

2.1.5 *Domination of persons with psychosocial disabilities by non-disabled persons*

Discipline is a dominating form of power that creates asymmetrical relationships of power between the disabled and the non-disabled.[34] In interactions between persons with psychosocial disabilities and the non-disabled, the latter is considered to be the dominant majority. Non-disabled persons, through the disciplinary power of unfitness declarations have limited the freedom of persons with psychosocial disabilities by influencing the choices they can make and even take when it comes to participation in access to justice. Non-disabled persons assume that persons with psychosocial disabilities need care and protection and that in order to protect the economic and social order, persons with psychosocial disabilities who are 'deviant members' of society should be segregated.[35] This approach has been used to establish asylums for persons with psychosocial disabilities because they are considered vulnerable.[36]

The word vulnerability stems from the Latin word *vulnerabilis*, which comes from the verb *vulnerare* and the noun *vulnus*, which means to wound. The term 'vulnerable' is commonly used in a negative sense to signify the possibility of being attacked or harmed, either physically or emotionally. It refers to a group of persons or individuals who due to risk factors, age, or disability are considered to be in need of special care, support, or protection. However, persons with psychosocial disabilities are not always powerless and there are situations, instances, and cases where they are powerful.[37] Thus, the

33 S Wendy et al. 'From criminalisation to individual choice: policy responses to changing constructions of intellectual disability in Western Australia' (2019) 21 *Scandinavian Journal of Disability Research* 102.

34 K McIntyre 'Foucault on freedom and domination' 31 January 2012 https://partiallyexaminedlife.com/2012/01/31/foucault-on-freedom-and-domination/ (accessed 4 September 2022).

35 MA Jackson 'Models of disability and human rights: Informing the improvement of built environment accessibility for people with disability at neighborhood scale?' (2018) 7 *Laws* 3.

36 Zheng (n 10).

37 EL Nuwagaba & PN Rule 'Power dynamics among PWDs during adult learning processes: motivator or demotivator?' (2015) 3 *Rwandan Journal of Education* 55.

assumptions of the dominant non-disabled that persons with psychosocial disabilities are always without power in their interactions with justice systems is untrue. Persons with psychosocial disabilities are capable of challenging and changing structures of oppression as the disability movement has demonstrated.[38] To this end, power is important to them if they are to overcome unequal power relations, which have bedevilled them for a long time despite the need for social justice for all.[39]

2.1.6 Challenging unfitness declarations through Foucault's counter-conduct ideology

Foucault has been faulted for not addressing the question of contemporary struggles for rights, including disability rights.[40] To combat the challenge of dominant power relations, Foucault adopts a counter-conduct ideology on the part of the governed.[41] However, even Foucault's counter-conduct ideology has been criticised for being limited only against the concept of the sovereign. It is argued that what is needed is not resistance against the sovereign but in combating the rationality of unfitness declarations in the freedom and knowledge of persons with psychosocial disabilities.[42] This is because persons with psychosocial disabilities, through the government, have been induced to accept that they are unfit.

Nevertheless, some scholars have argued that Foucault's counter-conduct ideology is related to the rights discourse. Counter-conduct through the rights discourse challenges 'anything as definitive, and untouchable, obvious, or immobile' in an attempt to 'bring things back to their original mobility, their openness to change'.[43] He considered rights as a basis from which to resist power relations of domination.[44] Thus, counter-conduct ideology is important when analysing the legality of unfitness declarations in Kenya. The result of counter-conduct ideology is law reform. However, it has been argued that the social control system needs law reform to perpetuate itself.[45] Therefore, it is important to avoid reproducing the control of persons with psychosocial disabilities under the guise of unfitness declaration reform.

38 As above.
39 As above.
40 Lacombe (n 16) 343.
41 M Foucault 'Va-t-on Extrader Klaus Croissant?' in D Defert & F Ewald (eds) *Dits et Ecrits III 1978–1979* (1994) 362.
42 Lacombe (n 16) 348.
43 O Louiza 'Human rights, self-formation and resistance in struggles against disposability: grounding Foucault's 'theorizing practice' of counter-conduct in Bhopal' (2016) 30 *Global Society* 9.
44 S Legg 'Subjects of truth: resisting governmentality in Foucault's 1980s' (2019) 37 *Environment and Planning D: Society and Space* 28.
45 Lacombe (n 16) 336.

The counter-conduct concept should be used to highlight and challenge modes of subjectification such as unfitness declarations that aim at the exclusion of persons with psychosocial disabilities. Like the social model, the Foucauldian theory's aim is to integrate persons with psychosocial disabilities as talented social participants.[46] However, it goes a step further to provide the disability community with a language of resistance.[47] Law is constantly transforming through its complex relations with that which it governs, not only the disciplines themselves but also those resistant and inventive subjects and processes that the disciplines also seek to govern. Disabled persons groups are urged to reject the subordinate place that unfitness declarations give to persons with psychosocial disabilities.[48]

2.1.7 Overall criticism of Foucauldian theory

One of the main criticisms of the Foucauldian theory is that it is a Western episteme about subjects in the South.[49] Some scholars from the Global South consider Foucault's theories to be Eurocentric particularly because they originated from Europe before being generalised to the rest of the world. Undoubtedly, European history is not world history. But even in Europe, some of Foucault's work has been criticised for being subjective and based on historical inaccuracies. An example is his observation that persons with mental disabilities were considered wise in renaissance Europe when in fact they were mistreated and viewed as objects possessed by demons, as will be discussed in Chapter 3.[50]

Africa, Asia, and Middle East also have their own histories and the use of Foucault's theoretical apparatus betrays the goal to produce subaltern studies. Moreover, Foucault provided no route map for escape, no revolutionary or reformist programme for how psychosocial disabilities and unfitness declarations ought to be governed in Kenya.[51] He never considered how indigenous Africans managed psychosocial disabilities. These knowledge gaps are filled by decolonial theory. In Africa, decolonisation provides an ideal opportunity for researchers to begin to consider fresh ways of addressing African social problems through African theories and methodologies. In Kenya's criminal justice system, decolonisation allows justice actors to consider alternative ways

46 Beaudry (n 8) 319.

47 Beaudry (n 8) 320.

48 As above.

49 E Ruíz 'The oxford handbook of feminist philosophy: "postcolonial and decolonial theories"' https://philarchive.org/archive/RUZPAD (accessed 15 December 2021) 5.

50 M Rowlinson & C Carter 'Foucault and history in organization studies' (2002) 9 *Organization* 533.

51 P O'Malley & M Valverde 'Foucault, criminal law, and the governmentalization of the state' in MD Dubber (ed) *Foundational texts in modern criminal law* (2014) 320.

of addressing the participation in access to justice of persons with psychosocial disabilities.

2.2 Decolonial theory

Decolonial theory offers pertinent insights into exclusion and the move towards more inclusive societies.[52] Decolonial theory has much to offer on the concept of disability and access to justice in participation which are frequently informed by the Eurocentric orientation. Decolonial analyses of unfitness declarations which question Eurocentric assumptions are scarce. Eurocentric assumptions are views from the epistemic West which implies that they are premised on the monotopic global design in which other cultures and peoples exist only as 'the other'. They are ghosts of the British empire which are filled with Eurocentric ideas of paternalism and justice. Kenya's unfitness declarations regimes are based on borrowed concepts from the colonial English common law. There is a need to rethink their usefulness by considering their effect in Kenya's community, being, and morality. Moreover, apart from rethinking the epistemic perspectives of disability, decolonial theory also directs attention beyond barriers inhibiting the participation of disabled people towards the revelation and disruption of ableist foundations of mainstream institutions and laws.

However, some scholars have argued that decolonial thinking draws on dichotomic opposition that relies on origins, identity, race, and location thus falling into the trap of essentialisation. For example, in discourses on decolonising unfitness declarations, the identity of the African is equated with the indigenous, ethnic or native without considering other grounds for an African identity. Mbembe states that the use of Africa implies unanimity within the continent about what is African and what is not which is not the case.[53] Ngwena surmises that what is Africanness is a construct that sits at the intersection of multiple discourses depending on the place, time, and culture of the people involved.[54] As a highly situated and contextualised concept, it means that some people may perceive it objectively as being all-embracing, dynamic, and cosmopolitan, while others may regard it subjectively as being static and exclusive.

Undoubtedly, Africa is much more an idea than it is a cartographic unit. Therefore, decolonial theory should be framed in a way that, while conscious of the history and subordinating effects of colonialism, does not assume that Africans are homogeneous. The mere fusion of Global South and Global North understandings of the concept of psychosocial disability is not sufficient to ensure the right of participation in access to justice for disabled persons in

52 SA Nixon et al. 'Using postcolonial perspectives to consider rehabilitation with children with disabilities: the Bamenda-Toronto dialogue' (2015) 2 *Disability and the Global South* 572.

53 A Mbembe *On the postcolony* (2015) 78.

54 Ngwena (n 2) 24.

Kenya. Moreover, the Global South is not the only neglected sphere in terms of knowledge apartheid relating to psychosocial disabilities. The decolonisation process needs to go beyond the North/South dichotomy to incorporate other cultures, knowledge traditions, and indigenous concepts of psychosocial disabilities from noncolonial powers, such as those of the 'Second World', which includes Russia and China.[55]

The decolonial theory does not call for the rejection of all aspects of colonial unfitness declaration laws, especially those that are capable of being adapted if deemed appropriate and beneficial to accused persons with psychosocial disabilities. The West is not a homogenous component and unfitness declaration views by Western societies are not monolithic or unanimous. Differences also existed in the outlooks of unfitness declarations by colonial societies. Thus, this research does not reject all aspects of unfitness declarations. The author argues that to some extent unfitness declarations have ensured the rights of accused persons with psychosocial disabilities in access to justice. The right to fair trial has historically been used as a justification and very foundation of the unfitness declaration laws. For example, it has been argued that unfitness declarations act as a check against the mistrial of accused persons with psychosocial disabilities if they are unable to understand the legal process and the charges against them.[56] Accordingly, the process of decolonising unfitness declaration laws should begin by negotiating all the liberating strands of colonial and noncolonial epistemologies affecting persons with psychosocial disabilities, such as the demand for rights, autonomy, agency and disabled persons' capacity, with local implementations that involve long and located traditions of social power building.[57]

2.2.1 Persistence of coloniality in Kenya's unfitness declaration laws

Coloniality refers to the long patterns of colonial matrices of power that have emerged from colonialism.[58] Coloniality goes beyond the state of being colonised to include control over how people sense and perceive the world. Particularly, coloniality encompasses the production of disability from within intersubjective relations. Coloniality places persons with psychosocial disabilities in the 'zone of nonbeing' where their rights are overridden by that of the

55 A Glück 'De-westernization and decolonization in media studies' http://eprints.bournemouth.ac.uk/34139/13/De-Westernization_acrefore-9780190228613-e-898.pdf (accessed 13 December 2021) 20.

56 B McSherry et al. *Unfitness to plead and indefinite detention of persons with cognitive disabilities: addressing the legal barriers and creating appropriate alternative supports in the community* Melbourne: Melbourne Social Equity Institute, University of Melbourne (2017) 17.

57 O Acha 'The places of critical universalism: postcolonial and decolonial approaches in contexts' https://doi.org/10.1515/9783110492415-008 (accessed 15 December 2021) 104.

58 M Lugones 'Heterosexualism and the colonial/modern gender system' (2007) 22 *Hypatia* 186.

dominant group. Unfitness declaration laws are a product of colonial administrations, colonial cultures, and structures of Kenya's criminal justice system. Coloniality makes visible how the instrumentality of the colonial/modern unfitness declarations systems are subjecting persons with psychosocial disabilities in Kenya's criminal justice system. Coloniality has different strands, including coloniality of being, coloniality of knowledge, and coloniality of power.

Coloniality of being

The coloniality of being constructs different identities and categorisations of people.[59] It is the global ordering by dominant power structures to ensure the perpetual classification of people into invented binaries of inferior/superior, irrational/rational, primitive/civilised, traditional/modern, black/white, civilised/uncivilised, powerful/marginalised, and able/disabled.[60] These bipolar dichotomies and particularly in the context of fit and unfit persons, denies multiplicity, differences, and plurality.[61] The decolonisation movement is a struggle to include the unfit and ensure that their right to have rights is respected, protected, and promoted, beginning with their right to visibility. It is a struggle against minoritisation, invisibility, and stereotypes.

The standard measure of normalcy is what has constructed disability as 'the other'. The social ordering process uses a 'normal body and mind' as a measuring standard, and as a result all other individuals with different bodies and minds are viewed as deviating from the norm, and are hence labelled unfit. Differences are what brings about labels but if these distinctions were to be viewed as part of humanity, regardless of the peculiarities in bodies, in minds, in colour, in social and economic status, there would be no hierarchical identities, no notion of 'the other' and no inequalities.[62] More importantly, there would be no distinctions between the fit and unfit.[63]

Coloniality of knowledge

Coloniality of knowledge is about hegemony in knowledge production.[64] Epistemic barriers inhibit the redemption of positive African knowledge on psychosocial disability that is neither rooted in, nor oriented around colonialism. Epistemic coloniality in unfitness declaration laws is informed by

59 Ndlovu-Gatsheni (n 2) 36.

60 A Quijano 'Coloniality of power, ethnocentrism, and Latin America' (2000) 1 *Nepantla* 543.

61 S Ndlovu 'Obstacles and opportunities for students with disabilities in entering and in preparation to graduate into professions in higher learning: the case of a university in South Africa' PhD Thesis, University of South Africa, 2016, 138.

62 Ndlovu (n 61) 139.

63 As above.

64 Ndlovu-Gatsheni (n 2) 35.

legacies of colonialism, incomplete education and curated access to theory, information, and experience. An extract from an anonymous article appearing in 1860 stated as follows:

> 'English gentlemen' ought to be: 'the centres of civili[s]ation from whence enlightenment and knowledge shall radiate standing forth like beacon lights to illumine the darkness of a benighted land; an ever present example of the wonders which English justice, probity and independence can achieve'.[65]

The above extract reveals the ego-politics of knowledge by Western philosophy and sciences, which assumes a universalistic, neutral, and objective point of view.[66] Common law theology has disguised unfitness declarations as God-ordained; a law of nature; or as the Romans would have it, the *jus gentium*[67] for persons with psychosocial disabilities.

The issue regarding the non-participation of persons with psychosocial disabilities in access to justice following unfitness declarations in Kenya cannot be solved by Western knowledge alone.[68] There is no *deus ex machina*[69] process by means of which Western epistemology will automatically solve the challenges of participation of persons with psychosocial disabilities following unfitness declarations as would a mechanical arm in a staged play in ancient Greece.[70] Thinking about decolonisation invites justice actors to consider what kind of unfitness declarations features should be shaped beyond modernity/coloniality in order to ensure the participation in access to justice of persons with psychosocial disability, rather than imagining a return to a pre-colonial past. Cultures such as ubuntuism, *botho* (respect for all), Afriethics, and oramedia which value humanness, dialogue, public good, consensus, and community care have the potential of facilitating the participation of persons with psychosocial disabilities in access to justice.[71] These cultures have liberating strands. The process of decolonisation should involve the liberating strands of African cultures that promote human rights, autonomy, and agency of persons with psychosocial disabilities.[72]

65 S Mizutani 'Hybridity and history: a critical reflection on Homi K. Bhabha's "post-historical" thought' (2009) 41 *Zinbun* 4.
66 R Grosfoguel 'Decolonizing post-colonial studies and paradigms of political economy: transmodernity, decolonial thinking, and global coloniality' https://dialnet.unirioja.es/descarga/articulo/3998080.pdf (accessed 10 December 2021).
67 Literal meaning: 'law of nations'.
68 R Grosfoguel 'The epistemic decolonial turn: beyond political-economy paradigms' (2007) 21 *Cultural Studies* 212.
69 Literal meaning: 'a god from the machine'.
70 C Lombaard '*Deus ex Machina*? Religious texts, spiritual capital and inequalities: in continuation of a current debate (a response to colleague Farisani)' (2015) 36 *Verbum et Ecclesia* 6.
71 Glück (n 55) 13.
72 Acha (n 57) 104.

Admittedly, in some cultures in Kenya, as discussed in Chapter 3, psychosocial disability is based on the morality model, which situates disability as a result of a person's sins or moral lapse thus leading to shame to the individual and to the family. However, there are some cultures where, contrary to the morality model, psychosocial disability is seen as a gift, a source of wisdom or a welcome contact with the spirits or the spiritual or philosophical life.[73] It means that Kenya's views on psychosocial disability are not static and can affect disabled persons positively or negatively. However, colonial matrices of power remain deeply entrenched in spheres of psychosocial disability and unfitness declarations.[74] The adoption of colonial laws by Kenya implies legitimacy and universality of unfitness declaration laws in controlling persons with psychosocial disabilities which is not the case. Accordingly, the author argues for alternative frameworks to unfitness declarations to be considered without any censorship.[75] Decolonisation requires that positive discourse on psychosocial disability in Kenya should be given its own space.[76]

Coloniality of power

Coloniality of power in unfitness declarations is characterised by domination, oppression, and the persistence of a colonial mentality against persons with psychosocial disability. It emerged from Foucault's concept of disciplinary power.[77] In the conflict arena of unfitness, the two parties that are pitted against each other features unfit versus the fit persons. It is 'them versus us' whereby the 'us' are humanised able-bodied persons and the 'them' are de-humanised persons with psychosocial disabilities. Domination of persons with psychosocial disabilities is the goal of unfitness declarations in the present legal structure.

The effects of coloniality of power is felt by persons with psychosocial disabilities and has impacted negatively on all dimensions of their social lives. Unfitness declarations are insufficient to the task of acknowledging the participation power of persons with psychosocial disabilities in Kenya's criminal justice system. The binary construction of fit and unfit, serves to limit access to agency and they also reinforce colonial power relations that have legitimised the discrimination of persons with psychosocial disabilities. Unfitness declaration laws should be examined in order to bring about reforms, which are not only more inclusive but are also aligned with the circumstances of Kenya. In

73 KC Hari 'Disability discourse in South Asia and global disability governance' (2016) 5 *Canadian Journal of Disability Studies* 39.

74 T Chari 'Decolonising conflict reporting: media and election violence in Zimbabwe' in B Karam & B Mutsvairo (eds) *Decolonising political communication in Africa* (2022) 14.

75 Ndlovu (n 61) 141.

76 D Stienstra 'For Michael Charlie: including girls and boys with disabilities in the global South/North' (2015) 2 *Disability and the Global South* 634.

77 Ndlovu-Gatsheni (n 2) 35.

turn, this will lead to ensuring the right to participation in access to justice of persons with psychosocial disabilities.

2.3 Strengthening the social model of disability through the Foucauldian and decolonial theories

The social model of disability attributes the cause of disability to society.[78] It argues that disabled persons only have one important attribute in common, which is that they are all subject to oppression.[79] In this radical model, the limitations of people who are considered disabled result primarily from their societal context.[80] The soul of the social model was described by one activist as a political strategy aimed at countering social oppression and dismantling disabling barriers that have unnecessarily inhibited the inclusion and participation of persons with impairments in the mainstream society.[81]

The main criticism against the social model is that it over-emphasises the aspect of 'being disabled by society' while under-emphasising the impact of impairments in participation restrictions and activity limitations on individuals.[82] In other words, it theorises away the body thus resulting in a failure to interrogate disabled people's differences.[83] However, especially through the Foucauldian theory, legal reformists are able to interrogate how the life and body of disabled persons are constituted not only by the society but also how persons with psychosocial disabilities have internalised the stigma of their impairments.[84]

The social model of disability focuses more on physical impairments as opposed to non-physical impairments, such as psychosocial disabilities.[85] The emphasis on physical disabilities as opposed to non-physical disabilities implies that among disabled persons, certain groups are classified as powerless while others are seen as being more powerful. This is reinforced by the social model's emphasis on the need to speak with one voice about the experience of disability and disability oppression, which may lead to the suppression of intersectional experiences of disabled people who occupy other marginalised identity positions.[86] The social model prefers philosophising over disability as opposed to the application of more pragmatic medical and psychiatric expertise in order

78 F Kiuppisa & A Soorenianb 'Bridging continents, cultures, and crip theories: teaching comparative and international disability studies in education and sociology' (2017) 19 *Scandinavian Journal of Disability Research* 120.
79 Kiuppisa & Soorenianb (n 78) 121.
80 Kiuppisa & Soorenianb (n 78) 120.
81 M Oliver 'The politics of disablement' (1990) 11.
82 Kiuppisa & Soorenianb (n 78) 121.
83 Beaudry (n 8) 318.
84 Lacombe (n 16) 343.
85 Kiuppisa & Soorenianb (n 78) 120.
86 TP Dirth & GA Adams 'Decolonial theory and disability studies: on the modernity/coloniality of ability' (2019) 7 *Journal of Social and Political Psychology* 269.

to overcome the obstacles, as well as suffering and anguish, which disabled persons experience and must navigate.[87] On the contrary, power dynamics in the Foucauldian and decolonial theories offers ways of addressing injustices and powerlessness that deny persons with psychosocial disabilities their right of participation in access to justice.

Foucauldian and decolonial theories enable legal reformists to explore alternatives, such as mental health and community-based diversion programmes, which as discussed in Chapter 7 are able to address barriers of participation in access to justice that are caused by mental impairment. Psychological barriers such as stress and fear due to lengthy and complicated legal processes can result in lack of effective participation for persons with psychosocial disabilities in access to justice.[88] Persons with psychosocial disabilities who have stressful lives as a result of their impairment may find it difficult to participate in the legal process because of its potential to compound their stress. The latter may act as a barrier during the initial stage of the legal process, it may deter persons with psychosocial disabilities from continuing with a legal process, or prevent them from participating effectively during a legal process.[89] Other persons with psychosocial disabilities may be motivated by fear and shame about their disability and as a result end up disguising their lack of understanding from the police, lawyers, and other legal service providers who in turn will fail to provide them with the necessary support needed to help them participate effectively in the trial process.[90] Mental health and community-based diversion programmes provide treatment-based alternatives to criminal trials for accused persons with psychosocial disabilities. The main objective of mental health and community-based diversion programmes is to process persons with psychosocial disabilities away from the criminal justice system.[91]

The other concern regards, the genealogy of the social model of disability. While the social model of disability has had a positive approach to cultures that in a sense medicalised disability, its genealogy remains to be Eurocentric. The social model's hegemonic understanding of disability is based on Western values, thus the need to draw from the decolonial theory which includes epistemic perspectives of disability from Global South countries. The process of Africanisation in the continent is evident in the African Disability Rights Protocol which is informed by both the social and human rights model of disability. The African Disability Rights Protocol is concerned with the removal

87 L Gahman 'Crip theory and country boys: masculinity, dis/ability, and place in rural southeast Kansas' https://core.ac.uk/download/pdf/169433775.pdf (accessed 20 August 2021) 7.

88 M Karras et al. *On the edge of justice: the legal needs of people with a mental illness in NSW* Sydney: Law and Justice Foundation of NSW, 128.

89 As above.

90 A Gray et al. 'Cognitive impairment, legal need, and access to justice' (2009) 10 *Justice Issues* 6.

91 F Sirotich 'The criminal justice outcomes of jail diversion programs for persons with mental illness: A review of the evidence' (2009) 37 *The Journal of the American Academy of Psychiatry and the Law* 461.

of specific barriers that hinder the right of persons with psychosocial disabilities to access justice and the provision of accommodations.

However, the African Disability Rights Protocol does not secure a proper blueprint for the protection of persons with psychosocial disabilities in Kenya's unfitness declaration laws. The African Disability Rights Protocol does not address the common law's justifications of unfitness declarations, neither does it specify how reasonable accommodations should be achieved and the measures needed to enhance the participation of persons with psychosocial disabilities in the criminal justice sector. The decolonial theory especially, aims at filling these gaps by seeking to undo coloniality/colonial mechanisms of power, language, culture, and thinking that shape unfitness declarations. The decolonial theory interrogates the provenance and legitimacy of the common law origins, dominant forms of knowledge, values, norms, and assumptions regarding unfitness declarations. It also contributes towards making proposals on how the weaknesses of Kenya's unfitness declaration regimes can be remedied in order to ensure the effective participation of persons with psychosocial disabilities.[92]

Another criticism of the social model of disability is that it does not deal with the need to reform or remove the phenomena of unfitness declarations and put in place safeguards to protect the participation of persons with psychosocial disabilities. Stein and Lord correctly observe that '[t]he principal difficulty with this approach is that existing . . . obligations are not tailored to address the specific barriers faced by persons with disabilities in the realisation of their human rights'.[93] The Foucauldian and decolonial theories are used in this research in order to strengthen the social model of disability by considering the practice of unfitness declarations, the essence of unfitness declarations, and the mechanisms for improving the participation of persons with psychosocial disabilities in access to justice. The Foucauldian and decolonial theories also direct attention beyond barriers inhibiting the participation of disabled people towards the revelation and disruption of ableist foundations of mainstream institutions and laws. The Foucauldian and decolonial theories are also concerned with the freedom of persons with psychosocial disabilities to act freely. The capacity to act freely is what brings about power in individuals.[94] Article 12 of the CRPD also supports the notion of legal capacity.

Article 12 of the CRPD provides for the right to equal recognition before the law, which entails the right to legal capacity on an equal basis with others

92 M Sherry 'Intersecting gender and disability perspectives in rethinking postcolonial identities' (2007) 4 *Wagadu* 11.

93 MA Stein & JE Lord 'Future prospects for the United Nations Convention on the Rights of Persons with Disabilities' http://www.law.wisc.edu/m/zdq3n/2-20-09_steinlord_future_prospects_for_un_on_disability_rights.pdf (accessed 14 January 2022) 19.

94 M Bevir 'Foucault and critique: deploying agency against autonomy' (1999) 27 *Political Theory* 73.

in all areas of life.[95] It is derived from article 16 of the ICCPR which guarantees everyone the right to recognition everywhere as a person before the law. The right to legal capacity includes both the right to legal personhood and legal agency. Foucault also supports the idea of agency.[96] Through his concept of monstrous which is related to abnormal bodies he opines that disabled persons should not be barred from co-operating in, accountable to, or from being effective social participants on account of their disability.[97] Simply, they should not be cast away as monsters but should be considered part of the social contract. As such, no person's legal capacity should be denied on the basis of their difference as seen in the case of unfitness declarations in Kenya. The empirical research in Chapters 6 and 7 revealed that unfitness declarations violate the right of participation for persons with psychosocial disabilities. Instead of denying persons with psychosocial disabilities' legal capacity, article 12 of the CRPD requires that they be provided with support that assists with the determination and expression of their will and preference. This book supports the view that under the Foucauldian and decolonial theories, legal capacity is never denied on the basis of an individual's membership in a protected class, including psychosocial disability.

2.4 Conclusion

The Foucauldian and decolonial theories that this research relies upon consider the individual's body and mind as essential part of the disability phenomenon and not just the contextual factors.[98] Through these theories, this research is committed to studying the concept of unfitness declaration in Kenya's criminal justice system not only through the lens of attitudinal and environmental barriers that hinder the full and effective participation of persons with psychosocial disabilities in society, but also by taking into consideration the impact that impairments can have on them.

This chapter has discussed the theoretical framework underpinning this research. It has demonstrated how the Foucauldian and decolonial theories enriches the social model of disability in order to ensure the rights of disabled persons. The Focauldian and decolonial theories have the potential to empower persons with psychosocial disabilities and ensure their participation in justice systems. The Foucauldian and decolonial theories also helps to forge a collective politics on disability rights, make visible assumptions or taken-for-granted truths that shape the disability discourse and to invite alternative ways of understanding unfitness declarations. The theories are emancipatory in their aims, they seek

95 A Arstein-Kerslakea & J Blackb 'Right to legal capacity in therapeutic jurisprudence: insights from critical disability theory and the convention on the rights of persons with disabilities' (2020) 68 *International Journal of Law and Psychiatry* 3.

96 M Foucault *The hermeneutics of the subject* trans G Burchell (2005) 67.

97 Beaudry (n 8) 318.

98 Kiuppisa & Soorenianb (n 78) 120.

new ways of and more progressive forms of action in the realisation of access to justice rights for persons with psychosocial disabilities. The next chapter analyses the construction of psychosocial disability by applying the two theories.

References

Acha O 'The places of critical universalism: postcolonial and decolonial approaches in contexts' https://doi.org/10.1515/9783110492415–008 (accessed 15 December 2021).

Arstein-Kerslakea A & Black J 'Right to legal capacity in therapeutic jurisprudence: insights from critical disability theory and the convention on the rights of persons with disabilities' (2020) 68 *International Journal of Law and Psychiatry* 3. https://doi.org/10.1016/j.ijlp.2019.101535.

Beaudry J 'The vanishing body of disability law: power and the making of the impaired subject' (2018a) 31 *Canadian Journal of Family Law* 27.

Beaudry J 'Welcoming monsters: disability as a liminal legal concept' (2018b) 29 *Yale Journal of Law & the Humanities* 306.

Bednarz D 'Power, identity and social change as we enter degrowth' https://www.resilience.org/stories/2013-08-14/power-identity-and-social-change-as-we-enter-degrowth/ (accessed 19 July 2022).

Bevir M 'Foucault and critique: deploying agency against autonomy' (1999) 27 *Political Theory* 73.

Carlen P *Magistrates' justice* (1976).

'Chapter 1: the Foucauldean concept of power' https://www.lkouniv.ac.in/site/writereaddata/siteContent/202004021930365629saroj_dhal_socio_FOUCOULT.pdf (accessed 27 June 2021).

Chari T 'Decolonising conflict reporting: media and election violence in Zimbabwe' in B Karam & B Mutsvairo (eds) *Decolonising political communication in Africa* (2022) 14.

Criminal Procedure Code, Cap 75 (Laws of Kenya).

Dirth TP & Adams GA 'Decolonial theory and disability studies: on the modernity/coloniality of ability' (2019) 7 *Journal of Social and Political Psychology* 269. https://doi.org/10.5964/jspp.v7i1.762.

Donaldson EJ 'The corpus of the madwoman: toward a feminist disability studies theory of embodiment and mental illness' (2002) 14 *NWSA Journal* 100. https://doi.org/10.1353/nwsa.2003.0003.

Dubois M 'The governance of the third world: a Foucauldian perspective on power relations in development' (1991) 16 *Alternatives: Global, Local, Political* 1.

Foucault M *Madness and civilization: a history of insanity in the age of reason* (1965).

Foucault M *The order of things: an archaeology of the human sciences* (1970).

Foucault M *The birth of the clinic: archaeology of medical perception* (1973).

Foucault M *The history of sexuality: an introduction* trans R Hurley (1978) vol 1.

Foucault M *Discipline and punish: the birth of the prison* (1991).

Foucault M 'Va-t-on Extrader Klaus Croissant?' in Defert D & Ewald F (eds) *Dits et Ecrits III 1978–1979* (1994) 362.

Foucault M *Abnormal. Lectures at the Collège de France 1974–1975* (2003).

Foucault M *The hermeneutics of the subject G Burchell* (2005).

Gahman L 'Crip theory and country boys: masculinity, dis/ability, and place in rural southeast Kansas' https://core.ac.uk/download/pdf/169433775.pdf (accessed 20 August 2021).

Glück A 'De-westernization and decolonization in media studies' http://eprints.bournemouth.ac.uk/34139/13/De-Westernization_acrefore-9780190228613-e–898.pdf (accessed 13 December 2021).

Gray A et al. 'Cognitive impairment, legal need, and access to justice' (2009) 10 *Justice Issues* 6.

Grosfoguel R 'The epistemic decolonial turn. Beyond political-economy paradigms' (2007) 21 *Cultural Studies* 212. https://doi.org/10.1080/09502380601162514.

Grosfoguel R 'Decolonizing post-colonial studies and paradigms of political economy: transmodernity, decolonial thinking, and global coloniality' https://dialnet.unirioja.es/descarga/articulo/3998080.pdf (accessed 10 December 2021).

Hari KC 'Disability discourse in South Asia and global disability governance' (2016) 5 *Canadian Journal of Disability Studies* 39. https://doi.org/10.15353/cjds.v5i4.314.

Jackson MA 'Models of disability and human rights: informing the improvement of built environment accessibility for people with disability at neighborhood scale?' (2018) 7 *Laws* 3. https://doi.org/10.3390/laws7010010.

James N 'Law and power: ten lessons from Foucault' (2018) 30 *Bond Law Review* 39.

Karras M et al. *On the edge of justice: the legal needs of people with a mental illness in NSW* Sydney: Law and Justice Foundation of NSW (2006).

Kezia PE 'A radical relational agency: Foucault, complexity theory and environmental resistances' PhD Thesis, University of Nottingham, 2010.

Kiuppisa F and Soorenianb A 'Bridging continents, cultures, and crip theories: teaching comparative and international disability studies in education and sociology' (2017) 19 *Scandinavian Journal of Disability Research* 120. https://doi.org/10.1080/15017419.2016.1224200.

Lacombe D 'Reforming Foucault: a critique of the social control thesis' (1996) 47 *The British Journal of Sociology* 338.

Legg S 'Subjects of truth: resisting governmentality in Foucault's 1980s' (2019) 37 *Environment and Planning D: Society and Space* 28. https://doi.org/10.1177/0263775818801.

Lombaard C 'Deus ex Machina? Religious texts, spiritual capital and inequalities: in continuation of a current debate (a response to colleague Farisani)' (2015) 36 *Verbum et Ecclesia* 6. https://doi.org/10.4102/VE.V36I1.1378.

Louiza O 'Human rights, self-formation and resistance in struggles against disposability: grounding Foucault's 'theorizing practice' of counter-conduct in Bhopal' (2016) 30 *Global Society* 9. https://doi.org/10.1080/13600826.2016.1141178.

Lugones M 'Heterosexualism and the colonial/modern gender system' (2007) 22 *Hypatia* 186. https://doi.org/10.1111/j.1527–2001.2007.tb01156.x.

Mbembe A *Out of the dark night: essays on decolonisation* Columbia University Press (2021).

McIntyre K 'Foucault on freedom and domination' 31 January 2012 https://partiallyexaminedlife.com/2012/01/31/foucault-on-freedom-and-domination/ (accessed 4 September 2022).

McSherry B et al. *Unfitness to plead and indefinite detention of persons with cognitive disabilities: addressing the legal barriers and creating appropriate alternative supports in the community* Melbourne: Melbourne Social Equity Institute, University of Melbourne (2017).

Mizutani S 'Hybridity and history: a critical reflection on Homi K. Bhabha's 'post-historical' thought' (2009) 41 *Zinbun* 4.

Ndlovu S 'Obstacles and opportunities for students with disabilities in entering and in preparation to graduate into professions in higher learning: the case of a university in South Africa' PhD Thesis, University of South Africa, 2016.

Ndlovu-Gatsheni SJ *Decolonization development and knowledge in Africa: turning on a new leaf* (2020).

Ngwena C 'Developing juridical method for overcoming status subordination in disablism: the place of transformative epistemologies' (2014) 30 *South African Journal of Human Rights* 283.

Ngwena CG *What is Africanness? Contesting nativism in race, culture and sexualities* (2018).

Nixon SA et al. 'Using postcolonial perspectives to consider rehabilitation with children with disabilities: the Bamenda-Toronto dialogue' (2015) 2 *Disability and the Global South* 572.

Nuwagaba EL & Rule PN 'Power dynamics among PWDs during adult learning processes: motivator or demotivator?' (2015) 3 *Rwandan Journal of Education* 55.

Oliver M 'The politics of disablement' (1990) 11.

O'Malley P & Valverde M 'Foucault, criminal law, and the governmentalization of the state' in MD Dubber (ed) *Foundational texts in modern criminal law* (2014) 320.

Quijano A 'Coloniality of power, ethnocentrism, and Latin America' (2000) 1 *Nepantla* 543.

Rowlinson M & Carter C 'Foucault and history in organization studies (2002) 9 *Organization* 533.

Ruíz E 'The oxford handbook of feminist philosophy: "Postcolonial and decolonial theories"' https://philarchive.org/archive/RUZPAD (accessed 15 December 2021).

Sherry M 'Intersecting gender and disability perspectives in rethinking postcolonial identities' (2007) 4 *Wagadu* 11.

Sirotich F 'The criminal justice outcomes of jail diversion programs for persons with mental illness: a review of the evidence' (2009) 37 *The journal of the American Academy of Psychiatry and the Law* 461.

Stein MA & Lord JE 'Future prospects for the United Nations Convention on the Rights of Persons with Disabilities' http://www.law.wisc.edu/m/zdq3n/2-20-09_steinlord_future_prospects_for_un_on_disability_rights.pdf (accessed 14 January 2022).

Stienstra D 'For Michael Charlie: including girls and boys with disabilities in the global South/North' (2015) 2 *Disability and the Global South* 634.

Suntrup JC 'Michel Foucault and the competing alethurgies of law' (2017) 37 *Oxford Journal of Legal Studies* 301. https://doi.org/10.1093/ojls/gqw019.

Verovšek PJ 'The reluctant postmodernism of Jürgen Habermas: reevaluating Habermas's debates with Foucault and Derrida' (2022) 84 *The Review of Politics* 26. https://doi.org/10.1017/S0034670522000316.

Wendy S et al. 'From criminalisation to individual choice: policy responses to changing constructions of intellectual disability in Western Australia' (2019) 21 *Scandinavian Journal of Disability Research* 102. https://doi.org/10.16993/sjdr.571.

Zheng LE 'Colonial psychiatry in Africa: a distorted science? Practice, knowledge, and power' https://www.researchgate.net/publication/328051535 (accessed 30 June 2021).

3 Constructing psychosocial disability

3.0 Introduction

This chapter discusses the construction of psychosocial disability. It examines the concept of psychosocial disability with a view of deconstructing the ideologies inherent in the concept. In this chapter the Foucauldian and decolonial theories will be used to interrogate how psychosocial disability is constructed in the society. Defining and delimiting psychosocial disability is a complex, ambiguous, and controversial arena.[1] On the one hand, psycho indicates that the disability is of or about the mind. On the other hand, disability is a concept that is related to other concepts such as illness, disorder, medical condition, malady, and disease. However, what properly is encompassed by the category psychosocial disability is a matter on which consensus is not easily reached.[2]

There are competing explanations and theories of mental disability, including biological perspectives,[3] philosophical interpretations,[4] legal perspectives, and rejection of mental disability as anything other than a social construction.[5] In this study, mental disability refers to both psychosocial and intellectual disabilities.[6] However, 'psychosocial disabilities' should be differentiated from intellectual capacity, mental impairment, and cognitive disability. Intellectual disability is characterised by significant permanent limitations in intellectual

1 RL Woolfolk 'The concept of mental illness: an analysis of four pivotal issues' (2001) 22 *Journal of Mind and Behavior* 161.

2 Woolfolk (n 1) 161.

3 NC Andreasen *The broken brain: the biological revolution in psychiatry* (1984).

4 M Foucault *Madness and civilization: a history of insanity in the age of reason* (1965) & M Foucault *The history of sexuality* (1986).

5 T Szasz 'The use of naming and the origin of the myth of mental illness' (1961) 16 *American Psychologist* 59, T Szasz *The manufacture of madness* (1970), T Szasz *The myth of mental illness* (1974).

6 Human Rights Watch 'Deportation by default: mental disability, unfair hearings, and indefinite detention in the US immigration system' https://www.hrw.org/report/2010/07/25/deportation-gdefault/mental-disability-unfair-hearings-and-indefinite-detention-us (accessed 9 August 2021).

DOI: 10.4324/9781003647102-3

functioning and adaptive behaviour in everyday social and practical skills.[7] Limitations in intellectual functioning refers to the ability to learn, reason, and solve problems.[8] Limitations in adaptive behaviour relate to three types of skills: conceptual skills, interpersonal skills, and practical skills. Conceptual skills involve language and literacy, money, time, and arithmetic concepts. Social skills involve interpersonal skills, self-esteem, and gullibility and practical skills involve daily living skills, safety, and use of money.[9]

Psychosocial disability is a term that reflects the interaction between psychological differences and social or cultural limits for behaviour as well as the stigma that the society attaches to persons with psychosocial disabilities.[10] This chapter is divided into three sections. This section introduces the study. Section two begins by defining the concept of psychosocial disability in the pre-psychiatric and psychiatric periods. The section then traces how psychosocial disability is constructed in Kenya. For Kenya, three periods are considered: the pre-colonial, colonial, and post-colonial periods. The objective is to determine the manner in which persons with psychosocial disabilities are regarded in terms of their autonomy, self-determination, and decision-making. Different constructions are highlighted in order to achieve several aims: (1) to provide multiple ways of understanding psychosocial disabilities around the globe; (2) to establish a critical lens of thinking about how psychosocial disability is constructed in Kenya; and, (3) to promote dialogue between African and Western understanding of psychosocial disabilities. Finally, section three concludes by suggesting that the construction of psychosocial disability in both the scientific and non-scientific approaches is dehumanising towards persons with psychosocial disabilities as they are considered objects first, which is something less than human beings.

3.1 Definitions and classifications of psychosocial disabilities

Various conceptions of psychosocial disabilities exist around the globe depending on the attitudes of a particular society or profession. Even the psychiatric classification of psychosocial disabilities has its roots in antiquity.[11] Through an analysis of his symptoms, Sophocles' Ajax is reported to have suffered one

7 LM Mute 'Shattering the glass ceiling: ensuring the right to vote for persons with intellectual disabilities in Kenya' (2010) 2 *A Journal of the Philosophical Association of Kenya (PAK) New Series* 5.

8 As above.

9 As above.

10 Human Rights Watch 'Deportation by default: mental disability, unfair hearings, and indefinite detention in the US immigration system' https://www.hrw.org/report/2010/07/25/deportation-default/mental-disability-unfair-hearings-and-indefinite-detention-us (accessed 9 August 2021).

11 LA Clark et al. 'Three approaches to understanding and classifying mental disorder: *ICD-11*, *DSM-5*, and the National Institute of Mental Health's Research Domain Criteria (RDoC)' (2017) 18 *Psychological Science in the Public Interest* 73.

of the first depressions in Western literature.[12] He experienced loss of appetite, anhedonia, sadness, and suicidality which are symptoms of depression as is also described in the bible and other ancient sources.

The naturalist or biomedical view holds that the various types of psychosocial disabilities are underpinned by an identical biological deep structure.[13] The objectivist natural position is that psychosocial disability is necessary for psychopathology and involves a departure from the normal and proper functioning of the mind or the brain.[14] Two eras have been studied in this section in an attempt to define and classify psychosocial disability. They are the pre-psychiatric era and the psychiatric era. The dialectic of both pre-psychiatric and psychiatric eras classifies psychosocial disability into two categories between the 'normal' and 'abnormal' and is based on Foucault's concept of able-bodiedness.[15] For each of these, there are corresponding analyses of what the able-bodied consider to be normal and abnormal behaviour, each with various implications for the concept of psychosocial disability.

3.1.1 Psychosocial disability in the pre-psychiatric era

In the Western pre-psychiatric era, mental health was viewed under the lens of religion.[16] To be accepted in the society, an individual's character traits, personality traits and lifestyle habits, relationship with self, with others, with social norms, and nature had to be in compliance with religion. Religion provided the standards with which to measure the mental and spiritual health of a person. An individual who did not meet the standards was considered to be ill.[17]

The classification of psychosocial disability in the pre-psychiatric era was often attributed to the supernatural.[18] It was believed that psychosocial disability could be traced from demons.[19] One scholar generally concluded that medicine in all ancient civilisations, was shrouded in magic.[20] Not only witchcraft but demonology flourished as exorcistic practices and prayers were offered to the gods. In Egypt, medical papyri written towards the middle of the 2nd century abounded in incantations and occult explanations for diseases.

12 Woolfolk (n 1) 174.
13 As above.
14 Woolfolk (n 1) 169.
15 L Gahman 'Crip theory and country boys: masculinity, dis/ability, and place in rural southeast Kansas' https://core.ac.uk/download/pdf/169433775.pdf (accessed 20 August 2021) 9.
16 I Pajević & M Hasanović 'Antipsychiatry as the stigma' (2017) 29 *Psychiatria Danubina* 890.
17 As above.
18 Clark et al. (n 11) 73.
19 RK Bufford 'Demonic influence and mental disorders-Chapter 8 of "counseling and the demonic"' https://digitalcommons.georgefox.edu/cgi/viewcontent.cgi?referer=https://www.google.com/&httpsredir=1&article=1011&context=counselingandthedemonic (accessed 6 August 2021) 116.
20 LA Hamel 'Mental illness and demonisation' (2015) 11 *Journal of Adventist Mission Studies* 48.

Studies of ancient Babylon by archaeologists revealed that various demons of varying degrees of power were believed to be the cause of different diseases and causes of death. And for those who believed in God, death and disease lay in the hands of God.[21] For example, in John Chapter 9 verse 2, the following conversation took place between Jesus and his disciples:

> His disciples asked him, "Rabbi, who sinned, this man or his parents, that he was born blind?" "Neither this man nor his parents sinned," said Jesus, "but this happened so that the works of God might be displayed on him".[22]

This is proof that in Biblical times, disabilities were thought to happen because someone sinned.

Some of the characteristics of demonic influence include knowledge of supernatural, supernatural strength, going about naked, unable to hear or speak, seizures, blindness, use of different voice, presence of distinct personality, fierce violent behaviour, unusual behaviour or attitude, feeling of overpowering evil, and self-report of demonic influence.[23] These descriptions refer to psychosocial disabilities as opposed to intellectual disability, which is characterised by limited intellectual functioning, adaptive behaviours, and conceptual skills. As will be seen in the psychiatric era, psychosocial disability and demonic possession are two distinct phenomena.

3.1.2 Psychosocial disabilities in the psychiatric era

The psychiatric era began in the 1800s during the French Revolution, which ushered in the Age of Reason.[24] That was the period of social, intellectual, and religious change. These changes had a huge impact on society and its outlook on the world. Human beings, through medicine were able to gain control over death and diseases thus replacing faith in the measure of religion with faith in the measure of reason. The birth of science ushered in the era of medicine thus, the belief that the universe is governed by deterministic, causal principles. These concepts had a profound impact on the development of the fields of psychology and psychiatry.[25]

In 1904, the field known as social psychiatry emerged.[26] During this period, governments in the Western world attempted to control the social conditions and consequences of psychosocial disability, for example syphilis, alcoholism,

21 Hamel (n 20) 52.
22 Bible, 2 John 9:2–3 New International Version.
23 Bufford (n 19) 36.
24 Hamel (n 20) 52.
25 As above.
26 H Helmchen 'Different conceptions of mental illness: consequences for the association with patients' (2013) 4 *Frontiers in Psychology* 2.

asocial psychopathy, vagabondage, by social, particularly even eugenic measures.[27] Further, during the economic misery after World War I the aims of social psychiatry were radicalised by the eugenic and thereby biological ideas of racial hygiene and euthanasia.[28] 'Madness' was a term used to describe all manner of mental afflictions ranging from seizures to hallucinations during the psychiatric era.[29] Later, when madness came into conflict with the values of Western culture during the era of enlightenment, it was constructed to insanity, which was considered an illness.[30]

Asocial behaviour and incoherent speech were recognised as sick thus, warranting the removal of those affected from the human community since they were considered a human abstraction in a society that was pursuing the concrete.[31] They were confined as patients and were excluded from the world, the country, and common sense, which, in the community's eyes, was impaired in the mentally ill person.[32] This taking over of the body is what Foucault referred to as 'technologies of power' which act to objectivise the subject by determining the conduct of individuals and submitting them to certain ends or domination.[33] Using the technology of power, the object of the gaze is transformed to being the viewer who is able to gain expertise and control over those being gazed at.[34] According to Foucault, when human beings are 'made subjects' their 'subjective identity', who or what they understand themselves to be, is made or produced by being tied to a specific identity through a 'conscience or self-knowledge'.[35] This is known as the subjectivity problem.[36]

The most important point that Foucault extracts from his study of the conceptualisation of 'unreason' within the scientific age is that madness is an object of knowledge. The concept of madness and practices are beastlike which strips off the subject all senses and capacities.[37] The psychiatric subject is one which is to be returned to an idealised state. In theory the psychiatric subject possesses an identifiable nosological abnormality which needs to be degenerated into the normative ideal state. This can be done only through

27 As above.

28 As above.

29 N Hogan '"We're all mad here": Power and identity in the modern era of mental illness' (2016) 10 *Intersect* 73.

30 Hogan (n 29) 4.

31 L Joranger 'Psychology and the historical power–body conjunction: Foucault's different view of the history and philosophy of psychology' (2016) 26 *Theory & Psychology* 310.

32 As above.

33 HM Alenaizi 'Disability and Kuwaiti society: a critical realist approach to participatory research in contemporary Kuwaiti society' PhD Thesis, The University of Manchester 2017, 118.

34 As above.

35 M Roberts 'The production of the psychiatric subject: Power, knowledge and Michel Foucault' (2005) 6 *Nursing Philosophy* 34.

36 D Ninnis 'Foucault and the madness of classifying our madness' (2016) 21 *Foucault Studies* 125.

37 Ninnis (n 36) 128.

the relationship of doctor and patient as one where the latter subjects itself to the other. In both the scientific and non-scientific classification methods, the patient is reduced to a series of behaviours which are measured against a set of normative standards in order to determine whether the behaviours might be compulsive or symptomatic of an underlying mental condition.[38]

Early science conceptualised mental disability as a disease. Hippocrates, also referred to as the father of medicine, was the first to explain consistently all diseases on the basis of natural causes.[39] The father of medicine taught that it is nature that heals the patient and that the doctor is merely nature's assistant. The earliest natural-science theory of psychosocial disability was known as the Galen's typology.[40] The Galen's typology suggested that there were four categories of temperament-choleric, sanguine, melancholic, and phlegmatic. These categories were based on Hippocrates's theory that health required a balance among the body's purported four humors: yellow bile, blood, black bile, and phlegm. The individual temperament had an associated pathology, which was the result of excess in one of the humors. Contemporary scientific theories on the biological bases of psychosocial disability reference brain structures and various biological processes rather than the four humors. The psychiatric era has also eliminated supernatural conceptions of psychosocial disability although non-scientific ideas about mental disability are still prominent worldwide. As a result, the major classification systems are based almost exclusively on psychiatry.[41]

The conceptual model of psychiatry is also referred to as the medical or disease model.[42] This is aligned with Foucault's view that persons with psychosocial disabilities were conceptualised as mad or mentally ill.[43] The model conceptualises modern medicine as institutionalised, scientific, and technologically directed.[44] According to this model, illnesses and diseases are organic malfunctions located primarily within the body. They are entities with specific causal origins which can be objectively identified and treated.[45]

In terms of psychosocial disabilities, the conceptual model of psychiatry maintains a strict distinction between the normal and the abnormal that can be objectively recognised or diagnosed and classified as discrete disease entities, applying value neutral scientific reasoning. The model places emphasis on the notion that the causes of psychosocial disabilities are to be found in the disturbances of a biological kind. The disturbances present themselves as specific

38 Ninnis (n 36) 130.

39 Hamel (n 20) 49.

40 Clark et al. (n 11) 73.

41 As above.

42 G Baltruðaitytė 'Theorising mental disorder: a sociological approach' (2003) 1 *Sveikatos sociologija* 117.

43 Ninnis (n 36) 125.

44 Baltruðaitytė (n 42) 117.

45 As above.

symptoms for each particular disability that should be targeted by somatic treatments.[46]

The initial diagnostic manuals on psychosocial disability were founded on the normative standards first employed by the general public and then experts.[47] The first classification system was designed by Emil Kraepelin and it gained widespread popularity in the early 20th century.[48] Kraepelin's classification relied on the growing movement and not only classified disabilities as mental illnesses but also redefined asylum inmates as patients. It was designed with the intention of applying a clinical approach, instead of previous symptomatic methodologies, to the definitions of psychosocial disability. Currently, the two main classifications of psychosocial disabilities used internationally are based on the descriptive categorical approach. These classification systems are the American Psychiatric Association's (APA) Diagnostic Statistical Manuals (DSM) and the World Health Organisation's (WHO) International Classification of Disease (ICD).[49] These classification systems recognise both intellectual and psychosocial disabilities. The former was conceptualised as mental retardation and the latter are referred loosely as mental, cognitive, or psychiatric disorders.

The APA was created in 1844 in the United States of America.[50] The APA is characterised by a history of institutionalisation of those deemed insane. It provided mid-20th century American psychiatrists with extensive powers over the lives of the persons with psychosocial disabilities. Moreover, as the discipline expanded, its authority over people's lives and clients grew. Unusual ideas and behaviours became increasingly medicalised and viewed as deviant, resulting in growing stigma and discrimination against psychosocial disability.[51] However, the social deviance perspective on psychosocial disabilities has been criticised for blurring the boundaries between psychosocial disability, on the one hand, and criminality, social ineffectiveness, or cultural variations, on the other.[52]

Mental disability was diagnosed by psychiatrists using the DSM manual, which was first published in 1952.[53] The DSM manual has been referred to as the bible of psychiatry, clinical social work, and psychology.[54] It is the main document used for organising psychiatric knowledge, research efforts

46 Baltruðaitytė (n 42) 117.
47 Hogan (n 29) 7.
48 As above.
49 Baltruðaitytė (n 42) 117.
50 SJ Wurtzburg & ND Thomson 'Antipsychiatry perspective of mental illness' https://www.researchgate.net/publication/277668176_Anti-Psychiatry_Perspective_of_Mental_Illness (accessed 6 August 2021) 1.
51 As above.
52 Woolfolk (n 1) 163.
53 Wurtzburg & Thomson (n 50) 1.
54 S Kirk & H Kutchins *Making us crazy: DSM, the psychiatric bible and the creation of mental disorders* (1996) 71.

and therapeutic approaches.[55] DSM-described symptoms are linked to patients through various methods depending on the skills of the psychiatrist involved.[56] Psychiatrists would use skills ranging from persuasion and in cases of non-communicative individuals, observation. The data obtained would then be linked to the DSM-documented disorders. According to the DSM template, proof of psychosocial disability depends on behaviours or expressed beliefs that lie outside the boundaries of psychiatric normalcy. Basically, individuals must exhibit a certain number of these characteristics, often over a certain time span, in order to be diagnosed with the disorder.[57]

The DSM manual has gone through a number of changes since 1952 when it was first published but the diagnostic techniques have remained essentially the same.[58] For example, between 1987 and 1994 the number of categories and subcategories of mental disorders increased from 297 to 374.[59] Initially, the DSM manual did not question what does or does not constitute a psychosocial disability but instead represented an accretion of psychosocial problems brought into psychiatric practice from the field of medicine and penology. DSM-I organised mental disorders into three broad groups: disorders with an organic basis, subdivided into acute and chronic forms; disorders without an identified organic basis, subdivided into psychotic disorders, psychophysiological disorders, psychoneurotic disorders, personality disorders, and transient situational personality disorders; and mental retardation or intellectual disability.[60] The description of the disorders have been updated. In DSM-III, each mental disorder was operationally defined by a specific list of observable signs. According to DSM-III, mental disorders results from three distinct overlapping causes; biological, functional, and behavioural.[61]

DSM-IV notes that although it deals with the classification of mental disorders, no definition adequately specifies precise boundaries for the concept of mental disorder.[62] However, DSM-IV goes further to conceptualise a mental disorder as a clinically significant behavioural or psychological syndrome or pattern that occurs in an individual and that is associated with present distress, for instance a painful symptom, or disability which means an impairment in one or more important areas of functioning, or with a significantly increased risk of suffering death, pain, disability, or an important loss of freedom.[63]

55 As above.

56 Wurtzburg & Thomson (n 50) 2.

57 As above.

58 As above.

59 Smith T 'Pathology, bias and queer diagnosis: a crip queer consciousness' Masters Dissertation, Smith College, Northampton, 2012, 45.

60 Clark et al. (n 11) 77.

61 Bufford (n 19) 36.

62 DJ Stein et al. 'What is a mental/psychiatric disorder? From DSM-IV to DSM-V' https://www.ncbi.nlm.nih.gov/pmc/articles/PMC3101504/pdf/nihms291831.pdf (accessed 7 August 2021) 1.

63 As above.

Premenstrual dysphoric disorder and masochistic personality disorder were officially removed from the official status as mental illnesses after highly polemical and acrimonious conflicts among the parties who influenced the fashioning of DSM-IV.[64] In the conceptualisation of mental disorder, disability consists of impairment in one or more important areas of functioning which have been interpreted to include domains such as occupational, academic, social (including interpersonal), and role functioning.[65]

The latest edition is DSM-5 (APA 2013).[66] DSM-5 tries to separate the concepts of mental disorder and disability.[67] Although it ended up stabilising the alarming growth of psychiatric diagnoses, DSM-5 created controversies over the creation of new disorders involving grief, behavioural disturbances in children, and the conceptualisation of psychosomatic disorders.[68] The phrase disturbance has been interpreted to mean a deviation from the normal state or progression.[69] What counts as a disturbance is measured by not only what is normal or expected but also on what is considered bad.[70] Bad has been interpreted based on social norms and is continuously graded in severity, from its absence to severe psychopathology.[71] Overall, the DSM standard has been criticised for lack of clarity and the use of indiscriminate boundaries among classified disorders, resulting in the possibility of mislabeling, abuse, and rejection the unique needs and life story of embodied persons.[72] Others have argued that it represents the represent political, financial, and guild interests of the APA.[73]

Next, is the WHO's classification system. According to the WHO, the term mental disorders is broadly conceptualised to include mental illness, intellectual disability, personality disorder, substance dependence, and adjustment to adverse life events.[74] WHO is responsible for the development of the International Classification of Diseases (ICD), however, the ICD's historical lineage predates the founding of WHO and its roots can be traced back to the 19th

64 Woolfolk (n 1) 173.

65 Stein et al. (n 62) 3.

66 Wurtzburg & Thomson (n 50) 2.

67 D Singh & W Sinnott-Armstrong 'The DSM-5 definition of mental disorder' (2015) 29 *Public Affairs Quarterly* 11.

68 American Psychiatric Association (APA) *Diagnostic and statistical manual of mental disorders DSM-5* (2013) 20.

69 Singh & Sinnott-Armstrong (n 67) 10.

70 Singh & Sinnott-Armstrong (n 67) 11.

71 Clark et al. (n 11) 75.

72 J Aultman 'Mental illness: concept of' in H ten Have (ed) *Encyclopedia of global bioethics* Springer International Publishing (2016) 1897.

73 M Robertson 'Mental illness: treatment of' in H ten Have (ed) *Encyclopedia of global bioethics* Springer International Publishing (2016) 1903.

74 S Leighton & N Dogra 'Defining mental health and mental illness' https://www.researchgate.net/publication/255657987_Defining_mental_health_and_mental_illness (accessed 5 August 2021) 9.

century.[75] WHO was founded after World War II as a specialised agency of the United Nations (UN). Some of its responsibilities included establishing and revising international nomenclatures of diseases, causes of death, and public health practices, as well as standardising diagnostic procedures.[76]

The first version of ICD classified diseases by anatomical site and provided the conceptual basis for the subsequent international list of causes of death, which was adopted by the Institute of International Statistics.[77] With regards to mental disorders, the ICD-6 has 26 categories. These categories are grouped into three broad clusters: psychoses, psychoneurotic disorders, and disorders of character, behaviour, and intelligence. ICD-10 classifies mental disorders into ten categories; organic, including symptomatic, mental disorders, mental and behavioural disorders due to psychoactive substance use, schizophrenia, schizotypal and delusional disorders, mood (affective) disorders, neurotic, stress-related, and somatoform disorders, behavioural syndromes associated with physiological disturbances and physical factors, disorders of adult personality and behaviour, mental retardation, disorders of psychological development, and behavioural and emotional disorders with onset usually occurring in childhood and adolescence.[78]

The current WHO's classification system of mental disorders is the International Classification of Diseases-11 (ICD-11). ICD-11 classifies mental disorders to include the following groupings: neurodevelopmental disorders, schizophrenia and other primary psychotic disorders, mood disorders, anxiety and fear-related disorders, obsessive–compulsive and related disorders, disorders specifically associated with stress, dissociative disorders, bodily distress disorders, feeding and eating disorders, elimination disorders, disorders due to substance use, impulse control disorders, disruptive behaviour and dissocial disorders, personality disorders, paraphilic disorders, factitious disorders, neurocognitive disorders, and mental and behavioural disorders due to disorders or diseases classified elsewhere.[79] One of the departure points between ICD-10 and ICD-11 is the renaming of 'mental retardation' and disorders of psychological development of ICD-10 to disorders of intellectual development, a move that is aimed at decreasing stigmatisation against persons with intellectual disabilities.[80] Furthermore, ICD-11 conceptualises intellectual disability as a health condition or a disorder as opposed to a disability.[81]

75 Clark et al. (n 11) 76.

76 As above.

77 As above.

78 D Goldberg 'The classification of mental disorder: a simpler system for DSM–V and ICD–11' (2010) 16 *Advances in Psychiatric Treatment* 15.

79 U Volpe 'The development of the ICD-11 chapter on mental disorders' https://sajp.org.za/index.php/sajp/article/view/1105/848 (accessed 20 August 2021).

80 A Gozi 'Highlights of ICD-11 classification of mental, behavioral, and neurodevelopmental disorders' (2019) 13 *Indian Journal of Private Psychiatry* 14.

81 SC Girimaji & AJ Pradeep 'Intellectual disability in international classification of diseases-11: a developmental perspective' (2018) 34 *Indian Journal of Social Psychiatry* 69.

3.1.3 *Criticism of the conceptualisation of psychosocial disability in psychiatry*

Psychiatry has not been without criticism. In fact, the science of psychiatry has been criticised severally throughout its history. The roots of psychiatry according to anti-psychiatrists, is the society, which was regarded as oppressive and required repression of human potentialities for its own effective functioning.[82] According to anti-psychiatrist theorists, the very notion of mental disorder referred to oppressive control for those deemed mentally disturbed. The movement of anti-psychiatry emerged during the 1960s and 1970s, and it included a diverse group of theorists such as Michel Foucault in France, psychiatrists Ronald Laing in England, Thomas Szasz in the United States of America (USA), Franco Basaglia in Italy, and David Cooper (1931–1986) from South Africa.[83] However, its main proponents, Laing and Szasz, were psychiatrists.[84]

Laing is referred to as the psychiatrist who wanted to make madness normal. A Laingian perspective to psychiatry considers psychosocial disability a normal response of human beings to a mad world.[85] Laing advocated for a new paradigm for managing psychosocial disabilities apart from psychiatry.[86] According to Laing psychiatry constituted persons with psychosocial disabilities as the other. They were subjected to various paternal acts of moral treatment methods, such as compulsory restraint, psychiatric observation, isolation in total institutions, such as mental hospitals whose effect was which deprived them of their autonomy, liberty, and invalidated their humanity due to their perceived lack of rationality.[87] One of the ideas that made Laing infamous is the revelation that psychosocial disabilities, for example schizophrenia are labels that should be attributed to the society, rather than an individual. In other words, the social construct of mental illness was heavily dependent on ideologies of the then medical and scientific communities who were driven by politics and economics as opposed to science, resulting in illegitimate diagnoses, disease labels, stigmatisation, and discrimination of persons with psychosocial disabilities.[88]

Szasz considered the concept of mental disorder to be a metaphor, given the contentious nature of the mind.[89] With reference to insanity, Szasz argued that that insanity does not exist in any objective sense, that it is an imprecise,

82 Baltruðaitytė (n 42) 121.

83 Pajević & Hasanović (n 16) 890.

84 Baltruðaitytė (n 42) 121.

85 MT Berlim et al. 'Notes on antipsychiatry' (2003) 253 *European Archives of Psychiatry and Clinical Neuroscience* 64.

86 N Crossley 'RD Laing and the British anti-psychiatry movement: a socio-historical analysis' (1998) 47 *Journal of Social Science & Medicine* 883.

87 RD Laing 'What is schizophrenia?' (1964b) 28 *New Left Review* 64.

88 F Lolas 'Mental illness and institutionalization' in H ten Have (ed) *Encyclopedia of global bioethics* Springer International Publishing (2016) 1891.

89 D Telles-Correia et al. 'Mental disorder – the need for an accurate definition' (2018) 9 *Frontiers in Psychiatry* 3.

all-encompassing concept, culturally defined.[90] He viewed psychological suffering as part of life problems and not diseases.[91] The body and mind are two different entities. The mind cannot be explained by mechanical causes because of its intentionality and rationality. According to Szasz, mental disorder is simply a socially disapproved mental condition.[92] Therefore, one should not speak of mental disorders but of deviations from socially accepted norms and values.[93] With regards to the naturalist or biomedical view that mental disabilities are universals, natural kinds that are constant across culture and history, Szasz argued that there is nothing like a violation of the natural order but only violations of the social order.[94]

Basaglia, in Italy found the conditions of accommodation or custody of persons with psychosocial disabilities in large psychiatric hospitals, such as in Görz and Triest in northern Italy to be unbearable.[95] The Italian theorist and activist called for the liberation of persons with psychosocial disabilities and the closure of mental hospitals.[96] He was convinced that the asylum system was morally bankrupt, had no therapeutic benefits towards patients and reduced persons with psychosocial disabilities to non-persons or hollow men.[97] Basaglia advocated for mutual understanding between the society and persons with psychosocial disabilities and not diagnosis that isolates the latter from the community.[98] The aim of medicine and psychiatry was viewed by philosophers such as Szasz and Basaglia as a way of enforcing social control or what Foucault described as 'discipline and punish'.[99]

People are labelled mentally ill when their personal conduct violates certain ethical, political, and social codes.[100] Both the scientific and non-scientific classification of mental disorders results in placing labels on people. For example, DSM-III sought to define what is and is not a disorder using the criteria of dysfunction and distress and recognising that disorders exist in psychosocial circumstances and environments.[101] Basically, it conceptualised mental disorder as a dysfunction of the mind.[102] The concept of abnormal, which is pivotal

90 M Vaughan 'Idioms of madness: Zomba lunatic asylum, Nyasaland, in the colonial period' (1983) 9 *Journal of Southern African Studies* 233.

91 Telles-Correia et al. (n 86) 3.

92 JCWakefield 'The concept of mental disorder: diagnostic implications of the harmful dysfunction analysis' (2007) 6 *World Psychiatry* 150.

93 Telles-Correia et al. (n 86) 3.

94 As above.

95 Helmchen (n 26) 2.

96 As above.

97 J Foot 'Franco Basaglia and the radical psychiatry movement in Italy, 1961–78' (2014) 2 *Critical and Radical Social Work* 237.

98 As above.

99 T Szasz *The manufacture of madness* (1970) 23.

100 As above.

101 Smith (n 59) 48.

102 Woolfolk (n 1) 164.

to both the scientific and non-scientific classification of psychosocial disability, is intelligible only in relation to a conceptualisation of proper or normal functioning.[103] Equally, normal functioning is intelligible only in relation to the concept of a function.[104] Such labels have a profound influence on how people perceive themselves and how society perceive others.[105]

Behaviours and conduct that receive attention from the psychiatric community are largely dependent on the social climate of the time. For instance, in the Union of Soviet Socialist Republics (USSR), psychiatrists performed an Orwellian manoeuvre of medicalising opposition to the state when they employed the diagnosis 'sluggish schizophrenia' to incarcerate political dissidents.[106] In Germany, Adolf Hitler ordered the elimination of patients or inmates with psychosocial disabilities, held in the country's hospitals, under the auspices of Operation (Aktion) T4, so as to prevent them from bearing disabled children.[107] Relatedly, in the year 1938 in America, listed in a leading textbook, were conditions such as moral deficiency, masturbation, misanthropy, and vagabondage, which are no longer psychiatric disabilities. Universally, homosexuality was also regarded as a manifestation of mental illness by Western psychiatry but was officially depathologised in 1973 after a contentious political struggle by a vote of the board of trustees of the APA.[108] Another famous example of a socially deviant behaviour of its time is the 19th century psychiatric diagnosis, draptomania, which was used to discipline and regulate maladjusted slaves with a pathological compulsion to run away. Therefore, psychiatry embraces a social construction model of mental disability depending on the common *topoi* of the society.

Foucault was also considered an anti-psychiatrist. Like Szasz, Foucault was also of the view that psychosocial disability is a present sociocultural situation in which the norms of social behaviour have become unbearable for the persons with psychosocial disabilities.[109] Foucault's power–knowledge dyad plays a prominent role in this construction. Knowledge plays a prominent role in the field of psychiatry and the acquisition of knowledge does not merely justify an intrusion of power, it is an intrusion of power.[110] The science of psychiatry is essentially a knowledge seeking undertaking that is used to justify the moral power of the physician.[111] Power produces knowledge and psychiatry is a source of power.

103 Woolfolk (n 1) 169.
104 As above.
105 RT Hare-Mustin & J Marecek 'Abnormal clinical psychology: the politics of madness' in D Fox & I Prilleltensky (eds) *Critical psychology: an introduction* (1997) 105.
106 Woolfolk (n 1) 174.
107 Robertson (n 73) 1901.
108 Woolfolk (n 1) 173.
109 Joranger (n 31) 310.
110 Dubois M 'The governance of the third world: a Foucauldian perspective on power relations in development' (1991) 16 *Alternatives: Global, Local, Political* 8.
111 Telles-Correia et al. (n 86) 3.

Foucault's discourse of power and knowledge are central to the process by which persons with psychosocial disabilities are made subjects and therefore how psychiatric identities are produced.[112] As the sane publics were constructing an identity for the mad based on normative standards for behaviour, experts in the then emerging field of psychology were utilising scientific process to obtain knowledge.[113] Scientific objectivity implied that madness needed to be seen in the context of physical observation instead of relying on abstract theories, for it is through the former that psychological factors affecting the patient could be seen.[114]

Normalising discourses construct epistemologies about disabled bodies thereby generating ontological control. The discourses that have been analysed in this chapter all operate under an ableist dynamic. The classification of psychosocial disability objectifies persons with psychosocial disabilities in the psychiatric discourse and therefore is a form of knowledge.[115] As a form of knowledge, objectifying persons with psychosocial disability in psychiatry, provides a distinct way of conceptualising the subject.[116]

The control, coordination, and observation of persons with psychosocial disabilities within the confines of psychiatric hospitals is a way of exercising power which enables knowledge to be produced through research and experiments that are carried out.[117] A clinical interview is considered the gold standard for diagnosing psychosocial disability but there are no biological laboratory tests for any psychosocial disability that confirms or disconfirms a diagnosis derived from a clinical interview.[118] Due to lack of biological theory of aetiology for any major disorders, it has been argued persuasively that some mental disorders, like multiple personality disorder, are roles that are created by the theories and practices of the mental health professions and subsequently enacted by patients.[119] Both the scientific and non-scientific conceptualisation of psychosocial disability can be seen as a manifestation of one of the most pervasive examples of the power–knowledge relation that has existed in the society.[120] In this instance, clinical theory and practice are not only mirrors of cultural norms but shapers of those norms as well, a fact that has produced what Foucault terms as 'the confession'.[121]

Confessions are manifested when persons with psychosocial disabilities are invited to disclose their thoughts and feelings so that they can be observed

112 Roberts (n 35) 34.
113 Hogan (n 29) 7.
114 Alenaizi (n 33) 117.
Alenaizi (n 33) 118.
115 Ninnis (n 36) 125.
116 As above.
117 Roberts (n 35) 35.
118 Woolfolk (n 1) 175.
119 As above.
120 Roberts (n 35) 35.
121 Woolfolk (n 1) 175.

and monitored by doctors.[122] In this doctor-patient relationship, the doctor is not a neutral, value-free, and passive observer. They are not neutral because they possess a body of knowledge or a theoretical framework which provides the conception of normality and abnormality and how the latter should be addressed. Therefore, their work is to interpret and act upon what is disclosed by the client by way of that theoretical framework. In the end, as Foucault laments, we are judged, condemned, classified, determined in our undertakings, destined to a certain mode of living or dying, as a function of the true discourses which are the bearers of the specific effect.[123]

The exclusion of persons with psychosocial disabilities in psychiatry is characterised by institutionalisation and naturalised by social norms and encoded in language. Particularly, persons with psychosocial disabilities are symbolically violated in the public domain by either not being represented or through misrepresentation. The latter can be tracked back to psychiatry and its creation of docile bodies. In psychiatry, docile bodies are segregated and concealed because they are considered vulnerable.[124] Here, vulnerability is defined according to the medical model of disability. It is a product of society's stigmatisation against disabled persons who are viewed as objects in need of special care and protection.

Foucault's ideas were tilted against the notion of normality and encouraged by urging the 'abnormal' 'do what thou wilt', 'obey only yourself', 'be as autonomous as possible'.[125] Psychiatry urges the notion of compulsory able-bodiedness, which is fundamentally structured to limit access for persons with psychosocial disabilities and perpetuates their oppression by figuratively and literally constructing a world that only privileges to very narrow conceptions of ability.[126] Normality is a straitjacket that limits the autonomy and freedom of persons with psychosocial disabilities leading to stigmatisation.[127]

Psychosocial disability within the context of Kenya

The discourse on psychosocial disability in Kenya is dehumanising. A dehumanising discourse is one that fails to acknowledge people's humanness.[128] It stigmatises, excludes or dissociates, immobilises and silences, devaluates and invalidates by stripping a person of any self-worth.[129] Consequently, as was revealed by the empirical research, when a person is dehumanised, that individual is viewed as falling outside the scope of morality and justice, thus

122 Roberts (n 35) 37.
123 Dubois (n 106) 8.
124 As above.
125 As above.
126 R McRuer 'Composing bodies; or, de-composition: queer theory, disability studies, and alternative corporealities' (2004) 24 *JAC* 52.
127 As above.
128 ST Tesemma & SA Coetzee 'Conflicting discourses on conceptualising children with disabilities in Africa' (2019) 7 *African Disability Rights Yearbook* 63.
129 As above.

making it easy for others to regard any harm done to such a person as morally justified and warranted.[130]

Native Africans in Kenya had a complex system of cultural beliefs, customs, and practices that control their worldview and prescribe norms of interpersonal relations. Psychosocial disability existed and was conceptualised differently by different cultures.[131] Culture has been defined as the shared behaviour patterns and interaction among a certain group of people.[132] It involves cognitive, emotional, and psychological construct, which is learnt through socialisation.[133] Although the concept of psychosocial disability is particular to the Western world, different communities in Kenya have different systems of health beliefs which help to explain what causes disability, how it can be cured or treated, and who should be involved in the process.[134]

The contemporary understanding of psychosocial disability relies on a Western nosology that might not be generalisable across diverse cultures around the world.[135] What is psychosocial disability is relative depending on the cultural values of a society.[136] In many other parts of the globe, especially the Global South, there are varying folk understandings of health and disability, and the extent of these differences have not been recognised by Western-trained physicians.[137] In certain instances, the colonialists' attempts to study the African brains led to odd conclusions and misunderstanding of culture.[138]

From a decolonial viewpoint, it is not in doubt that there are various cultural definitions of psychosocial disability. Furthermore, there are clear categories of psychosocial disability, which can be relatively easy to identify cross-culturally. However, the creation of psychosocial disability and mental institutions in Western societies destroyed what Foucault refers to as the 'stammered' dialogue which had previously existed between madness and reason, and replaced it with a chilling silence, punctuated only by the monologue of the psychiatrist.[139] African conceptualisations of psychosocial disability were classified on the basis of European standards.[140] Contemporary African psychiatry

130 See Chapter 7.

131 Vaughan (n 87) 234.

132 M Nyaga 'Connectedness of cultural dynamics and mental health' https://www.researchgate.net/publication/328513448_CONNECTEDNESS_OF_CULTURAL_DYNAMICS_AND_MENTAL_HEALTH (accessed 7 August 2021).

133 As above.

134 BO Ojwang 'Linguistic conceptualizations of disease among the Luo of Kenya' (2018) 28 *Qualitative Health Research* 434.

135 TL Osborn et al. 'The experience of depression among the Luo in western Kenya' https://osf.io/qu9kb/ (accessed 7 August 2021).

136 Wakefield (n 89) 151.

137 Wurtzburg & Thomson (n 54) 1.

138 RE Edgerton 'Conceptions of psychosis in four East African societies' (1966) 68 *American Anthropologist* 408.

139 Vaughan (n 87) 218.

140 HL Gordon 'The mental capacity of the African' (1934) 33 *Journal of the Royal African Society* 228.

focuses exclusively on Western developments, and advances a narrative of reform, professionalisation, and technological innovation relevant to Europe and America.[141] Studies in ethnopsychiatry are rare and they offset the discourse of Western psychiatry to some extent, but like their counterparts, they ignore the role of contact between Western and alternative psychiatric medicine.[142]

The perceptions of psychosocial disability among Kenyans falls well within the purview of the labelling approach which emphasises the social meanings imputed to deviant behaviour and focuses on the unfolding process of interaction whereby self-definition is influenced by others.[143] What is normal or abnormal depends on the society. Frequently, persons with psychosocial disability play the social roles assigned to them either incompetently or with great distress, and their actions often are objectionable to others.[144] Thus, psychosocial disability and diagnosis are social constructions created to enforce social mores and norms.[145] The Europeans labelled a variety of African institutions that interacted with insanity as witchcraft.[146] Both the psychiatric and non-psychiatric classification systems of psychosocial disability reveal prejudices, biases, and assumptions reflective of societies' norms and values at any given time in history.[147]

Law embodies the society's informal preferences, desires, and notions of order and justice. This is known as the mirror thesis and it stipulates that positive law historically evolved out of the social order, the contents of which were inscribed in customs and practices of the people. It means that positive law is supposed to mirror societal usages and habits as closely as possible, failure of which they may be considered ineffectual or illegitimate. In short, customs, habits, and usages are what forms the law.[148] This thesis is reflected in Roscoe Pound's notion that in any conflict between law and social norms, social norms would eventually prevail.[149] The relationship between law and society is one of close integration and association. Max Weber considered law as an institutionalised enforcement of norms, Joseph Raz defined it as an institutionalised normative system, and Kent Greenawalt reflected that law echoes dominant cultural norms, unless it is imposed from the outside by an alien power.[150]

141 R Keller 'Madness and colonization: psychiatry in the British and French empires 1800–1962' (2001) 35 *Journal of Social History* 295.

142 Keller (n 141) 297.

143 HMK Maithya 'The awareness and management of mental illness among the Babukusu of Bungoma District' LLM Dissertation, University of Nairobi, 1992, 84.

144 Woolfolk (n 1) 163.

145 Smith (n 59) 49.

146 Vaughan (n 90) 234.

147 Smith (n 59) 49.

148 B Tamanaha *A general jurisprudence of law and society* (2001) 5.

149 R Pound 'The need for a sociological jurisprudence' (1907) 19 *Green Bag* 615.

150 MA Edwards 'The alignment of law and norms: of mirrors, bulwarks, and pressure valves' (2015) 10 *Faculty Scholarship* 21.

These views are aligned with Foucault's notion of 'biopolitics,' which assumes the mirror principle that law as a form of power should reflect society if it is to ensure social order. Therefore, concepts of mental health and normality cannot be understood without looking at cultural norms and values.[151]

Kenya's cultural norms on psychosocial disability

Since the emphasis of this research is on Kenya, historical accounts of five ethnic groups in Kenya, the Luo, Kamba, Swahili, Pokot and the Babukusu will be considered in order to indicate their conceptualisation of psychosocial disability. In these five ethnic groups, there was no consensus towards what constituted psychosocial disability and each ethnic group had its beliefs about disability and attitudes towards persons with psychosocial disabilities which were either positive or negative.

3.1.4 Aspects of psychosocial disabilities

The Kambas, Pokots, and Babukusu of Kenya characterised mental disability to mean psychosocial disabilities and not intellectual disability as seen in the behaviour of persons they considered to be abnormal. Among the behaviours the Babukusu and Kambas consider to be abnormal are laughing alone, eating dirt, going naked or in tattered clothes, wandering, hearing voices (hallucinations), shouting, anti-social behaviours such as violence, insulting other people for no apparent reason and even raping.[152] According to the Pokots, some of the most obvious aspect of the many behaviours ascribed to psychosis, include talking nonsense and committing murder and arson.[153] However, the Pokots differentiate between wild and mild psychosis but do not seem to regard them as mutually exclusive types.[154]

3.1.5 Construction of psychosocial disability

In historical Kenya, psychosocial disability was construed as an illness. In a study conducted by Maithya in Bungoma, Kenya, the Babukusu's definition or perception of psychosocial disability was obtained as follows: 37.5% defined mental disability as a disease of the head, 35.6% of the respondents said it is abnormal behaviour, while 26.9% gave a combination of answers. The definitions ranged from 'loss of senses', 'traditional illness', and 'unstable head'. The Babukusu have a concept of what it means to have a 'disease of the head', which they described as a situation where an individual's head is affected to

151 Smith (n 59) 49.
152 Maithya (n 143) 82.
153 Edgerton (n 138) 414.
154 As above.

the extent that the victim loses touch with reality. It was concluded that the Babukusu use the concept head to refer to mind.[155]

Likewise, the Kambas and Pokot believe that psychosocial disabilities are curable diseases.[156] The Kambas attribute all misfortunes, including psychosocial disabilities, to human malevolence. However, in the case of psychosis, not all of it is due to witchcraft. According to the Kambas, some of the key factors that may lead one to have psychosis are the shame of poverty, grief over the death of a beloved child, worry over personal incompetence, or excessive drinking. These factors can tire the brain and cause it to malfunction. According to the Kambas, the treatment used is a combination of drugs with incantations. The Pokot have two major terms for psychosis implying different causes rather than different symptoms. 'Kipoiyin' means a severe loss of sense that is caused by a disease called 'chegugna', and 'yoiyon', which is a mild and temporary depression and confusion caused by worry or grief. The first is immensely difficult to cure, the second is easily cured by relocating the patient to a new location.[157]

However, in other societies such as the Swahilis, most of what is defined in the American Diagnostic Statistical Manual for Mental Disorders is not considered as psychosocial disability.[158] To some extent, their worldview is consistent with the normativism or cultural relativism espoused by social constructionist where the norm is what modern psychiatrists term pathological.[159] Their conceptualisation of psychosocial disability is very narrow.[160] It includes people who manifest obvious signs of abnormality and where the victim finds the abnormality to be a distress for self and others.[161] Neurodevelopmental disorders like intellectual disability, autism, communication disorder and developmental delays are not considered serious mental issues but merely inherited genes.[162] Intellectual disability, also known as 'koko' or 'zuzu' is not recognised as part of mental health problem. People with autism and down syndrome are treated with a lot of respect despite their conditions because they are considered to have been sacrificed by their families to the spirits in order for them to earn riches. They are mostly referred to as 'kiti'.[163]

Anxiety disorders are also not taken seriously.[164] Panic disorders, agro-phobia, dissociative disorders and somatic symptoms disorders, personality disorders and social anxiety disorders are collectively known as 'maradhi ya wasiwasi' and are usually seen to be genetic as its symptoms runs in certain families.

155 As above.
156 Edgerton (n 138) 416.
157 Edgerton (n 138) 410.
158 MS Khamis et al. 'The Swahilis traditional approach to mental health issues: a case of Swahilis of Mombasa' (2018) 23 *IOSR Journal of Humanities and Social Science* 60.
159 Woolfolk (n 1) 174.
160 Khamis et al. (n 158) 60.
161 As above.
162 Khamis et al. (n 158) 61.
163 As above.
164 As above.

Certain illnesses such as trauma and stress disorders are considered normal life challenges which can be treated by psychosocial support from family and friends. The only condition the Swahilis perceive as serious is schizophrenia. It is attributed to what is termed a 'jinn' (spiritual creatures) and intervention can only be successful when the jinn is cast out of the body of the victim.[165]

3.1.6 Denigrating expressions of persons with psychosocial disabilities

Most of the communities use expressions that denigrate persons with psychosocial disabilities. Descriptions of mental disability in Dholuo include 'janeko' (mad man), 'raura' (imbecile), 'orana' (mentally retarded), 'wiye rach' (has a bad head), 'wiye okethore' (has a spoilt head), 'wiye omoko' (has a stagnated head), 'wiye otop' (rotten head), 'wuotho duk' (walking naked), and 'ringo neko' (to run mad).[166] From the foregoing descriptions, it is clear that the Luo community abhor both the condition and symptoms of mental disability. On the one hand, the reference to 'bad head', 'spoilt head' stagnated head' 'rotten head', 'walking naked' and 'to run mad' refers to psychosocial disabilities. On the other hand, the reference to 'imbecile' and 'mentally retarded' in the Dholuo language implies a severe form of intellectual disability requiring extensive and pervasive support as opposed to intermittent support which would have gone unnoticed in traditional societies.

The descriptions are belittling towards persons with mental disabilities and portray them as worthless.[167] They are considered as 'brainless' and not in control of their reasoning capacity, hence socially dysfunctional. Furthermore, the labels of 'mad man' and 'imbecile' leads to persons with psychosocial disabilities being viewed as undesirable characters whose existence is inconsequential in society. In fact, in the Luo society, persons with mental disabilities are usually segregated from the mainstream society. They are barred from associating and mingling with guests or those of a high social status. Their isolation is necessary because their condition is considered an abomination in society. Mental disability is constructed by the Luo as debilitating and irreversible.[168]

Psychosocial disabilities under the common law

Kenya became a Crown colony in 1920 under the name Kenya colony.[169] As a result, the whole country became known as the Colony and Protectorate of Kenya.[170] In the colonial era, the English common law was the main source of

165 As above.

166 Ojwang (n 134) 436.

167 As above.

168 Ojwang (n 134) 437.

169 HF Morris 'A history of the adoption of codes of criminal law and procedure in British colonial Africa 1876–1935' (1974) 18 *Journal of African Law* 13.

170 S Chanan 'The Republican Constitution of Kenya: historical background and analysis' (1985) 14 *International and Comparative Law Quarterly* 883.

law. English common law referred to persons with mental disabilities as idiots and lunatics.[171] The term 'idiots' was ascribed to people with intellectual disabilities while the term 'lunatics' referred to persons with psychosocial disabilities. 'Idiocy' was considered to be permanent and incurable while 'lunacy' was temporary and curable. 'Idiots' were also referred to as 'fools naturalle' 'imbeciles' or 'feeble-minded'.[172] On the one hand, 'idiocy' was characterised by factors such as heightened dependence on others, ineducability, a lack of normalcy or maturity, and sometimes idiocy's congenital origins and accompanying physical abnormalities.[173] On the other hand, lunacy was marked by its intermittent periods of madness.[174] However, when compared with the permanent mental state of an idiot, there was often a heightened emphasis on the lunatic's phrenzy.[175] And, if lunacy became permanent it was considered to be idiocy.[176]

The law protecting lunatics and idiots in England before the 18th century was the English common law which was carried over to the colonies, including Kenya.[177] Generally, the colonialists conceptualised psychosocial disability as an illness to be treated thus the unfitness declarations and the resultant detentions in asylums.[178] Foucault termed this form of control by the powerful towards the less powerful as 'power relations'.[179] The political use of psychiatry in Kenya was informed by differences between African cognitive abilities and that of Europeans. Cognitive differences between Africans and Europeans were used by the British colonialists to crack down on political rebellion.[180] Africans who were agitating for freedom were believed to be suffering from 'Mau Mau perplexity fear syndrome' thus the rationale for their medicalisation and detention.[181] Medicalisation is the construction of 'non-medical problems' into 'medical problems' and labelling them 'illness' and 'disorders'.[182]

171 F Woodbridge 'Some unusual aspects of mental irresponsibility in the criminal law' (1938–1939) 29 *American Institute of Criminal Law and Criminology* 823.
172 Gordon (n 140) 228.
173 M Clemente 'A reassessment of common law protections for "idiots"' 124 (2015) *The Yale Law Journal* 2776.
174 Gordon (n 140) 228.
175 Clemente (n 173) 2777.
176 As above.
177 Clemente (n 173) 2757.
178 Vaughan (n 90) 223.
179 M Foucault 'The subject and power' in HL Dreyfus & P Rabinow (eds) *M Foucault: beyond structuralism and hermeneutics* (1983) 223.
180 PD Coene 'Therapeutic trajectories in 1950s Usumbura, Ruanda-Urundi. A historical research into colonial psychiatry and its limits' Masters Dissertation, Ghent University, 2020, 17.
181 S Mahone 'Forgotten histories: eugenics, racism and colonial mental doctors in Kenya' https://www.theelephant.info/culture/2021/06/11/forgotten-histories-eugenics-racism-and-colonial-mental-doctors-in-kenya/The Elephant-Speaking truth to power (accessed 3 September 2021).
182 P Conrad 'Medicalization and social control' (1992) 18 *Annual Review of Sociology* 209.

The domineering nature of Western culture in the discourse on mental disability excludes Africans leading to cultural imperialism which is the universalisation and establishment of a dominant group's experience and culture as the norm.[183] Ngwena cautions against universalissing the views, values, and standards of dominant groups because they are not neutral, but serve to demarcate the subjective ideas of mainstream institutions from the objective norms of the majority, including historically excluded and marginalised persons. Inevitably, the absolute nature of such master narratives ends up being based on abstract assumptions, whose effect is the perpetuation of structural injustices and imbalances of power, resulting in further disempowerment and dehumanisation against minorities and socially disadvantaged groups.[184]

To counter universalism and recognise diversity, however, does not merely imply constructing a rainbow world, where legitimacy is given to a multiplicity of congealed and competed differences. It must involve dominant groups with the potential of perpetuating subjectivity.[185] The medicalisation of Africans and the introduction of asylums was a way of exerting power by the colonialists in order to 'compare, differentiate, hierarchise, homogenise, exclude and ultimately normalise' the colonised.[186] Their physical traits coupled with resistance of colonial rule was construed as a pathological condition requiring medical control. This form of medicalisation is also what has created a social milieu where disabled persons are labelled as unfit and new categories of persons are created.

3.1.7 Interrelatedness of 'idiocy' and 'lunacy' under the common law

Under the English common law, the distinction between idiocy and lunacy existed in both property and criminal law. In property law, as part of the King's prerogative powers, the rights and duties in the land of subjects who could not manage their property reverted to the King.[187] The King exercised this right by seizing an idiot's land. In turn, the Crown would provide the subject with necessaries and then transfer the land to his or her heirs upon the idiot's death. Similarly, that was the practice with lunatics. However, since a lunatic's insanity was intermittent, the King only assumed custody of their land and diverted the profits to the lunatic subject.[188]

In criminal law, the distinction between idiocy and lunatic was constructed in terms of punishment.[189] Generally, idiots were protected from punishment

183 IM Young *Justice and the politics of difference* (1990) 47.
184 CG Ngwena *What is Africanness? Contesting nativism in race, culture and sexualities* (2018) 21.
185 Ngwena (n 184) 34.
186 M Foucault *Discipline and punish: the birth of the prison* trans A Sheridan (1977) 183.
187 Clemente (n 173) 2777.
188 Woodbridge (n 171) 823.
189 Clemente (n 173) 2778.

throughout their life. However, since lunacy was intermittent, additional investigation was conducted in order to determine whether an accused had acted under such a disability. In the 17th century, the English common law recognised the institutionalisation of persons with psychosocial disabilities if found to be mentally ill during plea-taking until recovery, and without any further trial.[190] The law stipulated as follows:

> If a man in his sound memory commits a capital offense and before his arraignment he becomes absolutely mad, he ought not by law to be arraigned during such his phrenzy, but be remitted to prison until that incapacity be removed; the reason is, because he cannot advisedly plead to the indictment.[191]

It means that no conceptual distinction was drawn between 'insanity at trial', during arraignment, and the 'insanity plea', which is a defence related to the commission of an offence. In both instances, an accused was imprisoned until the end of his or her 'incapacity'.[192]

3.1.8 *Legal status of a person with psychosocial disability in the common law criminal justice system*

In the 18th and 19th century one of the first pieces of legislation to deal with persons with psychosocial disabilities who have been declared unfit was the 1800 Criminal Lunatics Act (CLA).[193] Under the CLA, unfitness declarations against persons with psychosocial disabilities who committed an offence placed them in legal limbo as they were confined with neither a trial nor a guilty verdict.[194] The CLA was passed due to public demand following the acquittal and release of James Hadfield on grounds of insanity after attempting to assassinate King George III.[195] The CLA stated as follows in section 2,

> [i]f any person indicted for any offence shall be insane, and shall on arraignment be found so to be, by a jury lawfully impanelled for that purpose, so that such person cannot be tried upon such indictment, it

190 D Collins 'Re-evaluating competence to stand trial' https://scholarship.law.duke.edu/cgi/viewcontent.cgi?article=1002&context=mjs (accessed 24 February, 2020) 16.

191 M Hale *The history of the pleas of the crown* (2007) 34.

192 A Loughnan *Manifest madness: mental incapacity in the criminal law* (2012) 72.

193 Criminal Lunatics Act 1800 (CLA).

194 P Bartlett 'Legal madness in the nineteenth century' http://eprints.nottingham.ac.uk/1667/2/SOURCES3.SHM.pdf (accessed 10 February, 2020) 1.

195 P Brown 'Unfitness to plead in England and Wales: historical development and contemporary dilemmas' (2019) 59 *Medicine, Science and the Law* 190.

> shall be lawful for the Court to direct such finding to be recorded, and thereupon to order such person to be kept in strict custody until His Majesty's pleasure shall be known.[196]

The above sections of the CLA did not differentiate between insanity at trial and insanity during the commission of an offence. It was primarily concerned with the disposal of accused persons with psychosocial disabilities who committed offences in a more systematic manner. This meant that accused persons with psychosocial disabilities could be detained indefinitely, in whatever manner the Crown saw fit, which almost always meant prison.[197]

The earliest case where the accused was detained indefinitely was the matter of *Rex v Dyson*,[198] involving Esther Dyson who had been charged with the murder of her child. At the time she was deaf and mute thus not capable of taking plea. For this reason, she was declared to be insane and as a result was detained indefinitely under the CLA until further orders from the Crown.[199] That case was followed by that of *Rex v Pritchard*,[200] where the accused was facing a charge of bestiality which was considered a capital offence at the time.[201] Baron Alderson told the jury to consider whether the prisoner was

> of sufficient intellect to comprehend the course of proceedings of the trial, so as to make a proper defence – to know that he may challenge any of you to whom he might object – and to comprehend the details of the evidence, which in a case of this nature must constitute a minute investigation.[202]

Pritchard was found 'not capable of taking his trial' and was confined indefinitely in prison, without the option of making his defence after recovery.[203] Here again, the conceptual interdependency between insanity at trial and insanity during the commission of the offence resulted in the indefinite detention of an accused to the exclusion of any further trial.[204]

However, the rule in *Pritchard* did not exclude all deaf-mutes from the trial, those who were able to communicate through an interpreter using sign language or 'by gesture merely, the prisoner being imperfectly acquainted with the alphabetical language of the dumb' were ordered to proceed with the trial.[205] There were also other several interesting cases where the trial was

196 CLA, sec 2.
197 Loughnan (n 192) 76.
198 (1831) 7 C & P 305.
199 Brown (n 191) 189.
200 (1836) 7 C & P 303.
201 A Shah 'Making fitness to plead fit for purpose' (2012) 1 *International Journal of Criminology and Sociology* 179.
202 *Rex v Pritchard* (1836) 7 C & P 303.
203 Loughnan (n 192) 77.
204 As above.
205 Trial of Samuel Adams, London Times, 29 May 1879.

ordered to proceed. In *King v Jones*[206] in 1773, the accused, a deaf-mute, was charged with the offence of stealing five guineas. The jury found that he stood mute by 'visitation of God'. The phrase 'mute by visitation of God' originally meant that an accused could be tried despite the absence of a plea, but in the 19th century such accused persons were equated with the insane and declared 'unfit to plead' and so unfit to be tried.[207] However in *King v Jones*, it appeared that the accused could communicate his ideas to a witness, and be communicated with, consequently he was placed upon trial, convicted of simple larceny, and sentenced to be transported.

In *John Ruston's* case[208] in 1786, Ruston, a man *mutus et surdus a nativitate,* which means deaf-mute, was a Crown witness. When it appeared that he could communicate with his sister by signs, he was held a competent witness. The leading case on the point, however, is *The King v Steel*.[209] The accused was charged with simple larceny, refused to plead, and was found to stand mute by visitation of God. She complained that she could not hear and refused to plead on a second arraignment. The court, after saying that such cases should be tried with 'great diligence and circumspection' and every right of the defendant protected, ordered the trial to proceed. The accused was convicted of simple larceny and sentenced to transportation for seven years. In the case of Edward Haines, also a deaf-mute, illiterate, married shepherd, accused of stealing a piece of bacon. When Haines was ordered to be detained at Her Majesty's pleasure, Her Majesty's Secretary of State for Home Affairs and his officials protested that 'there can be no sense in detaining this man in a lunatic asylum all his life'.[210] After unsuccessful attempts to send him either to prison or to a workhouse, the Home Secretary, Sir William Harcourt, wrote, 'he really is quite sensible: and the common sense course would be to treat him as a criminal, try him as such (by the help of an interpreter) and punish him'. He was absolutely discharged within a month of trial.[211]

Overall, the common law seeks to regulate the conduct of persons with psychosocial disabilities to varying degrees through compulsory admission and treatment, control and restraint, seclusion, and the covert administration of medicines which can all be interpreted as explicit of the exercise of state powers within psychiatry.[212] The common law's outlook of persons with psychosocial disabilities is a manifestation of one of the most pervasive examples of the power–knowledge relation that has existed in the society.[213] Independent Kenya has largely maintained and glorified the colonial status quo on

206 (1773) 1 Leach CC 102.
207 T Ward 'Standing mute' (2012) 24 *Law & Literature* 3.
208 (1786) 1 Leach CC 408.
209 (1787) 1 Leach CC 451.
210 Ward (n 207) 13.
211 As above.
212 Roberts (n 35) 35.
213 As above.

psychosocial disability.[214] The power exercised by independent Kenya over persons with psychosocial disabilities is similar to the control exhibited by British colonial masters during the era of colonisation.

Psychosocial disabilities in Kenya's legislation

The manner in which psychosocial disability is perceived in post-colonial Kenya can be found in government documents and in legislation. Kenyan laws conceptualise psychosocial disability under the status model, functional model, or the outcome model.[215] Under the status model, the presence of a psychosocial disability alone presumes a lack of capacity.[216] As for the functional model, the law treats disability as a threshold condition under which a person is incapable if by reason of such disability that person is unable to perform a specified function.[217] It has four dimensions where one is tested for abilities to understanding the information required to make a decision, appreciating how the information being given pertains to the person's own life, and circumstances, logical reasoning using the information presented, and expression of choice.[218] Finally, the outcomes approach, determines incompetence on the basis of the quality of decision arrived at by the person with psychosocial disability.[219] The conceptualisation of psychosocial disabilities in laws influences the society's response towards persons with psychosocial disabilities.

The Constitution of Kenya provides for fundamental rights and freedoms to all persons, including 'persons of unsound mind'.[220] 'Persons of unsound mind' and 'mentally incapacitated' are the terms used to refer to persons with mental disabilities. 'Unsoundness of mind' is a label. Labelling is the use of names or other terms to alter a person's status thus transforming essentially normal actors into deviant ones.[221] The Constitution does not define who is a person of unsound mind.[222] However, being of unsound mind is a limited concept compared to mental disability.[223] According to Oxford Dictionary,

214 M Ibrahim 'Mental health in Kenya: Not yet uhuru' (2014) 1 *Disability and the Global South* 397.

215 L Mute 'Moving from the norm to practice towards ensuring legal capacity for persons with disabilities in Kenya' (2012) 9 *The Equal Rights Review* 139.

216 LO Oyaro 'Rearticulating ubuntu as a viable framework for the realisation of legal capacity in sub-Saharan Africa' (2018) 6 *African Disability Rights Yearbook* 85.

217 Mute (n 215) 140.

218 Miller (n 4) 12.

219 As above.

220 Constitution of Kenya, arts 83(1)(b) & 99(2)(e) & DM Ndetei, J Muthike, & ES Nandoya 'Kenya's mental health law' (2017) 14 *Bjpsych International* 97.

221 A Jiménez & A Elena 'Criminalizing disability: the urgent need of a new reading of the European Convention on Human Rights' (2015) 30 *American University International Law Review* 307.

222 Mute (n 7) 5.

223 As above.

the term unsound can have different meanings. When referring to a person, it means, 'not physically sound'; 'unhealthy', 'diseased'; 'suffering from wounds or injuries'.[224] It also has both legal as well as medical purports.[225] Legally, it is a judicially determined term referring to a person's mental functioning. If a trier of fact is satisfied there is a possibility an accused is mentally impaired they will allow the issue of unsoundness of mind to be raised and determined on a balance of probabilities.[226]

Courts around the globe have defined the phrase unsound mind variously. One judge states that it exists only where there is an essential privation of the reasoning faculties, or where a person is incapable of understanding and acting with discretion in the ordinary affairs of life.[227] In America, some courts have equated it to insanity in accordance with the M'Naghten standard which state that an individual is not 'guilty by reason of insanity' if he or she does not know the nature and quality of the act or does not know the act was wrong.[228] Insane is defined to include both idiots and lunatics.[229] In other cases, unsound mind has been found to exist where there is an essential privation of the reasoning faculties, or where a person is incapable of understanding and acting with discretion in the ordinary affairs of life.[230] According to the European Court of Human Rights, the threshold of unsound mind is dependent on objective reliable medical expertise coupled with the presence of a mental disorder.[231] The latter is construed widely to encompass abnormal personality traits which do not amount to mental illness.[232] Furthermore, 'unsoundness of mind' is not dependent on whether the mental disorder can be effectively treated.[233] It means that the concept of unsound mind covers both intellectual and psychosocial disabilities.[234]

The phrase 'unsoundness of mind' is based on the medical model of disability which locates the problem of disability within the body and prioritises

224 Oxford English Dictionary 'Unsound definition' http://www.oed.com/view/Entry/218175?rskey=BWCa8R&result=7&isAdvanced=false# (accessed 2 September 2021).
225 Mute (n 7) 5.
226 T Venning 'Intellectual disability in the Australian criminal justice system what effect, if any, does general and specific deterrence play in sentencing offenders with an intellectual disability? How can these and the other sentencing principles be applied when sentencing Noel?' https://espace.cdu.edu.au/eserv/cdu:46276/Venning_46276.pdf (accessed 20 February, 2022) 5.
227 *Turner v Howerton et al.* (1997) 22689-VA.
228 *M'Naghten's* Case (1843) 8 Eng Rep 718.
229 RI Simon et al. 'On sound and unsound mind: the role of suicide in tort and insurance litigation' (2005) 333 *Journal of the American Academy of Psychiatry and the Law* 177.
230 *Turner v Howerton et al.* (1997) 22689-VA.
231 *Winterwerp v Netherlands* (1979) ECtHR, para 39.
232 *X v Germany* (1976) ECtHR.
233 *Hutchison Reid v the United Kingdom* (2003) ECtHR, para 52.
234 M Szwed 'The notion of 'a person of unsound mind' under article 5 § 1(e) of the European Convention on Human Rights' (2020) 38 *Netherlands Quarterly of Human Rights* 291.

the normalising of such persons through medicine or rehabilitation.[235] The medical model is informed by notions of compulsory able-bodiedness and able-mindedness, which is both a relational and obscured cultural ideal that governs the society and serves as a mechanism of classification that disciplines subjects who fall outside a given society's arbitrarily constructed norms pertaining to both physical ability and mental health.[236] Medically, unsoundness of mind is closely related to mental illness.[237] The latter is a medical condition determined by medical professionals and not legislators or judicial officers. However, the law recognises that mental illness may have various legal effects. Individuals who are mentally ill are considered to suffer from a psychiatric or other disease, which substantially impairs their mental health. 'Mental illness' is also synonymous with insanity.[238]

It has been argued that the Constitution is informed by the outcomes model of determining disability.[239] For example, it bars persons of unsound mind from registering as a voter during elections or referenda.[240] Persons of unsound mind are considered to be not in control of their faculties thus not being able to know the magnitude of any election let alone the referendum, which makes their exclusion obvious and self-explanatory.[241] It means that the Constitution determines unfitness on the basis of the quality of decision arrived at by the person with disability.[242] Apart from unsound mind in the Constitution, other Kenyan legislation have also placed labels on persons with psychosocial disabilities.

The Criminal Procedure Code[243] refers to persons with mental disabilities derogatorily also as persons of unsound mind. Although, the Criminal Law (Amendment) Act[244] amended the Penal Code,[245] the Evidence Act,[246] and the Criminal Procedure Code by deleting such derogatory terms as imbecile, which was insensitive and derogatory to disabled persons, it never made any amendments with regards to the derogatory terms used to refer to persons with mental disabilities such as insanity or unsound mind. The Criminal Procedure Code recognises unfitness declarations.

The Criminal Procedure Code uses a functional approach to capacity by looking at the decision-making ability at a particular moment in time and

235 Jiménez & Elena (n 221) 291.
236 Gahman (n 15) 9.
237 Mute (n 7) 5.
238 As above.
239 Mute (n 215) 143.
240 Constitution of Kenya, art 83.
241 *Priscilla Nyokabi Kanyua v AG* (2010) eKLR.
242 Mute (n 211) 141.
243 Criminal Procedure Act Cap. 75, Laws of Kenya.
244 Criminal Law (Amendment) Act, 2003, Laws of Kenya.
245 Penal Code, Cap 63, Laws of Kenya.
246 Evidence Act, Cap 80, Laws of Kenya.

not the more general decision-making capacity of a person. Sections 162, 163, 164, and 280 of the Criminal Procedure Code establish the procedure through which a court may determine that a person is of unsound mind and the subsequent consequences, including that once so declared a person may be consigned to a mental hospital or, in the wording of section 280, a 'lunatic asylum' until such time as the medical officer or the court or the Attorney General deem such person to be of sound mind. This is similar to the common law's distinction of idiocy and lunacy in terms of curability. Under the common law, lunacy is considered a curable condition as opposed to idiocy.

The Evidence Act allows only witnesses who are competent to testify in a court of law.[247] The competency threshold is centred on a person's current mental status and functional abilities.[248] Persons who are prevented from understanding the questions put to them, or from giving rational answers to those questions, by tender years, extreme old age, disease (whether of body or mind) or any similar cause are considered unable to testify.[249] Section 125 conceptualises persons with mental disabilities as having no capacity to give evidence in court. Their disability makes them incompetent and unreliable witnesses in court.[250]

The Penal Code (Code) presumes sanity.[251] However, the burden of proving insanity rests on the person that alleges.[252] An accused person is either wholly sane or wholly insane.[253] Unlike psychiatry, criminal law allows for no gradations and requires a final decisive moral judgement of the culpability of the accused. For the purposes of conviction there is no twilight zone between abnormality and insanity.[254] The code provides that a person is not criminally responsible for an act or omission if at the time of doing the act or making the omission that person is suffering from any disease affecting his mind thus, incapable of understanding the act in question or of knowing the consequences of the action or omission.[255] The Penal Code perceives persons with mental disability as being incapable of reason and thus should not be subjected to blame.[256] The insanity defence gives life to the perception that there is no jail time for those found guilty but insane. However, the law in Kenya stipulates

247 Evidence Act, sec 125.
248 Miller (n 4) 13.
249 Evidence Act, sec 125.
250 D Msipa 'How assessments of testimonial competence perpetuate inequality and discrimination for persons with intellectual disabilities: an analysis of the approach taken in South Africa and Zimbabwe' (2015) 3 *African Disability Rights Yearbook* 64.
251 Penal Code, sec 11.
252 Penal Code, sec 12.
253 ML Perlin 'The insanity defense in English-speaking African countries' (1969) *African Law Studies* 73.
254 As above.
255 Penal Code, sec 12.
256 Perlin (n 253) 73.

that once a person is found not guilty by reason of insanity or guilty but insane, the person is detained in a mental hospital, usually Mathare Hospital.[257] The detention is indefinite and at the pleasure of the president.[258] The main reason for the detention of the criminally insane in mental asylums is to separate them from other prisoners.[259]

The Mental Health Act[260] defines a 'person with mental disorder' as a person who has been found to be suffering under the Mental Health Act and includes a person diagnosed as a psychopathic 'person with mental illness' and 'person with mental impairment' due to alcohol or substance abuse.[261] The Act is predicated on John Stuart Mill's 'harm principle', which considers 'persons with mental disorders' as dangerous to themselves and others, unable to manage their own affairs, or likely to act in a manner offensive to public decency.[262] As a result of this inability, guardians are appointed. The purpose of the guardian is to manage the estate of a person with mental disorder, including providing for them and their dependants. Such extensive powers to guardians of persons with mental disorders result in unnecessary restrictions of the rights to work, education, marriage and participation in community or family functions.[263] Although Kenya reformed its Mental Health Act in 2022, through the Mental Health Amendment Act (Amendment Act),[264] the reforms are vestiges of the old law that are based on a person's mental status and functional abilities. For example, the definition of a person with mental disorder has largely remained the same as the one found in the Mental Health Act.[265] Part XII of the Amendment Act contains provisions on care and administration of property of persons with mental illness. While Part XII has eliminated the use of guardians, it allows the court to appoint managers to make decisions concerning the affairs of persons with psychosocial disabilities without the participation of the latter after examining their mental capacity.[266]

A person with mental disability is defined under the Sexual Offences Act to mean a person affected by any mental disability irrespective of its cause, whether temporary or permanent.[267] The Act refers to both psychosocial and intellectual disabilities. Under the Sexual Offences Act, mental disability is

257 Criminal Procedure Code, sec 166.
258 Criminal Procedure Code, sec 166.
259 Vaughan (n 90) 218.
260 Mental Health Act Cap 248, Laws of Kenya.
261 Mental Health Act, sec 2.
262 Mental Health Act, sec 26(3).
263 EM Ngui et al. 'Mental disorders, health inequalities and ethics: a global perspective' https://www.ncbi.nlm.nih.gov/pmc/articles/PMC2935265/pdf/nihms226164.pdf (accessed 5 August 2021) 5.
264 Mental Health Amendment Act of 2022 (Laws of Kenya).
265 Mental Health Amendment Act, sec 22.
266 Mental Health Amendment Act, sec 26.
267 Sexual Offences Act 3 of 2006, Laws of Kenya.

not a fixed status that disqualifies people from any consensual sexual activity. However, it is an offence to have sex with a person affected by such mental disability to the extent that he or she, at the time of the alleged commission of the offence in question, was

> (a) unable to appreciate the nature and reasonably foreseeable consequences of any act described under this Act; (b) able to appreciate the nature and reasonably foreseeable consequences of such an act but unable to act in accordance with that appreciation; (c) unable to resist the commission of any such act; or (d) unable to communicate his or her unwillingness to participate in any such act.[268]

This section conceptualises mental disability situationally, in a functional manner that maximises a person's sexual self-determination while still recognising when they are exploited in situations of power imbalance.[269]

The courts, on various occasions, have also been called upon to address the concept of mental disability, as distinct from insanity. In Kenya, for the most part, judicial officers have been content to defer to psychiatric authority. Mental disability is regarded from precisely the same point of view as organic disease.[270] An organic disease is a term used to describe any health condition in which there is an observable and measurable disease process, such as inflammation or tissue damage.[271] Illustrating this trend, a court in Kenya held that an accused person will not succeed in pleading insanity unless a scientific witness can conclude with certainty that a disease of the mind exists as in the case of a bodily disease, which can be deduced from specific symptoms such as rashes, a coma, or other physical signs.[272] Insanity is classified as a form of mental disability requiring treatment rather than punishment.[273]

Interestingly, Kenyan courts have also held that medical evidence is not essential to prove insanity. Evidence of insanity may also be proved by not only lay witnesses, but also by the surrounding circumstances based on the conduct of the accused person.[274] This implies that there is conduct, which the society may consider abnormal. This view is not based on the human rights approach because it presumes that anyone who goes against societal norms is a person with mental disability.[275]

268 Sexual Offences Act, sec 2.

269 Mute (n 215) 140.

270 Perlin (n 253) 75.

271 B Bolen 'How an organic disease differs from a functional disorder' https://www.verywellhealth.com/organic-disease-1944921 (accessed 8 August 2021).

272 *Ellis v R* (1965) EACA 751.

273 *Leonard Mwangemi Munyasia v Republic* (2015) eKLR.

274 As above.

275 J Benedet & I Grant 'A situational approach to incapacity and mental disability in sexual assault law' (2013) 43 *Ottawa Law Review* 6.

3.2 Conclusion

From the foregoing, it is not in doubt that the conception of psychosocial disability within both the scientific and non-scientific eras constitutes them as objects first, which is something less than human beings. Both categories of practices are dehumanising towards persons with psychosocial disabilities. The chapter has also shown that psychosocial disability is portrayed differently depending on people's professions, locality, and culture. Consequently, how disabled persons are regarded in terms of personhood and participation in the society, depends on how disability is constructed in a particular society.

The existing Western orientation in the conceptualisation of psychosocial disability limits the global understanding of psychosocial disability thus creating mental health inequality. As opposed to psychiatrists, anthropologists have emphasised the transcultural dissimilarity of psychosocial disability.[276] To this end, the social model approach to disability might not be the answer to addressing the violations of the rights of persons with psychosocial disabilities especially in Global South countries. In this chapter, the study has conceptualised psychosocial disability. It has deconstructed the various principles attached to and affecting the concept of psychosocial disability. The next chapter interrogates participation in access to justice.

References

Alenaizi HN 'Disability and Kuwaiti society: a critical realist approach to participatory research in contemporary Kuwaiti society' PhD thesis, The University of Manchester, 2017.

American Psychiatric Association (APA) *Diagnostic and statistical manual of mental disorders DSM-5* (2013).

Andreasen NC *The broken brain: the biological revolution in psychiatry* (1984).

Baltruðaitytė G 'Theorising mental disorder: a sociological approach' (2003) 1 *Sveikatos sociologija* 117. https://doi.org/10.15388/SocMintVei.2003.1.5934.

Bartlett P 'Legal madness in the nineteenth century' http://eprints.nottingham.ac.uk/1667/2/SOURCES3.SHM.pdf (accessed 10 February 2020).

Benedet J & Grant I 'A situational approach to incapacity and mental disability in sexual assault law' (2013) 43 *Ottawa Law Review* 6.

Berlim MT et al. 'Notes on antipsychiatry' (2003) 253 *European Archives of Psychiatry and Clinical Neuroscience* 64. https://doi.org/10.1007/s00406-003-0407-8.

Bible, 2 John 9:2–3 New International Version.

Bolen B 'How an organic disease differs from a functional disorder' https://www.verywellhealth.com/organic-disease-1944921 (accessed 8 August 2021).

Brown P 'Unfitness to plead in England and Wales: historical development and contemporary dilemmas' (2019) 59 *Medicine, Science and the Law* 190. https://doi.org/10.1177/0025802419856761.

Bufford RK 'Demonic influence and mental disorders-Chapter 8 of "counseling and the demonic"' https://digitalcommons.georgefox.edu/cgi/viewcontent.cgi?referer=https://www.google.com/&httpsredir=1&article=1011&context=counselingandthedemonic (accessed 6 August 2021).

276 Edgerton (n 138) 430.

Chanan S 'The Republican Constitution of Kenya: historical background and analysis' (1985) 14 *International and Comparative Law Quarterly* 883.
Clark LA et al. 'Three approaches to understanding and classifying mental disorder: ICD-11, DSM-5, and the National Institute of Mental Health's Research Domain Criteria (RDoC)' (2017) 18 *Psychological Science in the Public Interest* 73. https://doi.org/10.1177/1529100617727266.
Clemente M 'A reassessment of common law protections for "idiots"' 124 (2015) *The Yale Law Journal* 2776.
Coene PD 'Therapeutic trajectories in 1950s Usumbura, Ruanda-Urundi. A historical research into colonial psychiatry and its limits' Masters Dissertation, Ghent University, 2020.
Collins D 'Re-evaluating competence to stand trial' https://scholarship.law.duke.edu/cgi/viewcontent.cgi?article=1002&context=mjs (accessed 24 February, 2020).
Conrad P 'Medicalization and social control' (1992) 18 *Annual Review of Sociology* 209.
Constitution of Kenya (2010).
Criminal Law (Amendment) Act, 2003, Laws of Kenya.
Criminal Lunatics Act 1800 (CLA).
Criminal Procedure Act Cap. 75, Laws of Kenya.
Crossley N 'RD Laing and the British anti-psychiatry movement: a socio-historical analysis' (1998) 47 *Journal of Social Science & Medicine* 883.
Dubois M 'The governance of the third world: a Foucauldian perspective on power relations in development' (1991) 16 *Alternatives: Global, Local, Political* 8.
Edgerton RE 'Conceptions of psychosis in four East African societies' (1966) 68 *American Anthropologist* 408.
Edwards MA 'The alignment of law and norms: of mirrors, bulwarks, and pressure valves' (2015) 10 *Faculty Scholarship* 21.
Ellis v R (1965) EACA 751.
Evidence Act, Cap 80, Laws of Kenya.
Foot J 'Franco Basaglia and the radical psychiatry movement in Italy, 1961–78' (2014) 2 *Critical and Radical Social Work* 237. https://doi.org/10.1332/204986014X14002292074708.
Foucault M *Madness and civilization: a history of insanity in the age of reason* (1965).
Foucault M *Discipline and punish: the birth of the prison* trans A Sheridan (1977).
Foucault M 'The subject and power' in Dreyfus HL & Rabinow P (eds) *M Foucault: beyond structuralism and hermeneutics* (1983) 223.
Foucault M *The history of sexuality* (1986).
Gahman L 'Crip theory and country boys: masculinity, dis/ability, and place in rural southeast Kansas' https://core.ac.uk/download/pdf/169433775.pdf (accessed 20 August 2021).
Girimaji SC & Pradeep AJ 'Intellectual disability in international classification of diseases-11--: a developmental perspective' (-2018-) 34 *Indian Journal of Social Psychiatry* 69. https://doi.org/10.4103/ijsp.ijsp_35_18.
Goldberg D 'The classification of mental disorder: a simpler system for DSM–V and ICD–11' (2010) 16 *Advances in Psychiatric Treatment* 15. https://doi.org/10.1192/apt.bp.109.007120.
Gordon HL 'The mental capacity of the African' (1934) 33 *Journal of the Royal African Society* 228.
Gozi A 'Highlights of ICD-11 classification of mental, behavioral, and neurodevelopmental disorders' (2019) 13 *Indian Journal of Private Psychiatry* 14. https://doi.org/10.5005/jp-journals-10067–0030.
Hale M *The history of the pleas of the crown* (2007).
Hamel LA 'Mental illness and demonisation' (2015) 11 *Journal of Adventist Mission Studies* 48.

Hare-Mustin RT & Marecek J 'Abnormal clinical psychology: the politics of madness' in Fox D & Prilleltensky I (eds) *Critical psychology: an introduction* (1997) 105.

Helmchen H 'Different conceptions of mental illness: consequences for the association with patients' (2013) 4 *Frontiers in Psychology* 2. https://doi.org/10.3389/fpsyg.2013.00269.

Hogan N '"We're all mad here": power and identity in the modern era of mental illness' (2016) 10 *Intersect* 73.

Human Rights Watch 'Deportation by default: mental disability, unfair hearings, and indefinite detention in the US immigration system' https://www.hrw.org/report/2010/07/25/deportation-gdefault/mental-disability-unfair-hearings-and-indefinite-detention-us (accessed 9 August 2021).

Hutchison Reid v the United Kingdom (2003) ECtHR.Ibrahim M 'Mental health in Kenya: not yet uhuru' (2014) 1 *Disability and the Global South* 397. https://doi.org/10.4324/9781003082583–25.

Jiménez A & Elena A 'Criminalizing disability: the urgent need of a new reading of the European Convention on Human Rights' (2015) 30 *American University International Law Review* 307.

John Ruston's case (1786) 1 Leach CC 408.

Joranger L 'Psychology and the historical power–body conjunction: Foucault's different view of the history and philosophy of psychology' (2016) 26 *Theory & Psychology* 310. https://doi.org/10.1177/0959354315623655.

Keller R 'Madness and colonization: psychiatry in the British and French empires 1800–1962' (2001) 35 *Journal of Social History* 295.

Khamis MS, et al. 'The Swahilis traditional approach to mental health issues: a case of Swahilis of Mombasa' (2018) 23 *IOSR Journal of Humanities and Social Science* 60.

King v Jones (1773) 1 Leach CC 102.

The King v Steel (1787) 1 Leach CC 451.

Kirk S & Kutchins H *Making us crazy: DSM, the psychiatric bible and the creation of mental disorders* (1996) 71.

Laing RD 'What is schizophrenia?' (1964b) 28 *New Left Review* 64.

Leighton S & Dogra N 'Defining mental health and mental illness' https://www.researchgate.net/publication/255657987_Defining_mental_health_and_mental_illness (accessed 5 August 2021).

Leonard Mwangemi Munyasia v Republic (2015) eKLR.

Loughnan A *Manifest madness: mental incapacity in the criminal law* (2012) 72.

Mahone S 'Forgotten histories: eugenics, racism and colonial mental doctors in Kenya' https://www.theelephant.info/culture/2021/06/11/forgotten-histories-eugenics-racism-and-colonial-mental-doctors-in-kenya/The Elephant-Speaking truth to power (accessed 3 September 2021).

Maithya HMK 'The awareness and management of mental illness among the Babukusu of Bungoma District' LLM dissertation, University of Nairobi, 1992.

McRuer R 'Composing bodies; or, de-composition: queer theory, disability studies, and alternative corporealities' (2004) 24 *JAC* 52.

Mental Health Act Cap 248 'Laws of Kenya'.

Mental Health Amendment Act of 2022 'Laws of Kenya'.

M'Naghten's Case (1843) 8 Eng Rep 718.

Morris HF 'A history of the adoption of codes of criminal law and procedure in British colonial Africa 1876–1935' (1974) 18 *Journal of African Law* 13.

Msipa D 'How assessments of testimonial competence perpetuate inequality and discrimination for persons with intellectual disabilities: an analysis of the approach taken in South Africa and Zimbabwe' (2015) 3 *African Disability Rights Yearbook* 64. https://doi.org/10.17159/2413–7138/2015/v3n1a3.

Mute L 'Moving from the norm to practice towards ensuring legal capacity for persons with disabilities in Kenya' (2012) 9 *The Equal Rights Review* 139.

Mute LM 'Shattering the glass ceiling: ensuring the right to vote for persons with intellectual disabilities in Kenya' (2010) 2 *A Journal of the Philosophical Association of Kenya (PAK) New Series* 5.

Ndetei DM et al. 'Kenya's mental health law' (2017) 14 *Bjpsych International* 97. https://doi.org/10.1192/s2056474000002117.

Ngui EM et al. 'Mental disorders, health inequalities and ethics: a global perspective' https://www.ncbi.nlm.nih.gov/pmc/articles/PMC2935265/pdf/nihms226164.pdf (accessed 5 August 2021).

Ngwena CG *What is Africanness? Contesting nativism in race, culture and sexualities* (2018).

Ninnis D 'Foucault and the madness of classifying our madness' (2016) 21 *Foucault Studies* 125. https://doi.org/10.22439/fs.v0i0.5016.

Nyaga M 'Connectedness of cultural dynamics and mental health' https://www.researchgate.net/publication/328513448_CONNECTEDNESS_OF_CULTURAL_DYNAMICS_AND_MENTAL_HEALTH (accessed 7 August 2021).

Ojwang BO 'Linguistic conceptualizations of disease among the Luo of Kenya' (2018) 28 *Qualitative Health Research* 434. https://doi.org/10.1177/1049732317747875.

Osborn TL et al. 'The experience of depression among the Luo in western Kenya' https://osf.io/qu9kb/ (accessed 7 August 2021).

Oxford English Dictionary 'Unsound definition' http://www.oed.com/view/Entry/218175?rskey=BWCa8R&result=7&isAdvanced=false# (accessed 2 September 2021).

Oyaro LO 'Rearticulating ubuntu as a viable framework for the realisation of legal capacity in sub-Saharan Africa' (2018) 6 *African Disability Rights Yearbook* 85. https://doi.org/10.29053/2413-7138/2018/v6a4.

Pajević I & Hasanović M 'Antipsychiatry as the stigma' (2017) 29 *Psychiatria Danubina* 890.

Penal Code, Cap 63 'Laws of Kenya'.

Perlin ML 'The insanity defense in English-speaking African countries' (1969) *African Law Studies* 73. https://doi.org/10.1080/07329113.1969.10756150.

Pound R 'The need for a sociological jurisprudence' (1907) 19 *Green Bag* 615.

Priscilla Nyokabi Kanyua v AG (2010) eKLR.

Rex v Pritchard (1836) 7 C & P 303.

Roberts M 'The production of the psychiatric subject: power, knowledge and Michel Foucault' (2005) 6 *Nursing Philosophy* 34. https://doi.org/10.1111/j.1466-769X.2004.00196.x.

Sexual Offences Act 3 of 2006 'Laws of Kenya'.

Shah A 'Making fitness to plead fit for purpose' (2012) 1 *International Journal of Criminology and Sociology* 179. https://doi.org/10.6000/1929-4409.2012.01.17.

Simon RI et al. 'On sound and unsound mind: the role of suicide in tort and insurance litigation' (2005) 333 *Journal of the American Academy of Psychiatry and the Law* 177.

Singh D & Sinnott-Armstrong W 'The DSM-5 definition of mental disorder' (2015) 29 *Public Affairs Quarterly* 11.

Smith T 'Pathology, bias and queer diagnosis: a crip queer consciousness' Master's dissertation, Smith College, Northampton, 2012.

Stein DJ et al. 'What is a mental/psychiatric disorder? From DSM-IV to DSM-V' https://www.ncbi.nlm.nih.gov/pmc/articles/PMC3101504/pdf/nihms291831.pdf (accessed 7 August 2021).

Szasz T 'The use of naming and the origin of the myth of mental illness' (1961) 16 *American Psychologist* 59. https://doi.org/10.1037/h0040842.

Szasz T *The manufacture of madness* (1970).
Szasz T *The myth of mental illness* (1974).
Szwed M 'The notion of 'a person of unsound mind' under article 5 § 1(e) of the European Convention on Human Rights' (2020) 38 *Netherlands Quarterly of Human Rights* 291. https://doi.org/10.1177/0924051920968480.
Tamanaha B *A general jurisprudence of law and society* (2001).
Telles-Correia D et al. 'Mental disorder – the need for an accurate definition' (2018) 9 *Frontiers in Psychiatry* 3. https://doi.org/10.3389/fpsyt.2018.00064.
Tesemma ST & Coetzee SA 'Conflicting discourses on conceptualising children with disabilities in Africa' (2019) 7 *African Disability Rights Yearbook* 63.
Trial of Samuel Adams, London Times, 29 May 1879.
Turner v Howerton et al. no. 22689-VA, April 2, 1997.
Vaughan M 'Idioms of madness: Zomba lunatic asylum, Nyasaland, in the colonial period' (1983) 9 *Journal of Southern African Studies* 233. https://doi.org/10.1080/03057078308708058.
Venning T 'Intellectual disability in the Australian criminal justice system what effect, if any, does general and specific deterrence play in sentencing offenders with an intellectual disability? How can these and the other sentencing principles be applied when sentencing Noel?' https://espace.cdu.edu.au/eserv/cdu:46276/Venning_46276.pdf (accessed 20 February, 2022).
Volpe U 'The development of the ICD-11 chapter on mental disorders' https://sajp.org.za/index.php/sajp/article/view/1105/848 (accessed 20 August 2021).
Wakefield JC 'The concept of mental disorder: diagnostic implications of the harmful dysfunction analysis' (2007) 6 *World Psychiatry* 150.
Ward T 'Standing mute' (2012) 24 *Law & Literature* 3. https://doi.org/10.1525/lal.2012.24.1.3.
Winterwerp v Netherlands (1979) ECtHR Ser A 33.
Woodbridge F 'Some unusual aspects of mental irresponsibility in the criminal law' (1938–1939) 29 *American Institute of Criminal Law and Criminology* 823.
Woolfolk RL 'The concept of mental illness: an analysis of four pivotal issues' (2001) 22 *Journal of Mind and Behavior* 161.
Wurtzburg SJ & Thomson ND 'Antipsychiatry perspective of mental illness' https://www.researchgate.net/publication/277668176_Anti-Psychiatry_Perspective_of_Mental_Illness (accessed 6 August 2021).
X v Germany (1976) ECtHR.
Young IM *Justice and the politics of difference* (1990).

4 Participation of persons with psychosocial disabilities in access to justice

4.0 Introduction

This chapter discusses the right of participation for persons with psychosocial disabilities in Kenya's justice sector. The post-2010 constitutional era[1] not only ushered in a new political dispensation but more importantly a new legal dispensation. For the first time the participatory and representation rights of all Kenyans in all aspects of life, including in justice matters were acknowledged by supreme law. Generally, the right of an accused to effective participation in any criminal process includes not only the right to be present during the proceedings, but also to hear and follow the proceedings.[2] However, the main hindrances to consultative and empowering participation in access to justice as revealed by Foucault and during the empirical study, are paternalistic attitudes by justice system actors towards persons with psychosocial disabilities.[3]

Lack of understanding of the value and benefits of participation, along with insufficient training and skills of professionals involved in these processes also limit the participation of persons with psychosocial disabilities.[4] This chapter adopts the premise that persons with psychosocial disabilities experience limited participation in Kenya's criminal justice process as a result of stigma-related unfitness declarations. In order to ensure effective participation of persons with psychosocial disability in Kenya's criminal justice system, this chapter applies Foucault's theory of power and the provisions of the CRPD on participation. The CRPD's provisions on participation are important because they advance Foucault's counter-conduct ideology against unfitness declarations as discussed in Chapter 2.

The aim of this chapter is to lay down the foundations of participation in regards to unfitness declarations in Kenya. Section one, briefly maps out the

1 Starting 27 August 2010.

2 *Stanford v the United Kingdom* (1994) ECtHR.

3 Chapter 7.

4 A Nylund 'Children's right to participate in decision-making in Norway: paternalism and autonomy' https://munin.uit.no/bitstream/handle/10037/17526/article.pdf?sequence=2&isAllowed=y (accessed 10 August 2021) 221.

DOI: 10.4324/9781003647102-4

extent of participation of persons with psychosocial disability in relation to Foucault's notion of power and the CRPD. Section two discusses the role of the state in ensuring the right of participation in access to justice for persons with psychosocial disabilities. The section analyses selected national legislation and policies on the right to participation in access to justice of persons with psychosocial disabilities. It assesses unfitness declarations and whether they violate the participation of persons with psychosocial disabilities in Kenya's justice sector. Section three is the conclusion.

4.1 Participation by persons with psychosocial disabilities in access to justice

Participation in access to justice has gained increasing acceptance since Aristotle who defined citizens, including citizens with psychosocial disabilities in terms of their ability to participate in deliberations or decision-making procedures.[5] Denis Diederot, a French philosopher wrote that 'the best order of things, as I see it, is the one that includes me; to hell with the most perfect of worlds, if I'm not part of it' illustrating the importance of participation in access to justice.[6] Participation in access to justice is a human right. Human rights connote laws, practices and projects, movements or groupings of lawyers, non-governmental organisations, and others who seek to secure and defend a particular right, group of rights, or human rights in general.[7]

Participation is the right of rights.[8] It cannot be delinked from other human rights.[9] It is a civil and political right as well as an economic, cultural, and social right.[10] The principle of participation in decision-making is an essential tool for the exercise of the right of access to justice.[11] It can be defined as a process of sharing information, expressing ideas, taking an active role in different steps of the justice process, being informed and consulted on decisions concerning public interest, analysing situations, and even making personal choices.[12] It means that there is a place for involvement by persons

5 E Puri 'Understanding participation: theoretical foundations and practical implications' (2004) 39 *Economic and Political Weekly* 2511.

6 D Diederot *Rameau's nephew/D'Alembert's dream* (1976) 50.

7 ML Flear & A Vakulenko 'A human rights perspective on citizen participation in the EU's governance of new technologies' (2010) 10 *Human Rights Law Review* 665.

8 SF Halabi 'Participation and the right to health: lessons from Indonesia' (2009) 11 *Health & Human Rights* 49.

9 United Nations Human Rights Office of the High Commissioner 'OHCHR and equal participation in political and public affairs' https://www.ohchr.org/EN/Issues/Pages/EqualParticipation.aspx (accessed 11 August 2021).

10 L Villa-Torres & J Svanemyr 'Ensuring youth's right to participation and promotion of youth leadership in the development of sexual and reproductive health policies and programs' (2015) 56 *Journal of Adolescent Health* 552.

11 Universal Rights Group 'The right to participate in environmental decision-making' http://www.universal-rights.org/wp-content/uploads/2015/02/EHRD-portal-Right-to-participation.pdf (accessed 11 August 2021).

12 Villa-Torres & Svanemyr (n 10) 553.

with psychosocial disabilities or their representatives alongside other groups, classes, or individuals exercising power and authority in the justice system.[13] Sharing connotes that each individual with psychosocial disability claims the right to play his or her part, along with the equal part played by all other individuals, in the justice system.[14]

The concept of participation in access to justice is not an abstract ideal, but a continuous act of inclusion. Participation in access to justice is of special importance to persons with psychosocial disabilities who are disempowered through unfitness declarations on the assumption that others can protect their interests through alternative measures.[15] Discussions on disempowerment and resistance to unfitness declarations have their foundations from Foucault's work.[16] Unfitness declarations in Kenya is always permeated by power. Participation in access to justice is also a practice whose ideal is not a utopian absence of power.[17]

4.1.1 Role of participation in empowering persons with psychosocial disabilities in access to justice

The role of participation in access to justice is closely linked to Foucault's theory of power.[18] Power simply means the ability to influence decisions in criminal justice systems.[19] Therefore, the right of participation in access to justice is about empowerment of persons with psychosocial disabilities.[20] Empowerment in access to justice is a process of involving the transformation of a person with psychosocial disability from being an object into an agent who can exercise influence and control in the trial process.[21] Empowerment increases the opportunities of persons with psychosocial disabilities in Kenya's criminal justice sector as they are able to make independent choices.[22]

Mere involvement or engagement of persons with psychosocial disabilities in criminal justice systems alone does not amount to being able to influence decisions in the trial process.[23] Power determines not only who is included

13 J Waldron 'Participation: the right of rights' (1998) 98 *Proceedings of the Aristotelian Society* 311.

14 Waldron (n 13) 312.

15 V Shikhelman 'Access to justice in the United Nations Human Rights Committee' (2018) 39 *Michigan Journal of International Law* 457.

16 A Aylett 'Participatory planning, justice, and climate change in Durban, South Africa' (2000) 42 *Environment and Planning* 103.

17 As above.

18 ML Flear & A Vakulenko 'A human rights perspective on citizen participation in the EU's governance of new technologies' (2010) 10 *Human Rights Law Review* 664.

19 A Mubita et al. 'The importance and limitations of participation in development projects and programmes' (2017) 13 *European Scientific Journal* 241.

20 Flear & Vakulenko (n 18) 664.

21 R Stern 'The child's right to participation – reality or rhetoric?' PhD Thesis, Uppsala University, 2006, 129.

22 As above.

23 Mubita et al. (n 19) 242.

Table 4.1 Arnstein's ladder

Level (from the top)	*Type of participation*
8	Citizen's control
7	Delegated power
6	Partnership
5	Placation
4	Consultation
3	Informing
2	Therapy
1	Manipulation

in participatory processes, but the way in which people participate and the conclusions that are reached.[24] Participation in access to justice is about the redistribution of power where persons with psychosocial disabilities, who are excluded through unfitness declarations, are given power to have control and influence in the trial process.[25] Participation in access to justice is power to persons with psychosocial disabilities.[26] A clearer understanding of participation as power is illustrated in Arnstein's ladder as follows:[27]

The ladder illustrates the level of power in each stage compared to the amount of power that persons with psychosocial disabilities have in influencing outcomes in access to justice.[28] The higher the ladder, the more the power in terms of influencing outcomes in access to justice. The citizen's control stage is the highest level of participation for persons with psychosocial disabilities in access to justice. It implies that persons with psychosocial disabilities have absolute power when it comes to influencing outcomes in access to justice. Mid-way, partnership begins to develop and the degree of participation in access to justice moves from mere tokenism to degrees of citizen power.[29] Conversely, the manipulation level is characterised by fake participation in which there is no power at all.[30] Persons with psychosocial disabilities are deceived that they are being involved but outcomes are influenced and determined by the power holders. It is merely a window dressing ceremony in which there is no participation in access to justice at all.[31]

24 S Arnstein quoted in A Aylett 'Participatory planning, justice, and climate change in Durban, South Africa' (2000) 42 *Environment and Planning* 103.

25 Mubita et al. (n 19) 242.

26 As above.

27 S Arnstein 'A ladder of citizen participation' (1969) 35 *Journal of the American Institute of Planners* 216.

28 As above.

29 SB Rifkin & M Kangere 'What is participation?' https://asksource.info/cbr-book/cbr03.pdf (accessed 10 August 2021) 43.

30 Arnstein (n 27) 216.

31 As above.

Participation is the basic right of persons with psychosocial disabilities to have a say in Kenya's criminal justice system.[32] Persons with psychosocial disabilities are right-bearers and their voices should not only be heard, but should count in the decision-making processes of the criminal justice system.[33] When persons with psychosocial disabilities demand the right to participate in access to justice, they are acknowledging that they are not the only voice in the society and that their voice should count for no more in the process than the voices of all other right-bearers. Although, they aspire that their voices be decisive, their aspiration is tempered by principles of fairness and equality, which is implied in the universalisation of their claim.[34] Participation in access to justice for persons with psychosocial disabilities is formally expressed in the CRPD and the African Disability Protocol.

4.1.2 Participation in access to justice under the CRPD

The CRPD is the most emancipatory document for disabled persons, and hence it can be of much use when it comes to the realisation of the right to participation for persons with psychosocial disabilities. The slogan 'nothing about us without us', was applied not only during the drafting and negotiations on the text of the CRPD, but it is also found throughout its provisions.[35] The five principles of the CRPD are equality, accessibility, autonomy, participation, and inclusion.[36] Apart from the CRPD, none of the other international human rights treaties contain disability-specific provisions on the right of access to justice in participation.

Participation under the CRPD is fully oriented towards a human rights perspective, which is focused on engendering empowerment. It creates a platform for the assertion of agency and sovereignty of persons with psychosocial disabilities. Agency implies capacity, which means that individuals are able to see themselves as the main decision-makers with the ability to make choices for their lives.[37] Therefore, an agent is a person who is empowered to act and brings about change.[38] The concept of agency embodies a person's ability to individually and collectively engage in processes that can lead to social transformation, question the power dynamics that contribute to

32 Halabi (n 8) 50.

33 Waldron (n 13) 312.

34 As above.

35 A Callus & A Camilleri 'Nothing about us without us': disabled people determining their human rights through the UNCRPD' (2017) 1 *Mediterranean Review of Human Rights* 8.

36 RM White et al. 'Transformative equality: court accommodations for South African citizens with severe communication disabilities' (2020) 9 *African Journal of Disability* 2.

37 GM Babulal et al. 'Measuring participation for persons with mental illness: a systematic review assessing relevance of existing scales for low and middle income countries' (2015) 3 *BMC Psychology* 2.

38 As above.

inequality, and improve the well-being of both individuals and the community as a whole.[39]

Active participation is a quintessential element in respecting the human dignity of persons with psychosocial disabilities. Participatory rights of persons with psychosocial disabilities become evident when analysing the CRPD. Starting with the preamble to the CRPD, concern is shown by the fact that although there exists a plethora of international instruments, disabled persons continue to face barriers in their participation as equal members of society and violations of their human rights in all parts of the world.[40] It stipulates that disabled persons should have the opportunity to actively be involved in decision-making process about policies and programmes, including those directly concerning them.[41] Article 7 deals with the rights of children with disability in relation to their right to participation. It provides that state parties should ensure that children with disabilities have the right to express their views freely on all matters affecting them, their view being given due weight in accordance with their age and maturity, on equal basis with other children and to be provided with assistive devices.[42]

The CRPD also casts participation as part of the right to access of justice both as an underlying determinant of justice and as a right to have a say in justice matters. Article 13 of the CRPD specifically addresses access to justice, directing state parties to ensure effective access to justice for disabled persons on an equal basis with others, including through the provision of specified accommodation, in order to facilitate their effective role as direct and indirect participants.[43] Following from ensuring effective access to justice, states are obligated to facilitate appropriate training for those working in the field of administration of justice, including police and prison staff on effective access to justice.[44] Participation in this regard is rights-based which means that according to the CRPD disability is a natural part of human diversity that must be respected and supported in all its forms and that disabled persons have the same rights as everyone else in society and that impairment must not be used as an excuse to deny or restrict people's rights.[45]

Moreover, article 29 of the CRPD provides that states parties should ensure that disabled persons are able to participate fully and effectively in political and public life on an equal basis with others.[46] Notwithstanding

39 As above.

40 CRPD, preamble.

41 CRPD, preamble.

42 CRPD, art 7.

43 CRPD, art 13.

44 CRPD, art 13.

45 DARU 'Understanding models of disability' https://www.daru.org.au/wp/wp-content/uploads/2019/03/Human-rights-info-sheet-for-website.pdf (accessed 13 August 2021).

46 CRPD, art 29 provides that: Participation in political and public life States Parties shall guarantee to persons with disabilities political rights and the opportunity to enjoy them on an equal basis with others (. . .).

the Human Rights Committee's (HRC) interpretation of article 25 of the ICCPR, the CRPD guarantees the active participation of persons with psychosocial disabilities. This means that it is grounded in values, which inform the society's belief in the importance of rights, most notably the values of autonomy and responsibility.[47] Every person has to have autonomy in order to feel free to make decisions.[48] Respect for people's autonomy is a principle that gives rise to an obligation to empathically engage with another person's experience and to imagine their situation, given their cares, values, and concerns.[49]

Autonomy denotes capacity for ethical evaluation and self-control and competency for self-rule or self-government.[50] The latter is based on personal rationale, deliberations, choices, and motivations, and, more importantly, freedom from external manipulations, distortions, and coercions.[51] In the context of effective participation in criminal proceedings, autonomy is not simply a matter of comprehension, it is also a matter of an ability to make evaluative judgements.[52] In practice, individuals often encounter the power of state control in matters related to their autonomy especially when exercising their right of participation in access to justice. The state often imposes restrictions and rules, which interferes with individuals' right to participate especially when they are mentally disabled. The CRPD Committee has also expressed concern that persons with psychosocial disabilities are not allowed to participate effectively in access to justice in its opinions in *Noble v Australia (Noble)*, *Doolan v Australia*[53] *(Doolan)*, *Leo v Australia*[54] *(Leo)*, and *Arturo Medina v Mexico*[55] *(Arturo)*.

The claimants in *Noble*, *Doolan*, *Leo*, and *Arturo* were all persons with mental disabilities. They were all deemed unfit to stand trial due to their mental impairments, and ordered to remain in custody. They were held indefinitely in prison where they stayed for periods longer than the sentence period had they been tried and convicted. The CRPD Committee found that state authorities did not provide them with the accommodation and supports needed to stand

47 A Kavanagh 'Participation and judicial review: a reply to Jeremy Waldron' (2003) 22 *Law and Philosophy* 452.

48 J Gumbis et al. 'Do human rights guarantee autonomy?' (2008) 62 *Cuadernos Constitucionales de la Cátedra Fadrique Furió Ceriol* 77.

49 C MacKenzie 'Relational autonomy, normative authority and perfectionism' (2008) 39 *Journal of Ethics & Social Philosophy* 512.

50 A Franklin-Hall 'On becoming an adult: autonomy and the moral relevance of life's stages' (2013) 63 *Philosophical Quarterly* 251.

51 R Arthur 'Giving effect to young people's right to participate effectively in criminal proceedings' (2016) 28 *Child and Family Law Quarterly* 224.

52 J Herring & J Wall 'Autonomy, capacity and vulnerable adults: filling the gaps in the Mental Capacity Act' (2015) 35 *Legal Studies* 711.

53 *Doolan v Australia (Doolan)* (2019) CRPD/C/22/D/18/2013.

54 *Leo v Australia (Leo)* (2019) CRPD/C/22/D/17/2013.

55 *Arturo Medina Vela v Australia (Arturo)* (2019) CRPD/C/22/D/17/2013.

trial, to exercise legal capacity and access justice as required by articles 12(2), 12(3) and 13(1) of the CRPD.

The CRPD Committee held that, first, unfitness declarations are discriminatory and should be replaced by reasonable accommodation provisions in order to ensure the rights of persons with mental disabilities in the criminal justice system.[56] Secondly, that the detention of accused persons with mental disabilities based solely on the nature of their disability without considering any available alternatives and support mechanisms to ensure their right to participation in the trial amounts to a violation of their right to equality before the law, access to justice, freedom from deprivation of liberty, and freedom from cruel, inhuman and degrading treatment under the CRPD.[57]

By being declared 'unfit to testify', the claimants were denied the possibility of exercising their legal capacity to plead not guilty, challenge the evidence against them, designate a defence lawyer of their choosing and challenge any decisions not in their favour. While states parties have some leeway to determine what procedural arrangements could enable persons with psychosocial disabilities to exercise their legal capacity, they must respect procedural safeguards and the person's rights. States parties must ensure effective access to justice for persons with psychosocial disabilities on an equal basis with others, including through the provision of support or necessary accommodations to exercise their rights such as procedural accommodations, in order to facilitate their effective role as direct and indirect participants in all legal proceedings.[58]

4.1.3 Participation in access to justice under the African Disability Protocol

Kenya ratified the African Disability Protocol on 15 November 2021 and entered into force on 5 May 2024.[59] The African Disability Protocol adds depth to the rights of persons with psychosocial disabilities in a manner that is not captured in the CRPD. Particularly, the right of participation in access to justice has been contextualised by the African Disability Protocol to suit the African experience. Article 13 of the African Disability Protocol provides, among other things, that persons with psychosocial disabilities have a right of access to justice on an equal basis with others, including through the provision of procedural, age and gender-appropriate accommodations, in order to facilitate their effective roles as participants in all legal proceedings.

56 *Noble v Australia* (2016) (2016) CRPD/C/16/D/7/2012, para 8.4.

57 *Noble v Australia* para 8.7.

58 P Gooding et al. 'Unfit to plead: imprisoned without conviction' https://findanexpert.unimelb.edu.au/news/1005-unfit-to-plead-imprisoned-without-conviction (accessed 9 March 2022).

59 https://au.int/sites/default/files/treaties/36440-sl-PROTOCOL_TO_THE_AFRICAN_CHARTER_ON_HUMAN_AND_PEOPLES_RIGHTS_ON_THE_RIGHTS_OF_PERSONS_WITH_DISABILITIES_IN_AFRICA_0.pdf (accessed 24 January 2021).

Unlike the CRPD, which makes no reference to African traditional forms of justice, article 13 of the African Disability Protocol has taken a more accommodating approach towards African culture while simultaneously charging states to ensure that those practices and attitudes that infringe on disabled persons rights, but are cloaked as culture, are dealt with. States are obliged to ensure that traditional forms of justice are not used to deny disabled persons their right to access appropriate and effective justice.[60] Article 13 continues with the empowerment ethos towards disabled persons by requiring all law enforcement and justice personnel to be trained at all levels so that they can effectively engage with and ensure that the rights of disabled persons are recognised and implemented without discrimination. Finally, article 13(4) obliges states parties to ensure availability of legal assistance, including legal aid to disabled persons. These rights are applicable to all disabled persons, including persons with psychosocial disabilities in Kenya. Following from the above, Kenya is expected to set up structures within the administration of justice system to assist persons with psychosocial disabilities enjoy the right of access to justice in participation.

4.2 Participation of persons with psychosocial disability in Kenya's justice sector

Kenya's laws do not sufficiently guarantee the right of disabled persons to participate in access to justice. Although participatory rights existed in Kenya as early as the pre-independence period, human rights violations were widespread.[61] At independence period, the 1963 Constitution made an attempt to prohibit discrimination under section 82 but this was also not sufficient to guarantee participation rights for the people of Kenya.[62]

Article 10(1)(a) of the Constitution of 2010 provides for equal participation of marginalised groups. Under article 38, disabled persons, including persons with psychosocial disabilities have a right to political participation, which includes the right to vote, right to participate in any political party among others.[63] The Constitution also makes provision for the right to a fair hearing under article 50.[64] As part of the right to fair hearing, the Constitution

60 African Disability Protocol, art 13(2).

61 MK Mbondenyi 'Entrenching the right to participate in government in Kenya's Constitutional order: some viable lessons from the African Charter on Human and Peoples' Rights' (2011) 55 *Journal of African Law* 39.

62 Sec 82 of the constitution partly provides: 1. Subject to subsections (4), (5) and (8), no law shall make any provision that is discriminatory either of itself or in its effect; 2. Subject to subsections (6), (8) and (9), no person shall be treated in a discriminatory manner by a person acting by virtue of any written law or in the performance of the functions of a public office or a public authority (. . .).

63 Constitution, art 38.

64 Constitution, Art 50 provides that (1) Every person has the right to have any dispute that can be resolved by the application of law decided in a fair and public hearing before a court or, if

provides for intermediation that facilitates participation of vulnerable groups in access to justice. The Constitution allows for the appointment of intermediaries for purposes of assisting the victim or the accused person to communicate with the court.[65] Participation in this instance is defined in terms of verbal communication. However, intermediaries in general are critical to the participation of persons with psychosocial disabilities in Kenya's criminal justice sector. They are not simply the mouth piece of a vulnerable witness.[66]

Article 50(7) of the Constitution has been interpreted in different ways by Kenyan courts. The judiciary in Kenya is divided into two categories; superior courts and subordinate courts. Superior courts are made up of the Supreme Court, Court of Appeal, and the High Court in the order of seniority, while subordinate courts comprise the Magistrates' Courts and Kadhis Courts. The decisions of the Court of Appeal are binding on the High Court. The judicial view on participation in Kenya inadvertently stresses verbal communication, which gives a disadvantage to persons with psychosocial disabilities.

According to the High Court, an intermediary under the Constitution is one who assists a complainant or an accused person to communicate with the court.[67] The Court of Appeal in the case of *MM v Republic*[68] affirmed this position. In that case, the accused was convicted for the offence of defilement contrary to section 8(1) as read with section 8(2) of the Sexual Offences Act. The complainant was unable to testify on account of her tender age and was declared a vulnerable witness under section 31 of the Sexual Offences Act. She never testified. In her stead, her mother who had been appointed as an intermediary testified. The mother's evidence served as that of the victim. The Court of Appeal was of the view that the evidence presented by the intermediary should not be that of the intermediary but that of the witness relayed to court through the intermediary. The Court affirmed the role of an intermediary to merely being that of acting as a medium through which the accused person or complainant communicates with the court.[69]

Similarly, in the case of *Republic v Elijah Weru Mathenge*,[70] the accused who had been charged with the offence of murder contrary to section 203 as read with section 204 of the Kenyan Penal Code was diagnosed with psychogenic conversion disability with aphonia, which resulted in him losing his voice while in custody. The High Court, in an attempt to safeguard the accused person's

appropriate, another independent and impartial tribunal or body. (2) Every accused person has the right to a fair trial (.).

65 Constitution, art 50(7).

66 *MM v Republic* (2012) eKLR.

67 See *Francis Ogoti Otundo v Republic* (2012) eKLR and *Kennedy Chimwani Mulokoto v Republic* (2011) eKLR, *TCK v R* Milimani (2010) eKLR, *Joseph Kamau Kirubi v Republic* (2010) eKLR, & *Marcus Muriuki v Republic* Meru (2009) eKLR.

68 *MM v Republic.*

69 As above.

70 (2017) eKLR.

right to participation in his trial ruled in favour of the appointment of an intermediary but went further to state that even pre-recorded statements are admissible in such cases. Participation of vulnerable witnesses may be enhanced by, admitting in evidence a recorded statement made by the witness or by holding a special sitting for the purpose of examining, in full or in part, the vulnerable witness. All these goes to participation in terms of communication.

However, the scope of the intermediary scheme under article 12 of the CRPD is not limited only to communication with vulnerable witnesses. The intermediary should not only seek to improve communication, but also the participation of vulnerable witnesses and accused persons.[71] Furthermore, intermediaries should pay attention to other factors affecting the communication and participation of vulnerable people, such as monitoring whether the questions are developmentally appropriate and whether the witness is becoming fatigued.[72] The intermediary scheme in Kenya is limited, a position that is exacerbated by a lack of guidelines which provides for the procedure for appointment, qualifications, and functions of intermediaries.

Although the Constitution provides an extensive catalogue of participatory rights for persons with psychosocial disabilities, it is not a guarantee that it or any other law with similar provision will be implemented. The Constitution of Kenya contains a bill of rights that has even domesticated international human rights and freedoms in the national legal system, for instance, the provision on discrimination.[73] However, this does not mean they will be fully implemented. The responsibility for ensuring that participation as a right in Kenya's criminal justice system exists, is functional, and accessible falls on the government under the national law and international law. The reality, however, is that the realisation of the right to participation in access to justice for persons with psychosocial disabilities under the Constitution is yet to be achieved. Participation in the criminal justice system follows the practice of the archaic laws, institutions, and attitudes that existed under colonialism.[74]

Kenya's criminal justice system classifies persons with psychosocial disabilities as vulnerable. The law that deals with individuals whose disabilities significantly impair their functioning and ability to prepare their case and participate in court is the Criminal Procedure Code. Criminal courts recognise that it is fundamentally unfair to prosecute a person who cannot understand the case against him or her. However, not all psychosocial disabilities raise competency concerns.[75] For instance, a person who suffers from depression, anxiety, or schizophrenia may be able to effectively advocate for their rights. Nevertheless,

71 P Cooper & M Mattison 'Intermediaries, vulnerable people and the quality of evidence: an international comparison of three versions of the English intermediary model' (2017) 21 *The International Journal of Evidence and Proof* 365.

72 Cooper & Mattison (n 70) 366.

73 Constitution, art 27(3).

74 Mbondenyi (n 61) 39.

75 As above.

accused persons with psychosocial disabilities in Kenya's criminal courts are always considered incompetent and denied their right of access to justice in participation. Usually, they are simply informed that they have been declared unfit. Informing is not participation.[76]

A substantive participation approach stresses the intrinsic value of a person's unique perspective, regardless of whether it will aid the decision-maker when making decisions. It follows that the intrinsic value of participation creates a presumption in favour of participatory decision-making, and places non-participatory decision-making mechanisms, such as unfitness declarations, under a burden of justification. Unfitness declarations regulate the participation of persons with psychosocial disabilities in highly overly-invasive ways. Unfitness declarations removes their legal capacity by essentially refusing to recognise the decision-making ability of the individual and gives that power to a source that is external from the individual. This results in a variety of restrictions of the individual's capability to participate effectively in the justice process. In Kenya, an accused person with psychosocial disability can be involuntarily placed in an institution or denied access to justice rights as a result of these declarations.

4.2.1 Role of the state in ensuring the participation of persons with psychosocial disabilities in access to justice

Generally, states are obliged by international law to guarantee basic human rights by all legitimate means, including legislation and law enforcement.[77] Kenya is a party to the CRPD which is the main international human rights instrument protecting the rights of persons with psychosocial disabilities. Under the CRPD state parties have three main obligations. These are the obligations to respect, protect and fulfil the rights of disabled persons. Moreover, in articles 54–57 of the Constitution, the state is required to take measures, including affirmative action programmes, to ensure that youth, disabled persons, minorities, and marginalised groups have access to relevant education and training, opportunities to associate, be represented, and participate in political, social, economic, and other spheres of life, access employment, and to be protected from harmful cultural practices and exploitation.

The obligation to respect is defined as the obligation not to interfere with the enjoyment of the rights of disabled persons.[78] Respect in participation in access to justice requires states not to stop any disabled persons from freely taking part in the justice process. In ensuring the respect of the right to

76 J Kaler 'Understanding participation' (1999) 21 *Journal of Business Ethics* 37.

77 Gumbis et al. (n 48) 78.

78 United Nations 'Chapter 2: the convention in detail – obligations of states parties under the convention' https://www.un.org/development/desa/disabilities/resources/handbook-for-parliamentarians-on-the-convention-on-the-rights-of-persons-with-disabilities/chapter-two-the-convention-in-detail–4.html (accessed 12 August 2021).

participation, the state should refrain from actions that deprive disabled persons of the right to participation and put in place measures to prevent non-state actors and private persons from interfering in their ability to realise and enjoy their human rights, including the right to participation in access to justice.[79]

The obligation to protect means that, the state must take positive steps to protect the rights of disabled people against violations by third parties, including private individuals and organisations.[80] The state should prevent private entities from prohibiting a disabled person from freely participating in the justice sector. It should abolish any systems that empower other actors to exercise power to deny the participation of persons with psychosocial disabilities in the criminal justice process. Particularly, steps should be taken to promote the ability of persons with psychosocial disabilities to understand and participate in court proceedings. Effective participation requires an accused person with psychosocial disabilities to have a broad understanding of the nature of the trial process and of what is at stake for him or her, including the significance of any penalty, which may be imposed. Understanding of what is said in court is paramount despite any assistance of, for example, an interpreter, lawyer, social worker, or friend. Accused persons with psychosocial disabilities should be able to follow what is said by the prosecution witnesses and, if represented, to explain to their own lawyers their version of events, point out any statements with which they disagree with and make them aware of any facts which should be put forward in their defence.[81]

The obligation to fulfil requires states to adopt appropriate measures towards the full realisation of the right to participation in access to justice, including executive, legislative, administrative, budgetary, and judicial actions.[82] States in this connection should therefore review all the laws that deprive persons with psychosocial disabilities of their right to participation and replace them with laws and policies that facilitates this right.

4.2.2 *Selected national legislation and policies fulfilling the right of persons with psychosocial disabilities of participation in access to justice*

The laws of Kenya are structured to take away the participation of persons with psychosocial disabilities. However, the country is also progressively making efforts of her own through the Constitution, statutes, and administrative

79 CRPD Committee General Comment 1: Article 12: Equal recognition before the law (2014) UN Doc CRPD/C/GC/1 dated 19 May 2014, para 20.

80 United Nations 'Chapter 2: the convention in detail – obligations of states parties under the convention' https://www.un.org/development/desa/disabilities/resources/handbook-for-parliamentarians-on-the-convention-on-the-rights-of-persons-with-disabilities/chapter-two-the-convention-in-detail–4.html (accessed 12 August 2021).

81 *SC v the United Kingdom* (2004) ECtHR.

82 As above.

reforms to project the paramountcy of participation rights of persons with psychosocial disabilities. Several legal enactments, including the Sexual Offences Act, Criminal Procedure Code, and the Children Act, have been enacted in order to facilitate the participation of persons with psychosocial disabilities. The Sexual Offences Act makes provision for the appointment of intermediaries who include any[83]

> [P]erson authorised by a court, on account of his or her expertise or experience, to give evidence on behalf of a vulnerable witness and may include a parent, relative, psychologist, counsellor, guardian, children's officer or social worker.

Although the Sexual Offences Act makes provisions for intermediaries, it does not facilitate the participation of accused persons with psychosocial disabilities as it applies only to witnesses. Under section 31, the court is authorised to declare a witness vulnerable if the witness is a person with mental disabilities. Further, the court is allowed to call any intermediary who will advise it on the vulnerability of such witnesses. However, the court will not convict an accused person solely on the uncorroborated evidence of an intermediary.[84]

As a means of enhancing the participation of vulnerable witnesses, the Sexual Offences Act also allows the court to adopt other necessary measures such as, allowing such persons to give evidence under the protective cover of a witness protection box, directing that the proceedings may not take place in open court, prohibiting the publication of the identity of the complainant or the family, including the publication of information that may lead to their identification, or any other measure which the court deems just and appropriate.[85] These are merely considerations accorded to vulnerable witnesses such as children in order for the right to participate effectively to be satisfied.[86]

The other measure that the state has adopted in order to fulfil the right to participation in access to justice is through legal aid. Legal aid is one way of ensuring the participation of disabled persons in Kenya's criminal justice system. Legal aid in Kenya is provided for under the Legal Aid Act.[87] It is guided by fundamental values and principles of access to justice, equality before the law, inclusiveness, and non-discrimination.[88] Legal aid includes: Legal advice, legal representation, recommending law reform and undertaking advocacy work on behalf of the community, creating awareness through the provision

83 Sexual Offences Act, sec 2.
84 Sexual Offences Act, sec 31(10).
85 Sexual Offences Act, sec 31(10).
86 Arthur (n 51) 224.
87 Legal Aid Act 6 of 2016.
88 ES Wabuke et al. 'Promoting access to justice in Kenya: making the case for law clinics' 11 October 2018 https://theplatform.co.ke/promoting-access-to-justice-in-kenya-making-the-case-for-law-clinics/ (accessed 22 September 2020).

of legal information and law-related education, and assistance in, resolving disputes by alternative dispute resolution, drafting of relevant documents; and effecting service incidental to any legal proceedings, and reaching or giving effect to any out-of-court settlement.[89] The main aim of the Legal Aid Act is to facilitate access to justice and social justice.[90]

Legal aid is available in both criminal and civil cases.[91] The Legal Aid Act also establishes the National Legal Aid Service (Service) which is mandated with administering an affordable and accessible national legal aid scheme, promoting research in the area of access to justice and conducting public interest litigation.[92] Section 36 of the Legal Aid Act provides for the categories of persons who are eligible for legal aid services which includes: Citizen of Kenya, a child, a refugee under the Refugees Act,[93] a victim of human trafficking, an internally displaced person, or a stateless person. Article 50(2)(h) states that

> [e]very accused person has the right to a fair trial, which includes the right to have an advocate assigned to the accused person by the State and at State expense, if substantial injustice would otherwise result, and to be informed of this right promptly.[94]

In determining whether substantial injustice will occur, the court must consider the severity of the charge and sentence, the complexity of the case, and the capacity of accused persons to defend themselves.[95] Other factors, which the court may consider includes the literacy level of the accused and whether the accused is a minor.[96]

In instances where the accused is unrepresented and seems not to understand the court procedures, Kenya's criminal process allows the presiding judicial officer to assist.[97] The Judiciary Criminal Procedure Bench Book (JCBB) stipulates that where an accused is unrepresented, the court is expected to provide her or him with some guidance on the court process.[98] According to Hawkins and Blackstone 'the judges of the court . . . are to be of counsel for the prisoner, and to see that he hath law and justice'.[99] Therefore, a judge or magistrate must not preside on a trial like a football match referee.

89 Legal Aid Act, sec 2.
90 Legal Aid Act, preamble.
91 As above.
92 As above.
93 (13 of 2006).
94 Constitution of Kenya, art 50(2)(h).
95 Legal Aid Act s 43(1A).
96 *R v Karissa Chengo & 2 Others* (2005) KESC.
97 P Juma 'Right to self-representation for people with mental disabilities in Kenya's courts' (2019) 7 *African Disability Rights Yearbook* 83.
98 The Judiciary *Criminal procedure bench book* (2018) 35.
99 W Hawkins *Pleas of the Crown* (1973) 327 and W Blackstone *Commentaries* (1783) 319.

Instead, they must ensure that an unrepresented party, and especially, a party with a mental disability, is assisted in order 'to present his case as fully as possible, without the court appearing to lose its impartiality'. Be that as it may, it is also noteworthy to point out that the court cannot act as an advisor to the accused as to the tactical possibilities open to him as the trial unfolds. Since *Pritchard*, it is no longer sufficient for a judge or magistrate to act as 'counsel for the prisoner'.[100] In an adversarial system, the parties bear the responsibility of putting their cases before the court, either in person or through counsel. An arbiter of the facts is not expected to descend into the arena and give the impression of acting as advocate on behalf of any of the parties involved.[101]

The Legal Aid Act does not specifically mention disabled persons. However, it can be inferred that it applies to everybody irrespective of their disability status. Most importantly, it fails to make provision for reasonable accommodations that enable better involvement of disabled persons in the legal aid process. Moreover, despite its reforms, the established offices exist only on paper and not 'in vivo', in realistic environments.[102] The National Legal Aid and Awareness Programme (NALEAP) was launched on 18 September 2008 with the objective of improving access to justice in Kenya.[103] A Steering Committee appointed by the president was established in late 2007 and includes representatives from a number of government departments, the Law Society of Kenya (LSK) and a number of civil society organisations.

The establishment of the NALEAP is a positive development and represents a significant step in addressing some of the barriers preventing access to justice among the poor. However, the pilot for the programme is limited in scope, both geographically and thematically. At present, the scheme is being piloted in five urban centres, each of which is focused on one area of law (for example family law, criminal law, or capital offences). It is a cause of concern that the scheme does not specifically cover disability, particularly given the strong link identified between disability and poverty. There is a significant risk, therefore, that disabled persons will remain unable to participate in access to justice, which have been so carefully protected in the Kenyan legal system. NALEAP has been largely ineffective due to lack of adequate budget. This programme is still at pilot stage 12 years after establishment, a clear demonstration of the government's lack of commitment to facilitating access to justice. That failure of the state to fulfil its obligations defeats the purpose of article 50 of the Constitution which provides for the right of access to justice.

100 *Rex v Pritchard.*

101 Juma (n 97) 83.

102 As above.

103 Kenya National Commission on Human Rights 'Report to the Human Rights Committee to inform its review of Kenya's third periodic report on implementation of the provisions of the International Covenant on Civil and Political Rights' https://www2.ohchr.org/english/bodies/hrc/docs/ngos/KNCHR_Kenya_HRC105.pdf 6.

Guarantees towards the participation of persons with psychosocial disabilities have also been provided for in the Persons Deprived of Liberty Act (Liberty Act).[104] Under the Liberty Act, every person deprived of liberty is entitled to the protection of all fundamental rights and freedoms subject to such limitations as may be permitted under the Constitution.[105] In this regard, all the rights under article 50 and 51 of the Constitution regarding arrested persons who are held in lawful custody in relation to any criminal proceedings are applicable. They are entitled to the due process of law, including a fair hearing and trial in accordance with the law relating to criminal procedure and the right to access the services of an interpreter or other intermediary during detention and legal proceedings.[106]

The Liberty Act also makes specific provisions in respect of disabled persons. Section 23 provides that disabled persons who have lawfully been deprived of liberty should be treated on an equal basis with others in terms of the Constitution and other relevant laws. They should be accommodated in facilities that adequately meet their personal needs, taking account of the condition and nature of their disabilities. The Act requires the competent authorities to take appropriate measures to facilitate humane treatment and respect for the privacy, legal capacity, and inherent dignity of disabled persons deprived of liberty. Despite these protections, the Liberty Act does not guarantee substantive rights to participation in access to justice. There is also an implication that persons with psychosocial disabilities who have been declared unfit in the criminal process are incarcerated because of their disabilities or that disability exacerbates their incarceration.[107]

The Persons with Disabilities Act[108] defines disability in terms of participation to mean a physical, sensory, mental, or other impairment, including any visual, hearing, learning, or physical incapability, which impacts adversely on social, economic, or environmental participation. The very acknowledgement of participation for disabled persons is an expression of empowerment towards them. However, although the Persons with Disabilities Act provides for participation, it has been criticised for focusing more on physical accessibility and employment of persons with disabilities.[109] On participation in access to justice, the Persons with Disabilities Act does not expressly provide for legal aid. However, the Attorney General in consultation with the National Council for

104 Persons Deprived of Liberty Act 23 of 2014, Laws of Kenya.

105 Persons Deprived of Liberty Act, sec 3(1).

106 Persons Deprived of Liberty Act, sec 7.

107 African Policing Civilian Oversight Forum (APCOF) and the National Gender and Equality Commission (NGEC) *Pre-trial detention for persons with disabilities in correctional institutions* African Policing Civilian Oversight Forum (2017) 15.

108 Persons with Disabilities Act (Act 14 of 2003), Laws of Kenya.

109 H Mudora 'Review of Kenya persons with disabilities act overdue' http://globaldisability.org/2016/04/01/review-kenya-persons-disabilities-act-2003-overdue (accessed 12 August 2021).

Persons with Disabilities (NCPWD) and the LSK have been mandated under section 38 of the Persons with Disabilities Act to make regulations providing for free legal services for disabled persons, including in respect of matters affecting the violation of their rights and in cases involving capital punishment. The chief justice is also required to make rules relating to the exemption of disabled persons from paying fees in relation to matters relating to the violation of their rights and the provision to disabled persons who attend court of free sign language interpretation, braille services, and physical guide assistance.[110] Disabled accused persons are also to be held in custody or in facilities, which have been modified appropriately in order to accommodate their disabilities.[111] The Chief Justice is obligated to ensure that cases involving disabled persons are disposed of expeditiously, having due regard to the disability and suffering of such persons.[112]

4.2.3 Unfitness declarations and participation of persons with psychosocial disabilities

Unfitness declaration systems in Kenya were created and maintained by colonial legal technocrats-lawyers and bureaucrats-who were guided by norms of the common law rather than the wider Kenyan society.[113] This is what Foucault termed as 'governmentality' where power is exercised by institutions to maintain social order. Colonial state institutions created and maintained complex unfitness declarations laws, which had no basis in norms of the Kenyan people. As such, this book shares the views of Oliver Wendel Holmes, who like Foucault, was of the opinion that law is not merely a set of rules, but 'simply a prediction of how state power will be deployed in particular circumstances'.[114] In the case of psychosocial disability, oppressive and archaic doctrines, for instance unfitness declarations in Kenya's Criminal Procedure Code have created a perception that persons with psychosocial disabilities lack capacity to participate effectively in access to justice.[115]

The Criminal Procedure Code provides for the dual concept of insanity at trial and insanity during the commission of an offence. Insanity at trial is what results in unfitness declarations. Unfitness declarations present legal barriers that affect the interactions between persons with psychosocial disabilities, legal systems, and the nature of the law.[116] Such barriers hinder the mainstreaming

110 Persons with Disabilities Act, sec 38.

111 African Policing Civilian Oversight Forum & the National Gender and Equality Commission (n 106) 15.

112 Persons with Disabilities Act, sec 38.

113 MA Edwards 'The alignment of law and norms: of mirrors, bulwarks, and pressure valves' (2015) 10 *Faculty Scholarship* 23.

114 RA Posner *The problems of jurisprudence* (1993) 223.

115 Users & Survivors of Psychiatry in Kenya (USP-K) *Advancing the rights of persons with psychosocial disability in Kenya* USP-K (2017) 15.

116 A Gray et al. 'Cognitive impairment, legal need, and access to justice' (2009) 10 *Justice Issues* 5.

of disability rights in national law and corresponding policy responses in a country. Section 162 and 167 of the Criminal Procedure Code are the often-cited provisions by courts when dealing with the issue of unfitness declaration against accused persons with psychosocial disabilities in Kenya. These provisions are so permissive that their effect in many instances is to deprive persons with psychosocial disabilities of their right to participation in access to justice and instead detain them forcefully and indefinitely.[117]

Section 162 provides that when in the course of a trial or committal proceedings the court forms the opinion that the accused is of unsound mind and consequently incapable of making his defence, the court after inquiring into the fact of unsoundness must postpone further proceedings in the case if it forms the opinion that the accused is incapable of defending himself or herself. On the one hand, if the accused person is entitled to bail, the court may release the accused person on the condition that he or she will be properly taken care of and prevented from doing injury to himself or herself or to any other person. The accused is also required to give security for his or her appearance before the court or such officer as the court may appoint in that behalf. On the other hand, if the case is one in which the accused person is not entitled to bail, or if sufficient security is not given, the court must order that the accused be detained in safe custody in such place and manner as it may think fit. The court shall transmit the record or a certified copy of the order of detention to the minister (today Cabinet Secretary) for the time being responsible for prisons, for consideration by the president. Upon consideration of the record, the president may by order under his or her hand addressed to the court direct the detention of the accused person in a mental hospital or other suitable place of custody. In turn, the court shall issue a warrant in accordance with the president's directives. The warrant shall be sufficient authority for the detention of the accused until the president makes a further order in the matter or until the court, which found him or her incapable of making his or her defence orders him or her to be brought before it again in the manner provided by the law.

Section 167 provides for the procedure where an accused person, though not insane, cannot be made to understand the proceedings. If the matter is being tried by a subordinate court, the court must proceed to hear the evidence. If at the close of the evidence for the prosecution, and, if the defence has been called upon, of any evidence for the defence, the court is of the opinion that the evidence, which it has heard would not justify a conviction, it must acquit and discharge the accused. However, where the court is of the opinion that the evidence justifies a conviction, it must order the accused to be detained during the president's pleasure, subject to confirmation by the High Court. In cases tried by the High Court, the court shall try the case and at the close of the prosecution case, either acquit the accused person or, if satisfied

117 African Policing Civilian Oversight Forum & the National Gender and Equality Commission (n 106) 18.

that the evidence would justify a conviction, order that the accused person be detained during the president's pleasure.

Any person ordered to be detained during the president's pleasure will be detained in such place and under such conditions as the president may from time to time by order direct, and while so detained shall be deemed to be in lawful custody. The president may at any time of his own motion, or after receiving a report from any person or persons thereunto empowered by him, order that a person detained be discharged. The president may also make orders for the supervision of an accused person with psychosocial disabilities in any place or by any person and any such other conditions for ensuring the welfare of the detained person and the public, as the president thinks fit. When a person has been ordered to be detained during the president's pleasure, the confirming or presiding judge must forward to the minister a copy of the notes of evidence taken at the trial, with a report in writing signed by him or her containing any recommendation or observations on the case he or she may think fit to make.

Barriers to participation following unfitness declaration detentions

Generally, persons with psychosocial disabilities are more likely to be refused bail and held on remand than others, once a trial is postponed following unfitness declarations.[118] The law presumes that persons with psychosocial disabilities are insane, mad, irrational, and are likely to cause harm to themselves or others thus the need for their detention.[119] Detention is often a barrier to their right to participation in access to justice. In this instance, participation involves not only the end product events such as taking part in advice session, a court appearance, or obtaining a piece of legal information, but also the steps in the process leading to those end products, such as being able to obtain the requisite documents such as witness statements and charge sheet, making an appointment with advocates, getting access to a library, or just getting some assistance to know what will be the next step in a process.[120] According to section 162 of Kenya's Criminal Procedure Code, unfit accused persons who are unable to raise bail or who have been charged with non-bailable offences are to be detained until a psychiatrist finds them fit to plead.[121] If released on bail, a person with psychosocial disability is ordered to seek treatment and come back to stand trial.[122]

118 Gray et al. (n 116) 5.

119 USP-K (n 115) 15.

120 A Grunseit et al. *Taking justice into custody: the legal needs of prisoners* Law and Justice Foundation of New South Wales, 93.

121 L Matata 'Kenyans living with mental illness get lost in the criminal justice system' https://pettyoffences.org/kenyans-living-with-mental-illness-get-lost-in-the-criminal-justice-system/ (accessed 16 August 2021).

122 As above.

Detentions do not consider the needs of incarcerated persons with psychosocial disabilities. Detention limits the abilities of persons with psychosocial disabilities to obtain legal information because they cannot actively seek it in the same way as their non-incarcerated counterparts. Their range of choice of sources of information is narrower due to limited sources of information such as public libraries or internet facilities. Moreover, opportunities to consult available sources are hampered due to strictures generated by other prison functions.[123] Detention also means that it is likely that the process of accessing or interacting with an advocate would be hampered due to the fact of incarceration.[124] It is easier to access an advocate and interact with an advocate while out of prison than when one is in prison. Persons with psychosocial disabilities may also require other forms of support, which are strictly not legal.[125] Persons with psychosocial disabilities may need their carers to assist them participate effectively in court, such as assisting them with filling out forms or for general support in court or tribunal.[126] However, they may be denied the opportunity for such assistance due to the legal constraints caused by unfitness declarations thus inhibiting their ability to participate effectively in court processes.[127]

The detention of accused persons at the pleasure of the president has been declared by the courts to be in contravention of their right to freedom from torture and cruel, inhuman or degrading treatment or punishment and freedom and security of the person under the Constitution of Kenya as discussed in Chapter 1 in the cases of *Hassan Hussein Yusuf v Republic* and in *Joseph Melikino Katuta v Republic.*[128] These cases dealt with the detention of persons with psychosocial disabilities at the president's pleasure but did not address the extent to which section 162 and 167 violate the rights of persons with psychosocial disabilities to legal capacity by denying them their right to participation.

Barriers to participation following unfitness declarations on account of not understanding proceedings

Evidently, under section 167 of the Criminal Procedure Code, it is legal to convict or acquit persons with psychosocial disabilities without them participating in the trial process. It means that persons with psychosocial disabilities, in the words of Young, will both externally and internally be excluded

123 As above.

124 Grunseit et al. (n 120) 97.

125 M Karras et al. *On the edge of justice: the legal needs of people with a mental illness in NSW* Sydney: Law and Justice Foundation of NSW, 144.

126 Gray et al. (n 116) 6.

127 As above.

128 *Hussan Hussein Yusuf v Republic* (2016) eKLR & *Joseph Melikino Katuta v Republic* (2016) eKLR.

from participating in the democratic space of access to justice.[129] Persons with psychosocial disabilities, after being declared unfit on account of lack of understanding are barred from participating not only in the justice process, but also from influencing the legal outcome, thus external exclusion. Persons with psychosocial disabilities are also excluded from participating in access to justice under section 167 of the Criminal Procedure Code due to limited opportunities, thus internal exclusion.[130] Unfitness declarations do not take into consideration the disability-specific needs of persons with psychosocial disabilities such as support and reasonable accommodation in access to justice. The major drawback of section 167 is the lack of investigation as to the necessity of appropriate accommodations to enhance the participation of persons with psychosocial disabilities in access to justice. The law does not make any provision for reasonable accommodation. Moreover, there are no provisions for alternatives to unfitness declarations, such as diversion and probation. In short, section 167 does not reflect the special needs of persons with psychosocial disabilities.

Effective participation goes beyond simple legal status and serves to establish the worth of persons with psychosocial disabilities by allowing them to exercise their legal capacity, feel a sense of ownership and take an active part in justice determinations.[131] Their notion of self-worthiness is increased when they are able to express, assert, and act upon their moral convictions and commitments, not just in their personal lives, but also in the criminal justice domain.[132] This is the intrinsic value of participation. One legal commentator urged for the application of the three Vs as voice, validation, and voluntariness, arguing that it is only fair that all litigants, including persons with psychosocial disabilities be heard before accepting a decision, especially in the criminal justice system. This creates a sense of voluntary as opposed to coercive participation, which in turn can improve trust in the outcome of the judicial process, contribute to any healing of the parties involved, and bring about a change of behaviour on the part of an accused persons in the future.[133] The intrinsic value of participation is concerned with the ability of persons with psychosocial disabilities to take part in Kenya's criminal justice process and not the outcome of a decision-making procedure.[134] Thus, what matters is the opportunity of persons with psychosocial disability to participate and not the moral standing of judicial decisions.

129 IM Young *Inclusion and democracy* (2000) 54.
130 Young (n 129) 55.
131 DP Moynihan 'Normative and instrumental perspectives on public participation: citizen summits in Washington, DC' (2003) 33 *The American Review of Public Administration* 168.
132 Kavanagh (n 47) 459.
133 AD Ronner 'Songs of validation, voice, and voluntary participation: therapeutic jurisprudence, miranda and juveniles' (2002) 71 *University of Cincinnati Law Review* 94–95.
134 As above.

Unfitness declarations as part of fair trial rights of persons with psychosocial disabilities in Kenya

For a long time, unfitness declarations have been viewed as promoting the right to a fair trial of accused persons with psychosocial disabilities.[135] In *Charles Mwangi Muraya v Republic*[136] the appellant was tried, convicted, and sentenced to death in the High Court of Kenya. Among the appellant's grounds of appeal was that the learned trial judge erred in disregarding medical evidence pertaining to his mental status, particularly failing to carry out an inquiry into the appellant's mental fitness to stand trial upon receiving the evidence of Dr Victor Ombaka Otieno who testified as one of the prosecution witnesses. The psychiatrist testified that at the time of examination he formed the opinion that the appellant was unfit merely because he could not tell the time and stated that he was hearing voices, or what in medical history is referred to as hallucinations.[137] The Court of Appeal agreed that the appellant was unfit and should not have been allowed to participate during the trial because according to section 162

> [I]t is a fundamental requirement in criminal trials that an accused person should understand, follow and fully participate in his trial. Section 162 CPC as a whole, is a safeguard meant to achieve that fundamental requirement. That is the reason why the section makes it mandatory for an inquiry to be done immediately when the issue arises, and if, upon inquiry, there is evidence of unsoundness of mind, further proceedings must be adjourned and further consequences follow to ensure the accused is medically treated and becomes mentally fit to understand, follow and participate in the trial.

Although the Court of Appeal reiterated the long-standing principle in criminal law that accused persons must be able to understand and participate effectively in the criminal proceedings of which they are a part, the judiciarisation of persons with psychosocial disabilities under section 162 does not achieve this effect.[138]

Indeed, persons with psychosocial disabilities have the same fair hearing right as all other accused persons. However, unfitness declarations violate the fair trial rights of persons with psychosocial disabilities because they are based solely on the nature of their disability. The participation of persons with psychosocial disabilities in access to justice is based on the fitness or unfitness of

135 A Kirby et al. 'Effective participation or passive acceptance: how can defendants participate more effectively in the court process?' https://howardleague.org/wp-content/uploads/2016/04/HLWP_9_2014_2.pdf (accessed 12 August 2021) 6.

136 *Charles Mwangi Muraya v Republic* (2001) eKLR.

137 *Charles Mwangi Muraya v Republic*.

138 Kirby et al. (n 135) 5.

their mind, which according to the CRPD Committee amounts to discrimination.[139] The Committee has maintained that such declarations, including that of unfitness to stand trial and non-responsibility as well as their resultant detentions, contradict the provisions of article 14 of the CRPD since they were meant and have had the effect of depriving persons with mental disabilities of their right to due process and safeguards, which should be applicable to every accused person.[140] This makes Kenya's mental disability-based orders obtaining under sections 162 and 167 of the Criminal Procedure Code inconsistent with the provisions of the CRPD as they inhibit the participation and liberty of persons with psychosocial disabilities in the criminal justice system.

Mental incapacity tests as a barrier to participation of persons with psychosocial disabilities following unfitness declarations

In practice, as will be discussed in Chapter 7, the test of unfitness in Kenya is not one of participation but of determining whether an accused person is mentally disabled or in need of hospitalisation. In part, the substitution of the participation standard with the one of mental disability has occurred because of the reliance by courts on psychiatric opinion, which fail to focus on the purposes of the incompetency test. The criticism is that courts loosely apply the unfitness standard on the basis of an accused person's mental capacity without finding out whether it impacts on their ability to understand proceedings or to assist counsel.[141]

Mental assessment tests deprive persons with psychosocial disabilities of their right to make decisions which subsequently impacts on the exercise of their right to participation in access to justice.[142] A person with psychosocial disability may simply be very poor at being a witness rather than unfit.[143] A slight cognitive impairment may act as a barrier to the effective participation of persons with psychosocial disabilities in the legal system. Persons suffering from schizophrenia may experience a degree of memory loss and problems with concentrating or planning. Drug and alcohol abuse may also lead to cognitive impairment as well as depression, which may result in concentration and memory problems.[144]

In *Nyawa Mwajowa v Republic*[145] the appellant was convicted and sentenced for the offence of murder contrary to section 203 as read with section 204 of the Penal Code. He appealed arguing that his conviction was

139 *Noble v Australia*, paras 8.4.

140 Guidelines on the right to liberty and security of persons with disabilities, adopted September 2015, para 16.

141 Anonymous 'Incompetency to stand trial' (1967) 81 *Harvard Law Review* 460.

142 USP-K (n 115) 15.

143 Karras et al. (n 125) 132.

144 As above.

145 *Nyawa Mwajowa v Republic* (2016) eKLR.

unlawful on two grounds, namely that the trial court, having found him to be of unsound mind, erred by failing to comply with section 162(4) of the Criminal Procedure Code and further that the trial court erred by convicting him of murder instead of proceeding as provided in section 167 of the Criminal Procedure Code. The doctor's report indicated that the accused persons was unfit to stand trial because his concentration was relatively impaired and he suffered from mental illness on account of his abnormal belief and on account of his recollection of his behaviour. According to the Court of Appeal,

> there was evidence that the appellant could have been of unsound mind at the time of commission of the offence, the High Court restricted its consideration of his mental status only to the time of the appellant's trial. In *Leonard Mwangemi Munyasia v Republic* (supra), this Court reiterated that it is the duty of the trial court where the defence of insanity is raised or where it becomes apparent from the accused person's history and antecedent, to inquire specifically into the question and that the trial court cannot ignore evidence on record suggestive of the appellant's insanity merely because the defence has not specially raised it.

It can be argued that the Court of Appeal conflated the issue of mental capacity and legal capacity. The reasoning of the courts implies that the participation of persons with psychosocial disability is solely based on the nature of their disability without considering any available alternatives and support mechanisms to ensure their legal capacity thus amounting to violations of their right to participation.[146]

The reasoning in *Nyawa Mwajowa v Republic* was followed in *Republic v GKN*[147] where the accused who was on trial for murder was found to have a history of mental disability despite being declared fit to stand trial. The court directed that a fresh mental status report be carried out. Later, the accused was detained at Mathare Hospital for a period of one month which was later extended for a period of three (3) months and further extended severally. According to the High Court, the accused could not comprehend the charges and therefore formed an opinion that the accused was also unlikely to understand the court process and proceedings. The trial was postponed and the accused detained at Mathare National Hospital under the provisions of section 162(4) of the Criminal Procedure Code. The case reveals that in an adversarial system, the common law tradition requires the active participation of an accused in the criminal process.[148] The role of the accused and his or her ability

146 B McSherry et al. *Unfitness to plead and indefinite detention of persons with cognitive disabilities: addressing the legal barriers and creating appropriate alternative supports in the community* Melbourne: Melbourne Social Equity Institute, University of Melbourne (2017) 26.

147 *Republic v GKN* (2018) eKLR.

148 L Anker et al. 'Fitness to stand trial: a general principle of European criminal law?' (2011) 7 *Utrecht Law Review* 121.

to actively participate is considered to be in line with the notion of unfitness declarations.[149]

From the foregoing, the author argues that sections 162 and 167 are merely procedures which do not provide for the legal test of whether or not an accused person is unfit to plead or to proceed with trial. The sections are not based on the accused persons' ability to participate but on their cognitive abilities. Merely being considered to be of unsound mind or incapable of understanding or incapable of defending oneself is sufficient to be considered unfit. These phrases have not even been comprehensively defined. This reflects the general principle of legality, which is universally applicable.[150] The principle of legality requires that laws should be drafted with reasonable clarity to avoid unfair enforcement.[151] Procedures established by law and their implementation should be clear, accessible, and precise.

4.3 Conclusion

Despite the obvious need, the rights of disabled persons in Kenya were not recognised by the courts and legislature until the 2010 Constitution. Prior to this, disabled persons had few resources to which to turn for assistance. However, Kenya is still lagging behind when it comes to ensuring the right to participation for persons with psychosocial disabilities. Although our judicial system is attempting to alleviate and ensure that persons with psychosocial disabilities are able to participate effectively in the judicial process, Kenya's laws are outdated and most of them are still based on the era of colonialism. The lack of guidelines and rules to protect and ensure that those with psychosocial disabilities are able to adequately participate in court has compounded the matter further. However, where clear provisions are in place, they are not implemented because of lack of awareness and inadequate training. Legal change is not enough if people are unaware of existing law because laws will not be implemented. Human rights are about realities of peoples' lives on the ground. It is not enough to make good law, if it does not have real benefits in peoples' actual lives. Implementation is key.

Although this book is mainly grounded on Foucault's theory of power, this chapter has also drawn from the CRPD's provisions in order to effectively counter unfitness declarations and ensure the rights of persons with psychosocial disabilities. The CRPD makes provision for participation as a principle and as a right. The country has tremendous opportunity to change the present situation by giving effect to article 13 of the CRPD, which requires the full and effective participation of persons with psychosocial disabilities in access to justice. Participation in court processes can benefits accused persons with

149 As above.
150 Arthur (n 51) 237.
151 Arthur (n 51) 236.

psychosocial disabilities in many ways because it allows them to tell their version of events and feel believed. More importantly, it assists them to experience the effective fulfillment of their human rights. In this chapter, the study has analysed participation of persons with psychosocial disabilities in Kenya's justice sector, the next chapter will examine the principle of reasonable accommodation and its role in enhancing the participation of persons with psychosocial disabilities in access to justice.

References

African Policing Civilian Oversight Forum (APCOF) and the National Gender and Equality Commission (NGEC) *Pre-trial detention for persons with disabilities in correctional institutions* African Policing Civilian Oversight Forum (2017).

Anker L et al. 'Fitness to stand trial: a general principle of European criminal law?' (2011) 7 *Utrecht Law Review* 121. https://doi.org/10.18352/ulr.174.

Anonymous 'Incompetency to stand trial' (1967) 81 *Harvard Law Review* 460.

Arnstein S 'A ladder of citizen participation' (1969) 35 *Journal of the American Institute of Planners* 216. https://doi.org/10.1080/01944366908977225.

Arthur R 'Giving effect to young people's right to participate effectively in criminal proceedings' (2016) 28 *Child and Family Law Quarterly* 224.

Arturo Medina Vela v Australia (2019) CRPD/C/22/D/17/2013.

Aylett A 'Participatory planning, justice, and climate change in Durban, South Africa' (2000) 42 *Environment and Planning* 103. https://doi.org/10.1068/a4274.

Babulal GM et al. 'Measuring participation for persons with mental illness: a systematic review assessing relevance of existing scales for low and middle income countries' (2015) 3 *BMC Psychology* 2. https://doi.org/10.1186/s40359-015-0093-0.

Blackstone W *Commentaries* (1783).

Callus A & Camilleri A 'Nothing about us without us': disabled people determining their human rights through the UNCRPD' (2017) 1 *Mediterranean Review of Human Rights* 8.

Charles Mwangi Muraya v Republic (2001) eKLR.

Constitution of Kenya (1963).

Constitution of Kenya (2010).

Cooper P & Mattison M 'Intermediaries, vulnerable people and the quality of evidence: an international comparison of three versions of the English intermediary model' (2017) 21 *The International Journal of Evidence and Proof* 365.

CRPD Committee General Comment 1: Article 12: Equal Recognition Before the Law (2014) UN Doc CRPD/C/GC/1 dated 19 May 201.

DARU 'Understanding models of disability' https://www.daru.org.au/wp/wp-content/uploads/2019/03/Human-rights-info-sheet-for-website.pdf (accessed 13 August 2021).

Diederot D *Rameau's nephew/D'Alembert's dream* (1976) 50.

Doolan v Australia (2019) CRPD/C/22/D/18/2013.

Edwards MA 'The alignment of law and norms: of mirrors, bulwarks, and pressure valves' (2015) 10 *Faculty Scholarship* 23.

Flear ML & Vakulenko A 'A human rights perspective on citizen participation in the EU's governance of new technologies' (2010) 10 *Human Rights Law Review* 665. https://doi.org/10.1093/hrlr/ngq039.

Francis Ogoti Otundo v Republic (2012) eKLR.

Franklin-Hall A 'On becoming an adult: autonomy and the moral relevance of life's stages' (2013) 63 *Philosophical Quarterly* 251. https://doi.org/10.1111/1467–9213.12014.

Gooding P et al. 'Unfit to plead: imprisoned without conviction' https://findanexpert.unimelb.edu.au/news/1005-unfit-to-plead-imprisoned-without-conviction (accessed 9 March 2022).

Gray A et al. 'Cognitive impairment, legal need, and access to justice' (2009) 10 *Justice Issues* 5.

Grunseit A et al. *Taking justice into custody: the legal needs of prisoners* Law and Justice Foundation of New South Wales (2008).

Guidelines on the right to liberty and security of persons with disabilities, adopted September 201.

Gumbis J et al. 'Do human rights guarantee autonomy?' (2008) 62 *Cuadernos Constitucionales de la Cátedra Fadrique Furió Ceriol* 77.

Halabi SF 'Participation and the right to health: lessons from Indonesia' (2009) 11 *Health & Human Rights* 49. https://doi.org/10.2139/ssrn.1743704.

Hawkins W *Pleas of the crown* (1973).

Herring J & Wall J 'Autonomy, capacity and vulnerable adults: filling the gaps in the Mental Capacity Act' (2015) 35 *Legal Studies* 711. https://doi.org/10.1111/lest.12094.

Hussan Hussein Yusuf v Republic (2016) eKLR.

Joseph Kamau Kirubi v Republic (2010) eKLR.

Joseph Melikino Katuta v Republic (2016) eKLR.

The Judiciary *Criminal procedure bench book* (2018).

Juma P 'Right to self-representation for people with mental disabilities in Kenya's courts' (2019) 7 *African Disability Rights Yearbook* 83. https://doi.org/10.29053/2413-7138/2019/v7a4.

Kaler J 'Understanding participation' (1999) 21 *Journal of Business Ethics* 37. https://doi.org/10.1023/A:1006230712569.

Karras M et al. *On the edge of justice: the legal needs of people with a mental illness in NSW* Sydney: Law and Justice Foundation of NSW (2006).

Kavanagh A 'Participation and judicial review: a reply to Jeremy Waldron' (2003) 22 *Law and Philosophy* 452. https://doi.org/10.1023/A:1025450827929.

Kennedy Chimwani Mulokoto v Republic (2011) eKLR.

Kenya National Commission on Human Rights 'Report to the Human Rights Committee to inform its review of Kenya's third periodic report on implementation of the provisions of the International Covenant on Civil and Political Rights' https://www2.ohchr.org/english/bodies/hrc/docs/ngos/KNCHR_Kenya_HRC105.pdf.

Kirby A et al. 'Effective participation or passive acceptance: how can defendants participate more effectively in the court process?' https://howardleague.org/wp-content/uploads/2016/04/HLWP_9_2014_2.pdf (accessed 12 August 2021).

Legal Aid Act 6 of 2016.

Leo v Australia (2019) CRPD/C/22/D/17/2013.

MacKenzie C 'Relational autonomy, normative authority and perfectionism' (2008) 39 *Journal of Ethics & Social Philosophy* 512. https://doi.org/10.1111/j.1467-9833.2008.00440.x.

Marcus Muriuki v Republic (2009) eKLR.

Matata L 'Kenyans living with mental illness get lost in the criminal justice system' https://pettyoffences.org/kenyans-living-with-mental-illness-get-lost-in-the-criminal-justice-system/ (accessed 16 August 2021).

Mbondenyi MK 'Entrenching the right to participate in government in Kenya's Constitutional order: some viable lessons from the African Charter on Human and Peoples' Rights' (2011) 55 *Journal of African Law* 39. https://doi.org/10.1017/S0021855311000027.

McSherry B et al. *Unfitness to plead and indefinite detention of persons with cognitive disabilities: addressing the legal barriers and creating appropriate alternative supports in the community* Melbourne: Melbourne Social Equity Institute, University of Melbourne (2017).

MM v Republic (2012) eKLR.

Moynihan DP 'Normative and instrumental perspectives on public participation: citizen summits in Washington, DC' (2003) 33 *The American Review of Public Administration* 168. https://doi.org/10.1177/0275074003251379.

Mubita A et al. 'The importance and limitations of participation in development projects and programmes (2017) 13 *European Scientific Journal* 241. https://doi.org/10.19044/esj.2017.v13n5p238.

Mudora H 'Review of Kenya persons with disabilities act overdue' http://globaldisability.org/2016/04/01/review-kenya-persons-disabilities-act-2003-overdue (accessed 12 August 2021).

Noble *v Australia* (2016) CRPD/C/16/D/7/2012.

Nyawa Mwajowa v Republic (2016) eKLR.

Nylund A 'Children's right to participate in decision-making in Norway: paternalism and autonomy' https://munin.uit.no/bitstream/handle/10037/17526/article.pdf?sequence=2&isAllowed=y (accessed 10 August 2021).

Persons Deprived of Liberty Act 23 of 2014 'Laws of Kenya'.

Persons with Disabilities Act (Act 14 of 2003) 'Laws of Kenya'.

Posner RA *The problems of jurisprudence* (1993).

Protocol to the African Charter on Human and People's Rights on the Rights of Persons with Disabilities, 29 January 2018.

Puri E 'Understanding participation: theoretical foundations and practical implications' (2004) 39 *Economic and Political Weekly* 2511. https://doi.org/10.2307/4415152.

R v Karissa Chengo & 2 Others (2005) KESC.

Refugees Act (13 of 2006).

Republic v Elijah Weru Mathenge (2017) eKLR.

Republic v GKN (2018) eKLR.

Rex v Pritchard (1836) 7 C & P 303.

Rifkin SB & Kangere M 'What is participation?' https://asksource.info/cbr-book/cbr03.pdf (accessed 10 August 2021).

Ronner AD 'Songs of validation, voice, and voluntary participation: therapeutic jurisprudence, miranda and juveniles' (2002) 71 *University of Cincinnati Law Review* 94–95.

SC v the United Kingdom (2004) ECtHR.

Shikhelman V 'Access to justice in the United Nations Human Rights Committee' (2018) 39 *Michigan Journal of International Law* 457.

Stanford v the United Kingdom (1994) ECtHR.

Stern R 'The child's right to participation – reality or rhetoric?' PhD thesis, Uppsala University, 2006.

TCK v R (2010) eKLR.

United Nations 'Chapter two: the convention in detail – obligations of states parties under the convention' https://www.un.org/development/desa/disabilities/resources/handbook-for-parliamentarians-on-the-convention-on-the-rights-of-persons-with-disabilities/chapter-two-the-convention-in-detail–4.html (accessed 12 August 2021).

United Nations Human Rights Office of the High Commissioner 'OHCHR and equal participation in political and public affairs' https://www.ohchr.org/EN/Issues/Pages/EqualParticipation.aspx (accessed 11 August 2021).

Universal Rights Group 'The right to participate in environmental decision-making' http://www.universal-rights.org/wp-content/uploads/2015/02/EHRD-portal-Right-to-participation.pdf (accessed 11 August 2021).

Users and Survivors of Psychiatry in Kenya (USP-K) *Advancing the rights of persons with psychosocial disability in Kenya* USP-K (2017).

Villa-Torres L & Svanemyr J 'Ensuring youth's right to participation and promotion of youth leadership in the development of sexual and reproductive health policies and programs' (2015) 56 *Journal of Adolescent Health* 552. https://doi.org/10.1016/j.jadohealth.2014.07.022.

Wabuke ES et al. 'Promoting access to justice in Kenya: making the case for law clinics' 11 October 2018 https://theplatform.co.ke/promoting-access-to-justice-in-kenya-making-the-case-for-law-clinics/ (accessed 22 September 2020).

Waldron J 'Participation: the right of rights' (1998) 98 *Proceedings of the Aristotelian Society* 311. https://doi.org/10.1111/1467–9264.00039.

White RM et al. 'Transformative equality: court accommodations for South African citizens with severe communication disabilities' (2020) 9 *African Journal of Disability* 2. https://doi.org/10.4102/ajod.v9i0.651.

Young IM *Inclusion and democracy* (2000).

5 Realising participation in access to justice through reasonable accommodation in Kenya

5.0 Introduction

Participation in access to justice involves not only procedures and fair hearings, which are essential, but also reasonable accommodations. Providing accommodations for persons with psychosocial disabilities in criminal proceedings in essence removes specific barriers that may hinder their right of access to justice. Persons with psychosocial disabilities, from the perspective of the social model are holders of the fundamental right to reasonable accommodation.[1] Like Foucault's theory of power, the principle of reasonable accommodation enables the agency and social inclusion of persons with psychosocial disabilities in order to meet their special needs in access to justice. However, while Foucault's theory of power emphasises the body, the principle of reasonable accommodation largely focuses on the environment. As discussed in Chapter 2, humans, nonhumans, and environments are all participants within relations of unfitness declarations power. Therefore, in order to advance Foucault's empowerment ethos and ensure effective and holistic reforms of Kenya's unfitness declaration laws, it is important to leverage the CRPD's provisions on reasonable accommodation.

Persons with psychosocial disabilities who have challenges participating in access to justice should be afforded reasonable accommodation instead of being declared unfit.[2] The Committee on the Rights of Persons with Disabilities (CRPD Committee) considers the right to reasonable accommodation as essential to enabling persons with psychosocial disabilities to participate in legal proceedings and to achieve effective access to justice.[3] States parties under the CRPD are required to ensure that persons with psychosocial disabilities have access to reasonable accommodation. However, financial and bureaucratic restrictions under the law are some of the challenges affecting the provision of reasonable accommodation.[4] Where reasonable accommodation is provided, sometimes it does not fit the needs of persons with psychosocial

1 LV Martel 'Reasonable accommodation: the new concept from an inclusive constitutional perspective' (2011) 8 *International Journal of Human Rights* 105.

2 M Karras et al. *On the edge of justice: the legal needs of people with a mental illness in NSW* Sydney: Law and Justice Foundation of NSW 142.

3 E Flynn et al. *Final report: access to justice of persons with disabilities* OHCR (2019) 14.

4 Flynn et al. (n 3) 15.

DOI: 10.4324/9781003647102-5

disabilities. Kenya has not yet defined in its criminal procedure legislation the principle of reasonable accommodation in access to justice, in line with article 2 of the CRPD. The legislature should recognise that the denial of reasonable accommodation by authorities that do not impose undue burden amounts to discrimination.

The chapter aims to evaluate the principle of reasonable accommodation in ensuring the right of persons with psychosocial disabilities in access to justice. Section one discusses the international legal framework of reasonable accommodation of persons with psychosocial disabilities in access to justice. It analyses states parties' obligation to provide reasonable accommodation in relation to the concept of undue or disproportionate burden. It also evaluates the impact of financial and non-financial factors that amount to undue hardships. Section two discusses the need for reasonable accommodation when determining unfitness. Thereafter, in section three, an overview of the extent of the implementation of reasonable accommodation in Kenya's justice system is discussed. Section four is the conclusion.

5.1 Development and definition of reasonable accommodation

The concept of reasonable accommodations developed from employment law as a way of combating discrimination that resulted from the strict application of norms.[5] For example, in the United States of America (USA), reasonable accommodation was used to safeguard the religious beliefs of employees in the workplace.[6] In the European Union (EU), the Employment Equality Directive, placed an obligation on employers to provide disabled applicants and employees with reasonable accommodation.[7]

Accommodations in access to justice are variations to the way things are normally done to enable a person with psychosocial disability to have an equal opportunity to participate in court activities.[8] The CRPD defines reasonable accommodation as

> [N]ecessary and appropriate modification and adjustments not imposing a disproportionate or undue burden where needed in a particular case to ensure to persons with disabilities the enjoyment or exercise on an equal basis with others of all human rights and fundamental freedoms.[9]

5 G Bouchard & C Taylor *Building the future: a time for reconciliation abridged report* (Gouvernement du Quebec) 23.

6 Equal Employment Opportunity Act 1972 (amending Civil Rights Act 1964, 42 USC 2000e).

7 Council Directive 2000/78/EC establishing a general framework for equal treatment in employment and occupation [2000] OJ L303/16.

8 R White & D Msipa 'Implementing article 13 of the Convention on the Rights of Persons with Disabilities in South Africa: reasonable accommodations for persons with communication disabilities' (2018) 6 *African Disability Rights Yearbook* 103.

9 CRPD, art 2.

According to the CRPD Committee, the provision of reasonable accommodation is different from 'specific measures' such as affirmative action.[10] Reasonable accommodation is a non-discrimination duty while specific measures implies a preferential treatment of persons with psychosocial disabilities over others in order to address historic and/or systemic exclusion from the benefits of exercising rights of participation in access to justice.

Reasonable accommodation also varies from accessibility. While the latter applies to a group of persons and is broad and standardised, reasonable accommodation is individualised and requires immediate implementation.[11] Moreover, according to the CRPD Committee, 'the entity obliged to provide accessibility may not excuse the omission to do so by referring to the burden of providing access for persons with disabilities'.[12] However, in practice the difference between reasonable accommodation and accessibility is unclear. A breach of reasonable accommodation can also amount to a violation of the right to accessibility in access to justice. In *Michael Lockrey v Australia*,[13] the Applicant was summoned to serve as a juror. However, the applicant could not participate effectively as a juror because he had a hearing impairment. He requested for real-time steno-captioning of formal communications in order to communicate with others but was denied.

The applicant claimed that the state's refusal to provide steno-captioning amounted not only to discrimination but also violated his right to accessibility under the CRPD. The CRPD Committee agreed with the applicant's submissions. It said that the state party's refusal to provide steno-captioning without thoroughly assessing whether its provision would constitute an undue burden is discriminatory and violates the rights of reasonable accommodation and accessibility. The CRPD Committee considered that the accessibility provision was breached both alone and in conjunction with the provision on reasonable accommodation. Therefore, the concepts of reasonable accommodation and accessibility are complementary and can strengthen each other towards ensuring participation in access to justice for persons with psychosocial disabilities.

5.1.1 Intersection of power and reasonable accommodation

The concept of reasonable accommodation intersects with Foucault's notion of power.[14] Reasonable accommodation is a strategy of power, the exercise of

10 CRPD Committee General Comment 6: Article 5: Equality and nondiscrimination (2018) UN Doc CRPD/C/GC/6 dated 26 April 2018, paras 25–26.

11 D Ferri 'Reasonable accommodation as a gateway to the equal enjoyment of human rights: from New York to Strasbourg' (2018) 6 *Social Inclusion* 43.

12 CRPD Committee General Comment 2: Article 9: Accessibility (2014b) UN Doc CRPD/C/GC/2, para 25.

13 *Michael Lockrey v Australia* Communication (2016) CRPD/C/15/D/13/2013.

14 M Foucault 'The subject and power' in H Dreyfus & P Rabinow (eds) *Beyond structuralism and hermeneutics* (1983) 223.

which does not simply apply to relationships between the parties involved, but also to how persons with psychosocial disabilities interact with structures in the criminal justice system. As a strategy of power, reasonable accommodation may be used to enhance the participation of persons with psychosocial disabilities following unfitness declarations. However, every power relationship implies a struggle which may act to limit the actions of the parties involved. As discussed in Chapter 2, Foucault termed these limitations in the exercise of power between two parties as resistance.[15] Since the duty to accommodate is part of the power structure, productive relations between the state and persons with psychosocial disabilities requires that the law should provide for some form of resistance.

Reasonable accommodation aims to make easier the participation of persons with psychosocial disabilities in access to justice and at the same time can cause difficulties to the duty-bearers. It means that reasonable accommodation, like Foucault's notion of power, also has boundaries. Limitations of power in the strategy of accommodation take the form of reasonableness of adjustments geared towards empowering persons with psychosocial disabilities. As a result, the requirement for reasonableness allows relating the relevant modification to other parameters such as undue burden, interests, and other rights.[16]

5.1.2 *Legal obligation to provide reasonable accommodation in access to justice*

The CRPD Committee has expressed concerns regarding the inadequate application of the principle of reasonable accommodation to persons with psychosocial disabilities in situations beyond employment such as in access to justice.[17] The CRPD Committee is concerned about legislative barriers and lack of reasonable accommodation to ensure the effective participation of persons with psychosocial disabilities in access to justice.[18] Persons with psychosocial disabilities are prevented from participating in access to justice because of unfitness declarations in Kenya. Therefore, reasonable accommodation fits in with the decolonial theory due to its potential to bring about reforms in regards to the persistence of coloniality in unfitness declarations that continue to violate the rights of persons with psychosocial disabilities.

The duty to provide reasonable accommodation in access to justice can be broken down into two constituent parts.[19] The first part imposes a positive

15 As above.

16 RA Roig 'Reasonableness in the concept of reasonable accommodation' (2016) 6 *The Age of Human Rights Journal* 48.

17 CRPD Committee 'Concluding observations on the initial report of South Africa' UN Doc CRPD/C/ZAF/CO/1 (23 October 2018), para 8.

18 CRPD Committee 'Concluding observations on the initial report of Canada' UN Doc CRPD/C/CAN/CO/1(8 May 2017), para 29.

19 General Comment 6, para 25(a).

legal obligation to provide a reasonable accommodation while the second part ensures that those required accommodations do not impose a disproportionate or undue burden on the duty-bearer. The duty to provide reasonable accommodation in the CRPD extends to a broad array of social actors, including states parties.[20] States parties are required to take necessary steps to ensure that persons with psychosocial disabilities enjoy the right to reasonable accommodation in all levels of government, including in justice institutions. Article 13 of the CRPD obligates Kenyan courts to provide necessary accommodations in order to ensure that persons with psychosocial disabilities are able to play an effective role in criminal proceedings. State parties should also ensure that persons with psychosocial disabilities are not excluded, segregated, or otherwise treated differently than others because of the absence of reasonable accommodation.[21]

Within the courtroom, judicial officers have the burden of providing reasonable modifications necessary to assure competent participation during trial of persons with psychosocial disabilities.[22] According to Primor and Lerner, the object of making criminal proceedings accessible is to enhance the participation of accused persons with psychosocial disabilities by removing any legal restrictions or limitations placed by the law on account of their disability. They are not meant to ease the process or improve their well-being during any police inquiry or trial process.[23] It means that reasonable accommodation is an essential element, which if employed in the justice sector will improve the participation of persons with psychosocial disabilities.

According to the CRPD Committee, states parties must immediately ensure that reasonable accommodation is provided, since the duty to accommodate is not subject to progressive realisation.[24] In essence, states parties to the CRPD are under the obligation to consider the particular circumstances and needs of persons with disabilities and to accommodate these needs when applying domestic legislation. According to Du Plessis and Nienaber, the duty to ensure reasonable accommodation means that states parties must adjust the physical and social environment in order to ensure 'equality of outcomes'.[25]

20 J Lord & R Brown 'The role of reasonable accommodation in securing substantive equality for persons with disabilities: the UN Convention on the Rights of Persons with Disabilities' in MH Rioux et al. (eds) *Critical perspectives on human rights and disability law* (2011) 279.

21 Concluding observations on the initial report of South Africa, para 8.

22 K Gould 'And equal participation for all . . . the Americans with Disabilities Act in the courtroom' (1993–1994) 8 *Journal of Law & Health* 141.

23 S Primor & N Lerner 'The rights of persons with intellectual, psychosocial and communication disabilities to access to justice: accommodations in the criminal process' *Bizchut, The Israel Human Rights Centre for People with Disabilities* 7.

24 CRPD Committee General Comment 5: Article 19: Living independently and being included in the community (2017a) UN Doc CRPD/C/18/1, para 46.

25 I Grobbelaar-du Plessis & A Nienaber 'Disability and reasonable accommodation: *HM v Sweden* Communication 3/2011 (Committee on the Rights of Persons with Disabilities)' (2014) 30 *South African Journal on Human Rights* 376.

5.1.3 *Reasonable accommodation as part of substantive equality*

Comandé argues using a metaphor that 'the notion of reasonable accommodation is the offspring of both the notion of equality and the notion of discrimination'.[26] It means that reasonable accommodation has the potential to operate as a shield against the discriminatory practices of unfitness declarations by ensuring the participation of persons with psychosocial disabilities in access to justice.[27] Hence, reasonable accommodation embraces the idea of substantive equality as opposed to formal equality.[28]

Formal equality applies a universalist principle of justice, which embraces the 'fairness-as – hands-off' approach while substantive equality sees beyond identical treatment which can result in inequality. Justice Tanaka famously expressed the idea of substantive equality as follows:

> [T]he principle of equality before the law does not mean the absolute equality, namely the equal treatment of men without regard to individual, concrete circumstances, but it means the relative equality, namely the principle to treat equally what are equal and unequally what are unequal . . . To treat unequal matters differently according to their inequality is not only permitted but required.[29]

Substantive equality facilitates inevitable differences that exist between persons with psychosocial disabilities or groups of persons with psychosocial disabilities.[30] Therefore, in order to resolve psychosocial disability inequalities in access to justice, criminal rules and regulations cannot be strictly equal and justice institutions cannot be strictly neutral.

5.1.4 *Determining the reasonableness of accommodations*

One of the criticisms that have been raised against the principle of reasonable accommodation is that the concept is based on ableist norms and that questions of reasonableness have been left to be decided by judicial officers who may have very little familiarity with psychosocial disability.[31] Some scholars

26 G Comandé 'Discrimination and reasonable accommodation: "insight" from a (non) zero sum game' (2010) 2 *Opinio Juris in Comparatione* 14.

27 R McCallum & H Martin 'A forgotten cohort: citizenship through work and persons with disabilities' (2016) 41 *Queen's Law Journal* 341.

28 OP Fuente 'Reasonable accommodation based on religious beliefs or practices. A comparative perspective between the American, Canadian and European approaches' (2018) 10 *The Age of Human Rights Journal* 115.

29 *South West Africa (Ethiopia v South Africa; Liberia v South Africa)* (1966) ICJ Rep 6, 305 (Tanaka, J, dissent).

30 E Griffiths 'The "reasonable accommodation" of religion: is this a better way of advancing equality in cases of religious discrimination?' (2016) 16 *International Journal of Discrimination and the Law* 172.

31 A Lawson & M Orchard 'The anticipatory reasonable adjustment duty: removing the blockages?' (2021) 80(2) *Cambridge Law Journal* 319.

have argued that the concept of 'reasonable accommodation' should be abandoned and replaced by an entitlement to 'rightful access', without any 'reasonableness' or 'undue burden' limitations. Article 2 of the CRPD requires that accommodations should be reasonable which means that they should be tailored and adjusted to the individual's specific requirements.

According to the CRPD, what is reasonable is interpreted from an efficiency perspective.[32] 'Necessary and appropriate' implies that accommodations must be effective, which means that they must enable capabilities and remove the disadvantage that is inhibiting the participation of persons with psychosocial disabilities in access to justice.[33] Reasonable does not only mean the effective accommodation for the individual or group but also includes the prevention and elimination of segregation, humiliation, and stigma.[34] Martel has equated the concept of reasonableness to the principles of fairness, congruence with the law and equivalence between two measures.[35] Thus, the duty to provide reasonable accommodation under article 2 of the CRPD is not absolute. However, what is reasonable remains to be a contested issue and differing views have been offered.

Interpretation of reasonableness under foreign law

Generally, when the term reasonable is used, it weakens the obligation in question. However, determining what is reasonable is not a straightforward task as 'measures that states are expected to take' cannot be established in general terms but will be state-specific, meaning that it depends on certain factors such as the development level of a country. In the USA, the word reasonable is dictated by common sense. It means that the demand for accommodation is reasonable if it can be justified through the hypothetical legal standard of the ordinary man.[36] As an illustration to explain reasonableness, the court in *Vande Zande v Wisconsin Department of Administration*[37] used an analogy of 'reasonable effort', which it defined as the act of using 'less than the maximum possible effort'. Therefore, according to the court, reasonable does not require duty-bearers to make every conceivable accommodation. Authorities are only required to make accommodations if, and to the extent, that those accommodations are reasonable.

In Canada, as opposed to USA, reasonable accommodation is recognised as an equality principle in the country's federal legislation as well as in provincial human rights codes.[38] It is a mechanism that can be used for achieving equality

32 L Waddington 'When it is reasonable for Europeans to be confused: understanding a when disability accommodation is "reasonable" from a comparative perspective' (2008) 29 *Comparative Labor Law & Policy Journal* 339.

33 General Comment 6, para 25.

34 Martel (n 1) 106.

35 Martel (n 1) 103.

36 Roig (n 16) 49.

37 (1995) 44 F3d 538.

38 JL Pretorius et al. *Employment Equity Law* (2001, 2021 Update), Chapter 7, para 7.3.3. *Eaton v Brant County Board of Education* (1997) 1 SCR 24.

for persons with psychosocial disabilities. The duty to accommodate is not about finding the best solution but providing modification that is reasonable.[39] Reasonableness is defined broadly to signify the efforts made to accommodate up to the point of undue burden.[40] It means that in Canada, as was explained by Fuente, reasonable accommodation measures are conditional on the test of proportionality, the end result of which is undue or disproportionate burden.[41] To put it succinctly, the obligation is to make a 'genuine effort'.[42] However, the genuine effort parameter may be criticised on grounds that it enables what in the decolonial sense is considered coloniality of power, which is a dynamic that emboldens the accommodator to freely judge the unreasonability or reasonability of a disability accommodation.[43]

In South Africa, like in Canada, the doctrine of reasonable accommodation is grounded on the constitutional right of equality and non-discrimination.[44] Section 9 of the Constitution of South Africa[45] prohibits unfair discrimination, including on grounds of disability. According to Ngwena, the provision of reasonable accommodation should be applied in order to prevent the unfair discrimination of persons with disabilities and enable their effective participation on an equal basis with others in a given sector.[46] Reasonableness is associated with section 36 limitations under the South African Constitution. Reasonableness connotes a limitation of a right. According to Courtis, it is a general standard attributed to specific rights but also a criterion to be considered when assessing the proportionality of a limitation as well as appropriateness of an action as adopted by any political branch of government, either towards compliance of its duties or for achieving a legitimate state purpose.[47] It means that reasonable accommodation is not an absolute obligation. However, the Constitution of South Africa does not describe the circumstances under which accommodations will be considered reasonable or unreasonable.

Nevertheless, the courts in South Africa have assessed reasonableness from the standpoint of proportionality.[48] For example, in *SA Clothing and Textile*

39 *Central Okanagan School District No 23 v Renaud* (1992) 2 SCR 970.
40 Martel (n 1) 102.
41 Fuente (n 28) 89.
42 *Holmes v Canada (Attorney General)* (1997) CanLII 5101 (FC). See also *Holmes v Canada (Attorney General)* (1999) CanLII 7869 (FCA).
43 A Barras et al. 'Rethinking Canadian discourses of "reasonable accommodation"' (2018) 6 *Social Inclusion* 166.
44 *Independent Municipal and Allied Trade Union obo Strydom v Witzenburg Municipality and Others* (2012) ZALAC 1.
45 Constitution of the Republic of South Africa Act 108 of 1996.
46 Pretorius et al. (n 38) Chapter 7, para 7.5.
47 C Courtis 'Rationality, reasonableness, proportionality: testing the use of standards of scrutiny in the constitutional review of legislation' (2011) 4 *Constitutional Court Review* 35.
48 *Government of the Republic of South Africa v Grootboom* (2001) 1 SA 46 (CC) & *Minister of Health v Treatment Action Campaign* (2002) 5 SA 703 (CC).

Workers Union and Others v Berg River Textiles – A Division of Seardel Group Trading (Pty) Ltd,[49] where the Labour Court noted that

> [I]n particular, the employer must establish that it has taken reasonable steps to accommodate the employee's religious convictions. Ultimately the principle of proportionality must be applied. Thus[,] an employer may not insist on the employee obeying a workplace rule where that refusal would have little or no consequence to the business.

Accordingly, it can be argued that in terms of disability, the principle of reasonableness imports the notion of proportionality in South African jurisprudence.[50]

The reasonableness analysis is enshrined in the Kenyan Constitution. Article 24 of the Constitution stipulates that a right will only be limited if the restriction 'is reasonable and justifiable in an open and democratic society based on human dignity, equality and freedom, taking into account all relevant factors'. Kenyan courts have further developed the principle of reasonableness when interpreting article 24 of the Constitution by using the balance or proportionality approach.[51] However, some legal commentators have called for the reconciliation of competing rights rather than using the balanced approach, thus focusing on ensuring the realisation of each right as far as possible rather than curbing one in the interest of another.[52]

Interpretation of reasonableness by the CRPD Committee

When interpreting reasonable accommodation, the CRPD Committee has not always spoken with one voice. In General Comment 6, the CRPD Committee stated that 'reasonable accommodation is a single term' and the concept of reasonableness should 'not be misunderstood as an exception clause'. According to the CRPD Committee, reasonableness 'should not act as a distinct qualifier or modifier' to the obligation of accommodation.[53] Another clarification on reasonable accommodation as per the CRPD Committee is to the effect that reasonableness should only be considered relevant, appropriate, or effective from the perspective of persons with disabilities. Costs or availability of resources should not be assessed when determining reasonableness but when considering undue burden.

49 (2012) 33 *ILJ* 972 (LC), para 38.6.

50 *MEC for Education and Others v Pillay and Others* (2008) (2) BCLR 99 (CC), para 76.

51 *Geoffrey Andare v Attorney General & 2 others* (2016) eKLR, *Kijuki Kiambi Paul Kagia & 5 Others v Clerk Meru Municipal Council Municipal council* (2012) eKLR, and *Robert Alai v Attorney General & another* (2017) eKLR.

52 C Szurlej 'Reconciling competing human rights in Canada' (2015) 47 *Peace Research* 180.

53 General Comment 6, para 25(a).

Moreover, the key elements guiding the implementation of the duty to provide reasonable accommodation according to General Comment 6 include

> assessing whether an accommodation is feasible (legally or in practice)... c) Assessing whether the accommodation is relevant (i.e., necessary and appropriate) or effective in ensuring the realization of the right in question. d) Assessing whether the modification imposes a disproportionate or undue burden on the duty bearer . . . e) Ensuring that the reasonable accommodation is suitable to achieve the essential objective of the promotion of equality and the elimination of discrimination against persons with disabilities.[54]

However, in General Comment 4 on inclusive education, the CRPD Committee suggested a slightly different method of assessing reasonableness from the one contained in General Comment 6 on equality and non-discrimination. The CRPD Committee commented that the notion of reasonableness should be 'understood as the result of a contextual test that involves an analysis of the relevance and the effectiveness of the accommodation, and the expected goal of countering discrimination'.[55] A further distinct interpretation is found in the case of *Jungelin v Sweden*,[56] where the CRPD Committee used the term 'reasonableness and proportionality' interchangeably thus implying that there is no difference between the two tests when it comes to assessing accommodations. In *Jungelin*, a complaint by the applicant had been dismissed by a Swedish Labour Court on account that the suggested support and adaptation measures of altering the computer systems and employing a person to read the handwritten documents as a way of accommodating her visual impairment were, in all of the circumstances, not reasonable.

The issue before the CRPD Committee was whether the Swedish courts had carried out a thorough and well-balanced assessment of the factual circumstances relating to the accommodation of the applicant. The majority in the CRPD Committee found that the decision by the Labour Court to deem the accommodation requested as constituting an unreasonable burden was justified. However, the minority in *Jungelin* disagreed that the accommodation was unreasonable and stated that the test of reasonableness and proportionality in the context of employment should ensure,

> inter alia, that (i) the measures of accommodation were requested to promote the employment of a person with a disability, with the professional capacity and experience to perform the functions corresponding

54 General Comment 6, para 26.

55 CRPD Committee General Comment 4: Right to inclusive education UN Doc CRPD/C/GC/4 (2016) para 27.

56 *Marie-Louise Jungelin v Sweden* (2014) CRPD/C/12/D/5/2011.

to the position for which he or she applied; and (ii) the public or private company or entity to which the candidate applied can reasonably be expected to adopt and implement accommodation measures.[57]

The majority in *Jungelin* held that when assessing reasonableness and proportionality, a holistic evaluation of facts and evidence in each individual case needs to be considered.[58]

Further authoritative guidance on what is reasonable is set out in *Gemma Beasley v Australia* (*Gemma*),[59] where the CRPD Committee held that states parties have a wide margin of appreciation in determining what kind of accommodations might be reasonable in a particular situation. In *Gemma* the complainant was denied the opportunity to serve in the jury because she required an additional person, the interpreter, who was not permitted to be present for jury deliberations. The reasons cited for the denial of interpreter as part of reasonable accommodation was section 14(4) of the New South Wales Jury Act,[60] which states that a sheriff may exempt persons from jury service if there is good cause to do so. The CRPD Committee affirmed the obligation of states parties to take appropriate steps to ensure that reasonable accommodation is granted to further equality and eradicate discrimination. However, the state has a certain 'margin of appreciation' or discretion when assessing the reasonableness of an accommodation. The CRPD Committee stressed that states parties must determine reasonableness in a 'thorough and objective manner, assessing all pertinent elements, before reaching a conclusion'.[61] Therefore, any justification that denies reasonable accommodation, but is hinged on negative stereotypes or discrimination against persons with psychosocial disabilities is not legitimate.[62]

Overall, accommodations are reasonable if they achieve the aims for which they are being made and are tailored to meet the requirements of persons with disabilities. The decisions in *Jungelin* and *Gemma* shows support to the notion that the duty to provide reasonable accommodation under the CRPD is not absolute. The margin of appreciation principle allows a significant measure of autonomy and flexibility for state parties when discharging their international obligations.[63] However, allowing states parties to have a margin of appreciation when assessing reasonable accommodation can be decried because it places the rights to effective modifications of persons with psychosocial disabilities only within a domestic milieu. There have been calls for the introduction of

57 *Jungelin v Sweden*, para 4.

58 *Jungelin v Sweden*, para 10.5.

59 *Gemma Beasley v Australia* (2016) CRPD/C/15/11/2013.

60 New South Wales Jury Act of 1977.

61 *Gemma Beasley v Australia*, paras 8.3 & 8.4.

62 General comment 6, para 27.

63 ME Addadzi-Koom 'Of the women's rights jurisprudence of the ECOWAS court: the role of the Maputo Protocol and the due diligence standard' (2020) 28 *Feminist Legal Studies* 161.

regulations specifying 'circumstances in which it is, or in which it is not, reasonable for a person of a prescribed description to have to take steps of a prescribed description'.[64] Nonetheless, these calls have been rejected for reasons that they might unhelpfully restrict the flexibility of the reasonable accommodation duty. The important outcome is that the principle of reasonable accommodation cannot compensate absolutely for the disadvantages experienced by persons with psychosocial disabilities in access to justice because it is subject to limitations.

5.1.5 Duty to activate reasonable accommodation

According to the CRPD Committee, each request and application for reasonable accommodation should be evaluated on a case-by-case basis.[65] The principle of reasonableness requires some reciprocity on a voluntary basis in order to create the grounds for accommodation.[66] Accused persons with psychosocial disabilities in need of reasonable accommodations may self-identify their disability and make a request for reasonable accommodation. However, a model that requires persons with psychosocial disabilities to bear the burden of disclosing their impairment or requesting for modifications in order to activate the provision of reasonable accommodation may amount to discrimination against those who are unable to disclose or make requests.

The disclosure model to reasonable accommodation implicitly or explicitly assumes the idea that persons with psychosocial disabilities are part of a well-ordered public sphere. A well-ordered public sphere draws loosely from the ideal that persons with psychosocial disabilities are able to participate effectively in access to justice deliberations. For the process of disclosure to take effect, participants need to be on equal footing. However, the disclosure model to reasonable accommodation is blind to the participation challenges that persons with psychosocial disabilities face in access to justice. Particularly, the disclosure model is too vague and abstract about the reality of participation barriers resulting from the impairments of persons with psychosocial disabilities. Therefore, in order to avoid discrimination against persons with psychosocial disabilities, alternative models to disclosure should also be adopted.

By virtue of the individualised nature of modifications, the duty to provide reasonable accommodation in access to justice arises *ex nunc*, meaning that it takes effect at the moment when the person with a psychosocial disability is in need of accommodations.[67] Thus, the duty to provide reasonable accommodation arises from the moment a person with a disability requires the

64 Lawson & Orchard (n 31) 321.

65 General Comment 6, paras 26 & 27.

66 K Karjalainen & M Ylhäinen 'On the obligation to make reasonable accommodation for an employee with a disability' (2021) 12(4) *European Labour Law Journal* 562.

67 CRPD Committee General Comment 2: Accessibility (2014b) (UN Doc. CRPD/C/GC/2), para 25.

accommodation in access to justice.[68] The *ex nunc* model has been differently applied by states parties, such as Norway and Finland. In Norway, authorities are under a duty to provide reasonable accommodation when the duty-bearer knows or ought to know that a person has a disability that requires accommodation in order to participate effectively in the society.[69] Relatedly, in Finland, the duty to provide reasonable accommodation is not conditional on the disabled person expressly requesting reasonable accommodation from the state.[70] It means that the duty to provide reasonable accommodation in Finland and Norway adopts an anticipatory approach. An anticipatory approach to reasonable accommodation requires authorities to proactively consider the needs of persons with psychosocial disabilities in access to justice.[71] I argue that the duty to accommodate should arise when the duty-bearer knows or ought to know, using ordinary diligence about the psychosocial disability and specific needs of the individual involved.[72]

It is important to be sure that reasonable accommodations are feasible and in place before the trial begins. Individualised inquiries by the authorities will achieve its goal of protecting persons with psychosocial disabilities from deprivations based on prejudice, stereotypes or unfounded fears while giving weight to legitimate concerns. Placing the discussion of reasonable accommodations after an arrest, but before the trial commences, is a fair way to protect against discrimination. Doing so also ensures that an accused person with psychosocial disability will have reasonable accommodations in place to level the playing field and promote an atmosphere of participation. Once the duty to provide reasonable accommodation arises, the court is obligated to participate in the interactive process of seeking an accommodation. The interactive process is the primary vehicle for identifying and achieving effective adjustments because it allows disabled persons to participate in court activities without placing an undue burden on the state. However, it is not mandatory for the court to consult with a person with psychosocial disability in each and every case as long as the court ensures that there is meaningful participation in access to justice.[73]

Another alternative model to disclosure is the CRPD's concept of universal design. As defined in article 2 of the CRPD, universal design is the design of 'products, environments, programmes and services to be usable by all people, to the greatest extent possible, without the need for adaptation or specialised design'. Further, universal design 'shall not exclude assistive devices

68 CRPD Committee General Comment 3: Article 6: women and girls with disabilities (2016a) (UN Doc CRPD/C/GC/3).

69 *B v A Company* (2007) Norway, Equality and Anti-Discrimination Tribunal of Norway.

70 Finland, National Non-Discrimination and Equality Tribunal, 14 December 2015, YVTltk 21/2015.

71 European Network of Equality Bodies *Reasonable accommodation for persons with disabilities: exploring challenges concerning its practical implementation* Equinet (2020) 21.

72 General Comment 6, para 24b.

73 *Nano Nagle School v Marie Daly* (2019) IESC 63.

for particular groups of persons with disabilities where this is needed'. The universal design model encourages states to take a proactive rather than reactive approach towards making justice system structures accessible to persons with psychosocial disabilities. The universal design approach has the potential of reducing or eliminating the need for the reasonable accommodation system. Article 4 of the CRPD obligates states parties to undertake or promote research and development of universally designed goods, services, equipment and facilities. It further requires the promotion of 'universal design in the development of standards and guidelines'. The move towards universal design will enhance the participation of persons with psychosocial disabilities in access to justice due to its potential to mainstream disability.[74]

5.1.6 Undue or disproportionate burden

The second part of the obligation to ensure reasonable accommodation requires that the duty should not impose an undue or disproportionate burden on the parties involved.[75] According to the CRPD Committee 'disproportionate or undue burden' should be interpreted as a single concept that limits the obligation to provide reasonable accommodation. It means that the terms 'undue' and 'disproportionate' are synonyms insofar as they refer to reasonable accommodation.[76]

Undue burden is a defence that excuses the accommodating party from the obligation of providing reasonable accommodation. Therefore, although state parties are under a duty to provide reasonable accommodation in access to justice, they will not do so if it causes a 'disproportionate or undue burden' on them. However, the limitation of undue burden under article 2 of the CRPD does not always exempt duty-bearers from the obligation of providing reasonable accommodation. Rather, it simply limits the duty, which means that if the state has an option of two or more effective accommodation options, the duty-bearer is entitled to opt for the less burdensome accommodation.[77]

There is not only a lack of consistent meaning of what constitutes an undue burden, but jurisprudence in this area does not define the extent of accommodation that is needed in order to ensure participation in access to justice for persons with psychosocial disabilities. Courts have a margin of appreciation to determine what constitutes undue burden depending on domestic legislation.[78] For example, in the USA, the level of undue hardship above which

74 P Daly & D Whelan 'Disability in employment equality law: a reappraisal of the reasonable accommodation duty and issues arising in its implementation' (2021) 28 *Maastricht Journal of European and Comparative Law* 757.

75 General Comment 6, para 25(a).

76 General Comment 6, para 25(b).

77 A Broderick *Report on reasonable accommodation under the CRPD: the Georgian context* USAID (2017) 27.

78 *Jungelin v Sweden* para 10.5.

authorities are not obligated to provide accommodation has been set at the *de minimis* or negligible level.[79] It means that in the USA, employers are not required 'to bear more than a *de minimis* cost' when providing reasonable accommodation as that would amount to an undue hardship. The *de minimis* or negligible test has been criticised for only considering 'hardship' and not the qualifier 'undue', which makes it incompatible with the doctrine of 'undue or disproportionate burden'.[80] In Canada, undue hardship is determined depending on the case at hand using the test of proportionality.[81]

There is a distinction between the proportionality and the reasonableness test. Reasonableness is a general test meaning that it not only determines the proportionality of two or more actions but also considers other factors such as whether an act is rational. However, the test of proportionality covers a narrow field than reasonableness.[82] The former is a precise test that is applied negatively to a previously identified relationship. In short, proportionality is only a relationship test. In practice, a disproportionate accommodation will almost always be unreasonable but the vice-versa may not necessarily achieve the same result.[83] For example, a proportionate accommodation measure might be considered unreasonable, because of a lack of consultation.

The proportionality test requires decision-makers to balance any interference on the right to reasonable accommodation with the needs of persons with psychosocial disabilities.[84] Case law indicates that 'the more substantial the interference the more that is required to justify it'.[85] The burden lies on the state to justify whether an accommodation is disproportionate. Lack of reasonable accommodation will not amount to discrimination if there is an 'objective and reasonable justification'. Objective and reasonable justification implies either that there is a legitimate aim behind the denial of reasonable accommodation or that there is a reasonable relationship of proportionality between the means and the aim.[86]

According to the CRPD Committee, when determining undue burden, states parties should assess the proportional relationship between the means employed and its aim, which is the enjoyment of the right concerned.[87] An examination of undue hardship will only be made if states are unable to provide

79 Fuente (n 28) 94.

80 Martel (n 1) 96.

81 *Ontario Human Rights Commission, Theresa O'Malley v Simpsons-Sears* (1985) 2 SCR 536.

82 G Downes 'Reasonableness, proportionality and merits review' https://www.aat.gov.au/AAT/media/AAT/Files/Speeches%20and%20Papers/ReasonablenessSeptember2008.pdf (accessed 30 August 2022) 12.

83 As above.

84 M Curtice et al. 'The proportionality principle and what it means in practice' (2011) 35 *The Psychiatrist* 111.

85 *R (on the application of N) v Ashworth Special Hospital Authority and another* (2001) EWHC 339.

86 G Lurie 'Proportionality and the right to equality' (2020) 21 *German Law Journal* 188.

87 General Comment 6, para 26(d).

any accommodation deemed reasonable.[88] It follows that, necessary efforts to accommodate should be made up to the point of undue burden.[89] Reasonable accommodation must also be the product of a process of dialogue between the parties involved. Whether a burden is disproportionate or undue depends on the duty-holder.[90]

Denial of reasonable accommodation constitutes discrimination under the CRPD if the state receives adequate notice, and a reasonable accommodation is available that would not place an undue hardship on the operation of the state, which is prohibited.[91] The factors to be determined when considering whether the duty to ensure reasonable accommodation imposes an undue burden to the party involved according to the CRPD Committee include financial and non-financial considerations.

Financial

Conceptually, an accommodation can be limited by the unreasonable costs of its performance. According to Lisa Waddington, cost of a requested accommodation is the primary factor in determining whether an accommodation is reasonable or not.[92] The CRPD Committee has confirmed the issue of costs in General Comment 4, which explicitly affirms that the availability of resources and financial implications is recognised when assessing disproportionate burden.[93] The onus of proving undue burden due to cost lies with the duty-bearer. In *Gemma Beasley v Australia* and *Michael Lockrey v Australia* the State of Australia argued that the obligation to provide an Auslan interpreter and steno-captioning would have an undue 'impact on the complexity, cost and duration of trials'.[94] However, in deciding against the state, the CRPD Committee, held that the state had failed to provide sufficient evidence or analysis to support the conclusion that the accommodations would constitute an undue burden.

Even in circumstances where economic considerations are compelling, the duty to provide reasonable accommodation remains. Scarcity of funds should

88 Martel (n 1) 90.

89 Martel (n 1) 103.

90 H Kallehauge 'General themes relevant to the implementation of the UN Disability Convention into domestic law: who is responsible for the implementation and how should it be performed?' in OM Arnardottir & G Quinn (eds) *The UN convention on the rights of persons with disabilities: European and Scandinavian perspectives* (2009) 211.

91 Melbourne Social Equity Institute *Addressing the indefinite detention of people with cognitive and psychiatric impairment due to unfitness to plead laws* Melbourne Social Equity Institute (2016) 3.

92 L Waddington, 'Reasonable accommodation' in D Schiek et al. (eds) *Cases, materials and text on national, supranational and international non-discrimination law* (2007) 731.

93 CRPD Committee General Comment 4: Article 24: Right to inclusive education (2016b) (UN Doc CRPD/C/GC/4), para 27.

94 *Gemma Beasley v Australia*, para 8.5 & *Michael Lockrey v Australia*, para 8.5.

be balanced with budgetary allocations for non-disabled persons in situations such as in access to justice. In *GL v Italy*,[95] the applicant, a young girl suffering from nonverbal autism, filed a complaint that she was unable to receive specialised learning support during her first two years of primary education even though the support was provided for by law. The Italian government relied, in particular, on a lack of financial resources. The Court held that the state should have considered the possibility that a lack of resources could be compensated for by a reduction in the overall educational provision, so that it would be distributed equally between non-disabled and disabled pupils. This case sheds light on how the argument of budget restrictions to provide reasonable accommodations should be analysed. It means that any arguments regarding scarcity of the funds to provide for reasonable accommodation in access to justice should be analysed in relation to the costs allocated for non-disabled persons. Costs provided for reasonable accommodation should be proportionate and equivalent to budgetary allocations for non-disabled persons in access to justice.

Non-financial considerations

To constitute undue burden, costs may not necessarily be financial in nature, rather, they should extend to a consideration of the manner in which the accommodation alters the nature of the trial or causes excessive difficulties for authorities.[96] The negative impact of the accommodation to the duty-bearer was determined in the Kenyan case of *Wilson Macharia v Safaricom Plc*.[97] In that case, the respondent hired the petitioner, who was visually impaired after a rigorous interview process, but later withdrew the contract. The reason for withdrawing the contract was cited as a lack of a special software which was needed to reasonably accommodate the petitioner. The respondents argued that the company was unable to comply with its reasonable accommodation obligations because it would require making significant adjustments and technological incorporations to its entire system which was not viable in the short run. The Employment Court agreed and held as follows:

> [I]n view of statutory provisions and the demonstration by the Respondent as regards requiring special facility to accommodate the Petitioner, the Respondent cannot therefore be reasonably be expected to provide software due to budgetary constraints. In the circumstance the Respondent cannot be deemed to have discriminated therefore against the Petitioner. I find the Petitioner was not discriminated against.

95 *GL v Italy* (2020) ECtHR.

96 A Broderick 'The long and winding road to equality and inclusion for persons with disabilities: the United Nations Convention on the Rights of Persons with Disabilities' Doctoral Thesis, Maastricht University, 2015, 176.

97 Wilson Macharia v Safaricom Plc (2021) eKLR.

Nonetheless, the Court found that the respondents had violated the petitioner's right to human dignity as enshrined under articles 28 and 54(1) of the Kenyan Constitution. This decision suggests that non-financial costs, such as nature of the accommodation required and the time required to implement it are all relevant factors in determining whether and to what extent the duty-bearer can duly claim to be exempt. Therefore, an accommodation in access to justice may be considered unreasonable due to its complexity and duration of the trial. Other non-financial considerations when considering undue hardship include factors such as the health and safety rules laid down by national law in determining whether a requested accommodation imposes a disproportionate burden on the duty-bearer,[98] administrative burdens,[99] third-party rights,[100] and public interest.[101]

5.2 Provision of accommodations when determining unfitness

The determination of an accused fitness to stand trial should not be independent of the need for accommodations. The Supreme Court of Washington in *State v Ortiz-Abrego*[102] (*Ortiz*) answered this question. Although the case concerns intellectual disability, it is relevant also to psychosocial disability. In *Ortiz*, the accused was diagnosed with an auditory processing disability and borderline intellectual functioning, for which a neuropsychologist recommended trial accommodations to facilitate the accused person's participation. On appeal to the Court of Appeals, it was found that the trial court had inappropriately conflated competency with disability accommodation law.[103]

However, a further appeal to the Supreme Court of Washington upheld the trial court's decision recommending trial accommodations in order to facilitate the participation of the accused person with intellectual disability in access to justice. The Supreme Court of Washington stated that 'a criminal defendant's competency to stand trial and the need for disability accommodations at that trial are distinct, if at times overlapping, concerns'.[104] It means that the determination of accused person's fitness or unfitness in relation to accommodations which may facilitate the participation of persons with psychosocial disabilities in court does not amount to a violation of access to justice rights.

Reasonable accommodation reduces the risk of persons with psychosocial disabilities being inappropriately identified as unfit when modifications would be sufficient. In *State v Cleary*[105] (*Cleary*), an accused person with intellectual

98 *Gemma Beasley v Australia*, para 8.3.
99 *Rainey v Greater Glasgow Health Authority* (1987) 1 All ER 65, 1 AC 224 (HL).
100 *Guberina v Croatia* (2013) ECtHR.
101 Pretorius et al. (n 38) Chapter 5, para 5.5.1.2.
102 *State v Ortiz-Abrego* (2017) 387 P3d 638.
103 As above.
104 *State v Ortiz-Abrego* 15.
105 *State v Cleary* (2003) 824 A.2d 509.

disability appealed his conviction, arguing that the court was in error by finding him competent to proceed contingent upon the assistance of a cognitive facilitator. The accused had a documented Intelligence Quotient (IQ) of between 65 and 70, with evidence of variable functional capacities. During the plea hearing, the defence counsel asked questions, along with periodic conferences to ensure his understanding. On appeal, the accused argued the court had used predictive competence, rather than present ability in opining that he was competent with this accommodation. Present ability is concerned with the accused person's factual understanding of the proceedings against him or her.[106]

The Appeal Court disagreed, citing a prior case wherein a 'juvenile with a developmental disability' was considered competent with the assistance of a cognitive facilitator. In the discussion, the court noted,

> [t]here is nothing to prevent a court from qualifying its competency finding and suggesting accommodations that will enable the defendant to better capitalize on his capacity to understand and participate effectively in the proceedings.[107]

The Court qualified competency findings through accommodations in order to protect the rights of accused persons with psychosocial disabilities who may otherwise not be able to participate in the trial process. The decisions in *Ortiz* and *Cleary* are in line with the CRPD Committee's views that unfitness declarations are discriminatory and should be replaced by reasonable accommodation provisions in order to ensure the rights of persons with mental disabilities in the criminal justice system.[108]

5.3 Implementation of the CRPD's reasonable accommodation in Kenya

Kenya is subject to the monitoring of its treaty obligations by the CRPD Committee. Such monitoring of its obligations consists of, inter alia, the receiving and consideration by the CRPD Committee of periodic reports from state parties. The CRPD Committee has already issued its recommendations on Kenya's initial report.[109] The CRPD Committee was concerned about obstacles in the prosecution of cases involving persons with psychosocial disabilities as witnesses or victims and about the legal provisions that restrain the validity of corroborated evidence of persons with psychosocial disabilities.

106 *Dusky v United States* (1960) 362 US 402.
107 *State v Cleary* para 12.
108 *Noble v Australia* (2016) CRPD/C/16/D/7/2012, para 8.4.
109 CRPD Committee 'Concluding observations on the initial report of Kenya' UN Doc CRPD/C/KEN/CO/1 (30 September 2015).

The CRPD Committee also raised concerns regarding the absence of reasonable accommodations for persons with psychosocial disabilities in access to justice, which was confirmed during the empirical research.[110] Reasonable accommodation measures, such as technology can play a major role in enhancing the right of participation in access to justice for persons with psychosocial disabilities. To this end, the CPRD stipulates that[111]

> [S]tate parties to the Convention have the duty to make sure accessibility through, inter alia, promoting access for persons with disabilities to new information and communications technologies and systems, including the Internet and promoting the design, development, production and distribution of accessible information and communications technologies and systems at an early stage, so that these technologies and systems become accessible at minimum cost.

Kenya does not have a law that obliges courts to use appropriate technologies to ensure the right of participation in access to justice for persons with psychosocial disabilities in criminal proceedings. The Practice Directions to Standardise Practice and Procedures in the High Court of Kenya[112] (Practice Directions) stipulate in section 6(b) that '[a]n E-Support Centre shall be established in each High Court station to assist vulnerable litigants to access the ICT platform where needed'.[113] However, the Practice Directions apply only in civil and not criminal cases.

The most used information and communication technologies (ICT) by persons with disabilities in Kenya include mobile phones, television, and radio. Unfortunately, the majority of people that need these technologies do not have access to affordable and user-friendly assistive devices, and many are not even aware of the existence or exposed to such technologies and their functionalities. In many cases, the devices, including smartphones, accessibility features are often expensive and difficult to repair once broken down. Most of the time, they must be imported.[114] Further, the funding programmes by the government do not prioritise the purchase of ICT assistive devices such as laptops and computer software such as JAWS, owing to their high costs. Greater public awareness of the various affirmative action and waivers on taxes to enable persons with disabilities to acquire and access these devices could be a significant intervention to promote access to ICT.

110 Chapter 7.

111 CRPD art 9(2)(g) & (h).

112 Gazette Notice 189, Laws of Kenya (Nairobi, 14 January 2022).

113 Practice Directions to Standardize Practice and Procedures in the High Court of Kenya, sect 6(b).

114 CIPESA 'Assessing the barriers to accessing ICT by people with disabilities in Kenya' https://cipesa.org/?wpfb_dl=429 (accessed 16 February, 2022) 19.

Apart from adopting reasonable accommodation measures in its criminal justice legislation, the CRPD Committee recommended that Kenya should define explicitly in legal instruments the duty of the judiciary to provide procedural accommodations for persons with disabilities in accordance with article 13 of the CRPD. Justice system actors are not sufficiently flexible in their approach, and those working with persons with psychosocial disabilities are acutely aware of the degree of flexibility needed to elicit comprehensive accounts of their experiences. For example, the Office of Director of Public Prosecutions has a Diversion Policy,[115] which allows prosecutors to divert cases involving vulnerable people, including disabled persons as opposed to prosecuting them.[116] However, where it is not appropriate to prosecute persons with psychosocial disabilities in the ordinary criminal justice process, they must be subjected to section 162 of the Criminal Procedure Code.[117] Section 162 discriminates against persons with psychosocial disabilities as it denies them the right to participation in access to justice.

The CRPD Committee has also recommended that the state should develop a capacity-building strategy within the judicial branch, including lawyers, magistrates, judges, prison staff and the police on reasonable accommodation and rights of persons with disabilities. Structural and epistemic decolonisation requires that training of justice system actors should not only be based on the social model of disability, but also on indigenous knowledge processes that promote the participation of persons with psychosocial disabilities in access to justice such as alternative dispute resolution (ADR) and right-based diversionary strategies. ADR and diversionary strategies are part of the structural decolonisation mechanisms for empowering persons with psychosocial disabilities in order to enable them participate in access to justice.[118] The establishment of mobile courts in order to enhance the participation in access to justice of persons with psychosocial disabilities who cannot leave their homes or who are currently residing in hospitals is also part of structural decolonisation.

Epistemic decolonisation avoids reproducing Eurocentric assumptions about unfitness declaration laws by applying African concepts whose aim is to restore lost balance of power between persons with psychosocial disabilities and Kenya's criminal justice system. An attempt to build the capacity of justice system actors has been made through the use of the Judiciary Criminal Procedure Bench Book (JCBB).[119] However, the JCBB has provided limited information on reasonable accommodations in access to justice. Moreover, judges, magistrates, and other justice actors are not aware of the detailed guidance laid

115 Office of Director of Public Prosecutions Diversion Policy (2019).

116 Guideline 2.8 of the Diversion Policy.

117 Guideline A.6 of the Diversion Policy.

118 M Runo 'Independent living for persons with disabilities' (2012) 46 *Les Cahiers d'Afrique de l'Est/The East African Review* 11.

119 The Judiciary *Criminal procedure bench book* (2018).

out in the JCBB. It is almost unheard of for judges and magistrates to refer to the JCBB and provide reasonable adjustments for disabled persons. The nature of the JCBB is to provide guidance which can be accessed by judiciary on a needs basis and as such the Judicial Service Commission (JSC) needs to train judges and other justice actors on its contents.

Criminal justice actors should produce online e-learning materials aimed at helping all justice personnel faced with cases involving persons with psychosocial disabilities, which includes information and tips for effective preparation as well as effective communication. E-learning is aimed to help ensure that cases are dealt with fairly and justly and without avoidable problems with communication. E-learning materials should be advertised and drawn to the attention of the criminal justice actors in a variety of ways. All training should include an element of the social context within which judging occurs. This should include all issues of equal treatment and diversity and this approach means that case studies used in jurisdictional training can have social context issues woven into them. Overall, there is need for sufficient training in this area but all training needs are continually evaluated and reviewed.

5.4 Conclusion

Principles of inclusion and participation in access to justice dominate the discourse in the field of disability, criminal law, and human rights. One of the limitations of this chapter is that it relies heavily on the human rights approach to reasonable accommodation as opposed to Foucault's theory of power. However, the aim of reasonable accommodation is to address issues of inequalities thus cultivating Foucault's ideas of agency which aim at creating justice structures that advance the human rights of persons with psychosocial disabilities.[120] The provisions of reasonable accommodation are essential preconditions for any meaningful participation. While some measures to ensure the participation of persons with psychosocial disabilities have been implemented, more needs to be done to improve the position of persons with psychosocial disabilities in Kenya's criminal justice sector.

The measures needed to enhance the participation of persons with psychosocial disabilities in the criminal justice sector should not impair their ability to participate in proceedings, or to give their best evidence.[121] Accommodations do not necessarily involve large financial expenditures.[122] Many accommodations merely require procedural flexibility such as provision of public information, pretrial services, out-of-court hearings and trials, and

120 M Foucault *The hermeneutics of the subject* G Burchell (2005) 67.

121 Civil Justice Council *Vulnerable witnesses and parties within civil proceedings: current position and recommendations for change* Civil Justice Council (February 2020) 4.

122 K Gould 'And equal participation for all . . . the Americans with Disabilities Act in the courtroom' (1993–1994) 8 *Journal of Law & Health* 138.

access throughout the courthouse facility. Generally, a flexible approach to procedures should be adopted in order to challenge stakeholders to question ingrained attitudinal beliefs about the integration of people with psychosocial disabilities into the mainstream courtroom activities.[123] Apart from accommodations, alternative procedures and measures should be explored in order to support and enhance the legal capacity of accused persons with psychosocial disabilities and ensure their participation in Kenya's justice system. This chapter has examined the principle of reasonable accommodation and its role in enhancing the participation of persons with psychosocial disabilities in access to justice. The next chapter deals with the research methodology.

References

Addadzi--Koom Me 'Of the women's rights jurisprudence of the ECOWAS Court: the role of the Maputo Protocol and the due diligence standard' (2020) 28- *Feminist Legal Studies* 161. https://doi.org/10.1007/s10691-020-09432-4.

B v A Company (2007) 'Norway, equality and anti-discrimination tribunal of Norway'.

Barras A et al. 'Rethinking Canadian discourses of "reasonable accommodation"' (2018) 6 *Social Inclusion* 166. https://doi.org/10.17645/si.v6i2.1443.

Bouchard G & Taylor C *Building the future: a time for reconciliation abridged report* Gouvernement du Quebec.

Broderick A 'The long and winding road to equality and inclusion for persons with disabilities: the United Nations Convention on the Rights of Persons with Disabilities' Doctoral Thesis, Maastricht University, 2015. https://doi.org/10.26481/dis.20151120ab.

Broderick A *Report on reasonable accommodation under the CRPD: the Georgian context* USAID (2017).

Central Okanagan School District No 23 v Renaud (1992) 2 SCR 970.

CIPESA 'Assessing the barriers to accessing ICT by people with disabilities in Kenya' https://cipesa.org/?wpfb_dl=429 (accessed 16 February, 2022) 19.

Civil Justice Council *Vulnerable witnesses and parties within civil proceedings: current position and recommendations for change* Civil Justice Council (February 2020).

Comandé G 'Discrimination and reasonable accommodation: "insight" from a (non) zero sum game"' (2010) 2 *Opinio Juris in Comparatione* 14. https://doi.org/10.20935/AcadMed7615.

Constitution of the Republic of South Africa Act 108 of 1996.

Council Directive 2000/78/EC establishing a general framework for equal treatment in employment and occupation [2000] OJ L303/16.

Courtis C 'Rationality, reasonableness, proportionality: testing the use of standards of scrutiny in the constitutional review of legislation' (2011) 4 *Constitutional Court Review* 35.

CRPD Committee 'Concluding observations on the initial report of Kenya' UN Doc CRPD/C/KEN/CO/1 (30 September 2015).

CRPD Committee 'Concluding observations on the initial report of Canada' UN Doc CRPD/C/CAN/CO/1(8 May 2017).

CRPD Committee 'Concluding observations on the initial report of South Africa' UN Doc CRPD/C/ZAF/CO/1 (23 October 2018).

123 As above.

CRPD Committee General comment 2: article 9: accessibility (2014b) UN Doc CRPD/C/GC/2.

CRPD Committee General comment 4: article 24: right to inclusive education (2016b) (UN Doc CRPD/C/GC/4).

CRPD Committee General comment 6: article 5: equality and nondiscrimination (2018) UN Doc CRPD/C/GC/6 dated 26 April 2018.

CRPD Committee General comment 5: article 19: living independently and being included in the community (2017a) UN Doc CRPD/C/18/1.

CRPD Committee General comment 3: article 6: women and girls with disabilities (2016a) (UN Doc CRPD/C/GC/3).

Curtice M et al. 'The proportionality principle and what it means in practice' (2011) 35 *The Psychiatrist* 111. https://doi.org/10.1192/pb.bp.110.032458

Daly P & Whelan D 'Disability in employment equality law: a reappraisal of the reasonable accommodation duty and issues arising in its implementation' (2021) 28 *Maastricht Journal of European and Comparative Law* 757. https://doi.org/10.1177/1023263X211035268.

Downes G 'Reasonableness, proportionality and merits review' https://www.aat.gov.au/AAT/media/AAT/Files/Speeches%20and%20Papers/ReasonablenessSeptember2008.pdf (accessed 30 August 2022).

Dusky v United States (1960) 362 US 402.

Eaton v Brant County Board of Education (1997) 1 SCR 24.

Equal Employment Opportunity Act 1972 (amending Civil Rights Act 1964, 42 USC 2000e).

European Network of Equality Bodies *Reasonable accommodation for persons with disabilities: exploring challenges concerning its practical implementation* Equinet (2020).

Ferri D 'Reasonable accommodation as a gateway to the equal enjoyment of human rights: from New York to Strasbourg (2018) 6 *Social Inclusion* 43. https://doi.org/10.17645/si.v6i1.1204.

Finland, National Non-Discrimination and Equality Tribunal, 14 December 2015, YVTltk 21/2015.

Flynn E et al. *Final report: access to justice of persons with disabilities* OHCR (2019).

Foucault M 'The subject and power' in Dreyfus H & Rabinow P (eds) *Beyond structuralism and hermeneutics* (1983).

Foucault M *The hermeneutics of the subject* trans G Burchell (2005).

Fuente OP 'Reasonable accommodation based on religious beliefs or practices. A comparative perspective between the American, Canadian and European approaches' (2018) 10 *The Age of Human Rights Journal* 115. https://doi.org/10.17561/tahrj.n10.5.

Gazette Notice 189 *Laws of Kenya* Nairobi (14 January 2022).

Gemma Beasley v Australia Communication (2016) CRPD/C/15/11/2013.

Geoffrey Andare v Attorney General & 2 others (2016) eKLR.

GL v Italy (2020) ECtHR.

Gould K 'And equal participation for all . . . the Americans with disabilities act in the courtroom' (1993–1994) 8 *Journal of Law & Health* 141.

Government of the Republic of South Africa v Grootboom (2001) 1 SA 46 (CC) & *Minister of Health v Treatment Action Campaign* (2002) 5 SA 703 (CC).

Griffiths E 'The 'reasonable accommodation' of religion: is this a better way of advancing equality in cases of religious discrimination?' (2016) 16 *International Journal of Discrimination and the Law* 172.

Grobbelaar-du Plessis I & Nienaber A 'Disability and reasonable accommodation: *HM v Sweden* Communication 3/2011 (Committee on the Rights of Persons with Disabilities)' (2014) 30 *South African Journal on Human Rights* 376. https://doi.org/10.1080/19962126.2014.11865113.

Guberina v Croatia (2013) ECtHR.
Holmes v Canada (Attorney General) (1997) CanLII 5101 (FC).
Holmes v Canada (Attorney General) (1999) CanLII 7869 (FCA).
Independent Municipal and Allied Trade Union obo Strydom v Witzenburg Municipality and Others (2012) ZALAC 1.
The Judiciary *Criminal procedure bench book* (2018).
Kallehauge H 'General themes relevant to the implementation of the UN Disability Convention into domestic law: who is responsible for the implementation and how should it be performed?' in Arnardottir OM & Quinn G (eds) *The UN convention on the rights of persons with disabilities: European and Scandinavian perspectives* (2009) 211.
Karjalainen K & Ylhäinen M 'On the obligation to make reasonable accommodation for an employee with a disability' (2021) 12(4) *European Labour Law Journal* 562. https://doi.org/10.1177/20319525211027430.
Karras M et al. *On the edge of justice: the legal needs of people with a mental illness in NSW* Sydney: Law and Justice Foundation of NSW (2006).
Kijuki Kiambi Paul Kagia and 5 Others v Clerk Meru Municipal Council Municipal council (2012) eKLR.
Lawson A & Orchard M 'The anticipatory reasonable adjustment duty: removing the blockages?' (2021) 80(2) *Cambridge Law Journal* 319. https://doi.org/10.1017/S0008197321000568.
Lord J & Brown R 'The role of reasonable accommodation in securing substantive equality for persons with disabilities: the UN Convention on the Rights of Persons with Disabilities' in Rioux MH et al. (eds) *Critical perspectives on human rights and disability law* (2011) 279.
Lurie G 'Proportionality and the right to equality' (2020) 21 *German Law Journal* 188. https://doi.org/10.1017/glj.2020.8.
Marie-Louise Jungelin v Sweden (2014) CRPD/C/12/D/5/2011.
Martel LV 'Reasonable accommodation: the new concept from an inclusive constitutional perspective' (2011) 8 *International Journal of Human Rights* 105.
McCallum R & Martin H 'A forgotten cohort: citizenship through work and persons with disabilities' (2016) 41 *Queen's Law Journal* 341.
MEC for Education and Others v Pillay and Others (2008) BCLR 99 (CC).
Melbourne Social Equity Institute *Addressing the indefinite detention of people with cognitive and psychiatric impairment due to unfitness to plead laws* Melbourne Social Equity Institute (2016).
Michael Lockrey v Australia Communication (2016) CRPD/C/15/D/13/2013.
Nano Nagle School v Marie Daly (2019) IESC 63.
New South Wales Jury Act of 1977.
*Noble v Au*stralia (2016) CRPD/C/16/D/7/2012.
Office of Director of Public Prosecutions Diversion Policy (2019).
Ontario Human Rights Commission, Theresa O'Malley v Simpsons-Sears (1985) 2 SCR 536.
Practice Directions to Standardize Practice and Procedures in the High Court of Kenya.
Pretorius JL et al. *Employment equity law* (2001, 2021 update).
Primor S & Lerner N *The rights of persons with intellectual, psychosocial and communication disabilities to access to justice: accommodations in the criminal process* Bizchut, The Israel Human Rights Centre for People with Disabilities.
R (on the application of N) v Ashworth Special Hospital Authority and another (2001) EWHC 339.
Rainey v Greater Glasgow Health Authority (1987) 1 All ER 65, 1 AC 224 (HL).
Robert Alai v Attorney General and another (2017) eKLR.

Roig RA 'Reasonableness in the concept of reasonable accommodation' (2016) 6 *The Age of Human Rights Journal* 48.

Runo M 'Independent living for persons with disabilities' (2012) 46 *Les Cahiers d'Afrique de l'Est / The East African Review* 11. https://doi.org/10.4000/eastafrica.432.

SA Clothing and Textile Workers Union and Others v Berg River Textiles – A Division of Seardel Group Trading (Pty) Ltd (2012) 33 ILJ 972.

South West Africa (Ethiopia v South Africa; Liberia v South Africa) (1966) ICJ Rep 6, 305.

State v Cleary, (2003) 824 A.2d 509.

State v Ortiz-Abrego (2017) 387 P3d 638.

Szurlej C 'Reconciling competing human rights in Canada' (2015) 47 *Peace Research* 180.

Vande Zande v Wisconsin Department of Administration (1995) 44 F3d 538.

Waddington L 'Reasonable accommodation' in Schiek D et al. (eds) *Cases, materials and text on national, supranational and international non-discrimination law* (2007).

Waddington L 'When it is reasonable for Europeans to be confused: understanding a when disability accommodation is "reasonable" from a comparative perspective' (2008) 29 *Comparative Labor Law and Policy Journal* 339.

White R & Msipa D 'Implementing article 13 of the convention on the rights of persons with disabilities in South Africa: reasonable accommodations for persons with communication disabilities' (2018) 6 *African Disability Rights Yearbook* 103. https://doi.org/10.29053/2413-7138/2018/v6a5.

Wilson Macharia v Safaricom Plc (2021) eKLR.

6 Empirical research methodology

6.0 Introduction

This chapter deliberates on the research methodology.[1] It explains how the empirical study was conducted, the research methods and procedures of the study. The chapter covers the research design, study area, target population, sampling techniques, data collection methods, and data quality control.

The purpose of the empirical research was to investigate and evaluate the views of the respondents regarding the law on unfitness declarations and the factors that limit the right of participation of persons with psychosocial disabilities in the criminal justice system of Kenya. The findings of the empirical study, CRPD provisions, Foucault's notion of power, and decolonial theory informed the recommendations made in Chapter 7 to reform unfitness declarations in Kenya.

6.1 Research design

Research is defined as an investigation into a subject for the purpose of discovering new information, reaching a new understanding, or obtaining additional information.[2] The primary focus of research is to increase knowledge and understanding of a particular subject in order to help solve relevant problems. A research design is the process of how research is conducted from the theoretical underpinning to the collection and analysis of the data.[3] It consists of specific methods of collecting data, deliberation on the significance of the results obtained, and an explanation of any limitations experienced.[4] The overall goal of a research design is to provide credible results.[5]

1 TA Schwardt *The SAGE dictionary of qualitative inquiry* (2007) 195.

2 Cambridge Dictionary 'Research' https://dictionary.cambridge.org/dictionary/english/research (accessed 1 September 2021).

3 J Hussey & R Hussey *Business research: a practical guide for undergraduate and postgraduate students* (1997) 54.

4 MN Saunders et al. *Research methods for business students* (1997) 1.

5 JH MacMillan & S Schumacher *Research in education: a conceptual introduction* (2001) 166.

DOI: 10.4324/9781003647102-6

The study adopted the mixed method research (MMR) approach, which involves the use of both qualitative and quantitative data collection and analysis.[6] On the one hand, quantitative research involves the use of numerical representation and manipulation of observations for the purpose of describing and explaining the phenomena that the observations reflect.[7] The objective of quantitative research is to collect facts about human behaviour that will lead to verification and extension of knowledge. On the other hand, qualitative research attempts to make sense of a phenomenon by studying it in its natural settings, and interpreting it in terms of the meanings people bring to it.[8] It means that the researcher is located as part of the study and is able to gain the perspective of members of the target audience through immersion in their culture or situation and direct interaction with them.

The MMR approach implies that any collected data will be integrated, related, or mixed at some stage of the research process.[9] The logic behind the mixed method research is that neither the qualitative nor quantitative methods are sufficient in themselves to analyse the subject under investigation thus the combination whose aim is to yield a more complete analysis and to complement each other.[10] According to Sale et al., MMR aims to combine multiple theories or data sources to study a single phenomenon, gain an in-depth understanding of a research issue, and ensuring convergence in results by using the strengths of each method to enhance the weaknesses of the other technique, otherwise known as independence of research methods.[11]

Apart from enhancing each other, the MMR also contributes to participant enrichment, instrument fidelity, treatment integrity, and significance enhancement.[12] Participant enrichment in terms of the research implies involvement of more respondents. In this regard, the larger the sample, the more reliable and valid the research findings.[13] In terms of this study, raw data was collected from employees at the judiciary, Office of the Director of Public Prosecutions (ODPP), doctors, defence counsels, and non-governmental institutions dealing with persons with psychosocial disabilities.

Instrument fidelity refers to the utility of the instruments employed. They should be used appropriately and optimally. For the purpose of this study,

6 EA Kemper et al. 'Mixed methods sampling strategies in social science research' in A Tashakori & C Teddlie (eds) *Handbook of mixed methods in social and behavioural research* (2003) 274.

7 E Babbie & J Mouton *The practice of social research* (2001) 646.

8 NK Denzin & YS Lincoln *The discipline and practice of qualitative research* (2005) 10.

9 JW Creswell et al. 'Designing a mixed methods study in primary care' (2004) 2 *Annals of Family Medicine* 7.

10 As above.

11 JEM Sale et al. 'Revisiting the quantitative – qualitative debate: Implications for mixed methods research' (2002) 36 *Quality and Quantity* 46.

12 AJ Onwuegbuzie & NL Leech 'Linking research questions to mixed methods data analysis procedure' (2006) 11 *The Qualitative Report* 479.

13 As above.

two instruments were used, namely questionnaires and focus group discussions (FGDs). A questionnaire contains a set of questions that are used for gathering information from the participants of the research.[14] Questionnaires can be administered in various ways, including through face to face interviews, telephone, by mail, as hand-outs, or electronically.[15] In this study, a self-administered questionnaire was compiled and data collected by means of distributing the questionnaire as part of the research design and its content was guided by the literature reviewed. The purpose of the questionnaire for the magistrates and prosecutors was to gather information concerning their perceptions with regard to the unfitness declarations, participation of persons with psychosocial disabilities, and reform mechanisms for improving participation in access to justice.

An FGD is a way of collecting data by gathering small groups of people from similar backgrounds or experiences in order to discuss a specific topic of interest.[16] FGDs are guided by moderators who facilitate the discussion by introducing topics for discussion and helping the group to participate in a lively environment. FGDs involve the use of distinct groups that are chosen in terms of the research purpose, size composition, and procedures. The participants are selected because they possess certain characteristics in common that relate to the topic or theme of the research. FGDs encourage participants to agree or disagree with each other thus providing the researcher with insights into how the group thinks about an issue, about the range of opinion and ideas, and the inconsistencies and variation that exists in terms of beliefs, experiences, and practices. In this study, FGD sessions were conducted only among selected members of the target population who shared and discussed their views about psychosocial disability, unfitness declarations, and participation of disabled persons in the criminal justice sector.

The use of questionnaires and FGDs provided the necessary information for determining the barriers that inhibit the participation of persons with psychosocial disabilities following unfitness declarations and possible reform mechanisms that may be incorporated to counter current violations. The data was analysed according to the barriers, psychosocial disabilities, and the right to participation. Although this research utilised both quantitative approach and the qualitative approach, the study relied heavily on the quantitative approach because it allowed the researcher to examine the relationship between unfitness declarations and the right to participation in Kenya's criminal justice system.

14 Centers for Disease Control and Prevention 'Data collection methods for program evaluation: questionnaires' https://www.cdc.gov/healthyyouth/evaluation/pdf/brief14.pdf (accessed 1 September 2021).

15 Centers for Disease Control and Prevention (n 14).

16 ODI Toolkit 'Research tools: focus group discussion' https://odi.org/en/publications/research-tools-focus-group-discussion/ (accessed 1 September 2021).

6.2 The study site

The study was conducted in the eight provinces of Kenya.[17] The participants of the study are magistrates, prosecutors, defence counsels, doctors, and non-governmental organisations (NGOs) dealing with psychosocial disability issues.

6.3 Target population

Target population refers to a group of people with shared characteristics who are recruited by the researcher to take part in a study.[18] The target population for this study was selected from a diverse group of professionals employed in both the private and public sector. The study's target population were judicial officers, prosecutors, defence counsels, doctors, and NGOs dealing with psychosocial disability issues. All these groups contribute in different capacities in Kenya's criminal justice sector. The population mentioned above is acquainted with the day-to-day running of the criminal justice sector and are able to provide the researcher with more information in relation to the factors of the unfitness declarations laws that lead to the limitation of persons with psychosocial disabilities' right to participation in the context of Kenya's criminal justice system.

6.4 Sampling and sampling techniques

A sample is a designated sub-group of a larger group called a population.[19] Sampling is the method for selecting a portion of individuals from the parent population for purposes of participating in research and generalise the outcomes to the entire populace of the research.[20] Use of samples instead of the parent population in research is advantageous because it saves on time and resources.[21] For instance, in this research, rather than using all the stakeholders working in Kenya's criminal justice sector, a sample was used. This study employed professionals and skilled employees from both the private and public sector who are aware of the day-to-day running of Kenya's criminal justice sector and unfitness declarations procedures. A purposive and snowball sampling was used to select participants.

In terms of administering questionnaires, the study employed snowballing sampling technique. Snowball sampling or chain-referral sampling is defined as a non-probability sampling technique in which existing subjects provide

17 J Gachohi et al. 'Epidemiology of East Coast fever (*Theileria parva* infection) in Kenya: past, present and the future' (2012) 5 *Parasites & Vectors* 4.

18 S Wilson & R MacLean *Research methods and data analysis for psychology* (2011) 161.

19 B Tyabashe 'Assessing the relationship between food insecurity, the child support grant and child care arrangements' Masters Dissertation, The University of Western Cape, 2019, 63.

20 As above.

21 A Fink *How to sample in surveys* (2003) 1.

referrals to recruit samples required for a research study.[22] In other words, the sample starts small but snowballs into a larger sample through the course of the research. Snowball sampling can be particularly useful for identifying hard-to-reach, information-rich participants when studying sensitive topics.[23] Thus, a sample of participants was recruited using the snowball sampling, through social media and word-of-mouth. Since the researcher used to practice in Kenya as an advocate, he had contacts for people working within Kenya's justice sector. Recruitment of participants was done using an information leaflet. The researcher emailed the information leaflet to would be participants with a request for them to participate. The researcher also asked them to recommend and share the information leaflet with any of their colleagues who may be interested or may know someone else who would like to participate in the study. The information leaflet contained the inclusion criteria to aid potential participants in self-selecting. In terms of administering questionnaires, participants were recruited randomly from the judiciary and ODPP since they are acquainted by the nature of their work with Kenya's criminal justice sector and are able to provide the researcher with more information in relation to unfitness declarations.

The study also employed purposive sampling method for the FGDs mainly because FGDs does not aim to achieve consensus on issues but to identify candid perceptions that may differ between participants through promoting an open discussion which encourages dynamic group interaction and allows contrasting opinions.[24] In this study purpose sampling was ideal because it focuses only on those individuals who have the competence in the phenomenon under study and are able to contribute widely to the subject under investigation.[25] Therefore, only those participants who are knowledgeable in the area of psychosocial disability and criminal justice were selected because of their potential to enrich existing knowledge on unfitness declarations.[26]

6.5 Inclusion criteria

The inclusion criteria used was the experience of participants with Kenya's criminal justice system and psychosocial disability. In general, research that focuses on participant experiences ensures there is sufficient material for discussion. However, requiring participants to have had a lot of experience may

22 QuestionPro 'Snowball sampling: definition, method, advantages and disadvantages' https://www.questionpro.com/blog/snowball-sampling/#:~:text=Snowball%20sampling%20or%20chain-referral%20sampling%20is%20defined%20as,to%20recruit%20samples%20required%20for%20a%20research%20study (accessed 16 February 2022).

23 As above.

24 L Jamieson & LM Williams 'Focus group methodology: explanatory notes for the novice nurse researcher' (2003) 14 *Contemporary Nurse* 274.

25 B Mastalgia et al. 'Ensuring validity in instrument development: challenges and innovative approaches' (2003) 14 *Contemporary Nurse* 281.

26 P Roberts 'Planning and running a focus group' (1997) 4 *Nurse Researcher* 79.

bias participation towards participants with more positive experiences, excluding those with less experience. Thus, participants who had engaged with Kenya's criminal system for a longer duration were given priority in order to ensure that the interviews could be as rich as possible. However, the concerns regarding potentially biasing the results by excluding participants with less experience was noted during participant selection.

6.6 Data collection techniques

Prior to conducting any thematic analysis, good data needs to be collected.[27] Good data reveals detailed insights into the research problem. The researcher used different approaches in collecting data. Introductory letters were prepared in order to enable the researcher apply for various approvals from the judiciary, ODPP, hospitals, and non-governmental organisations. Questionnaires for the study were sent by email. This is in keeping with the requirements of the University of Pretoria, Faculty of Law Research Ethics Committee. A cover letter accompanied the questionnaires to explain to the respondents the purpose of the study.

FGD sessions with prosecutors, doctors, and members of NGOs were arranged once all the participants had been recruited. A date and time for the FGDs were scheduled. The focus group discussions were conducted using Zoom Video technology (version 5.9.1). Face to face interviews were avoided in keeping with the conditions by the Faculty of Law Research Ethics Committee. The researcher moderated the FGDs and took the notes of the sessions. Recording of answers was done during the discussions. The researcher then read to the respondents and asked them to clarify any misreporting on the part of the researcher of what the respondent might have said. The collected data was subsequently transcribed but not all the data went through this process because some of it, especially those obtained from questionnaires was already in written format. However, for purposes of analysis all the collected data had to be organised and prepared. Any data that was received through email was copied to a word document for easier analysis. This enabled the researcher to ensure the anonymity and protect the privacy of participants.

6.7 Data collection instrument and procedures

This section discusses the research instrument that was used in the collection of data. The section discusses the following; FGD, the questionnaire, administration, and distribution of the questionnaire, forms of questions in the questionnaire and the response rate. The questionnaire comprises of both close and open-ended questions, which is divided into five sections. This approach is suitable for this research because the respondents were able to read and write

27 V Clarke et al. 'Thematic analysis' in JA Smith (ed) *Qualitative psychology: a practical guide to research methods* (2015) 220.

independently. The questionnaire comprised of several questions, which took the respondents approximately 20 minutes to answer.

The questionnaire for prosecutors and magistrates contained several items and was divided into five sections. The first section had three items and elicited demographic data from the target population. The second section comprised of two items relating to psychosocial disability, including questions about the respondents' training on and causes of psychosocial disability. Section three contained four items relating to the respondents' understanding about the CRPD and its concept of reasonable accommodation. The fourth section had four components pertaining to legal capacity and participation. The questions sought participants' views on the right to participation and legal capacity of persons with psychosocial disabilities following unfitness declarations. The fifth and sixth sections were made up of 30 items relating to causes and impact of unfitness declarations on persons with psychosocial disabilities. These were closed ended questions, which solicited the respondents' answers on the reasons that led to persons with psychosocial disabilities being declared unfit, the impact of unfitness declarations, and whether there is need for reforms on the law governing unfitness declarations. The researcher administered the questionnaires (Annexure A) to participants through email. Participants were requested to complete the questionnaire as soon as possible.

An interview schedule was also used to conduct FGDs aimed at obtaining in-depth information from doctors, senior prosecution counsels, defence counsels and representatives of non-governmental organisations. The interview schedules contained questions on the personal information of respondents excluding their names. They also had questions aimed at soliciting the opinions of the respondents on unfitness declarations, participation of persons with psychosocial disabilities in Kenya's criminal justice system, and their understanding of the CRPD and supported decision-making. The FGD interview schedules contained questions aimed at determining their personal and professional views on supported decision-making and the right to legal capacity of persons with psychosocial disabilities in terms of participation in access to justice. In total, four FGDs with members of each single profession were conducted. One FGD involved two to six participants at the same time, as they worked at the same organisation. Each interview lasted approximately 90 minutes. The researcher was primarily responsible for conducting the interviews. All interviews were audio recorded and subsequently transcribed verbatim.

6.8 Pilot testing

Background information about a research problem is essential before the commencement of any study.[28] A pilot study is an opportunity for the researcher to familiarise himself or herself with the research project. For these reasons,

28 H Stydom 'The pilot study' in De Vos (ed) *Research at grassroots: for social sciences and human sciences professions* (2002) 120.

the pilot study formed an essential part of this study. The pilot study gave the researcher an opportunity to test the effectiveness of the methods to be implemented and the data collection instruments to the respondents. The instruments were tested during pilot study with the end goal of improving their reliability and validity. The researcher used the results of the pilot study to rectify the questions, augment their readability and lessen the odds of misunderstanding. Moreover, piloting the questions gave an indication of the duration of the interview in real time. The questionnaire was administered to two prosecutors.

6.9 Validity and reliability of the questionnaires

Validity and reliability ensure transparency and reduces the possibility of bias in research.[29] Reliability refers to the stability, consistency, and repeatability of the research results.[30] It is concerned with the ability of the research method to consistently yield the same results on separate occasions. Validity refers to the extent to which a researcher can draw meaningful and justifiable inferences from the research results.[31] Messick defines it as the extent to which evidence and theory adequately and accurately supports a proposed interpretation and uses of test scores.[32] In other words, it refers to the accuracy and reasonability of data. It is an essential prerequisite for any research study.

This study focused on two types of validity, namely, face and content validity. Face validity examines whether an instrument is able to measure the intended concept.[33] Face validity was guaranteed in this study, because the instrument evidently appears to be measuring the factors of the unfitness declarations laws that lead to the limitation of persons with psychosocial disabilities' right to participation in the context of Kenya's criminal justice system. Content validity seeks to verify the degree with which the research instrument evidences all the components of variables to be measured.[34] The questionnaire has content validity. In this study, questionnaire items were developed from the reviewed literature. The items in the questionnaire were clearly formulated and the language used was understood by all the participants.

Moreover, content validity was attained after assessing the face validity of the questionnaire through a series of discussion between the researcher and the supervisor. The researcher also conducted a pilot study in order to establish content validity on the items covered in the questionnaire. Afterwards, the

29 HK Mohajan 'Two criteria for good measurements in research: validity and reliability' (2017) 17 *Annals of Spiru Haret University* 2.

30 Mohajan (n 29) 1.

31 M Joppe 'The research process' (2000) 8 *The Qualitative Report*41.

32 S Messick 'Validity' in RL Linn (ed) *Educational measurement* (1989) 13.

33 D Amakiri & BB Kuroakegha 'Unveiling the validity and reliability rambles of research outcomes' (2018) 4 *International Journal of Social Sciences and Management Research* 46.

34 RZF Costa et al. 'Content validity, reliability and construct validity of a checklist for dive roll evaluation' https://www.scielo.br/j/jpe/a/jmdM9ZQ36fdbkskmZ3J7R4P/?lang=en (accessed 6 October 2021).

questionnaires were reviewed by the supervisor for errors and vagueness. Final adjustments to wording and format were made prior to distributing the questionnaire to the participants. Therefore, the design of the instrument enjoys high content validity, and the pilot study ensured that the instrument was able to measure the concepts in this study.

6.10 Data analysis

The process of making sense of raw data, interpreting, and theorising it is known as data analysis.[35] The researcher must accurately represent the participants' perspectives in the findings.[36] Since the research study adopted both the qualitative and quantitative method of research, different approaches to analysing data were utilised. Descriptive statistics analysed the quantitative data while thematic analysis was used to analyse the qualitative data.

For quantitative data, the researcher invited participants to fill questionnaires through email and made follow-ups to make sure that all the respondents had completed the forms correctly. The statistics used in descriptive analysis are frequency distributions and percentage distributions. Frequency distribution refers to the number of times an outcome repeats itself. When the frequency is expressed in percentage, it is referred to as percentage distribution. The quantitative data was analysed using the software for statistics called Google Forms. The reason why the Google Forms software was utilised was because it reduced the time and energy needed to construct graphs and tables.

Qualitative data was analysed through thematic analysis, which involves taking one piece of data, for example, one interview, and constantly comparing it to others with the aim of conceptualising possible relationships between the different data sets. The researcher read and reread the transcripted data and made notes of unexpected or not obvious information, observations, and insights. The information was then coded and captured on Microsoft Excel spreadsheet through identification and labelling of key features in the data that were relevant to the research problem. The researcher then grouped together similar segments for proper organisation and identification of themes related to the research problem. The researcher reviewed themes in order to determine whether the research problem reflect the data contents. The key patterns and meaning in the data were captured before defining each theme in an effort to ensure conceptual clarity. This helped the researcher draw up conclusions, organise, and write the analysis easily.

The researcher analysed all interviews of the same respondent type separately, beginning with prosecutors. To understand the data as a whole, the researcher first read through all transcripts of the respondent type. The researcher then

35 W Schurink et al. 'Qualitative data analysis and interpretation' in AS De Vos et al. (eds) *Research at grass roots for the social sciences and human service professions* (2011) 397.

36 CA Lietz & LE Zayas 'Evaluating qualitative research for social work practitioners' (2010) 11 *Advances in Social Work* 191.

began coding one information-rich interview by reading through the interview and summarising important phrases, sections, or quotations. Using emergent patterns, the researcher rearranged the summarised sections through an iterative process based on how they relate to each other. Finally, the researcher labelled each arrangement to create a set of codes.

6.11 Methodological limitations

Limitations are normal occurrences in a study due to factors, which may be beyond the researcher's control. Such factors limit the extent to which the research can be carried out and sometimes affect the results and conclusions. Every study no matter how well it is conducted must have limitations. Therefore, it is imperative that the researcher prepares ways of dealing with limitations at the earliest time possible. However, in certain instances limitations may arise either during the research process or afterwards. Limitations of these types are difficult to counter due to time constraints.

This study utilised a small, purposive sample. Those who agreed to partake in the study did so because they have an interest in the research topic and therefore, participants cannot be said to represent the views of their professions as a whole. Additionally, the study was framed to assess the respondents' opinions on the factors of the unfitness declarations laws that lead to the limitation of persons with psychosocial disabilities' right to participation in the context of Kenya's criminal justice system as opposed to intellectual disability in their responses. For these reasons, the generalisability of results is low and should be done with caution.

6.12 Areas for further research

In the current research, it was not possible to hear the direct experiences of persons with psychosocial disabilities who have been accused in Kenya's criminal justice system. In order to deepen the understanding of accommodation practices in Kenya and learn from those who have experiential knowledge, this is essential. Additionally, if conducted sensitively, supportively and appropriately, such a study could challenge system level issues in disability research, namely, over-paternalism and the suppression of the voice of persons with psychosocial disabilities in the name of protection.

6.13 Ethical and confidentiality considerations

Ethics are norms that govern people's moral choices in relation to their conduct and interpersonal relationships.[37] Research ethics is the propriety of a researcher's behaviour in terms of the participants' rights.[38] An ethical research

37 DR Cooper & PS Schindler *Business research methods* (2006) 116.

38 M Saunders et al. *Research methods for business students* (2007) 183–184.

study is one that is methodologically sound and morally acceptable to the participants. Where human beings are involved, researchers must conduct the study with integrity by focusing on all the ethical implications surrounding the research. A researcher needs to be careful when handling sensitive information about participants.[39] Psychosocial disability is a very sensitive and private issue and precautions were taken in an attempt to preserve the anonymity and confidentiality of the participants. In concert with the university's rules and regulations on how research involving human subjects should be conducted, the following ethical considerations were taken into account during the course of the study. These considerations applied to both the quantitative and qualitative research sections of this study.

The researcher obtained approval from the Ethics Committee of the Faculty of Law and Faculty of Health, University of Pretoria under protocol number L031/21, to conduct this research. In addition, permission to conduct the research was obtained from Kenya's National Commission for Science Technology and Innovation and other relevant government departments and non-government organisations dealing with psychosocial disability. Letters requesting permission for the researcher to carry out the research in the selected stations were also submitted to the relevant state agencies and the researcher was granted approval in writing to carry out the research in the selected stations.

After approvals to undertake the research were granted by the relevant authorities, letters of introduction explaining the nature and purpose of the research were sent to the participants. Attached to the letters were the informed consent forms to signify voluntary participation of the respondents. Voluntary participation and informed consent are closely linked ethical considerations. Informed consent implies knowledge in the part of the participants of the research in which they intend to take part in and have an option to refuse to take part.[40] It ensures that the subjects' decision to participate is voluntary and also that they have understood the research process, the goals, strengths, and limitations, as well as the duration of the study.

Informed consent forms were sent to participants through email. They were informed in writing about the nature of the research. They were also sent participant information leaflets that contained the contact details of the interviewer as well as the duration, manner, and purpose of the study. Annexed to the given participant information leaflets were informed consent forms in order to ensure that those who took part in the research did so willingly. Prospective participants were given 14 days to read the information leaflets and decide on whether or not they would take part in the study. Those who volunteered to participate in the study completed and returned the informed consent forms to the researcher.

39 K Ranjit *Research methodology: a step-by-step guide for beginners* (2005) 213.
40 U Flick *Designing qualitative research* (2007) 69.

Regarding doctors, the researcher addressed would be respondents on the nature and goals of the study. Informed consent forms and participant information leaflets detailing the manner and purpose of the research were also sent electronically to prospective interviewees. They were allowed 14 days to go through the information leaflets and decide whether or not they would take part in the research. Those who chose to participate in the study completed and emailed back the informed consent forms to the researcher.

The right of would be respondents to decline participation in the research was also considered. They were informed of this right prior to them giving their consent as well as during the administration of questionnaires and the FGDs. The researcher emphasised that participation in the study was optional and that interviewees had the right to withdraw from the research at any time before its conclusion. The participant information leaflet also indicated that participation in the research was voluntary and that respondents could withdraw from the study at any stage. They were assured that their decision to withdraw would not affect their relationship with the researcher or the respective organisations. In addition, during the FGDs, interviewees were informed of their rights to decline to be recorded. For the respondents who refused to be audio recorded, notes were taken by the researcher while those who agreed to be taped signed consent forms permitting the interviewer to record them.

The participants have a right to privacy, which is important as it guarantees the validity of the research and encourages truthfulness among the respondents. In this regard, the researcher ensured the anonymity of the respondents and restricted access to participant's information. Respondents' names and the identities of their organisations were dealt with in the strictest confidence. Any material that could link respondents to the information provided or forms containing their names, addresses and institutions were stored electronically in a computer that only the researcher had access to. Moreover, participants were assured that all the obtained information would only be used for research purposes.

The data was ultimately forwarded to the Centre for Human Rights, University of Pretoria for storage. Completed questionnaires were saved electronically in a hard drive that only the researcher had access to and were eventually submitted to the Centre for Human Rights, University of Pretoria for safe keeping. Codes were allocated to the audio recordings of the FGDs, which were stored electronically in folders that were encrypted. Numerals and fictitious names were also used in data analysis to protect the confidentiality of the information obtained as well as conceal the identities of the respondents who participated in the research. Participants were also made aware that in the future, the investigator may refer to the data obtained from the study for further research purposes. There was no financial compensation offered for participation in the research project. The researcher kept all costs to a minimum to ensure that participants did not incur any expenses as a result of participating in the study. The University of Pretoria Policy Framework for

Research Data requires data to be stored for a minimum period of ten years after the completion of the project.[41] Accordingly, the data collected in this research will be stored until 2037, when it will be destroyed.

6.14 Conclusion

This chapter presented the methodology of the empirical component of the research and its implementation. The next chapter analysed, presented, and interpreted data collected in the form of focus group discussions and questionnaires.

References

Amakiri D & Kuroakegha BB 'Unveiling the validity and reliability rambles of research outcomes' (2018) 4 *International Journal of Social Sciences and Management Research* 46.

Babbie E & Mouton J *The practice of social research* (2001).

Cambridge Dictionary 'Research' https://dictionary.cambridge.org/dictionary/english/research (accessed 1 September 2021).

Centers for Disease Control and Prevention 'Data collection methods for program evaluation: questionnaires' https://www.cdc.gov/healthyyouth/evaluation/pdf/brief14.pdf (accessed 1 September 2021).

Clarke V et al. 'Thematic analysis' in Smith JA (ed) *Qualitative psychology: a practical guide to research methods* (2015).

Cooper DR & Schindler PS *Business research methods* (2006).

Creswell JW et al. 'Designing a mixed methods study in primary care' (2004) 2 *Annals of Family Medicine* 7.

Denzin NK & Lincoln YS *The discipline and practice of qualitative research* (2005).

Fink A *How to sample in surveys* (2003).

Flick U *Designing qualitative research* (2007).

Gachohi J et al. 'Epidemiology of East Coast fever (Theileria parva infection) in Kenya: past, present and the future' (2012) 5 *Parasites & Vectors* 4. https://doi.org/10.1186/1756-3305-5-194.

Hussey J & Hussey R *Business research: a practical guide for undergraduate and postgraduate students* (1997).

Jamieson L & Williams LM 'Focus group methodology: explanatory notes for the novice nurse researcher' (2003) 14 *Contemporary Nurse* 274. https://doi.org/10.5172/conu.14.3.271.

Joppe M 'The research process' (2000) 8 *The Qualitative Report* 41.

Kemper EA et al. 'Mixed methods sampling strategies in social science research' in Tashakori A and Teddlie C (eds) *Handbook of mixed methods in social and behavioural research* (2003) 274.

Lietz CA & Zayas LE 'Evaluating qualitative research for social work practitioners' (2010) 11 *Advances in Social Work* 191. https://doi.org/10.18060/589.

MacMillan JH & Schumacher S *Research in education: a conceptual introduction* (2001).

41 University of Pretoria 'Research data management policy' https://www.up.ac.za/media/shared/12/ZP_Files/research-data-management-policy_august-2018.zp161094.pdf (accessed 10 August 2022) 3.

Mastalgia B et al. 'Ensuring validity in instrument development: challenges and innovative approaches' (2003) 14 *Contemporary Nurse* 281. https://doi.org/10.5172/conu.14.3.281.

Messick S 'Validity' in RL Linn (ed) *Educational measurement* (1989).

Mohajan HK 'Two criteria for good measurements in research: validity and reliability' (2017) 17 *Annals of Spiru Haret University* 1. https://doi.org/10.26458/1746.

ODI Toolkit 'Research tools: focus group discussion' https://odi.org/en/publications/research-tools-focus-group-discussion/ (accessed 1 September 2021).

Onwuegbuzie AJ & Leech NL 'Linking research questions to mixed methods data analysis procedure' (2006) 11 *The Qualitative Report* 479. https://doi.org/10.46743/2160–3715/2006.1663.

QuestionPro 'Snowball sampling: definition, method, advantages and disadvantages' https://www.questionpro.com/blog/snowball-sampling/#:~:text=Snowball%20sampling%20or%20chain-referral%20sampling%20is%20defined%20as,to%20recruit%20samples%20required%20for%20a%20research%20study (accessed 16 February, 2022).

Ranjit K *Research methodology: a step-by-step guide for beginners* (2005).

Roberts P 'Planning and running a focus group' (1997) 4 *Nurse Researcher* 79.

RZF Costa et al. 'Content validity, reliability and construct validity of a checklist for dive roll evaluation' https://www.scielo.br/j/jpe/a/jmdM9ZQ36fdbkskmZ3J7R4P/?lang=en (accessed 6 October 2021).

Sale JEM et al. 'Revisiting the quantitative – qualitative debate: implications for mixed methods research' (2002) 36 *Quality and Quantity* 46. https://doi.org/10.1023/A:1014301607592.

Saunders M et al. *Research methods for business students* (2007).

Saunders MN et al. *Research methods for business students* (1997).

Schurink W et al. 'Qualitative data analysis and interpretation' in De Vos AS et al. (eds) *Research at grass roots for the social sciences and human service professions* (2011) 397.

Schwardt TA *The SAGE dictionary of qualitative inquiry* (2007).

Stydom H 'The pilot study' in De Vos (ed) *Research at grassroots: for social sciences and human sciences professions* (2002).

Tyabashe B 'Assessing the relationship between food insecurity, the child support grant and child care arrangements' Masters Dissertation, The University of Western Cape, 2019.

University of Pretoria 'Research data management policy' https://www.up.ac.za/media/shared/12/ZP_Files/research-data-management-policy_august-2018.zp161094.pdf (accessed 10 August 2022).

Wilson S & MacLean R *Research methods and data analysis for psychology* (2011).

7 Data analysis, presentation, and interpretation of results

7.0 Introduction

This chapter analysed, presented and interpreted data collected in the form of focus group discussions (FGDs) and questionnaires. The latter was distributed to the research participants who work in the public sector. The data gathered was analysed, presented and interpreted in the form of tables, bar graphs, and pie charts together with a brief discussion.

7.1 Characteristics of interviewees

The data in this study was from different professionals in Kenya's criminal justice system. Questionnaires were administered to prosecutors and magistrates and four FGDs were conducted with doctors, defence counsels, members of non-governmental organisations (NGOs) working with persons with psychosocial disabilities, and senior prosecutors. The interviews were recorded and stored in tapes. Immediately after the data collection, the researcher proceeded to transcribe the information and engage in further analysis. The results presented below are based on data that was validated from amongst the 56 interviews that were conducted on professionals engaged with Kenya's criminal justice system.

The researcher selected seven judges to participate in the FGD. However, due to time factor and busy schedules, the judges could not participate in the study. Despite the non-participation of the judges, the researcher carried out other FGDs with senior prosecutors, defence counsels, members of NGOs and doctors, whose narratives resulted into clear themes that were sufficient for this exploratory investigation. Moreover, the data collected was exceptionally rich and detailed due to the mixed method nature of the study. The research was able to attain a high degree of consensus among the interviewees regarding the extent of participation of persons with psychosocial disabilities in access to justice following unfitness declarations in Kenya. By the last few interviews, significant repetition of concepts was occurring, suggesting ample sampling. The respondents' quotes drawn on below were chosen as representative, and illustrate saturated themes. The principle of theoretical saturation means the

DOI: 10.4324/9781003647102-7

Table 7.1 Participant information

Participant	*Judges*	*Magistrates*	*Prosecutors*	*Senior Prosecutors*	*Defence Counsels*	*Members of NGOs*	*Doctors*
Questionnaire	0	20	21				
FGD	0	0	0	6	4	3	2
Total	0	20	21	6	4	3	2

point at which no new data, no new themes, and no new codes can be identified in a study.[1] Nonetheless, while it is the position that the study attained saturation, the fact that further interviews with judges could have identified additional themes or provided more nuanced explanations cannot be ruled out with certainty.

7.2 Analysis of the data

Qualitative data analysis was used to code and analyse data collected through individual responses and FGDs by defence counsels, senior prosecutors, members of NGOs working with persons with psychosocial disabilities, and doctors. Additionally, thematic analysis was used to generate the emerging themes, patterns, concepts, and insights. The process required several readings, initially looking for response patterns, which then emerged as themes that were generated from the data. Supporting quotations were chosen that showed the responses of different participants.

Based on the collected elements, data was analysed and presented using the following themes: county, gender, work experience, psychosocial disability, CRPD, legal capacity, participation, causes of unfitness declaration, and impact of unfitness declarations. Each theme was listed and described in turn. Included in each thematic section is a discussion of the sub-themes, including verbatim quotes from participants to bring the themes to life. It is important to understand that while these themes are explored individually, they are not strictly delineated, they are overlapping and interwoven, and each theme speaks to and informs the others.

7.2.1 Analysis of respondents' demographic information

The demographic data of the respondents was investigated in section one of the questionnaire. The respondents' demographic data is presented in this section in the form of bar graphs and pie charts, under the following headings: county, gender, and work experience in Kenya's justice sector.

1 K Vasileiou et al. 'Characterising and justifying sample size sufficiency in interview-based studies: systematic analysis of qualitative health research over a 15-year period' (2018) 18 *BMC Medical Research Methodology* 150.

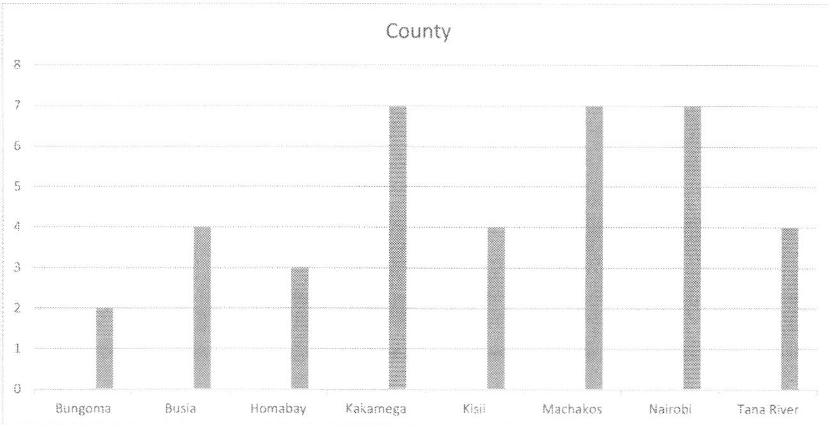

Figure 7.1 County

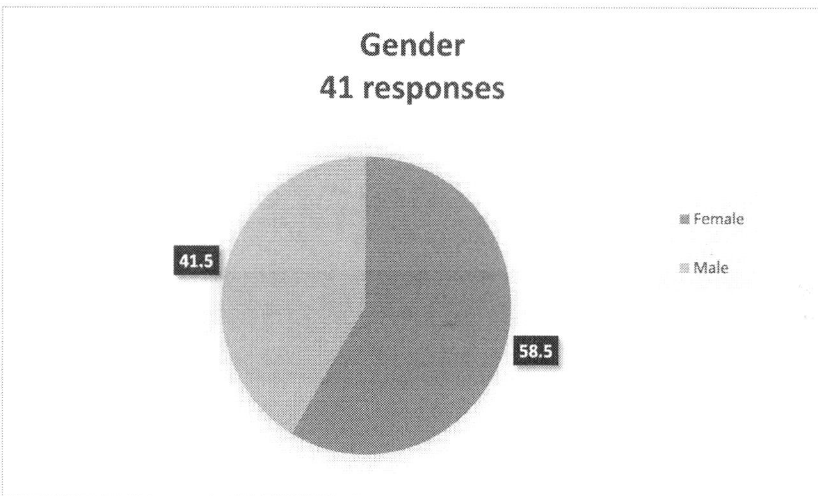

Figure 7.2 Gender

Figure 7.1 indicates the location of the survey respondents in Kenya. The results showed a balanced representation of criminal justice actors across different counties in Kenya. This suggests that the survey results are likely to be representative of the overall distribution of justice actors in the country.

Figure 7.2 indicates the gender of respondents. The sample of those who answered translated into 41.5% male respondents and 58.5% female respondents. It shows that Kenya's justice sector is an equal opportunity employer,

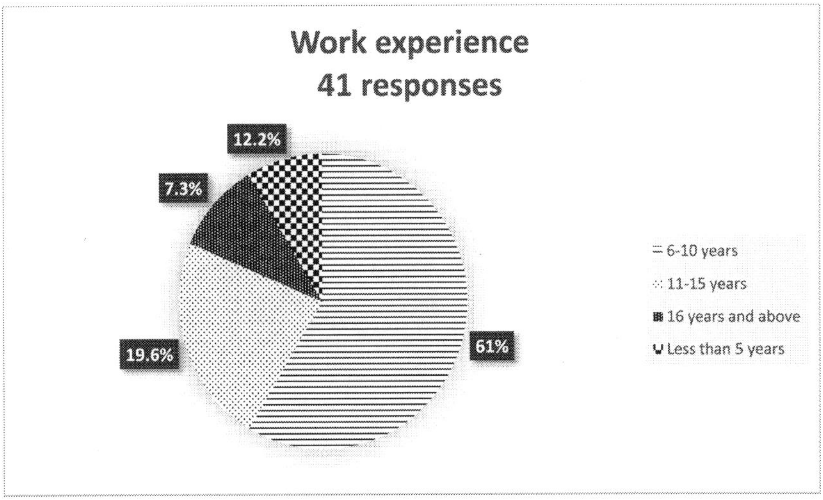

Figure 7.3 Work experience

which does not discriminate on the basis of gender. This means that both the male and female respondents were more accessible to the researcher.

Figure 7.3 indicates that majority (61%) of the respondents have been working in the public sector for 6 to 10 years, and 7.3% of the respondents reported that they have been working in the public sector for 16 years and above. In addition, 12.2% of the respondents have been working in the public sector for 11 to 15 years, and 19.5% have been working for less than 5 years. The results clearly show that majority of the respondents have been working for the justice sector for a long time.

7.2.2 *Absence of training*

Responses of prosecutors and magistrates in questionnaires revealed that training on psychosocial disability has been lacking in the judiciary and the Office of the Director of Public Prosecutions (ODPP). The data that was collected reveals that training is extremely necessary to understand the rights of persons with psychosocial disabilities in general and the right of access to justice in particular. 92.7% of the participants do not have never formal training on psychosocial disabilities.[2]

There is a paucity of data on trainings offered to judicial officers, prosecutors, and the support staff regarding the rights of persons with psychosocial disabilities in access of justice. Particularly, there is no compulsory training for

2 See Table 7.2.

Table 7.2 Do you have formal training on psychosocial disability?

Do you have formal training on psychosocial disability?					
		Frequency	*Percent*	*Valid percent*	*Cumulative percent*
Valid	Medical training	0	0%	0%	0%
	Special training	0	0%	0%	0%
	Training by Handicap International	1	2.4%	2.4%	2.4%
	Basic training	1	2.4%	2.4%	4.9%
	Legal training	1	2.4%	2.4%	7.3%
	None	38	92.7%	92.7%	100%
	Total	41	100%	100%	

criminal justice actors on the CRPD or forms of reasonable accommodation to ensure equal access to justice. Participants in the FGD agreed that

> The third barrier . . . at this point would be . . . lack of awareness in the criminal justice sector or among the criminal justice personnel on how to accommodate persons with psychosocial disabilities because it's one thing to have ways of accommodating persons with mental and psychosocial disabilities but also another thing for people working in the justice system to know how to accommodate such persons.[3]
>
> We can train their caregivers . . . to be their voice . . . And also having the . . . justice system having people trained . . . like intermediaries and prosecutors and even advocates trained on how to communicate interact and explain circumstances to persons with disabilities especially when they have mental disabilities.[4]

There is a need for improved and regularly reinforced education and training for judges, lawyers, prosecutors, police, social workers, language and sign language interpreters, legal aid centres, other judicial and administrative bodies intervening in judicial or quasi-judicial instances.

Article 8(1) of the CRPD obligates states parties to positively educate their populations on issues relating to disability. Training can include how to communicate effectively with persons with psychosocial disabilities, their needs, what it is like to have a mental disability, indicators of mental disability, referral and resource information, strategies to work effectively with persons with psychosocial disabilities, stress management, and general awareness-raising in order to combat stigma and discrimination.[5] Importantly, research should be conducted

3 FGD with defence counsels on 29 March 2022.

4 FGD with NGO members on 19 April 2022.

5 M Karras et al. *On the edge of justice: the legal needs of people with a mental illness in NSW* Sydney: Law and Justice Foundation of NSW, 121.

into the content of training manuals. The research should disclose not only good practices, such as the placement of staff with disability awareness training in court but also avoid reproducing Eurocentric assumptions about unfitness declaration laws as discussed in Chapter 5. The training should apply African concepts whose aim is to restore lost balance of power between persons with psychosocial disabilities and Kenya's criminal justice system. However, education and training have their limitations mainly because the problem of ineffective participation is systemic. Violation of participation rights resides in the very fabric of the criminal adversarial process, which promotes and entrenches unfitness declarations which not only is discriminatory but also impedes the effective participation of persons with disabilities in access to justice.

7.2.3 Psychosocial disability

Most of the participants indicated that the origin of psychosocial disability is biological. 36.6% attributed psychosocial disabilities to diseases, while others mentioned illness during pregnancy. The findings confirm Foucault's notions of compulsory able-bodiedness and able-mindedness, which is fundamentally structured to medicalise persons with psychosocial disabilities and limit their rights. Unfitness declarations, which are based on the idea of able-bodiedness and able-mindedness, disciplines persons with psychosocial disabilities as unfit thus creating relational barriers between justice system actors and disabled people.

The findings show that most participants view psychosocial disability from a medical model perspective, which might explain some of the interventions employed when dealing with persons with psychosocial disabilities in the criminal justice system, such as indefinite detention in hospitals and prisons. The medical model has been superseded by the social model of disability which emphasises that persons with disability are disabled by the society. Nonetheless, the social model of disability alone cannot ensure the participation of

Table 7.3 Which of these do you believe is the cause of psychosocial disability?

	Which of these do you believe is the cause of psychosocial disability?				
		Frequency	*Percent*	*Valid percent*	*Cumulative percent*
Valid	Witchcraft	0	0%	0%	0%
	Medical negligence	0	0%	0%	0%
	Parental negligence	0	0%	0%	0%
	Demonic possession	0	0%	0%	0%
	Accident	0	0%	0%	0%
	Anger of the gods	0	0%	0%	0%
	Others	2	4.9%	4.9%	4.9%
	Illness during pregnancy	3	7.3%	7.3%	12.2%
	Disease	15	36.6%	36.6%	48.8%
	Biological causes	21	51.2%	51.2%	100%
	Total	41	100%	100%	

Table 7.4 Have you heard about the CRPD?

	Have you heard about the CRPD?				
		Frequency	*Percent*	*Valid percent*	*Cumulative percent*
Valid	No	6	14.6%	14.6%	14.6%
	Yes	35	85.4%	85.4%	100%
	Total	41	100%	100%	

Table 7.5 If yes, how did you hear about the CRPD?

	If yes, how did you hear about the CRPD?				
		Frequency	*Percent*	*Valid percent*	*Cumulative percent*
Invalid		1	2.7%	2.7%	2.7%
Valid	Friends	3	8.1%	8.1%	10.8%
	Media	3	8.1%	8.1%	18.9%
	Others	5	13.5%	13.5%	32.4%
	Internet	12	32.4%	32.4%	64.9%
	Work	13	35.1%	35.1%	100%
	Total	37	100%	100%	

Table 7.6 Have you heard about CRPD's concept of reasonable accommodation?

	Have you heard about CRPD's concept of "reasonable accommodation"?				
		Frequency	*Percent*	*Valid percent*	*Cumulative percent*
Valid	Yes	16	40%	40%	40%
	No	24	60%	60%	100%
	Total	40	100%	100%	

persons with psychosocial disabilities in Kenya's criminal justice process as it focuses more on physical impairments as opposed to psychosocial disabilities. It does not mean that the social model has no role to play in Kenya's reform process. In fact, the social model of disability has been strengthened through the Foucault's concept of agency so as to empower persons with psychosocial disabilities and ensure their right to participation in access to justice.

7.2.4 CRPD

Overall, the level of knowledge of participants on the CRPD is high.[6] However, with respect to the concept of reasonable accommodation, less is known.[7] Also, whereas knowledge on the CRPD is high, majority learnt of it from work

6 See Table 7.4.
7 See Table 7.6.

Table 7.7 Do persons with psychosocial disabilities have a right to participate in the Kenyan criminal justice system?

	Do persons with psychosocial disabilities have a right to participate in the Kenyan criminal justice system?				
		Frequency	*Percent*	*Valid percent*	*Cumulative percent*
Valid	No	6	14.6%	14.6%	14.6%
	Yes	35	85.4%	85.4%	100%
	Total	41	100%	100%	

Table 7.8 Should persons with psychosocial disabilities have a right to participate in Kenya's criminal justice system?

	Should persons with psychosocial disabilities have a right to participate in Kenya's criminal justice system?				
		Frequency	*Percent*	*Valid percent*	*Cumulative percent*
Valid	No	6	14.6%	14.6%	14.6%
	Yes	35	85.4%	85.4%	100%
	Total	41	100%	100%	

Table 7.9 In your professional opinion, should persons with psychosocial disabilities have the right to participate in Kenya's criminal justice sector following unfitness declarations?

	In your professional opinion, should persons with psychosocial disabilities have the right to participate in Kenya's criminal justice sector following unfitness declarations?				
		Frequency	*Percent*	*Valid percent*	*Cumulative percent*
Valid	No	20	48.8%	48.8%	48.8%
	Yes	21	51.2%	51.2%	100%
	Total	41	100%	100%	

and the internet.[8] Their knowledge level was not influenced by any specialised disability rights training. This indicates that the level of training on CRPD in their workplace is low.

7.2.5 Legal capacity and participation

Although 51.2% of the respondents agreed that persons with psychosocial disabilities have the right to participate in Kenya's criminal justice sector following unfitness declarations, 48.8% disagreed. According to Table 7.10, 61.3%

8 See Table 7.5.

Table 7.10 If your answer to question 12 is no, who should make the determination as to whether they should participate?

If your answer to question 12 is no, who should make the determination as to whether they should participate?					
		Frequency	*Percent*	*Valid percent*	*Cumulative percent*
Valid	Defence Counsel	0	0%	0%	0%
	Witnesses	0	0%	0%	0%
	Prosecutor	2	6.5%	6.5%	6.5%
	Judicial Officer	10	32.3%	32.3%	38.7%
	Doctors	19	61.3%	61.3%	100%
	Total	31	100%	100%	

of the respondents also agreed that doctors should make the decision concerning the participation of persons with psychosocial disabilities. Generally, the analysis carried out shows that, the right of access to justice in participation for persons with psychosocial disabilities in Kenya's criminal justice system following unfitness declarations is marked by acts of discrimination, prejudice, and inequality. Table 7.9 indicate that persons with psychosocial disabilities are vulnerable to/or are likely to being denied their right of access to justice in participation after being declared unfit.

The role of doctors is linked to Foucault's ideas on power, knowledge, and truth. Foucault was interested in how the law produces mental disabilities.[9] The findings illustrate how advocacy and institutional (judiciary and hospitals) discourses have controlled and re-organised the discourse on psychosocial disability in Kenya's criminal justice sector, which has led to the belief that persons with psychosocial disabilities are incapable of participating in court. Foucault contends that when institutional discourses intersect, new forms of knowledge are bound to emerge.[10] According to the findings, it is inevitable for new forms of knowledge to be created in the form of unfitness declarations, due to the intersection of discourses among justice actors. The reliance of doctors is part of Kenya's justice system to link scientific knowledge and structures of legal power in order to produce and operationalise truths that persons with psychosocial disabilities are unfit. It does not mean that doctors have no role to play in the justice system. In fact, doctors can provide the court with important information on the effects of various types of psychosocial disabilities on an accused person's actions. Therefore, their role should not only be limited to giving opinions regarding the unfitness or otherwise

9 S Wendy et al. 'From criminalisation to individual choice: policy responses to changing constructions of intellectual disability in Western Australia' (2019) 21 *Scandinavian Journal of Disability Research* 102.

10 As above.

of an accused person. They should also be allowed to educate the court to understand that accused persons with psychosocial disabilities can participate effectively in court.[11]

7.2.6 Causes of unfitness declarations

Questions from section 2 of the questionnaire were used to obtain the first objective, which is the causes of unfitness declarations in Kenya's criminal justice system. Various themes were identified in Table 7.11.

Whether persons with psychosocial disabilities have a right to participate in criminal proceedings

Based on Table 7.11 below, 34.1% of the respondents strongly agreed that persons with psychosocial disabilities have a right to participate in criminal proceedings, 56.1% of the respondents agreed, 2.4% disagreed, whereas 7.3% of the respondents strongly disagreed. The overall analysis shows that most of the respondents (90%) are willing to ensure the right to participation of persons with psychosocial disabilities. Importantly, persons with psychosocial disabilities should not only be present in court, but they should also able to hear and follow the proceedings. Effective participation is the general principle behind the specific rights to defend oneself and to examine witnesses.[12]

Unfitness declarations offer no participation opportunities to persons with psychosocial disabilities who have a right to be heard

The results established that 25% of the respondents strongly agreed that unfitness declarations offer no participation opportunities to persons with psychosocial disabilities, 45% of the respondents agreed, 10% were neutral, 7.5% disagreed, whereas 12.5% of the respondents strongly disagreed. The overall analysis shows that most of the respondents believe that unfitness declarations violate the right of persons with psychosocial disabilities to participation. These results affirm the views of the Office of the High Commissioner for Human Rights' (OHCHR) that disability-based verdicts violate the rights of persons with psychosocial disabilities.[13]

11 R White et al. 'Court accommodations for persons with severe communication disabilities: a legal scoping review' (2021) 27 *Psychology, Public Policy and Law* 420.

12 *Stanford v UK* (2002) ECtHR.

13 United Nations Human Rights Council 'Thematic study by the United Nation High Commission for Human Rights on enhancing awareness and understanding on the Convention on the Rights of Persons with Disabilities' https://www.un.org/disabilities/documents/reports/ohchr/A.HRC.10.48AEV.pdf (accessed 19 March 2021) para. 48.

Table 7.11 Causes of unfitness declarations

Item	*Strongly Disagree*	*Disagree*	*Neutral*	*Agree*	*Strongly Agreed*
Persons with psychosocial disabilities have a right to participate in criminal proceedings.	7.3%	2.4%	0%	56.1%	34.1%
Unfitness declarations offer no participation opportunities to persons with psychosocial disabilities.	12.5%	7.5%	10%	45%	25%
Persons with psychosocial disabilities should be afforded an opportunity to be heard before they are declared unfit.	2.4%	4.9%	2.4%	46.3%	43.9%
Persons with psychosocial disabilities are not involved in decision-making following unfitness declarations.	14.6%	7.3%	9.8%	34.1%	34.1%
There is a lack of reasonable accommodation in Kenya's criminal procedure following unfitness declarations.	2.4%	19.5%	7.3%	39%	31.7%
Members of the organisation you work in have no knowledge on rights and needs of persons with psychosocial disabilities.	17.1%	43.9%	26.8%	9.8%	2.4%
The organisation, which you work in enhances the participation of persons with psychosocial disabilities in criminal proceedings.	9.8%	24.4%	25%	36.6%	4.9%
Persons with psychosocial disabilities have the ability to make decisions on their own.	26.8%	24.4%	26.8%	19.5%	2.4%
Persons with psychosocial disabilities have the ability to participate effectively in access to justice if given appropriate support.	4.9%	0%	17.1%	43.9%	34.1%
Judicial officers should make the decision whether an accused person is fit to participate.	14.6%	31.7%	4.9%	31.7%	17.1%
Judicial officers should involve, inform, and consult persons with mental disabilities before declaring them unfit.	7.3%	4.9%	7.3%	36.6%	43.9%
Experts should involve, inform, and consult persons with psychosocial disabilities when preparing mental assessment reports.	2.5%	0%	2.4%	29.3%	65.9%

(*Continued*)

Table 7.11 (Continued)

Item	*Strongly Disagree*	*Disagree*	*Neutral*	*Agree*	*Strongly Agreed*
Lack of support limits the participation of persons with psychosocial disabilities following unfitness declarations.	0%	2.4%	2.4%	34.1%	61%
Negative attitudes have a role in preventing the participation of persons with psychosocial disabilities following unfitness to plead declarations.	0%	7.3%	4.9%	51.2%	36.6%
Cultural beliefs play a role in preventing the participation of persons with psychosocial disabilities following unfitness to plead declarations.	7.3%	22%	12.2%	31.7%	26.8%
Social norms play a role in preventing the participation of persons with psychosocial disabilities following unfitness to plead declarations.	0%	14.6%	14.6%	51.2%	19.5%
Persons with psychosocial disabilities should be allowed to participate in criminal proceedings after being declared unfit.	7.3%	39%	22%	14.6%	17.1%
Persons with a history of mental problems are of unsound mind and should not be allowed to participate in a criminal trial.	46.3%	46.3%	2.4%	2.4%	2.4%
Persons suffering from hallucinations are of unsound mind and should not be allowed to participate in criminal trials.	34.1%	46.3%	7.3%	12.2%	0%

As indicated in Table 7.11, 43.9% of the respondents strongly agreed that persons with psychosocial disabilities should be afforded an opportunity to be heard before they are declared unfit, 46.3% of the respondents agreed, 2.4% were neutral, 4.9% disagreed whereas 2.4% of the respondents strongly disagreed. The overall analysis shows that most of the respondents, 90%, indicated that persons with psychosocial disabilities have a right to be heard before they are declared unfit. The opportunity to be heard will ensure that persons with psychosocial disabilities receive a fair trial and are equally protected under the law.[14]

14 *Leo v Australia* (2019) CRPD/C/22/D/17/2013.

There is lack of reasonable accommodation in Kenya's criminal procedure following unfitness declarations

The results show that 31.7% of the respondents strongly agreed that there is a lack of reasonable accommodation in Kenya's criminal procedure following unfitness declarations. Another 39% agreed, while 7.3% were neutral, 19.5% disagreed and only 2.4% of the respondents strongly disagreed. The overall analysis shows that most of the respondents believe that the law on unfitness does not enhance the legal capacity of persons with psychosocial disabilities in Kenya due to lack of reasonable accommodation. Therefore, it is imperative for the legislature to put in place measures to ensure the legal capacity of persons with psychosocial disabilities. Both decolonial and Foucauldian theories proposes ways of overcoming oppression and prejudices that are imposed by unfitness declarations on persons with psychosocial disabilities, which have been discussed in Chapter 2. Even if unfitness declaration laws are maintained, measures that account for the relational understanding of decision-making and safeguard the participatory rights of persons with psychosocial disabilities should be put in place.

Evidently, the provision of reasonable accommodation is a viable mechanism in enhancing the legal capacity of persons with psychosocial disabilities in Kenya's criminal justice system. Reasonable accommodation has the potential for transforming how justice actors treat persons with psychosocial disabilities in terms of their legal capacity to make participatory decisions. Justice actors must satisfy themselves that persons with psychosocial disabilities are able to participate effectively in access to justice. The process should not only consider how psychosocial deficits may interfere with participation in access to justice, but also assess which accommodations are best suited for an accused person with psychosocial disability.[15] In the end, the state should collect data on persons with psychosocial disabilities being convicted, the nature of their sentence, and whether they benefitted from safeguards of the right to fair trial on an equal basis with others.

The organisation which the respondents work in enhances the participation of persons with psychosocial disabilities in criminal proceedings and members of the organisation the respondents work in have no knowledge on rights and needs of persons with psychosocial disabilities

The results established that 17.1% of the respondents strongly disagreed and 43.9% disagreed that members of the organisation they work in have no knowledge on rights and needs of persons with psychosocial disabilities. While 26.8% were neutral, only 9.8% of the respondent agreed and 2.4% strongly agreed. The overall analysis shows that most of the respondents believe that

15 As above.

the members of their respective organisations have knowledge on the rights of persons with psychosocial disabilities. However, the results also established that only 41.5% of the respondents agreed that the organisation, which they work in enhances the participation of persons with psychosocial disabilities in criminal proceedings. The overall analysis shows that most of the respondents are either neutral or do not believe that the organisation they work in enhances the rights of persons with psychosocial disabilities.

Judicial officers should make the decision whether an accused person is fit to participate

The control of unfitness declarations by justice system actors was revealed during the study. Majority of the respondents (48.8%) agreed that judicial officers should make the decision whether an accused person is fit to participate. Only 4.9% of the respondents remained neutral, while another 46.3% disagreed. The findings reflect Foucault's position that unfitness declaration laws are strategies of power used by justice system actors and those with influence over the state's lawmaking processes to influence the thoughts, actions and, well-being of persons with psychosocial disabilities.[16] It means that unfitness declaration systems are created and maintained by legal technocrats who are guided by norms of their profession rather than their wider culture.[17]

Judicial officers should involve, inform and consult persons with psychosocial disabilities before declaring them unfit

The majority, 43.9% of the respondents strongly agreed that judicial officers should involve, inform, and consult persons with psychosocial disabilities before declaring them unfit while 36.6% agreed. Only, 7.3% were neutral, 4.9% disagreed and 7.3% strongly disagreed. From the analysis, it can be concluded that there is need to involve, inform and consult persons with psychosocial disabilities before declaring them unfit. In the FGD session with defence counsels, the phrase 'ask the person' (ATP) was articulated. This includes encouraging justice actors to relinquish control and to rely on autonomy and self-responsibility. One defence counsel said,

> When I am doing disability rights advocacy I use the abbreviation ATP . . . which is a short form of saying ask the person . . . persons with mental or psychosocial disabilities . . . are usually triggered by the environment around them . . . so the person with the psychosocial disabilities even before an assessment is conducted on them . . . they should be

16 N James 'Law and power: ten lessons from Foucault' (2018) 30 *Bond Law Review* 39.

17 MA Edwards 'The alignment of law and norms: of mirrors, bulwarks, and pressure valves' (2015) 10 *Faculty Scholarship* 23.

> asked whether . . . they are able to participate in that . . . set up . . . and even whether there is anything that can be done to make their participation comfortable.[18]

These findings dovetail with the decolonial theory's concept of relational decolonisation, which emphasises interdependence between non-disabled persons and persons with psychosocial disabilities.[19] The implication of this is that justice actors are willing to protect and ensure the right of persons with psychosocial disabilities of participation in access to justice. This means that a large number of justice actors who participated in the empirical component of the study believe that persons with psychosocial disabilities are capable of making decisions with appropriate support.

It is essential for justice actors to allow persons with psychosocial disabilities and provide them with the opportunity to speak for themselves when they choose to do so. Accordingly, in the justice system, states must provide the accommodations that are necessary to afford this opportunity. The controlling approach to advocacy should be to advance what the individual chooses, not what someone else decides is in the person's best interest. Likewise, tribunals should afford individuals every opportunity to present their own accounts and, where applicable, their own preferences. In reaching decisions in matters in which the individual's wishes are a factor, for example, whether to testify or not, fact finders should afford the individual's preference the strongest, even controlling, weight.

The 'ask the person' attitude is not common in Kenya's criminal justice sector, even during trials. Nevertheless, the 'ask the person' attitude is important for pragmatic reasons. There are situations, where persons with psychosocial disabilities may be willing to participate. In such instances, participation should be based on the person's needs. However, where persons with psychosocial disabilities are not able to express their needs, the court ought to find alternatives, beyond reasonable accommodation to ensure their participation in access to justice as discussed in Chapter 5. All criminal processes should be geared to the perspective of what the person, acting on his or her own behalf or through his or her representatives needs in order to participate. Based on this idea, participation should be implemented in all criminal processes. In certain instances, participation should be allowed with the adoption of the necessary support structures.

Experts should involve, inform and consult persons with psychosocial disabilities when preparing mental assessment reports

The results showed that 67.9% of those interviewed strongly agreed that experts should involve, inform, and consult persons with psychosocial disabilities when preparing mental assessment reports. A further 29.3% of the

18 FGD with defence counsels on 29 March 2022.

19 M Amuyunzu-Nyamongo 'The social and cultural aspects of mental health in African societies' (2013) 63 *Commonwealth Health Partnerships* 62.

population agreed. Only 2.4% remained neutral. Those strongly disagreeing with the position were 2.4%. Overall, there was consensus that experts should involve, inform, and consult persons with psychosocial disabilities when preparing mental assessment reports. A participant in the FGD sessions said that

> in most cases they [mental assessment reports] do not conform with views or the opinion of the person with the mental or psychosocial disability . . . who . . . are people who you can have conversation with . . . And some even know the form of accommodation that they would like for instance they would like someone who is close to them.[20]

Therefore, when conducting mental assessments, a holistic approach needs to be undertaken, taking into account a wide range of information, including medical opinion and variety of other circumstances.[21] This was the holding in *Chauke v The State (Chauke)*.[22]

In *Chauke,* the Supreme Court of Appeal held that the mental assessment report should include the previous psychiatric reports of the accused. Interviews should be conducted not only with the accused but also with any other person who can provide relevant information. The psychiatrist and psychologist if appointed, has to provide the court with reports and can be called to testify, in which case they will have to testify as expert witnesses. The witness should not express an opinion on hypothetical facts which have no bearing on the case or which cannot be reconciled with all the other evidence in the case. In short, expert witnesses should support their opinions with valid reasons.[23]

Ethical professional practice also requires experts to be mindful of appropriate accommodations during mental assessment processes.[24] According to Combrinck, functional tests of unfitness, which are solely based on mechanical, physical, and chemical factors and that are concerned more with the removal of legal capacity on account of limited decision-making ability of accused persons with psychosocial disabilities, are inconsistent with the provisions of the CRPD and should not be used.[25] As seen in Chapter 3, the process of mental assessment across the globe focuses largely on psychiatric symptoms

20 FGD with defence counsels on 29 March 2022.

21 *Kevin Kiprotich Amos alias Rotich v Republic* (2016) eKLR.

22 *Chauke v The State* (2015) ZASCA 181.

23 MC Van Hout & J Wessels 'Navigating the complexities of the mentally ill and mentally incapacitated in the criminal justice system in South Africa' (2021) 2 *Forensic Science International: Mind and Law* 3; FGD with prosecutors on 24 March 2022.

24 ME Wood et al. 'Reasonable accommodations for meeting the unique needs of defendants with intellectual disability' (2019) 47 *Journal of American Academy Psychiatry Law* 314.

25 H Combrinck 'Rather bad than mad? A reconsideration of criminal incapacity and psychosocial disability in South African law in light of the Convention on the Rights of Persons with Disabilities' (2018) 6 *African Disability Rights Yearbook* 23.

rather than concrete courtroom-related knowledge, leading individuals with expressive language deficits and impaired language comprehension to perform poorly on those instruments. In Kenya, it was revealed during the study that when conducting mental assessment tests, psychiatrists will consider the mental history of the person with psychosocial disability, ability to understand the charges, and assist in their own defence.[26] This confirmed that psychiatrists do not consider how persons with psychosocial disabilities should be accommodated in the criminal legal process in order to participate effectively in court. This book argues that doctors should be allowed to assess the individual needs of persons with psychosocial disabilities within the criminal justice system and make recommendations of appropriate accommodations.

Lack of support limits the participation of persons with psychosocial disabilities following unfitness declarations and persons with psychosocial disabilities have the right to participate effectively in access to justice if given appropriate support

The results showed that 61% of the respondents strongly agreed that lack of support limits the participation of persons with psychosocial disabilities following unfitness declarations. A further 34.1% of the respondents agreed while 2.4% of the respondents were neutral and another 2.4% disagreed. From the analysis, it can be concluded that there is a lack of support for persons with psychosocial disabilities in Kenya's criminal justice system.

Regarding the question on whether persons with psychosocial disabilities have the ability to participate effectively in access to justice if given appropriate support, 34.1% strongly agreed. A further 43.9% of the respondents agreed, 7.1% were neutral and only 4.9% disagreed strongly with this position. Overall, the respondents were satisfied that appropriate support would enhance the participation of persons with psychosocial disabilities in Kenya's justice sector.

To be able to stand trial, persons with psychosocial disabilities need both information that they can understand, together with adequate time, support, and teaching to assimilate and to understand the information.[27] Generally, the role of support persons in the process is to assist disabled persons and their presence can be of benefit in the whole process. One participant affirmed the need for support as follows:

> a better alternative would be to provide supported participation . . . for the persons with psychosocial disabilities to mean that if the court considered a person has psychosocial disabilities . . . who is incapable to some extent to participate in the process then they should provide

26 FGD with psychiatrists on 21 April 2022.

27 NSW Law Reform Commission 'People with an intellectual disability and the criminal justice system' Sydney (1996) 17.

> means for the person to get supported . . . decision making that's what I mean. Having someone else who is capable to support them in the court processes.[28]

Providing appropriate support tailored to the needs of persons with psychosocial disabilities will not only facilitate their participation in decision-making but will also help them exercise their legal capacity.[29] Professionals in the judicial system should be trained by disability practitioners to accommodate the needs of persons with psychosocial disabilities. Staff may need to learn how to make reasonable adjustments to aid persons with psychosocial disabilities.

The exact role of the support person should be flexible, with the court giving directions regulating the conduct of a person providing support to a witness. Regulations can specify, without limiting, the role of the support person. Support persons may relay and translate information between the court and the person with psychosocial disability.[30] However, they not only facilitate understanding and communication but also they enhance the quality of the process and participation of persons with psychosocial disabilities.[31] The use of support persons can eliminate any perceived difficulty in communication between lawyers and disabled clients from an early stage.[32] Naturally, the support person should sit near the witness in order to calm him or her and help the person understand the criminal process.[33] They assist in clarifying the wishes of disabled persons and giving them emotional support, as well as giving practical guidance to the lawyer during trial. Support persons can also assist the witness psychosocially during the proceedings, reduce his or her anxiety, and inspire confidence and reassurance. However, support persons cannot assist in facilitating the communication of the evidence of accused persons with psychosocial disabilities, particularly in the face of what can sometimes be confusing and difficult questions on the stand.[34] Support persons may include a family member, close friend who is familiar with the disabled person, or an advocacy service, either provided by state or by peer support group.[35]

Justice actors need to work with Disabled Persons Organisations (DPOs) in order to ensure the right support is given to persons with psychosocial disabilities in the criminal justice system. Often, the person who is best able

28 FGD with defence counsels on 29 March 2022.

29 N Clarke et al. 'Going to pot: Nick's journey through the criminal justice system' In E Flynn et al. (eds) *Global perspectives on legal capacity reform our voices, our stories* (2020) 30.

30 Karras et al. (n 5) 135.

31 Disability Council of NSW *A question of justice: access to participation for people with disabilities in contact with the justice system* Sydney: Disability Council of NSW (2003) 105.

32 E Flynn et al. *Final report: access to justice of persons with disabilities* OHCR (2019) 18.

33 N BenZeev et al. 'The right of people with disabilities to legal justice: a view from Israel' in DN Bryen & J Bornam (eds) *Stop violence against people with disabilities! An international resource* (2014) 127.

34 B Janine & G Isabel 'Taking the stand: access to justice for witnesses with mental disabilities in sexual assault cases' (2012) 50 *Osgoode Hall Law Journal* 29.

35 Flynn et al. (n 32) 18.

to understand and communicate with a person with psychosocial disability is a family member, who does not have formal interpreting qualifications, and may have some real or perceived interest in the outcome of the matter.[36] Providing some independent check on the quality of the interpreting offered may be almost impossible, as would be training and accrediting appropriate interpreters. This scheme should be an integral part of the justice process, and procedures should be adapted to value their contribution and assistance so as to avoid unnecessary, prolonged, and expensive proceedings in future.[37]

Role of negative attitudes, social norms, and cultural norms in preventing the participation of persons with psychosocial disabilities following unfitness to plead declarations

Studies by Sahu and Sahu[38] and Ashagre[39] show that unfitness declarations are largely attributed to attitudinal and social factors. These factors may be emotions, beliefs, or behavioural tendencies, negative or positive, which are specific to one individual or society and directed towards persons with psychosocial disabilities.[40] The study revealed that most respondents attributed the causes of unfitness declarations to negative attitudes and cultural and social norms.[41] These results confirm Foucault's hypothesis that the exclusion of persons with psychosocial disabilities in justice processes is first naturalised by social norms before being encoded in law.

Particularly, the findings imply an inclination towards a negative outlook of psychosocial disability at least by legal professionals in Kenya's criminal justice sector. Negative attitudes by justice system actors often result in denying persons with psychosocial disabilities basic human and civil rights, which are afforded to other members of the community.[42] Attitudinal barriers cannot merely be overcome by laws. Personal decolonisation is needed to sustain the relationship between justice system actors and persons with psychosocial disabilities. The relationship should be based on equity, mutuality, reciprocity, and continuous contact. Interaction between persons with psychosocial disabilities and justice system actors is an effective method of influencing positive attitudes towards disability.[43] An honest relationship between the justice

36 New South Wales Law Reform Commission 'People with an intellectual disability and the criminal justice system' Sydney (1996) 168–169.

37 Disability Council of NSW (n 31) 105.

38 KK Sahu & S Sahu 'Attitudinal barrier experienced by people with disabilities' (2015) 1 *Disability Studies* 1.

39 A Ashagre 'Access to justice for PWDs in Civil Proceedings before the Federal Courts of Ethiopia: the law and practice' (2020) 14 *Mizan Law Review* 25.

40 Sahu & Sahu (n 38) 2.

41 See Table 7.11.

42 Sahu & Sahu (n 38) 1.

43 JRR Freer 'The tripartite intervention: breaking down attitudinal barriers in education' (2021) *Journal of Disability Studies in Education* 10.

system actors and persons with psychosocial disabilities can also greatly aid in providing accommodations that are satisfactory to both parties.

The involvement of persons with psychosocial disabilities in decision-making following unfitness declarations, whether they should be allowed to participate in criminal proceedings after being declared unfit and their ability to make decisions on their own

The results established that majority of the respondents (68.2%) agreed that persons with psychosocial disabilities are not involved in decision-making following unfitness declarations. Only about 31% of the respondents indicated that persons with psychosocial disabilities should be allowed to participate in criminal proceedings after being declared unfit. It means that a majority of the respondents support the non-participation in access to justice of persons with psychosocial disabilities following unfitness declarations. These findings illustrate the protectionist attitude of justice professionals towards persons with psychosocial disabilities as highlighted in Chapters 2, 3 and 4.

Justice system actors are reluctant for persons with psychosocial disabilities to participate in access to justice on account that they are unable to make their own decisions. The overall analysis shows that most of the respondents (51.2%) disagreed that persons with psychosocial disabilities have the ability to make decisions on their own. In discussing how persons with psychosocial disabilities are viewed in Kenya's criminal justice system, FGD participants said,

> We just treat them like . . . objects once you establish that somebody maybe is mentally ill. Nobody wants to come near them nobody wants to understand what they are going through.[44]
>
> When a person is considered or viewed as a person with psychosocial . . . disability then . . . they are automatically viewed or considered as lacking capacity to participate in the criminal justice system so that's one of the main barriers.[45]

The findings demonstrate how colonial unfitness declaration structures sustain itself through Kenya's justice system. The study exposed how justice actors are largely not ready or willing to cede space for persons with psychosocial disabilities to participate in access to justice. The findings are also a reflection of the Foucauldian perspective on institutional discourse and power as discussed in Chapter 2. According to Foucault, criminal justice institutions have their own discourse and there are power relations within the justice sector

44 FGD with prosecutors on 24 March 2022.
45 FGD with defence counsels on 29 March 2022.

involving the exertion of institutional power over persons with psychosocial disabilities.[46] The findings illustrate institutional control over persons with psychosocial disabilities' bodies and how institutional discourse and knowledge on decision-making reifies the incapacity of persons with psychosocial disabilities.

Whether persons with a history of mental problems and persons suffering from hallucinations are of unsound mind and should not be allowed to participate in criminal trials

The respondents were requested to give their opinion on whether persons with a history of mental problems are of unsound mind and should not be allowed to participate in a criminal trial. The results obtained indicate that 46.3% strongly disagreed, 46.3% disagreed, 2.4% were neutral, 2.4% disagreed whereas the remaining 2.4% strongly disagreed. The findings reveal that majority of the respondents believe that persons with a history of mental problems are not of unsound mind and should be allowed to participate in a criminal trial. The respondents' opinions were also sought to determine whether persons suffering from hallucinations are of unsound mind and should not be allowed to participate in criminal trials. Hallucinations may result from both psychosocial and intellectual disabilities.[47] The findings indicate that 34.1% strongly disagreed, 46.3% simply disagreed, 7.3% were neutral, and 12.2% agreed. The data reveal that majority of the respondents perceive that persons suffering from hallucinations should be allowed to participate in criminal trials.

The findings are aligned with the case of *Liebreich v Germany*48 where the Court held that a person with a history of depression and who is under medication should not be denied the right to participation in access to justice on account of treatment alone. In *Liebreich v Germany*, the appellant was charged with insurance fraud. After conviction he filed an appeal under article 6 of the European Convention, alleging that he had been unable to participate effectively due to the effects of antidepressant medication. The ECtHR declared this complaint inadmissible since the appellant had been represented by a lawyer with whom he could consult. Apart from that, there was information during the trial from the doctor treating the accused that he was fit enough to plead. Moreover, there was nothing, in the Court's opinion to indicate that the applicant, due to his history of depression and the effects of his medication, was unable to have a broad understanding of the trial process and unable to understand the consequences.

46 Wendy et al. (n 9) 102.

47 SL Griffiths et al. 'Vulnerability to psychosocial disability in psychosis' (2019) 28 *Epidemiology and Psychiatric Sciences* 140.

48 *Liebreich v Germany* (2009) ECtHR.

Table 7.12 Have you dealt with any matter involving persons with psychosocial disabilities in the last few years?

	Have you dealt with any matter involving persons with psychosocial disabilities in the last few years?				
		Frequency	*Percent*	*Valid percent*	*Cumulative percent*
Valid	No	5	12.2%	12.2%	12.2%
	Yes	36	87.8%	87.8%	100%
	Total	41	100%	100%	

The majority of the respondents stated that the decision to declare persons with psychosocial disabilities as unfit depended on the individual's conduct in court, nature of their disability and recommendation of the doctor. One reason for unfitness declaration according to one participant is because

> the suspect could . . . not really understand the trial process according to the psychiatrist . . . his mental condition was such that he could not fully participate. He was disoriented as . . . the psychiatrist put it . . . to such a level that he could not fully understand the process of the trial.[49]

Evidently, the path of unfitness declaration laws in Kenya follows the predilections and idiosyncrasies of justice actors.[50] From the results, it is clear that the judicial making decision is based on sanism. Sanist decision-makers use flawed ordinary common sense, heuristic reasoning, and biased stereotyping to justify their verdicts.[51] Persons with psychosocial disabilities may not receive a good outcome in court, particularly if they behave in a manner deemed to be inappropriate.[52] Symptoms of disorientation, impaired memory, poor judgement, and thought and communication disturbances have been associated with findings of unfitness.[53]

Similarly, other variables such as unemployed status and previous history of hospitalisations also pose a higher risk of being declared unfit.[54] Persons with psychosocial disabilities may also be excluded from courtrooms when

49 FGD with prosecutors on 24 March 2022.

50 B Leiter 'American legal realism' in MP Golding & WA Edmundson (eds) *Blackwell's guide to the philosophy of law and legal theory* (2004) 55.

51 K Gould 'And equal participation for all . . . the Americans with Disabilities Act in the courtroom' (1993–1994) 8 *Journal of Law & Health* 139.

52 Karras et al. (n 5) 143.

53 D Miller 'Dementia and competency in United States courtrooms: a case law review' https://academicworks.cuny.edu/cgi/viewcontent.cgi?article=1157&context=jj_etds (accessed 10 September 2021) 15.

54 As above.

they have difficulty conforming their behaviour to the set rules.[55] One participant said,

> most judicial officers are not trained . . . in . . . how to communicate effectively with persons with psychosocial disabilities . . . sometimes they may misread ques from a person with psychosocial disabilities for example if the person participates in the trial and in the cause of the trial occasionally they . . . get a bit stubborn or they make faces at a victim of their crime.[56]

Depending on the nature of their disabilities, they may lack internal control to avoid speaking out of turn, may use unacceptable terminology, or engage in other behaviour generally considered improper within the courtroom setting. Unfitness declaration procedures, which are rigid and insensitive to the conditions of persons with psychosocial disabilities always lead to their non-participation in access to justice. This may occur when judicial officers demand strict conformity with Kenya's unfitness declaration rules and procedures in the courtroom.[57]

7.2.7 Objective 2: impact of unfitness declaration

Questions from section 3 of the questionnaire were used to obtain the second objective, which is the impact of unfitness declaration. Various themes were identified in Table 7.13.

Whether unfitness declarations violate the right to participation for persons with psychosocial disabilities

On being asked whether unfitness declarations violate the right to participation for persons with psychosocial disabilities, the respondents responded as follows: 12.2% strongly agreed, 26.8% agreed, 22% were neutral, 22% disagreed, and 17.1% strongly disagreed. Overall, this question was left undecided as the respondents were evenly split on the question.

Whether unfitness declarations are based on the mental capacity of an accused person

When asked whether unfitness declarations are based on the mental capacity of an accused person, 87.8% of the respondents agreed. Only 7.3% of the respondents remained neutral while 4.8% disagreed. Evidently, unfitness declarations are based on the mental capacity of persons with psychosocial disabilities. In practice, unfitness declarations are determined after considering a

55 Gould (n 51) 140.
56 FGD with defense counsels on 29 March 2022.
57 Gould (n 51) 139.

Table 7.13 Impact of unfitness declaration

Item	*Strongly Disagree*	*Disagree*	*Neutral*	*Agree*	*Strongly Agree*
Unfitness declarations violate the right to participation for persons with psychosocial disabilities.	17.1%	22%	22%	26.8%	12.2%
Unfitness declarations are based on the mental capacity of an accused person.	2.4%	2.4%	7.3%	61%	26.8%
Unfitness declarations violate the right of persons with psychosocial disabilities to legal capacity.	14.6%	34.1%	12.2%	26.8%	12.2%
Unfitness declarations constitute a barrier to the effective participation of persons with psychosocial disabilities.	12.5%	20%	12.5%	35%	20%
Unfitness declarations violate the accused person's right to be heard.	12.5%	27.5%	12.5%	32.5%	15%
The law on unfitness declarations should be reformed.	2.4%	2.4%	12.2%	36.6%	46.3%
Legal aid enhances the participation of persons with psychosocial disabilities.	2.4%	4.9%	0%	39%	53.7%
Diversion will enhance the participation of persons with psychosocial disabilities in access to justice.	0%	7.3%	4.9%	29.3%	58.5%
Alternative Dispute Resolution (ADR) will enhance the participation of persons with psychosocial disabilities.	0%	2.4%	9.8%	31.7%	56.1%
Procedural accommodations will enhance the participation of persons with psychosocial disabilities.	0%	0%	9.8%	43.9%	46.3%
Assistive technology enhances the participation of persons with psychosocial disabilities.	0%	0%	19.5%	36.6%	43.9%

person's mental capacity through the use of long and complex questions that are put to them or their caregivers.[58] A person's mental history is frequently a pretext to deny the person the same rights of access and participation in the

58 As above.

justice sector. These criterial are very subjective and may reflect the biases of the examiner more than the abilities of the person with psychosocial disability. The fact that an accused has a psychosocial disability is simply a circumstance to be considered in connection with not only other relevant evidence but also reasonable accommodation in determining whether he or she is unfit.

An argument raised during the empirical study related to persons with psychosocial disabilities with borderline cases, meaning that the degree of their understanding is such that they are neither fit nor unfit to plead.[59] Doubts emerged regarding whether it is feasible to simply declare one group of persons fit and another unfit with legal certainty. To simply assume that this is the position is not correct and may be discriminatory to persons who do not fall in either category. Challenges are likely to occur in cases involving persons who do not fall in either category. To prevent any violations of persons with psychosocial disabilities who fall under this category, participants agreed that they could be referred to a committee of experts involving lawyers, social workers, criminologists, sociologists, and psychiatrists in order to determine how their rights could be ensured in the criminal justice system. It should not be an option to be applied at the whim of the doctors alone. One legal commentator cautioned against the likelihood of doctors misunderstanding the extent, limitations, and legal effect of judicial declarations such as unfitness when they are being applied, interpreted, or altered under the aegis of the law.[60] Accordingly, many groups of experts should be allowed to make contributions on unfitness declarations enquiries beyond the particular expertise of psychiatrists. Currently there are no guidelines on unfitness declaration enquiries. Consequently, there is need for the state to formulate guidelines on procedure based on persons with psychosocial disabilities who have limited understanding of the criminal process.[61]

Whether unfitness declarations violate the right of persons with psychosocial disabilities to legal capacity?

The findings left a large discrepancy in the understanding of mental and legal capacity. The respondents, after agreeing that unfitness declarations are based on mental capacity, denied that they violate the right to legal capacity of persons with psychosocial disabilities. As per Table 7.13, when asked whether unfitness declarations violate the right of persons with psychosocial disabilities to legal capacity, 12.2% strongly agreed, 26.8% agreed, 12.2% remained neutral, 34.1% disagreed and 14.6% strongly disagreed. It means that a majority

59 FGD with psychiatrists on 21 April 2022.

60 JD Ball & AM Kidd 'The relation of law and medicine in mental disease' (1920) 9 *California Law Review* 14.

61 As above.

did not view unfitness declaration as a violation of the right to legal capacity of persons with psychosocial disabilities. However, according to article 12 of the CRPD, unfitness declarations violate the right to legal capacity of persons with psychosocial disabilities because they are based on their mental capacity, which then goes to constrain their participation in access to justice.

Mental capacity merely refers to a person's ability to make decisions and it has nothing to do with legal capacity which is the power of people to act upon their rights. Therefore, I argue that any legal restrictions, such as unfitness declarations that are based on the mental capacity of persons with psychosocial disabilities, cannot be considered to be promoting the right to participation of persons with psychosocial disabilities in access to justice. The ambivalence in the findings could be attributed to a lack of training on disability rights by the respondents. Lack of knowledge of disability rights on the part of justice actors is an impediment in the protection of the rights of persons with psychosocial disabilities. According to the CRPD Committee, lack of knowledge of disability issues in the justice sector is a key barrier to the right of participation in access to justice for persons with psychosocial disabilities which is compounded by practitioners inadvertently or explicitly failing to consult appropriately.[62]

Whether unfitness declarations constitute a barrier to the effective participation of persons with psychosocial disabilities and violate accused person's right to be heard

The respondents were requested to give their views on whether unfitness declarations constitute a barrier to the effective participation of persons with psychosocial disabilities. The results indicate that 20% strongly agreed, 35% agreed, 12.5% were neutral, 20% disagreed and the rest 12.5% strongly disagreed. The above analysis shows that majority of the respondents believe that unfitness declarations constitute a barrier to the right to participation of persons with psychosocial disabilities.

On whether unfitness declarations violate the accused person's right to be heard, 15% strongly agreed, 32.5% agreed, 27.5% disagreed whereas 12.5% strongly disagreed. 12.5% of the respondents were neutral. The responses recorded above indicate that a majority of the respondents are of the opinion that unfitness declarations violate the right to be heard of persons with psychosocial disabilities.

62 CRPD Committee 'Concluding observations on the initial report of the former Yugoslav Republic of Macedonia' UN Doc CRPD/C/MKD/CO/1 (29 October 2018) para 23; CRPD Committee 'Concluding observations on the initial report of Senegal' CRPD/C/SEN/CO/1 (13 May 2019) para 23; CRPD Committee 'Concluding observations on the initial report of Vanuatu' CRPD/C/VUT/CO/1 (13 May 2019) para 24; and CRPD Committee 'Concluding observations on the initial report of Oman' CRPD/C/OMN/CO/1 (17 April 2018) para 27.

Whether the law on unfitness declarations should be reformed

The respondents were asked to give their views on whether the law on unfitness declarations should be reformed. 46.3% strongly agreed, 36.6% agreed, 12.2% were neutral, whereas 2.4% disagreed and strongly disagreed respectively. None of the respondents disagreed with the statement. This analysis indicate that majority of the respondents were of the view that the law on unfitness declarations should be reformed.

The findings reveal the importance of Foucault's counter-conduct ideology against unfitness declarations. Resistance should be applied not just to criminal justice institutions or unjust relationships, but also to the ways in which unfitness declarations inequalities are rationalised. It is important to identify and resist underlying logics of the oppressive unfitness declaration systems.[63] However, oppressive relationships can persist despite seemingly positive institutional reform.[64] Therefore, fairness to accused persons with psychosocial disabilities is important and must be balanced against the interests of the victim and the society.[65]

Whether legal aid enhances the participation of persons with psychosocial disabilities

Lack of free legal aid also inhibits the rights of effective participation for persons with psychosocial disabilities in access to justice. The responses on whether legal aid enhances the participation of persons with psychosocial disabilities indicate that 53.7% strongly agreed, 39% agreed, none were neutral, 4.9% disagreed, and 2.4% strongly disagreed. The findings reveal that majority of the respondents believe that legal aid can enhance the participation of persons with psychosocial disabilities. Therefore, persons with psychosocial disabilities who have challenges expressing themselves and understanding the proceedings should be afforded the aid of a legal representative who can assist by explaining events, advocating, and ensuring the person makes it through the legal process.[66]

Representation by counsel is sometimes the most powerful tool for making the available remedies responsive to an individual's needs. One participant stated that 'the inability to afford basic legal services can hinder . . . access to justice' thus the need to 'have sufficient legal provision to ensure that these individuals are represented'.[67] The CRPD has not explicitly provided for the

63 M Foucault 'Omnes et singulatim: towards a criticism of "political reason"' (1981) 2 *The Tanner Lectures on Human Values* 254.

64 A Aylett 'Participatory planning, justice, and climate change in Durban, South Africa' (2000) 42 *Environment and Planning* 103.

65 P Bowden et al. 'Balancing fairness to victims, society and defendants in the cross-examination of vulnerable witnesses: an impossible triangulation?' (2014) 37 *Melbourne Law Review* 539.

66 Karras et al. (n 5) 142.

67 FGD with NGO members on 19 April 2022.

right to legal assistance or representation. However, meaningful participation requires that individuals have access to legal representation in order to fulfil their right of access to justice.[68] Moreover, the right to equality before the law and a fair trial is well established in human rights law and it includes the right to legal representation.[69] Building on the general framework of the CRPD to ensure for non-discrimination and equality by providing accommodations, the right to legal representation is clearly included under article 13,[70] and it includes the right to access free legal aid.[71] States are expected to take active measures to ensure equal access to justice systems by setting up legal aid schemes amongst other steps.[72]

However, the mere fact that an accused person with psychosocial disability is represented by skilled lawyers is not enough if it is difficult for him or her to participate effectively during the trial due to the formal nature of the process or the high public interest surrounding the case as was held in *T v United Kingdom* and *V v United Kingdom*.[73] T and V were tried and convicted of the murder and abduction of a two-year-old boy. During the trial, the procedure was modified to a certain extent in view of the accused persons' age. They were found guilty and they appealed to the ECtHR. In their appeal, they argued that they had been denied their fair trial rights under article 6 of the European Convention, because in the light of their youth, immaturity, and state of emotional disturbance, they had not been able to participate effectively in the trial against them. During the trial, evidence was adduced to show that T suffered from a post-traumatic stress disorder following the events of the offence, which limited his ability to instruct his lawyers and to adequately testify in his own defence.

On the part of V, there was psychiatric evidence during the trial that he functioned emotionally at far younger than his chronological age and that he suffered from post-traumatic stress disorder. He was also not able to give informed instruction to his lawyers. The ECtHR concluded in both cases that the applicants had been deprived of their right to a fair trial since they were

68 JA Bamberger 'Confirming the constitutional right of meaningful access to the courts in non-criminal cases in Washington State' (2005) 4 *Seattle Journal for Social Justice* 383.

69 International Covenant on Civil and Political Rights, arts 2, 3, 14, 26; see Human Rights Committee, General Comment 32 (2007) on the right to equality before courts and tribunals and to a fair trial. European Convention on Human Rights, art 6; African Charter on Human and Peoples' Rights, art 7; American Convention on Human Rights, art 8.

70 Human Rights Council 'Access to justice in the promotion and protection of the rights of indigenous peoples: restorative justice, indigenous juridical systems and access to justice for indigenous women, children and youth and persons with disabilities: study by the expert mechanism on the rights of indigenous peoples' (7 August 2014) A/HRC/27/65 para 62.

71 Human Rights Council *Right to access to justice under article 13 of the Convention on the Rights of Persons with Disabilities* Report of the Office of the High Commissioner for Human Rights (2017) para 40.

72 Flynn et al. (n 32) 16.

73 *T v United Kingdom* and *V v United Kingdom* (2000) ECtHR, 121.

not able to participate effectively in the criminal proceedings against them. The Court stated that in cases involving children, it is essential for them to be dealt with in a manner, which takes full account of their age, level of maturity and intellectual and emotional capacities. Furthermore, their immaturity and disturbed emotional state inhibited their capacity of co-operating with their lawyers and limited their ability to furnish them with information to use for their defence.

Whether diversion from formal criminal justice processes will enhance the participation of persons with psychosocial disabilities in access to justice?

The respondents' views on whether diversion from formal criminal justice processes will enhance the participation of persons with psychosocial disabilities in access to justice indicate that a majority represented by 58.5% strongly agreed, 29.3% agreed, 4.9% were neutral and 7.3% disagreed. None of the respondents strongly disagreed to the statement. The results affirm that diversion can enhance the participation of persons with psychosocial disabilities.

Generally, the characteristics of the diversion approach in Africa include the appointment of assessors during the trial, correctional supervision, and the use of special courts, such as family courts, employment courts, land courts, environmental courts, and customary courts.[74] One participant stated that

> we can introduce special courts within our judicial system . . . if you look in the case of Australia. They have established . . . special courts that try persons with mental illnesses. So, if people can bench mark and introduce the same within our justice system . . . it could be helpful.[75]

Examples of diversionary special courts for persons with psychosocial disabilities around the globe are the Drug Treatment Courts (DTC) and Mental Health Courts (MHC).[76] DTCs respond to drug offenders and their tendency to recycle through the criminal justice and treatment systems by affording them opportunities for personal growth and eventual sobriety. DTCs regard the cause of criminal behaviour in addicts to be addiction, which is considered a chronic brain disease that promotes or intensifies criminal behaviour.

MHCs are created to resolve three critical problems: The perceived public health risk posed by persons with psychosocial disabilities, the challenges and costs of housing persons with psychosocial disabilities in crowded local jails, and the criminal justice system's pervasive inability to respond effectively and

74 E Fourie 'Constitutional values, therapeutic jurisprudence and legal education in South Africa: Shaping our legal order' (2016) 19 *PER/PELJ* 5.

75 FGD with prosecutors on 24 March 2022.

76 DJ Farole et al. 'Applying problem-solving principles in mainstream courts: lessons for state courts' (2005) 26 *The Justice System Journal* 202.

humanely to persons with psychosocial disabilities.[77] The goal of MHCs is to divert persons with psychosocial disabilities away from the criminal justice system and into the mental health treatment system. Diversions may involve the use of mandated community-based treatment as a condition of programme participation; direct court supervision of clients, including attendance at regular status hearings in the court; and rewards and sanctions to encourage compliance with court mandates.

To be eligible for participation in MHCs, defendants must have an identifiable mental disability. Participation may be allowed in cases where the accused person's mental disability contributed directly to the offence for which they are being accused of, their availability for treatment, or the treatability of the accused person and willingness to take medication as part of the treatment plan. The type of offence committed may also be a guide for participation eligibility.[78] The failure of Kenya's laws to adequately spell out the unfitness declaration procedures and the conduct of mental assessments tests in court has resulted in a haphazard, ineffectual patchwork of safeguards. As shown in Chapter 4, unfitness declarations have yielded disparate and unreliable outcomes in the participation of persons with psychosocial disabilities in access to justice.

ADR will enhance the participation of persons with psychosocial disabilities

Unlike court process, which impose unfitness declarations systems on persons with psychosocial disabilities, ADR processes are free of disability related-verdicts and offer better opportunities for persons with psychosocial disabilities of participating and feeling involved.[79] The respondents gave their views on the statement ADR will enhance the participation of persons with psychosocial disabilities. The results obtained indicate that majority represented by 56.1% strongly agreed, 31.7% agreed, and 9.8% were neutral. 2.4% of the respondents disagreed. The results affirm that ADR has the potential of enhancing the right of persons with psychosocial disabilities of access to justice.

ADR mechanisms that emphasises human rights and person-centredness will enhance the participation of persons with psychosocial disabilities in access to justice.[80] ADR mechanisms involves the use of third-party authorities in dispute resolutions. Kenya's criminal justice system is not 'psychosocial-disability-friendly', in the sense that the court structure, procedures, and communication styles are all geared towards higher functioning witnesses, and are quite intimidating to persons with psychosocial disabilities and other vulnerable witnesses. ADR and traditional mechanisms aim to support conflict resolution at the local level and enhances access to justice by

77 Farole (n 76) 202.
78 Farole (n 76) 206.
79 Karras et al. (n 5) 139.
80 See Table 7.13.

improving the formal system.[81] ADR mechanisms should focus on voice, destigmatisation, and meaningful processes and outcomes in accordance section 12 of the CRPD. However, ADR mechanisms should not be used to coerce persons with psychosocial disabilities to admit to treatment. Although keeping persons with psychosocial disabilities out of the criminal justice system also keeps them out of the unfitness declaration process, there is a risk that they can become a vehicle for involuntary services and treatment.

Whether procedural accommodations will enhance the participation of persons with psychosocial disabilities

Unfitness declaration procedures should avoid stigmatising or marginalising persons with psychosocial disabilities.[82] The analysis recorded in Table 7.13 above on whether procedural accommodations will enhance the participation of persons with psychosocial disabilities indicates that majority of the respondents represented by 46.3% strongly agreed and 43.9% agreed. Only 9.8% were neutral. None of the respondents disagreed to the statement. These results are in line with Flynn's views that procedural accommodations can enhance the participation of persons with psychosocial disabilities in the justice system.[83]

Arguably, procedural accommodations may enhance the participation of persons with psychosocial disabilities. A participant said, 'I would propose that . . . we should come up with comprehensive guidelines touching on persons with mental . . . illnesses that . . . will enable us fast track their cases'.[84] The Supreme Court of Washington in *State v Ortiz-Abrego* also determined that courts may

> accommodate the needs of a particular defendant by modifying trial schedules and day-to-day courtroom procedures to make the proceedings more accessible to a party. Such accommodations, when appropriate, are permissible exercises of judicial discretion – but are distinct from the legal analysis of competency to stand trial.[85]

During the study, participants also agreed that the use of simple language, diagrams, visual aids, and pictures should be at the discretion of judicial officers.[86]

Courts should be granted the power to control the conduct of the questioning of accused persons with psychosocial disabilities. The law should allow

81 PK Mbote & M Akech *Kenya: justice sector and the rule of law* (2011) 175.
82 L Kennedy & D Tait *Court perspectives: architecture, psychology and Western Australian Law Reform* Western Australian Law Reform Commission, 1048.
83 E Flynn *Disabled justice? Access to justice and the UN Convention on the Rights of Persons with Disabilities* (2016) 16.
84 FGD with prosecutors on 24 March 2022.
85 *State v Ortiz-Abrego* (2017) 387 P3d 638.
86 FGD with psychiatrists on 21 April 2022.

for questioning of accused persons with psychosocial disabilities to be done through caregivers who will relay information to the accused and the court simultaneously.[87] A participant stated that 'the court may also consider repeated evidence given in different forms depending on the capacity of the individual to communicate to recall and . . . to express themselves coherently'.[88] Alternatively, accused persons with psychosocial disabilities should be accorded the right to make statements that are not subject to any questions. Out-of-court statements should also be admissible in court as truth of their contents without the witness being available for any questioning.[89] This is particularly important where an accused person with psychosocial disabilities has been declared unfit due to lack of understanding on his or her part.

The Court should also have sufficient procedural flexibility to change seating arrangements or move premises during a hearing, if necessary. The law should allow for mobile courts in order to enhance the participation in access to justice of persons with psychosocial disabilities who cannot leave their homes or who are currently residing in hospitals/institutions. One participant said,

> someone might have some reactions in court which would make them or as a result of which they would be considered as unfit . . . yet may be . . . they are afraid of the court seat . . . or the fact that there are so many people formally dressed in that room . . . Sometimes they can be able to speak in court but it is because there are so many people in court . . . So maybe they . . . proceed in camera . . . or participate in . . . environment which they are used to . . . for instance at homes or places around where they stay . . . because . . . they . . . become anxious . . . when they get to different settings like that of a court set up.[90]

The use of such special measures may reduce the trauma of giving evidence in court. However, it has been noted that the elimination of trauma may remove the distress, which may be perceived as supporting the veracity of the witness's evidence.[91]

Whether assistive technology enhances the participation of persons with psychosocial disabilities?

On whether assistive technology enhances the participation of persons with psychosocial disabilities, 43.9% strongly agreed, 36.6% agreed and 19.5% were neutral. None of the respondents disagreed to the statement. The above

87 As above.
88 FGD with NGO members on 19 April 2022.
89 Bowden et al. (n 65) 569.
90 FGD with defense counsels on 29 March 2022.
91 J Cashmore *The use of closed-circuit television for child witnesses in the ACT* (Children's Evidence Research Paper 1, Australian Law Reform Commission, 1992) (ALRC RP1) 62.

data reveal that majority of the respondents believe that assistive technology enhances the participation of persons with psychosocial disabilities in Kenya's criminal justice system. There are various assistive technologies that cater for the special needs of persons with psychosocial disabilities, including access to justice in criminal proceedings. Assistive technology is a broad term that encompasses items, pieces of equipment, or product systems, whether acquired commercially, modified, or customised, that may be used to increase, maintain, or improve functional capabilities of persons with psychosocial disabilities.[92]

Assistive technology enables and promotes the inclusion, participation, and engagement of persons with disabilities. Their aim is to facilitate communication between justice actors and persons with psychosocial disabilities.[93] A participant in the FGD session stated that

> I have never known how to deal or speak to such a person . . . I think it is important for key justice actors to also know how to communicate with some of this people . . . To know how to communicate with them so that once you establish somebody maybe has mental issues the next thing you should do is to see how you can seek help.[94]
>
> Nowadays courts are . . . fitted with communication devices . . . but not all courts . . . there is still a long way to go . . . but . . . the judiciary is doing something to . . . foster communication of this people during their trials.[95]

Article 2 of the CRPD, defines communication to include alternative ways of expressively communicating as opposed to speech or *viva voce*. Barriers affect persons with psychosocial disabilities differently and as such there is need for considering various factors, both individual and environmental before deciding on the assistive technology method to use depending on their communication output.[96]

7.3 Conclusion

The results of the quantitative and qualitative research revealed that social, cultural, and attitudinal factors shape the attitudes about psychosocial disability and unfitness declarations in Kenya's criminal justice sector. The study reflects

92 PH Wise 'Emerging technologies and their impact on disability. The future of children' https://www.researchgate.net/publication/224886619_Wise_P_H_Emerging_technologies_and_their_impact_on_disability_Future_Child_22_169-191 (accessed 23 February 2022) 173.

93 D Jonathan & D Lauran 'Non-verbal victims in the adversarial criminal process: Communication, competency, and credibility' https://shura.shu.ac.uk/18482/3/Doak-NonverbalVictmsintheAdversarialCriminalProcess%28AM%29.pdf (accessed 21 August 2021) 4.

94 FGD with prosecutors on 24 March 2022.

95 FGD with defence counsels on 29 March 2022.

96 Jonathan & Lauran (n 93) 4.

the discussions on the barriers that inhibit the participation of persons with psychosocial disabilities in Chapter 4, which exposed the substantial shortcomings in Kenya's unfitness declaration laws and its failure to adequately protect the rights of persons with psychosocial disabilities. The study also revealed that most respondents believed that persons with psychosocial disabilities have the right of access to justice in participation. The need for legal reforms whose aim is to decolonise the structure of Kenya's justice system was highlighted in this study. It was shown that provisions of support, legal aid, diversion, and alternative dispute resolution mechanisms would enhance the participation of persons with psychosocial disabilities in access to justice. Arguably, provision of reasonable accommodation is a viable way for enhancing the legal capacity of persons with psychosocial disabilities in Kenya's criminal justice system. The next chapter compares reform approaches to the decolonisation of unfitness declaration laws in selected jurisdictions across the globe.

References

African Charter on Human and Peoples' Rights, 27 June 1981, OAU Doc. CAB/LEG/67/3/Rev.5 (1981) (entered into force on 21 October 1986).

American Convention for the Protection of Human Rights, OAS TS No 36 at 1 OAS Doc OEA/ser L/V/II 23 Doc 21 rev 6 (entered into force on 8 July 1978).

Amuyunzu-Nyamongo M 'The social and cultural aspects of mental health in African societies' (2013) 63 *Commonwealth Health Partnerships* 62.

Ashagre A 'Access to justice for PWDs in Civil Proceedings before the Federal Courts of Ethiopia: the law and practice' (2020) 14 *Mizan Law Review* 25.

Aylett A 'Participatory planning, justice, and climate change in Durban, South Africa' (2000) 42 *Environment and Planning* 103. https://doi.org/10.1068/a4274.

Ball JD & Kidd Am 'The relation of law and medicine in mental disease' (1920) 9 *California Law Review* 14.

Bamberger JA 'Confirming the constitutional right of meaningful access to the courts in non-criminal cases in Washington State' (2005) 4 *Seattle Journal for Social Justice* 383.

BenZeev N et al. 'The right of people with disabilities to legal justice: a view from Israel' in Bryen DN & Bornam J (eds) *Stop violence against people with disabilities! An international resource* (2014) 127.

Bowden P et al. 'Balancing fairness to victims, society and defendants in the cross-examination of vulnerable witnesses: an impossible triangulation?' (2014) 37 *Melbourne Law Review* 539.

Cashmore J *The use of closed-circuit television for child witnesses in the ACT* (Children's Evidence Research Paper 1, Australian Law Reform Commission, 1992) (ALRC RP1).

Chauke v The State (2015) ZASCA 181.

Clarke N et al. 'Going to pot: nick's journey through the criminal justice system' in Flynn E et al. (eds) *Global perspectives on legal capacity reform our voices, our stories* (2020) 30.

Combrinck H 'Rather bad than mad? A reconsideration of criminal incapacity and psychosocial disability in South African law in light of the Convention on the Rights of Persons with Disabilities' (2018) 6 *African Disability Rights Yearbook* 23. https://doi.org/10.29053/2413-7138/2018/v6a1.

CRPD Committee 'Concluding observations on the initial report of Oman' CRPD/C/OMN/CO/1 (17 April 2018).

CRPD Committee 'Concluding observations on the initial report of Senegal' CRPD/C/SEN/CO/1 (13 May 2019).

CRPD Committee 'Concluding observations on the initial report of the former Yugoslav Republic of Macedonia' UN Doc CRPD/C/MKD/CO/1 (29 October 2018).

CRPD Committee 'Concluding observations on the initial report of Vanuatu' CRPD/C/VUT/CO/1 (13 May 2019).

Disability Council of NSW *A question of justice: access to participation for people with disabilities in contact with the justice system* Sydney: Disability Council of NSW (2003).

Edwards MA 'The alignment of law and norms: of mirrors, bulwarks, and pressure valves' (2015) 10 *Faculty Scholarship* 23.

European Convention for the Protection of Human Rights and Fundamental Freedoms (ECHR), 213 UNTS (entered into force on 3/09/1953).

Farole DJ et al. 'Applying problem-solving principles in mainstream courts: lessons for state courts' (2005) 26 *The Justice System Journal* 202.

Flynn E *Disabled justice? Access to justice and the UN Convention on the Rights of Persons with Disabilities* (2016).

Flynn E et al. *Final report: access to justice of persons with disabilities* OHCR (2019).

Foucault M 'Omnes et singulatim: towards a criticism of "political reason"' (1981) 2 *The Tanner Lectures on Human Values* 254.

Fourie E 'Constitutional values, therapeutic jurisprudence and legal education in South Africa: shaping our legal order' (2016) 19 *PER/PELJ* 5. https://doi.org/10.17159/1727-3781/2016/v19i0a732.

Freer JRR 'The tripartite intervention: breaking down attitudinal barriers in education' (2021) *Journal of Disability Studies in Education* 10. https://doi.org/10.1163/25888803-bja10006.

Gould K 'And equal participation for all . . . The Americans with Disabilities Act in the courtroom' (1993–1994) 8 *Journal of Law and Health* 139.

Griffiths SL et al. 'Vulnerability to psychosocial disability in psychosis' (2019) 28 *Epidemiology and Psychiatric Sciences* 140. https://doi.org/10.1017/S2045796018000495.

Human Rights Committee 'General Comment No 32 (2007) on the right to equality before courts and tribunals and to a fair trial'.

Human Rights Council 'Access to justice in the promotion and protection of the rights of indigenous peoples: restorative justice, indigenous juridical systems and access to justice for indigenous women, children and youth and persons with disabilities: study by the expert mechanism on the rights of indigenous peoples' (7 August 2014) A/HRC/27/65.

Human Rights Council *Right to access to justice under article 13 of the Convention on the Rights of Persons with Disabilities* Report of the Office of the High Commissioner for Human Rights (2017).

International Covenant on Civil and Political Rights (adopted 16 December 1966, entered into force on 23 March 1976) 999 UNTS 171 (ICCPR).

James N 'Law and power: ten lessons from Foucault' (2018) 30 *Bond Law Review* 39. https://doi.org/10.53300/001c.5658.

Janine B & Isabel G 'Taking the stand: access to justice for witnesses with mental disabilities in sexual assault cases' (2012) 50 *Osgoode Hall Law Journal* 29. https://doi.org/10.60082/2817-5069.1031.

Jonathan D & Lauran D 'Non-verbal victims in the adversarial criminal process: communication, competency, and credibility' https://shura.shu.ac.uk/18482/3/Doak-Non-verbalVictmsintheAdversarialCriminalProcess%28AM%29.pdf (accessed 21 August 2021).

Karras M et al. *On the edge of justice: the legal needs of people with a mental illness in NSW* Sydney: Law and Justice Foundation of NSW (2006).

Kennedy L & Tait D *Court perspectives: architecture, psychology and Western Australian Law Reform* Western Australian Law Reform Commission (1999).

Kevin Kiprotich Amos alias Rotich v Republic (2016) eKLR.
Leiter B 'American legal realism' in Golding MP & Edmundson WA (eds) *Blackwell's guide to the philosophy of law and legal theory* (2004).
Leo v Australia (2019) CRPD/C/22/D/17/2013.
Liebreich v Germany (2009) ECtHR.
Mbote PK & Akech M *Kenya: justice sector and the rule of law* (2011).
Miller D 'Dementia and competency in United States courtrooms: a case law review' https://academicworks.cuny.edu/cgi/viewcontent.cgi?article=1157&context=jj_etds (accessed 10 September 2021).
New South Wales Law Reform Commission *People with an intellectual disability and the criminal justice system* Sydney (1996).
Sahu KK & Sahu S 'Attitudinal barrier experienced by people with disabilities' (2015) 1 *Disability Studies* 1.
Stanford v UK (2002) ECtHR.
State v Ortiz-Abrego (2017) 387 P3d 638.
T v United Kingdom and *V v United Kingdom* (2000) ECtHR.
United Nations Human Rights Council 'Thematic study by the United Nation High Commission for Human Rights on enhancing awareness and understanding on the Convention on the rights of persons with disabilities' https://www.un.org/disabilities/documents/reports/ohchr/A.HRC.10.48AEV.pdf (accessed 19 March 2021).
Van Hout MC & Wessels J 'Navigating the complexities of the mentally ill and mentally incapacitated in the criminal justice system in South Africa' (2021) 2 *Forensic Science International: Mind and Law* 3.
Vasileiou K et al. 'Characterising and justifying sample size sufficiency in interview-based studies: systematic analysis of qualitative health research over a 15-year period' (2018) 18 *BMC Medical Research Methodology* 150. https://doi.org/10.1186/s12874-018-0594-7.
Wendy S et al. 'From criminalisation to individual choice: policy responses to changing constructions of intellectual disability in Western Australia' (2019) 21 *Scandinavian Journal of Disability Research* 102. https://doi.org/10.16993/sjdr.571.
White R et al. 'Court accommodations for persons with severe communication disabilities: a legal scoping review' (2021) 27 *Psychology, Public Policy and Law* 420. https://doi.org/10.1037/law0000289.
Wise PH 'Emerging technologies and their impact on disability. The future of children' https://www.researchgate.net/publication/224886619_Wise_P_H_Emerging_technologies_and_their_impact_on_disability_Future_Child_22_169-191 (accessed 23 February, 2022).
Wood ME et al. 'Reasonable accommodations for meeting the unique needs of defendants with intellectual disability' (2019) 47 *Journal of American Academy Psychiatry Law* 314. https://doi.org/10.29158/JAAPL.003855-19.

8 Comparative analysis of reform approaches to the decolonisation of unfitness declaration laws in selected jurisdictions

8.0 Introduction

Kenya's mental unfitness laws are still largely a reproduction of colonialism whose main aim was the socio-economic exclusion of certain groups of people, including persons with psychosocial disabilities. The solution to dismantling and replacing such discriminatory colonial structures of power and ideologies in criminal justice systems across the globe, lies with decolonial practices that value and respond to the rights of persons with psychosocial disabilities. Presently, laws on eligibility to stand trial are being decolonised with the aid of various instruments such as the Convention on the Rights of Persons with Disabilities (CRPD).[1] The decolonisation of mental health through the use of the CRPD is a real, viable, and ethical solution to the overrepresentation of persons with psychosocial disabilities in criminal justice systems across the globe. The imperative for such a reconsideration arises on account of the CRPD's article 12 which, recognises the rights of persons with psychosocial disabilities to equal recognition before the law. The provision prohibits the use of separate processes for disabled persons in criminal law especially, those which incorporate higher or lower standard when it comes to human rights protection.[2] States parties are obligated to recognise that persons with psychosocial disabilities enjoy legal capacity on an equal basis with others in all aspects of life.[3] The wide application of the CRPD's article 12 has the potential of pushing the boundaries of traditional practices in regards to unfitness declaration laws around the globe.

There is no one universal decolonial reform model for the implementation of the CRPD's article 12.[4] According to Bartlett, the CRPD requires

1 UN General Assembly, Convention on the Rights of Persons with Disabilities: Resolution adopted by the General Assembly, 24 January 2007, UN Doc A/RES/61/106 (2007) (CRPD) adopted on 13 December 2006 (entered into force on 3 May 2008).

2 Guidelines on the right to liberty and security of persons with disabilities, adopted September 2015.

3 CRPD, Art 12(2).

4 L Davidson 'From pipe dream to reality: a practical legal approach towards the global abolition of psychiatric coercion' in MA Stein et al. (eds) *Mental health, legal capacity, and human rights* (2021) 76.

DOI: 10.4324/9781003647102-8

the abolition of laws that permit detention and removal of legal capacity for those with psychosocial disabilities.[5] However, amendments aimed at transposing the provision of the CRPD into national law have adopted different approaches. Some countries have adopted a passive transformation approach to the CRPD which occurs by assessing the compliance of already existing domestic laws with the Convention in order to determine whether there is need for any adjustment.[6] In Sweden for instance, recognition of the need for changes to the provisions on the active legal capacity in criminal law for all persons, including persons with psychosocial disabilities occurred many years before the CRPD came into effect. The changes stemmed from the recognition of the inadequacies of earlier regulations and the wish to find a balance between the need to assist persons with psychosocial disabilities and extend their autonomy wherever possible.[7]

In other countries, the CRPD has been used to set new standards for the protection of persons with psychosocial disabilities thus, providing the impetus for further and ever deeper modifications to the regulation of active legal capacity.[8] This is known as active transformation which takes place by translating and introducing a corresponding domestic law in order to implement the CRPD.[9] On the flipside, some states have specifically rejected the recommendation of the Committee on the Rights of Persons with Disabilities (CRPD Committee) to eliminate declarations that are based partly or exclusively on the disability of accused persons with psychosocial disabilities from criminal justice systems. For example, Canada, Estonia, the Netherlands, Norway, Spain, and several Arab states entered reservations to article 12 of the CRPD on account of protection of those persons with severe mental disabilities.[10]

Other state parties, in their periodic reports to the CRPD Committee have continued to cite without apparent embarrassment aspects of their criminal procedure and mental health laws, as evidence of compliance with the CRPD,

5 P Bartlett 'The United Nations Convention on the Rights of Persons with Disabilities and mental health law' (2012) 25/5 *Modern Law Review* 752–778.

6 KH Søvig & AV Valvatne 'Implementation of article 12 of the UN Convention on the Rights of Persons with Disabilities in Norway' in M Domański & B Lackoroński (eds) *Models of implementation of article 12 of the Convention on the Rights of Persons with Disabilities (CRPD): private and criminal law aspects* (2023) 390.

7 Y Litins'ka 'Implementation of article 12 of the UN Convention on the Rights of Persons with Disabilities in the Kingdom Sweden' in M Domański & B Lackoroński (eds) *Models of implementation of article 12 of the Convention on the Rights of Persons with Disabilities (CRPD): private and criminal law aspects* (2023) 528.

8 C Devandas-Aguilar *Report of special rapporteur on the rights of persons with disabilities* (UNDoc. A/HRC/37/56, 12 December 2017), para 38.

9 Søvig & Valvatne (n 6) 390.

10 For the text of all reservations to the Convention, see https://treaties.un.org/Pages/ViewDetails.aspx?src=TREATY&mtdsg_no=iv-15&chapter=4&lang=en b (accessed 8 August 2014); see especially the reservations of Australia, Canada, and Norway.

that are quite incompatible with the Committee's published views.[11] In Kuwait for example, the law allows for the appointment of legal assistants to act as a representative and not a supporter, in this instance.[12] The reason behind such reservations/non-compliance is the non-unitary nature of psychosocial disabilities which may result in the inability to make decisions even when necessary accommodations are provided.[13]

The aim of this chapter is to analyse the extent of compliance of national laws on unfitness to stand trial in selected jurisdictions across the globe, with the demands of the CRPD. It is divided into three main sections. Section one is this introduction. Section two explores the reform approaches to unfitness declarations in light of interpretations by the CRPD Committee. This section addresses the targeted and abolitionist approaches as the two main reform models to unfitness declaration laws in different countries. Through a comparative analysis of laws on unfitness to stand trial, the section seeks to reveal potential conflicts and areas for further reform, emphasising the importance of article 12 of the CRPD so as to ensure the participation of persons with psychosocial disabilities and prevent any unlawful discrimination. Section three is the conclusion.

8.1 National and international reform approaches to unfitness declaration laws

Analyses of national and international solutions to changes in the regulation of unfitness declaration laws has revealed several discernible general reform directions and trends towards the realisation of article 12 and 13 of the CRPD. The latter provisions partly require states parties to recognise that persons with psychosocial disabilities enjoy legal capacity on an equal basis with others in all aspects of life and take appropriate measures to provide them with access to the necessary support systems that they may require in order to exercise their legal capacity.[14] However, there have been considerable arguments regarding the extent to which national laws should comply with article 12 of the CRPD. Among the most important are the targeted and abolitionist approaches. This section considers these approaches through a comparative

11 See, for instance, the country reports of Australia: CRPD/C/AUS/1 (7 June 2012), paras 76, 96; Sweden, CRPD/C/SWE/1 (18 September 2012), paras 137, 140; Denmark: CRPD/C/DNK/1 (7 May 2013), paras 142–147; and New Zealand: CRPD/C/NZL/1 (1 October 2013), paras 67–69, 83–89.

12 AA Matar 'Implementation of article 12 of the UN Convention on the Rights of Persons with Disabilities in Kuwait' in M Domański & B Lackoroński (eds) *Models of implementation of article 12 of the Convention on the Rights of Persons with Disabilities (CRPD): private and criminal law aspects* (2023) 336.

13 German Statement on the Draft General Comment on Article 12 CRPD. 20 February 2014. http://www.ohchr.org/Documents/HRBodies/CRPD/GC/FederalRepublicOfGermanyArt12.pdf (accessed 18 April 2015).

14 CRPD, Art 12.

analysis of laws on unfitness to stand trial throughout the globe, including consideration of national and international law reform trends in this area of regulation.

8.1.1 Targeted approach

One of the major components of colonisation is the perpetuation of unfitness declarations structures through value-laden judgements and colonially constructed nature of mental disability. The targeted approach takes into consideration these value systems as part of the reform standards against which unfitness declarations are to be assessed. It targets certain components of unfitness declarations that have long supported the colonial criminal justice system such as criteria for determining unfitness and disposition by way of detention. The argument here is that a conscientious implementation of the CRPD is not only vital but requires specific policy targets. In this regard, the transposition of CRPD's articles 12 and 13 have largely taken the form of amendments to provisions relating explicitly to unfitness declarations as opposed to abolition. Where there is a lack of legislative changes, however, the burden of implementation has largely shifted onto the judiciary. This situation has resulted in the *ad hoc* application of articles 12 and other relevant provisions of the CRPD.

The targeted approach has mainly been adopted by England and Wales, New Zealand, and Australia. In England and Wales, the Law Commission has argued that unfitness to plead rules may be construed as an 'accessibility measure' in which modified proceedings help secure substantive equality.[15] In Australia, the Tasmania Law Reform Institute, the Victorian Law Reform Commission, the New South Wales Law Reform Commission and the New Zealand Law Commission have each rejected the call for abolition of disability-based declarations, opting instead for various targeted reforms to the declaration's scope and matters of disposition as discussed in detail below.

The criteria for determining unfitness

Fitness assessments have historically been based on the presumption of incapacity, which is recognised as a threshold issue in the criminal justice system.[16] It generally, involves the use of various interviews, tests, and physical examinations.[17] In many jurisdictions, as discussed later in this part, a fitness test is either based on the mental capacity of those involved or is in the process of

15 Law Commission, Unfitness to Plead: Volume 1, Report 364 (2015) 100, para 3.171.

16 I Freckelton & P Keyzer 'Fitness to stand trial and disability discrimination: an international critique of Australia' (2017) 24/5 *Psychiatry, Psychology and Law* 770.

17 L Pienaar 'The unfit accused in the South African criminal justice system: from automatic detention to unconditional release' 2018 (1) *SACJ* 60.

reform. The essence of decolonialism is to offer alternative diagnostic epistemologies to persons with psychosocial disabilities.[18] Traditional tests for mental capacity have been found to offend the principle of indirect discrimination due to their disproportionate impact on persons with psychosocial disabilities.[19] Such criminal justice solutions largely locate the sources of non-participation in the bodies of persons with psychosocial disabilities. As a result, the programmes and practices that are based upon mental assessment instruments have failed to address other primary sources of disability such as, the environment. Mental assessments predict unfitness solely based on individual factors rather than on structural ones. They are applicable only within the framework of individual-level interventions. This hyper-focus on the individual is particularly visible when one considers the disposition of disabled bodies following unfitness declarations whose main focus is the provision of fitness-based medications.[20]

A related issue at the heart of the fitness debate is the adequacy of the criteria to be satisfied when fitness to plead is in issue and whether an exclusive focus on an accused person's mental abilities is an appropriate basis upon which to determine whether someone is unfit to stand trial. The common law threshold for unfitness is considered as being higher compared to the inability to participate effectively as it focuses on intelligence, understanding and communication as opposed to the more nuanced decision-making abilities such as weighing up information.[21] Generally, the criteria should not set too high a threshold for unfitness so as to make it impossible to apply to persons with psychosocial disabilities. It should also not set too low a threshold, otherwise, it would run the risk of violating the fair trial rights of defendants with psychosocial disabilities. The latter threshold implies that an offender need only possess a basic level of competence in order to be judged fit to stand trial, regardless of whether they are acting in their best interests or not.[22]

The mere presence of a psychosocial disability or reduced capacity should not be a ground to warrant a finding of unfitness. This is consistent with numerous cases from across the globe where several accused persons with psychosocial disabilities were declared fit to stand trial despite, 1) suffering from a 'high degree of abnormality',[23] 2) being diagnosed with grandiose and

18 PO Juma & C Ngwena 'Decolonizing African mental health laws: a case for Kenya' (2024) 68 *Journal of African Law* 76.

19 P Weller 'Legal capacity and access to justice: the right to participation in the CRPD' (2016) 5(1) *Laws* 13, 18.

20 G Ferguson 'Unfit to stand trial: Canadian law and practice' in R Mackay & WJ Brookbanks (eds) *Fitness to plead: international and comparative perspectives* (2018) 12.

21 P Brown 'Modernising fitness to plead' (2019) 59 *Medical Science Law* 131.

22 WJ Brookbanks & RD Mackay 'Decisional competence and "best interests": establishing the threshold for fitness to stand trial' (2010) 12 *Otago Law Review* 277.

23 *R v Berry* (1978) 66 Cr App R 156.

paranoid delusions,[24] and 3) suffering from an undiagnosed brain tumour.[25] According to these cases, the degree of disability should not be used to declare one incapable of following criminal proceedings. Caution should, however, be exercised in order to avoid what Sherry Arnstein has termed fake participation which may result from power imbalances between the state and accused persons with psychosocial disabilities, on account of the latter's rudimentary understanding of the criminal process.[26]

The question of whether there ought to be a best interests component when assessing unfitness has also become a matter of some debate in certain jurisdictions. In Canada, Australia, the UK, and New Zealand for example, it has uniformly been held that the mere fact that an accused person with psychosocial disability is incapable of acting in his or her own best interests is not a conclusive sign that he or she is unfit to stand trial.[27] In the same vein, the provision of minimal assistance to the defence effort is also not a sufficient ground for a declaration of unfitness as has been stated in various court decisions. In *Heffernan v The Queen* for instance,[28] the accused person with psychosocial disability refused to raise a mental illness defence because his delusions prevented him from knowing he was mentally ill. It was held that this is not a reason for an unfitness declaration. According to the court, an accused person with psychosocial disabilities is not required to act in their best interests or to present a good defence.[29] This position has been heavily criticised by scholars and legal practioners alike, for contradicting the notions of justice and fairness, as it puts accused persons with psychosocial disabilities at a great risk of alienating the judge or jury or of being convicted.[30]

The criteria for determining unfitness should 'focus on whether, and to what extent, a person can be supported to play their role in the justice system, rather than on whether they have capacity to play such a role at all'.[31] According to the CRPD Committee's General Comment 1: Article 12: Equal Recognition Before the Law (General Comment 1), support is a broad term which must be personalised in form and intensity as there is no 'one size fits all'.[32] Countries have been directed to abandon the emphasis on identifying the point at which a person should be deemed unfit to plead, and instead

24 *R v Cain* (2010) QCA 373.

25 *R v Rivkin* (2004) 59 NSWLR 284.

26 S Arnstein 'A ladder of citizen participation' (1969) 35 *Journal of the American Institute of Planners* 216.

27 See *R v Berry* (1977) 66 Cr App R 156, *R v Taylor* (1992) 77 CCC (3d) 551, at 564–565, & *Eastman v the Queen* (2000) HCA 29.

28 (2005) 194 FLR 370.

29 GA Blake et al. 'Special considerations to the assessment of fitness to stand trial in Australia' (2023) 30/5 *Psychiatry, Psychology and Law* 682.

30 Brookbanks & Mackay (n 22) 268.

31 ALRC *Equality, capacity and disability in Commonwealth laws* (2014) 192.

32 CRPD Committee General Comment 1: Article 12: Equal recognition before the law (2014) UN Doc CRPD/C/GC/1 dated 19 May 2014, para 17.

places an obligation on states parties to provide support to exercise legal capacity.[33] It means that reform objectives in this area requires the legislature and judiciary to sufficiently consider the possible role of assistance and support for accused persons with psychosocial disabilities.

In 2005, Israel enacted the Investigation and Testimony Procedural Act (Accommodations for Persons with Mental or Cognitive Disabilities).[34] This law permits a court to allow a witness or accused person with psychosocial disability to give evidence using alternative augmentative communication, including the assistance of people, computerised aids, communication panels, photos, symbols, letters or words.[35] Finland's open dialogue model and Sweden's personal ombudsman approach are other examples of how states are attempting to support the participation of accused persons with psychosocial disabilities.

In England and Wales, similar support measures were made in January 2016 by the Law Commission which, made a series of recommendations about reforming the law on unfitness to plead. In particular, they called for the introduction of a statutory defendant intermediary scheme.[36] The Commission recommended for the replacement of the common law criteria for determining an accused's fitness with a new statutory test aimed at establishing whether the defendant lacked the 'capacity to participate effectively' with the trial process.[37] In Scotland, the law underwent significant reform in 1995 and 2010, and the test for fitness for trial now explicitly includes consideration of effective participation and related decision-making capacity.[38]

In Australia, the Australian Law Reform Commission (ALRC) has called for the simplification the procedure for assessment and shifting the focus from mental ability to decision-making.[39] In other words, it prefers a 'functional mental capacity' test as the one found in the Mental Capacity Act[40] of England and Wales due its low threshold for determining capacity. The latter depends on the extent with which a person's impairment or disturbance in the functioning of the mind or brain contributes to his or her inability to understand,

33 P Gooding & C O'Mahony 'Laws on unfitness to stand trial and the UN Convention on the Rights of Persons with Disabilities: comparing reform in England, Wales, Northern Ireland and Australia' (2016) 44 *International Journal of Law, Crime and Justice* 122.

34 The Investigation and Testimony Procedural Act (Accommodations for Persons with Mental or Cognitive Disabilities) of 2005.

35 Investigation and Testimony Procedural Act (Accommodations for Persons with Mental or Cognitive Disabilities) 2005, sec 22(7).

36 Law Commission, Unfitness to Plead Volume 1: Report, Report No. 364 (January 2016) 48–49 [2.66]–[2.69].

37 Law Commission 'Unfitness to plead, vol 2: draft legislation' (Law Com No 364, London 2016) at cl 1.

38 G Maher 'Unfitness for trial in Scots law' in R Mackay & WJ Brookbanks (eds) *Fitness to plead: international and comparative perspectives* (2018) 103.

39 ALRC (n 31) 201, para 7.41–47.42.

40 Mental Capacity Act 2005 (UK).

retain, use, or weigh information relevant to a decision.[41] As regards support, several provisions of the law are applicable, including sections 33BA-33BB of the Australian Youth Justice and Criminal Evidence Act (the 1999 Act).[42] The provisions were introduced by the Coroners and Justice Act[43] and are meant to enable accused youths with psychosocial disabilities to participate through intermediaries.

Prior to the amendments, the 1999 Act only allowed intermediaries to be employed when examining witnesses and not in trials involving accused youths with psychosocial disabilities.[44] In April 2016, similar limitations were introduced to the Criminal Practice Directions (Directions), which generally applies to accused persons, including those with psychosocial disabilities.[45] Among the amendments to the Directions, was the introduction of wide restrictions to the duration and manner in which defendant intermediaries should be applied.

As regards the manner, the new provisions require that defendant intermediaries should be rarely employed and for a limited time during the trial, except in extremely rare cases.[46] Such wide limitation it can be argued, are unreasonable and unjustifiable in an open and democratic society that is based on human dignity, equality, and freedom. According to the Victorian Law Reform Commission (VLRC), the use of defendant intermediaries can 'optimis[e] an accused's fitness where they might otherwise be unfit'.[47] This view has found support with other states like Canada, specifically in the governments of Ontario,[48] and Northern Ireland,[49] which have all settled on a similar continuum of support systems to the implementation of the CRPD.

Criteria for determining unfitness – case law

Case laws across the globe show a divide in the criteria for determining unfitness. Some jurisdictions have adopted a single or minimalist approach, which is based on the decision-making capacity of a person, while others have adopted a multiple issue test which considers several factors other than mental

41 EE Jang 'Mental capacity: reevaluating the standards' (2015) 43 *Georgia Journal of International and Comparative Law* 540.

42 Youth Justice and Criminal Evidence Act 1999.

43 Coroners and Justice Act 2009.

44 Youth Justice and Criminal Evidence Act 1999, sec 29.

45 Criminal Practice Directions, 2016 (Australia).

46 Criminal Practice Directions, 2016, para 3F.13.

47 Victorian Law Reform Commission *Review of the Crimes (Mental Impairment and Unfitness to Be Tried) Act 1997* (Report 28 of 2014) 89. (VLRC *Unfitness Report*).

48 Law Commission of Ontario, Legal Capacity Decision Making and Guardianship, Discussion Paper (2014).

49 Department of Health, Social Services and Public Safety (Northern Ireland) and Department of Justice (Northern Ireland) *Draft Mental Capacity Bill (NI)* (Consultation Summary Report, 2015).

incapacity.[50] The latter has been adopted by several courts for instance, the *Dusky v United States*[51] standard for competence to stand trial which explicitly considers the ability of a defendant to rationally and factually understand criminal proceedings, as well as consult with counsel.[52] A similar approach is found in the New Zealand case of *R v Friend*, where, included as part of the common law test, is the question of whether an accused can 'understand and reply rationally to the indictment'.[53] This criterion and several others are laid down in section 4 of the Criminal Procedure (Mentally Impaired Persons) Act.[54]

Both the single and multiple issue test have been criticised for being too narrow and for failing to answer the question whether a failure to meet one of the tests particularly, under the expanded criteria would necessarily result in a finding of unfitness, respectively.[55] In some cases the factors that make up the multiple issues test have been treated as separate constructs for example, it has been held that competence to waive the right to counsel does not automatically translate to competence to represent oneself at trial.[56] This inherent paternalism, found in both tests may be criticised for being discriminatory for failing to both respect the autonomy of persons with mental disabilities and take into account their trial needs.[57]

To resolve the challenge of discrimination, other courts have demonstrated a willingness to focus on participation and treat the availability of support as a critical factor in determining whether a person is unfit to stand trial. For example, in *R v Fisher*,[58] Refshauge J reviewed the authorities and identified the following principle:

> Where steps can reasonably be taken to accommodate the difficulties of the accused, including adjournments, 'one-on-one' assistance to follow the proceedings, insistence on brief, clear questions to the accused if he or she is examined on oath, an opportunity for the accused to narrate his or her version of events without interruption and the like[,] the implementation of these will mean the accused is not unfit to plead.

Further examples of case law indicate that such accommodations have played a decisive role in participation outcomes. In *GAE v Western Australia*,[59] a psychiatrist gave evidence that, while a professional communicator would not

50 Brookbanks & Mackay (n 22) 273.
51 *Dusky v United States* 362 US 402 (1960).
52 *Dusky* (n 51) 788.
53 (1997) 2 All ER 1011.
54 Criminal Procedure (Mentally Impaired Persons) Act 2003 (CPMIPA).
55 Brookbanks & Mackay (n 22) 282.
56 *Edwards v Indiana* (2008) 554 US 164.
57 Justice Scalia's dissent, *Faretta v California* (1975) 422 US 806.
58 (2011) 210 A Crim R 199, 205, para 29.
59 (2015) WADC 5, para 31.

be of assistance, a family member or colleague would be a suitable supporter. Wager DCJ found GAE fit to plead and allowed his sister to help defence lawyers communicate with her accused brother. The Court was also told that GAE could better follow proceedings if parties used short sentences, simple terms, and repetition of key issues.[60] The decision proves that the provision of support promotes rather than undermines the fairness of trial or an accused's ability to help produce the strongest possible defence. An accused person with psychosocial disabilities has no right therefore, to avoid adjudication or to avoid the consequences of guilt after plea or conviction because he or she proceeded by way of support. This will be against the interest of all parties, including the state, of ensuring a fair process for adjudicating guilt or innocence.[61]

In *R v JG*,[62] the existence of appropriate supports for the accused prompted the court to conclude that JG, whom the court determined had a 'mild intellectual impairment', was fit to stand trial. These supports which included the taking of regular breaks to allow the accused to consult with counsel and using short, simple questions during examination showed a willingness on the part of the court to engage with adapted processes in order to ensure effective participation of those involved. In *C v Sevenoaks Magistrates' Court*[63] it was held that it was within the court's discretion to appoint an intermediary for an accused person with psychosocial disabilities as part of its inherent powers to ensure the right to fair trial. Such an intermediary may be appointed for the whole trial or only to assist an accused person with psychosocial disability while he or she is testifying as was further held in *R (on the application of OP) v Secretary of State for Justice*.[64]

In England and Wales, the case of *R v Walls* affirmed the scope of the ruling in *GAE v Western Australia* in terms of assistance to accused persons with disabilities when it held as follows:

> Plainly[,] consideration should be given to the use of . . . ways in which the characteristics of a defendant . . . can be accommodated with the trial process so that his limitations can be understood by the jury, before a court takes the very significant step of embarking on a trial of fitness to plead.[65]

Relatedly, in *C v Sevenoaks Youth Court*, a High Court in the UK concluded that courts enjoy an inherent common law discretion to appoint a defendant

60 See *R v JG* (2014) ACTSC 120, para 14; *R v Haines* (2013) NSWSC 1609, para 25.

61 SJ Morse 'Involuntary competence in United States criminal law' in R Mackay & WJ Brookbanks (eds) *Fitness to plead: international and comparative perspectives* (2018) 222.

62 (2014) ACTSC 120.

63 *C v Sevenoaks Magistrates' Court* (2009) EWHC 3088.

64 *R (on the application of OP) v Secretary of State for Justice* (2014) EWHC 1944.

65 (2011) EWCA Crim 443.

intermediary 'if necessary to ensure a fair trial'.[66] In America, the case of *United States v Delaware*, mandated statewide crisis services to '[p]rovide timely and accessible support to individuals with mental illness experiencing a behavioral health crisis, including a crisis due to substance abuse'.[67] This shows that the willingness of the judiciary to remain proactive in being able to identify and take measures to support the participation of accused persons with psychosocial disabilities in the justice system.

The foregoing supports the need for reformulating the test of unfitness in order to ensure that those accused persons with psychosocial disabilities who are able to participate effectively with the use of both reasonable and procedural accommodations, are given the opportunity to do so with the aid of necessary modifications. Such adjustments may include sitting with their legal team in the courtroom as an accommodation measure, having extra breaks if they have problems concentrating, and advising counsel to avoid taking a confrontational approach in cross-examination and to use simple, concise language and ask one question at a time if there are problems with vulnerability or understanding.[68]

Procedural accommodations

According to Juma and Ngwena, one of the objectives of health activities in colonial territories was to treat unfit bodies.[69] This system resulted in what may be referred to as 'fitnessibilisation', where the responsibility to change was placed almost entirely on the person with psychosocial disability. In most jurisdictions, even those seen as having the most up-to-date laws, concerns have been raised that the procedures following a finding of unfitness to stand trial do not secure due process rights on an equal basis with others.[70]

A strict interpretation of the CRPD considers any declaration of unfitness to plead as a breach of the right to legal capacity on an equal basis with others, and incompatible with the rights of those with psychosocial disabilities. The criminal justice system was designed to deter, punish, incapacitate, and rehabilitate as opposed to healing, administering treatment, or making people whole.[71] The South African criminal justice system for example, was found to be lacking in facilities for providing psychological services to accused persons with mental disabilities.[72] According to the CRPD Committee,

66 (2010) 1 All ER 735, 742.

67 *Settlement Agreement at 3, United States v. Delaware*, 1:11-cv-00591-LPS (D. Del. 6 July 2011).

68 *R v Mathews* (2013) QCA 203.

69 Juma & Ngwena (n 18) 76.

70 Baldry E 'Disability at the margins: limits of the law' (2014) 23 *Griffith Law Review* 357, 370–388.

71 G West 'Insanity and incompetency: courts, communities, and the intersections of mental illness and criminal justice in the wake of Kahler and Trueblood' (2023) 53 *Golden Gate University Law Review* (2023) 253.

72 *De Vos NO v Minister of Justice and Constitutional Development* (2015a) ZACC 21, para 43.

wherever practicable a full criminal trial should be preferred to a finding of unfitness.[73] As such, the removal of an accused person with psychosocial disabilities from full trial process should be employed as a measure of last resort, and with great caution.[74] This view is part of what Juma and Ngwena has referred to as relational decolonisation, which is largely premised on human agency and equity.[75] It has been endorsed by the Australian Human Rights Commission, which has stated that a full trial is best for accused persons with psychosocial disabilities, the victims, and the society in general.[76]

Likewise, the ALRC has recommended the consideration of accommodations in fitness evaluations because being fit to stand trial is inevitably in the accused person with disability's best interests.[77] This expansive approach is increasingly getting traction with courts across the globe through their acknowledgement of the ability of accused person with psychosocial disabilities to participate effectively in criminal trials if given appropriate procedural and reasonable accommodations.[78] In certain instances, however, the judiciary has missed the opportunity of ensuring the participation of accused person with mental disabilities because, in its view, the process and practice of employing accommodations is 'potentially laborious'.[79] In the end, they have failed to allow parties to employ the use of necessary procedural modifications that would enable an accused person with psychosocial disabilities to better understand the trial process, such as taking breaks so as to enable counsel explain to the defendant what was happening as seen in the case in *R v Muller*.[80] The decision suggests a need for regular training on the part of the judiciary as was stated in *Noble v Australia*, to better understand and apply available support and accommodation mechanisms by which an accused person's effective participation can be facilitated.[81]

As far as possible, accused persons with psychosocial disabilities should be supported to take part in the trial process, for example by using special measures, intermediaries or delaying trials so that they can be rendered fit after treatment. In Estonia, section 41(3) of the Code of Criminal Procedure

73 Committee on the Rights of Persons with Disabilities *Guidelines on article 14 of the convention on the rights of persons with disabilities: the right to liberty and security of persons with disabilities* UNCRPD (2015).

74 M Bevan & D Ormerod 'Reforming the law of unfitness to plead in England and Wales: a recent history' in R Mackay & WJ Brookbanks (eds) *Fitness to plead: international and comparative perspectives* Oxford: Oxford University Press (2018) 71.

75 Juma & Ngwena (n 18) 86.

76 Australian Human Rights Commission, Submission No 6 to the Senate Community Affairs References Committee, Inquiry into the Indefinite Detention of People with Cognitive and Psychiatric Impairment in Australia, March 2016, 16–17 [62].

77 Australian Law Reform Commission *Equality, capacity and disability in Commonwealth laws* (Discussion Paper 81, 2014) Proposal 7–2.

78 *Noble v Australia* (2016) CRPD/C/16/D/7/2012 & *R v Jeffries* (2012) NZCA 608, para 36.

79 *R v Muller* (2013) ACTSC 154.

80 As above.

81 Recommendation iii, *Noble v Australia*.

(CCRP)[82] allows a person with restricted active legal capacity to participate in criminal proceedings personally or through a representative with the option of replacing the latter with someone providing state legal aid if the body conducting the proceedings realises that there is a conflict of interest. Appropriate resources should also be allocated for the expansion of available support programmes so as to reach all those people who are likely to be declared unfit.[83]

Procedural accommodations – special hearings

In other states such as Australia, reforms have gone as far as addressing the absence of a trial or special hearing process to determine the guilt or innocence of accused persons with psychosocial disabilities. A special hearing has been defined as an adversarial process in which the evidence against an accused is tested.[84] The procedure affords several advantages to an unfit accused person, including the benefit of the right to presumption of innocence, opportunity to put the evidence to scrutiny, especially under an accusatorial trial process, the possibility of acquittal. in which event the charges will cease to hang over the head of those involved, and where treatment is necessary, it may be issued outside the criminal justice system.[85] In Australia, with the exception of Western Australia or Queensland,[86] an accused person with psychosocial disabilities, who is declared unfit to stand trial, is assumed to have pleaded not guilty in relation to the charge which removes the benefits of entering an early guilty plea in sentence mitigation.[87]

Once a determination of unfitness has been made, special hearings are conducted to test the merits of the charge against the accused person with psychosocial disability.[88] The special hearings are essentially truncated trials designed to ensure that an individual's liberty is not restricted without proper basis and may be considered part of the diversion process.[89] Such alternative trial processes, according to Anna Lawson and Rebecca Parry which are akin to

82 *Kriminaalmenetluse seadustik* (*Code of criminal procedure*) (CCRP), RT I, 22 December 2021, 45. The English translation of the CCRP as of 27 December 2021.

83 Freckelton & Keyzer (n 16) 780.

84 F McGaughey et al. 'UN decision on Marlon Noble case: imprisonment of an aboriginal man with intellectual disability found unfit to stand trial in Western Australia' (2017) 42(1) *Alternative Law Journal* 68.

85 *Subramaniam v The Queen* (2004) 79 ALJR 116, para 40.

86 Jurisdictions such as the ACT, NSW (District and Supreme Court proceedings), the Northern Territory (NT), South Australia (SA), and Victoria).

87 K Eagle & A Ellis 'The widening net of preventative detention and the unfit for trial' (2016) 90 *Australian Law Journal* 172.

88 Australian Capital Territory, New South Wales, Victoria, South Australia, Tasmania, and Northern Territory. Crimes Act 1900 (ACT) s 316; Mental Health (Forensic Provisions) Act 1900 (NSW) s 21; Crimes (Mental Impairment and Unfitness to be Tried) Act 1997 (Vic) s 16; Criminal Law Consolidation Act 1935 (SA) s 269M; Criminal Justice (Mental Impairment) Act 1999 (Tas) s 16; Criminal Code Act 1983 (NT) s 43W.

89 See e.g. Mental Health (Forensic Provisions) Act 1900 (NSW), sec 19.

special hearings available in most Australian jurisdictions, may be considered part of accommodations of the type demanded by the CRPD.[90] While this may be so, caution should be exercised in order to prevent perpetuating hurtful stereotypes within the context of coloniality and patriarchy that views all accused persons with psychosocial disabilities as vulnerable and thus, the need for special protection mechanisms. Such hierarchised structures may reinforce stigmatisation and marginalisation against defendants with psychosocial disabilities thus, resulting in a further impairment of their human dignity.[91]

On the flipside, apart from entering a plea of not guilty, certain jurisdictions such as England and Wales, the state is considering other solutions such as one, permitting a guilty plea when the defendant understands the issues relevant to making such a decision, despite the nature of their disability or two, postponing consideration of fitnessibility where the accused is entitled to an acquittal.[92] The first one concerns separating between capacity to plead guilty and capacity for trial. It is premised on the idea that one can be unfit for trial without necessarily lacking in decisional capacity which has been defined as the ability to understand the information relevant to a decision, retain that information, use or weigh it as part of the process of making the decision, or communicate the decision.[93] The emerging separate test of ability to plead guilty is said to be rights-based as it ensures the autonomy of persons with psychosocial disabilities in decision-making and therapeutic.[94] The latter is due to its potential to provide accused persons with psychosocial disabilities who are unfit to participate in a full trial with the option of being sentenced to imprisonment.[95] It can also lead to the fast-tracking of proceedings for those who wish to accept moral responsibility for their offences and benefit from sentence reduction in return for a guilty plea or in situations where proceeding with the trial is in the best interest of a defendant.

For postponement of fitness considerations, an examination/trial of facts procedure applies, where only the external elements of the relevant offence are considered.[96] The accused person's advocate may concede at the outset that the state has established a *prima facie* case,[97] or make no such concession and compel the prosecution to establish an evidentiary basis for the alleged offence.[98] Where a hearing is conducted, the court may, after examining the

90 Law Commission (England and Wales) *Unfitness to plead* (Report No 364 (2016) vol 1) (Law Commission Report) 100.

91 *De Vos NO* (n 72), para 46.

92 *Marcantonio v R* (2016) EWCA 9.

93 Bevan & Ormerod (n 74) 63.

94 R Fortson 'Unfitness to plead in England and Wales: a practitioner's view of a plea in evolution' in R Mackay & WJ Brookbanks (eds) *Fitness to plead: international and comparative perspectives* (2018) 44.

95 Law Commission 2016 (n 90).

96 Criminal Procedure (Insanity) Act 1964, sec 4 as substituted by the Criminal Procedure (Insanity and Unfitness to Plead) Act 1991, sec 5.

97 Accepted as correct until proved otherwise.

98 Ferguson (n 20) 120.

adduced evidence, decide whether the accused committed or omitted the act that is subject of the charge in question.[99]

On the one hand, if the court finds in the negative, the accused is acquitted.[100] On the other hand, if the court finds in the affirmative, a special verdict to that effect is entered, whose effect is to result in neither a conviction nor punishment.[101] Instead of a sentence, the court is obligated to choose among three disposition options, namely, an absolute discharge, a supervision order, or a hospital order, with or without restrictions.[102] The examination of facts procedure has also been adopted in South Africa,[103] Scotland,[104] and Canada.[105] The practice is advantageous and a welcome development due to among others, its wide range of disposition orders available, which may act as an adequate safeguard against arbitrary detention.[106] Potential disadvantages of the trial of facts approach, however, include a lack of the full range of defences and less opportunities to test the prosecution's case.[107] The procedure may also be criticised for creating a separate and lesser form of justice for accused persons with psychosocial disabilities. Apart from that, it is based on mental disability which is inconsistent with the CRPD Committee recommendations.[108]

Procedural accommodation-diversion

Another procedural accommodation option that may be available to the courts in cases involving accused persons with psychosocial disabilities is diversion. These programmes offer benefits such as being able to access a specialist court, having charges dismissed, or referral to a support programme. However, most diversion systems are pre-sentenced based meaning, they require a person to plead guilty to some, or all charges before they can access them, a fact that has been criticised by several legal scholars.

According to the ALRC, diversion programmes should not require an admission of guilt so as to reduce the risk factors for pleading guilty under pressure.[109] They should instead, be developed and evaluated in order to determine whether they are capable of providing a wide range of supports to

99 Domestic Violence, Crime and Victims Act 2004, sec 22.
100 *R v H* (2003) 1 All ER 497 & *R v Antoine* (2003) ECtHR.
101 *H* (2003) UKHL 1, para 18.
102 Criminal Procedure (Insanity) Act 1964, sec 5.
103 CPA, sec 77(6).
104 Maher (n 38) 90.
105 Criminal Code (Canada), as it stood in January 1992, sec 672.25.
106 Pienaar (n 17) 81.
107 A Owusu-Bempah & N Wortley 'Unfit to plead or unfit to testify? *R v Orr* [2016] EWCA Crim 889' (2017) 80/6 *The Journal of Criminal Law* 396.
108 F Khan '*De Vos NO v Minister of Justice and Constitutional Development*: The constitutionality of detaining persons unfit to stand trial' (2017) 59 *SA Crime Quarterly* 42.
109 Commonwealth of Australia (CoA) *Royal commission into violence, abuse, neglect and exploitation of people with disability. Final report – volume 8, criminal justice and people with disability* (29 September 2023) 296–299.

persons with psychosocial disabilities charged with lesser offences, including providing assessment and diagnosis so as to allow for access to support services.[110] The latter is especially important when diverting to mental health services, under a civil voluntary treatment order.[111] Under this diversion scheme, an accused person with psychosocial disability would fall outside the criminal justice system, with treatment and discharge decisions resting with the clinician or a civil mental health tribunal only after consulting with the accused person with psychosocial disability.

The challenge, however, is that reforms in the area of diversion especially for mental health purposes have not gone far enough in addressing the CRPD Committee's concerns, especially as regards involuntary detention and treatment. In England and Wales for example, there is a proposal for a statutory requirement to consider postponing determinations of fitness to participate for up to 12 months, with a corresponding extension of the time limitation on hospital orders aimed at remanding a person for inpatient medical treatment under section 36 of the Mental Health Act of 1983.[112] It may be argued that this reform proposal merely reinforces the coercive provisions of the unfitness regime thus, contradicting the recommendations of the CRPD Committee.[113]

Disposition

After a finding of unfitness to plead, courts have the responsibility of determining how to deal with an accused person with psychosocial disability. During colonialism, the primary concern of unfitness declarations was confinement which involved the removal of persons with psychosocial disabilities from the society.[114] Individuals who the colonialists considered disruptive were labelled unfit and jailed or committed in mental asylums in order to maintain docile communities.[115] Laws provided for their involuntary detention until they were fit to return to the community.[116] Detention facilities resembled penitentiaries rather than medical facilities.[117] Presently, dispositions available following a finding of unfitness to stand trial differ between jurisdictions. They may involve the issuance of custodial or non-custodial supervision orders.[118]

110 As above.

111 P Gooding et al. 'Supporting accused persons with cognitive disabilities to participate in criminal proceedings in Australia: Avoiding the pitfalls of unfitness to stand trial laws' (2017) 35/2 *Law in Context a Socio-Legal Journal* 73.

112 Law Commission 2016 (n 46) para 4.81.

113 McGaughey et al. (n 84) 68.

114 R Edgar & H Sapire *African apocalypse: the story of Nontetha Nkwenkwe, a twentieth-century South African Prophet* (2000) 34.

115 Juma & Ngwena (n 18) 78.

116 AH Westbrook "Mental health legislation and involuntary commitment in Nigeria: a call for reform" (2011) 10 *Washington University Global Studies Law Review* 404.

117 Juma & Ngwena (n 18) 79.

118 Gooding et al. (n 111) 69.

Article 14(1)(a) of the CRPD obliges states parties to ensure that persons with psychosocial disabilities enjoy the right to liberty and security on an equal basis with others. Article 14(1)(b) of the CRPD further, prohibits both criminal and civil detentions based solely on a psychiatric diagnosis. Psychosocial disabilities are not on their own sufficient to warrant detentions.[119] This means that 'unfitness-based detentions' are prohibited as they are largely hinged on the nature of a person's impairment and the functioning of the mind or brain.[120]

Reforms in this area have involved the use of structural decolonisation mechanisms that do not echo and reproduce colonial relations for example through the use of non-custodial supervision orders.[121] These type of orders places accused persons with psychosocial disabilities under the supervision of a probation officer or social worker.[122] They often include conditions aimed at rehabilitation through for example non-resident medical treatment, counselling, and other forms of service provision. In New Zealand for example, unfit accused persons may be bailed to a place approved by the court, a hospital, or a secure facility[123] within 30 days of the finding of unfitness.[124] Subsequent orders may be made for the accused person to receive mental health treatment, disability support, imprisonment, or immediate release.[125]

The CRPD Committee's jurisprudence on unfitness to stand trial laws indicates that the loss of liberty flowing from a determination of unfitness to plead is in violation of the articles 12, 13 and 14 of the CRPD.[126] For instance, the Committee in its concluding observations to Ecuador expressed concern that declarations of unfitness to stand trial were a pretext for applying security measures involving the indefinite deprivation of liberty for persons with psychosocial disabilities who were not entitled to the same guarantees as their counterparts without disabilities in the criminal justice system.[127] It recommended that deprivation of liberty should be applied as a matter of last resort and when other diversion programmes, including restorative justice and community rehabilitation are insufficient to deter future crime.[128] Most jurisdictions, however, are yet to make provision for this social safety net of last resort for persons with psychosocial disabilities.[129]

119 A Nilsson *Compulsory mental health interventions and the CRPD: minding equality* (2021) 59.
120 Art 14(1)(b), CRPD.
121 S Kessi et al. 'Decolonizing African studies' (2020) 12 *Critical African Studies* 273.
122 Maher (n 38) 101.
123 Criminal Procedure (Mentally Impaired Persons) Act 2003 (NZ), sec 23(2).
124 Criminal Procedure (Mentally Impaired Persons) (NZ), sec 23(4).
125 Criminal Procedure (Mentally Impaired Persons) Act (NZ), sec 25(1a-d).
126 *Noble v Australia*.
127 CRPD Committee 'Concluding observations on the initial report of Ecuador' 27 October CRPD/C/ECU/CO/1 (2014).
128 CRPD Committee 'Concluding observations on the initial report of New Zealand' 31 October CRPD/C/NZL/ CO/1 (2014e).
129 West (n 71) 257.

Be that as it may, several countries such as Australia have moved away from the widely used regime of detention such as those given under the president/governor's pleasure, which saw individuals with psychosocial disabilities being detained until released by an executive order. This form of indefinite detention has been criticised for being antiquated, unjust, and prone to arbitrariness and political interference as they are subject to the discretion of the executive government.[130] As such, the law should make allowance for persons with psychosocial disabilities who are unable to effectively participate in the criminal process and who do not present a risk to others to be released through the use of early diversion court programmes.

The most common form of this programme has historically been diversion by way of hospital orders, especially in common law countries such as England and Wales.[131] These orders may require persons with psychosocial disabilities to be transferred and committed to or participate in mental health services, on the basis of their free and informed consent. For example, section 20BC of the Australia's Crimes Act provides that, if a court determines that a person is unfit to be tried and will not become fit to be tried within 12 months, the court may order that the person be detained in a hospital, but only if treatment is available, and the individual agrees to be transferred to a hospital or other place, including a prison.[132] In some countries, however, provisions have been enacted allowing for the overriding of decisions by accused persons with psychosocial disabilities in certain circumstances. For example, the proposed UK mental health legislation is expected to allow advance directives to be ignored when there are 'compelling reasons'.[133]

In other jurisdictions, if the court makes a custody order where it would have imposed imprisonment if the hearing involved a non-disabled person, the court must indicate a sentence that would have been appropriate, and the person cannot be detained for longer than this term.[134] In Italy, Croatia and Portugal for example, the length of a hospital order should not generally be longer than a prison sentence for a similar offence. In the case of Italy, however, a conditional discharge may continue long beyond the custodial phase, and in Croatia, the order may be extended by two years on multiple occasions.[135] The decision-making capacity is not a prerequisite for involuntary treatment in any of those jurisdictions.

130 See, eg, Victoria, Parliamentary Debates, Legislative Assembly, 19 September 1997, 185 (Jan Wade, Attorney-General).

131 Under section 36 of the Mental Health Act.

132 Crimes Act 1914 (Cth) s 20BC(2).

133 Final Report of the Independent Review of the Mental Health Act 1983 'Modernising the Mental Health Act'.

134 Mental Health Act 2015 (ACT) s 183.

135 G Szmukler 'Offenders with a mental impairment under a "fusion law": non-discrimination, treatment, public protection' (2020) 1 *International Journal of Mental Health and Capacity Law* 41.

In some countries, compulsory hospitalisation procedures are extremely arbitrary, blatantly discriminatory, and founded purely on disability. Malawi's hospital orders for instance, a country that ratified the CPRD in 2009, are based on 'unsoundness of mind', with no regard for circumstances of the case, including the severity or medical diagnosis of the accused person.[136] The failure to take into account the circumstances of accused persons with psychosocial disabilities and the warrantless use of involuntary medication, whether through psychotherapy and psychopharmacology has been found to be in violation of the right to freedom of thought and expression due to the high likelihood of iatrogenic harm, resulting from enforced use of antipsychotic treatment.[137] The practice of mandatory psychiatric medicalisation has been likened, albeit in derogatory terms, to 'manipulation of material evidence' because of their extremely serious and unpleasant side effects on those involved. For this reason, some courts have adopted strict measures that require the state to show that the relevant medication will not unduly prejudice the trial rights of affected persons.[138]

The CRPD Committee has criticised therapeutic aims in criminal law 'according to which persons considered "unfit to stand trial" on account of their impairment are not punished but are sentenced to treatment'.[139] For the Committee, regimes under which people are effectively 'sentenced to treatment' should be 'replaced by formal criminal sanctions for offenders whose involvement in crime has been determined'.[140] The purpose of this substitution is to eliminate separate processes which indirectly discriminates against accused persons with psychosocial disabilities.

According to the Office of the High Commissioner for Human Rights (OHCHR), 'legislation authorising the institutionalisation of persons with disabilities on the grounds of disability without their free and informed consent must be abolished'.[141] This includes situations 'where the deprivation of liberty is grounded in the combination between a mental or intellectual disability and other elements such as dangerousness, or [the need for] care and treatment'.[142] Article 14 of the CRPD prohibits forced hospitalisation and treatment of all persons with disabilities, including accused persons with psychosocial disability. To remedy this, certain jurisdictions have adopted a fusion

136 Laws of Malawi Chapter 34.02, Mental Treatment Act 2005, s. 11.

137 Brookbanks & MacKay (n 22) 265.

138 *Riggins v Nevada* 504 US 127 (1992).

139 CRPD Committee, Concluding Observations on the Initial Report of Denmark, 12th sess, 169th mtg, UN Doc CRPD/C/DNK/CO/1 (30 October 2014) 5 [34].

140 As above.

141 United Nations (UN) High Commissioner for Human Rights (UNHCHR) 'Thematic study on enhancing awareness and understanding of the Convention on the Rights of Persons with Disabilities' (47, U.N. Doc. A/HRC/10/48 (26 January 2009) 48.

142 As above.

of laws approach, which involves amalgamating mental health and mental capacity laws in one standalone piece of legislation.[143]

Disposition-fusion model

Proponents of the fusion model argue for a law that applies to all persons who are considered unable to make important decision for themselves, irrespective of the reason for that inability.[144] Currently, most Western legal systems such as England and Wales and Scotland operate two distinct legal schemes regulating involuntary disposition treatment schemes. Among them is the civil commitment scheme, usually found under the mental health regime, which is responsible for a majority of involuntary psychiatric treatment and hospital placement of persons with psychosocial disabilities who pose serious danger or risk to themselves or others.[145] The main aim of the fusion approach is elimination of discrimination against persons with psychosocial disabilities, through fostering respect for their dignity. The approach is lauded due to its ability to reduce stigma, protect autonomy, and remove confusing parallel mental health and mental capacity legislation.[146]

The scheme also applies to criminal involuntary commitments in hospital or prisons following the unfitness to plead declarations and guilty but insane verdicts.[147] Under a fusion law, the conventional recourse to an unfitness order would only be available if the accused person with psychosocial disability lacked decision-making capacity and treatment was in their best interests. The effect of this proposal would be to abolish specific mental health laws that coerce hospital admission and treatment on the basis of perceived risk and/or the severity of mental illnesses. It seeks to ensure that all involuntary, health-related interventions are based on capacity principles, whether the lack of capacity was due to a physical or mental disorder. For an accused person with decision-making capacity, treatment if considered appropriate, should only be considered on a voluntary basis.[148] However, the requirement for consent or non-consent to medication should not be used for the sole purpose of avoiding criminal trial or otherwise delaying or impeding the criminal process.[149]

143 J Dawson & G Szmukler 'Fusion of mental health and incapacity legislation' (2006) 188 *British Journal of Psychiatry* 504–509.

144 J Dawson & G Szmukler 'The "fusion law" proposals and the CRPD' in MA Stein et al. (eds) *Mental health, legal capacity, and human rights* (2021) 107.

145 G Szmukler et al. 'A model law fusing incapacity and mental health legislation' (2010) Special Edition *Journal of Mental Health Law* 12.

146 G Lynch et al. 'Mental capacity act (Northern Ireland) 2016' (2017) 41/6 *BJPsych Bulletin* 357.

147 C O'Mahony 'Implementation of article 12 of the UN Convention on the Rights of Persons with Disabilities in Northern Ireland' in M Domański & B Lackoroński (eds) *Models of implementation of article 12 of the Convention on the Rights of Persons with Disabilities (CRPD): private and criminal law aspects* (2023) 570.

148 Szmukler (n 135) 51.

149 Morse (n 61) 220.

The first principle of a fusion law stipulates therefore, that involuntary criminal detentions or treatments are only justified when an accused person with psychosocial disability lacks treatment decision-making capacity and the intervention is in their best interests.[150] In the unfitness system, however, this exceptions can also extend to those individuals who pose a substantial risk of serious harm to themselves and others, even though they possess the requisite mental capacity to make decisions regarding their medical treatment.[151] A second principle follows from the need to eliminate discrimination against accused persons with psychosocial disabilities when compared to non-disabled offenders charged with the same offence and with a similar level of seriousness. The management of those with psychosocial disabilities should be, as far as possible, on an equal basis with other offenders. Most importantly, the total duration of a deprivation of or a restriction of liberty for example, following a discharge order to the community, should be no longer than that imposed on non-disabled offenders.

Northern Ireland is considered the first country to have passed a law that is based on a fusion of law scheme.[152] The law repealed the then existing separate mental health legislation and merged aspects of that legislation into a single legal scheme based on capacity principles. In particular, non-consensual detention for purposes of treatment is based on incapacity to consent and on the accused person's best interests, as opposed to mental disability or risk. Certain steps are taken to support the accused person with psychosocial disability reach their own decision before they are declared unfit to participate, including providing adequate information, in the right environment, and ensuring the right persons were present.[153]

However, it has been argued that the Mental Capacity Act (Northern Ireland) (NI Act) is only anchored on the first principle of the fusion of law approach, which is the exception to the use of involuntary treatment.[154] According to the NI Act, before an order of involuntary treatment can be made against an offender, it must first be shown that the person is lacking in decision-making capacity and two, that treatment is the individual's best interest.[155] This functional capacity element, however, has been criticised for being excessively flexible thus, resulting in the erosion of the rights of persons with psychosocial disabilities.[156] According to Flynn, the 'impairment in the functioning of the mind or brain' requirement translates to a functional assessment of mental capacity which disproportionately affects persons with psychosocial disability.[157] The second principle, on the need to eliminate discrimination is

150 Szmukler, Daw, & Dawson (n 145) 12.

151 E Flynn 'Mental (in)capacity or legal capacity? A human rights analysis of the proposed fusion of mental health and mental capacity law in Northern Ireland' (2020) 64/4 *NILQ* 493.

152 Mental Capacity Act (Northern Ireland) 2016 (NI Act).

153 NI Act, secs 1(4) & (5).

154 Dawson & Szmukler (n 144) 107.

155 As above.

156 Flynn (n 151) 485–505.

157 Flynn (n 151) 497.

not fully recognised, which means that an accused person with psychosocial disability who has been declared unfit may be detained in a hospital or care home against their capacitous wishes, even when they have the capacity to make decisions and refuse the treatment.

While a detailed discussion of the NI Act is outside the scope of this book, it is noteworthy that the discourse surrounding the review of mental health and capacity law in Northern Ireland and the fusion model generally, predates the drafting and entry into force of the CRPD. The phrase best interests does not appear anywhere in article 12 of the CRPD. Such safeguard principles have been criticised for being paternalistic in nature as they permit the use of substitute decision-making, which are not permitted under article 12 of the CRPD.[158] To the CRPD Committee, the fusion model does not fully realise the supported decision-making approach of articles 12(3), 12(4) and 14(1)(b) of the CRPD, since it is based on mental capacity assessments. Such regimes should accordingly, be abolished and replaced with systems of supported decision-making.[159] This view, however, does not sit well with some state judiciaries who have faulted the Committee's absolutist demands on support measures for being unrealistic and failing to make provision for persons who are unable to defend their own interests.

The European Court of Human Rights in *AM-V v Finland*[160] for instance, found no breach of either the European Convention for the Protection of Human Rights and Fundamental Freedoms (European Convention)[161] or the CRPD when a person with psychosocial disability was treated against their will as long as it was considered necessary to protect them from life-threatening or irreversible harm.[162] In *Rooman v Belgium* the Grand Chamber upheld the detention of a convicted offender for psychiatric treatment on grounds of social protection and therapeutic aims.[163] Likewise, in *Fernandes de Oliveira v Portugal*, the same Court when addressing the duty of public hospitals to prevent voluntary patients from leaving the premises and killing themselves premised its arguments on the need for states to prevent harm to those concerned.[164]

These courts have declared approaches employing functional capacity tests, including in criminal law, as not amounting to discrimination on the basis of

158 Flynn (n 151) 498.

159 See, for example, Consideration of Reports Submitted by States Parties under Article 35 of the Convention: Concluding Observations, Tunisia, Committee on the Rights of Persons with Disabilities (CRPD), 5th Session, 4, UN Doc CRPD/C/TUN/CO/1 (11–15 April 2011) & Consideration of Reports Submitted by States Parties under Article 35 of the Convention: Concluding Observations, Spain, Committee on the Rights of Persons with Disabilities (CRPD), 6th Session, 5, UN Doc CRPD/C/ESP/CO/1 (19–23 September 2011).

160 *A-MV v Finland* (2017) ECtHR.

161 European Convention for the Protection of Human Rights and Fundamental Freedoms (ECHR), 213 UNTS (entered into force on 3/09/1953).

162 *Rappaz v Switzerland* (2013) ECtHR 508 paras 66–72.

163 *Rooman v Belgium*, App no. 18052/11 (ECtHR 2019), para 205.

164 *Fernandes de Oliveira v Portugal* (2019) ECtHR, para 124.

disability under the CRPD. The Federal Constitutional Court of Germany (GFCC) has argued that the CRPD Committee's statements on capacity tests are vague as they do not 'give an answer to the question of what, according to its understanding of the text of the Convention, should happen to persons who cannot form a free will and are in a helpless situation'.[165] According to the GFCC, it is the state's duty to provide medical care to persons who lack capacity to decide on their own need for treatment.[166] It held that article 12 of the CRPD does not prohibit such measures, including those making provision of treatment contrary to the preferences of accused person with psychosocial disability or when the person's 'capacity of self-determination' is 'limited due to illness'.[167]

Such views are in line with the Human Rights Committee's (HRC) standards which does not regard all forms of involuntary treatment as always arbitrary *per se*.[168] For instance, unconsented criminal hospitalisations may be allowed where it is proportionate and necessary for the purpose of protecting the individual in question from serious harm or preventing injury to others.[169] The Subcommittee on Prevention of Torture and Other Cruel, Inhuman or Degrading Treatment or Punishment also shares the similar views to those of the HRC.[170] Notwithstanding, these different interpretations of article 12 by various international human rights bodies, the author is of the opinion that the fusion model does not achieve compliance with article 12 of the CRPD and the requirement for state parties to ensure that their domestic law guarantees accused persons with psychosocial disabilities the right to exercise their legal capacity on an equal basis with others, including through the use of support or accommodation as was held in *Noble v Australia*.[171] However, this does not mean that everyone with a psychosocial disability must stand trial and receive equal punishment on account of their impaired decision-making capacity.

Disposition – substantive and procedural safeguards

Admittedly, it may be impractical to subject for example, an accused person with severe psychosocial disability to a full hearing in situations where they are unable to understand their trials, even with the provision of necessary

165 Judgment of 26 July 2016, 1 BvL 8/15 (BVerfG), para 91.

166 Federal Constitutional Court of Germany (2016) GFCC.

167 GFCC (n 166) para 88.

168 By or in itself.

169 Para 19, Human Rights Committee, General comment 35: Article 9 (Liberty and security of person), UN Doc. CCPR/C/GC/35 (2014).

170 'Approach of the Subcommittee on Prevention of Torture and Other Cruel, Inhuman or Degrading Treatment or Punishment regarding the Rights of Persons Institutionalized and Treated Medically without Informed Consent' (26 January 2016) UN Doc CAT/OP/27/2, paras 8, 11.

171 *Noble v Australia* as cited in Freckelton & Keyzer (n 16) 775.

adjustments.[172] Where this is the case and the person is not restorable to fitness within a reasonable period of time, the US Supreme Court has held in *Jackson v Indiana*[173] that the criminal jurisdiction should come to an end unless, there is proof that the individual poses a threat to self or others as was held in *O'Connor v Donaldson*.[174]

The holding in *O'Connor* was reiterated by the South African Constitutional Court in *De Vos NO v Minister of Justice and Constitutional Development*,[175] when it declined to strike down section 77(6)(a)(ii) of the Criminal Procedure Act (CPA),[176] that allowed for the detention of unfit accused persons who are likely to inflict harm on themselves or others, or who require care, treatment, and rehabilitation. Substantively, it can be argued that the exception for the deprivation of liberty in *O'Connor* and *De Vos No* is fair as it prohibits states' paternalistic action over individuals,[177] unless their actions are harmful to self and others.[178] The two decisions imply that not all persons with psychosocial disabilities are inclined to take part in full criminal trials. In such circumstances, other alternative less restrictive[179] disposition measures should be considered so as to avoid the risk of unreliable adjudications which, according to Slobogin, may be too great if such an individual proceeded with the trial.[180] The use of alternative disposition measures appears to be aligned with the CRPD, so long as the legal grounds which form the basis of such restrictions are de-linked from disability and apply to everyone, regardless of their medical conditions.[181] This substantive solution nevertheless, is still not as straightforward due to the risk of civil rights violation especially, by the political class, thus the need for the institution of procedural safeguards as per article 12 of the CRPD.

According to Perlin, persons with mental disabilities who have been deemed unfit are likely to spend more time in detention compared to their non-disabled counterparts.[182] Stronger safeguards and more regular review of detention orders have been touted as some of the solutions to this

172 GL Neuman 'Divergent human rights approaches to capacity and consent' in MA Stein et al. (eds) *Mental health, legal capacity, and human rights* (2021) 64.
173 (1972) 406 US 715.
174 *O'Conner v Donaldson* (1975) 422 US 563.
175 (2015a) ZACC 21.
176 Criminal Procedure Act 51 of 1977 (South Africa).
177 Pienaar (n 17) 70.
178 JS Mill quoted in M Robertson 'Mental illness: treatment of' in H ten Have (ed) *Encyclopedia of global bioethics* (2016) 1904.
179 *Lake v Cameron* (1966) 364 F 2nd 657.
180 C Slobogin 'Eliminating mental disability as a legal criterion in deprivation of liberty cases: the impact of the Convention on the Rights of Persons with Disability on the insanity defense, civil commitment, and competency law' (2015) 40 *International Journal of Law & Psychiatry* 41.
181 UN High Commissioner (n 141) para 48.
182 West (n 71) 250.

challenge.[183] In Australia, the key relevant Royal Commission's recommendation to the issue of disposition has been for a review of the National Principles and repeal of legislation that allow for indefinite detention of persons with psychosocial disabilities.[184] All jurisdictions are required to impose maximum terms of detention (also known as limiting terms). For example, in Western Australia, the Criminal Law (Mental Impairment) Act which was enacted in December 2023 legislates limiting terms for people found guilty of an offence but unfit to stand trial, and those acquitted due their mental impairment.[185] While such procedural safeguards are welcome, magistrates and judges should not over-rely on detentions.

Seclusion and solitary confinement may amount to inhuman and degrading treatment or torture or ill-treatment as per articles 15 and 16 of the CRPD, a fact that has been affirmed by courts and legislation across the globe.[186] The Humane Alternatives to Long-Term Solitary Confinement Act (HALT Act) of New York for instance, prohibits 'segregated confinement' for incarcerated persons with serious psychosocial disabilities.[187] The HALT Act was preceded by the decision in *Olmstead v LC*, where the Supreme Court of America had made an order for states to deinstitutionalise persons with disabilities who had been unjustifiably assigned to receive various state-provided services in segregated institutions rather than in the community.[188] The verdict acknowledged that persons with psychosocial disabilities are disproportionately held in solitary confinement, a fact that has also been recognised by several other states in the US and countries. Connecticut's General Assembly for instance, passed a law limiting the use of 'isolated confinement' for members 'of a vulnerable population', including persons who have historically grappled with psychosocial disabilities.[189] Similar laws exist in other countries, including Australia, Bangladesh, Canada, India, Serbia, and Ukraine, where limits exist on the use of solitary confinement for accused persons with psychosocial disabilities.[190]

183 *Winterwerp v Netherlands* (1979) ECtHR, 24 October 1979 & M Perlin 'God said to Abraham/kill me a son: why the insanity defense and the incompetency status are compatible with and required by the Convention on the Rights of Persons with Disabilities and basic principles of therapeutic jurisprudence' (2017) 54 *Criminal Law Review* 505.

184 CoA (n 109), para 8.12.

185 Criminal Law (Mental Impairment) Act 2023.

186 B McSherry 'Regulating seclusion and restraint in health care settings: the promise of the Convention on the Rights of Persons with Disabilities' (2017) 53 *International Journal of Law & Psychiatry* 41.

187 (2021) NY AB 2277 (NS).

188 (1999) 527 US 581.

189 Connecticut SB 1059, LegiScan (2021).

190 BA Barsky & MA Stein 'The United Nations Convention on the Rights of Persons with Disabilities, neuroscience, and criminal legal capacity' (2023) 10/1 *Journal of Law and the Biosciences* 16.

Disposition community-based alternatives

The promotion of alternatives to seclusion and restraint has particularly, been read into article 16 of the CRPD which, obligates state parties to protect persons with disabilities from all forms of exploitation, violence, and abuse.[191] It means that domestic laws should be interpreted in a manner that promotes community-based alternatives that allow for the right to live in the community as opposed to the blanket use of institutional detention. In Europe, laws governing deprivation of liberty of persons considered to lack mental capacity were found to be in breach of the right to liberty in as far back as 2005.[192] The Constitutional Courts of Germany and South Africa have also questioned their respective domestic regulations that allow for both detention and compulsory treatment of persons with psychosocial disabilities.[193] In South Africa, the Court dealt with the disposition of two accused persons following a finding of 'unfitness to stand trial' in terms of section 77(6) of the CPA. Before 2017, the law allowed the court a narrower range of options for disposition and specifically excluded the release of the accused (with or without conditions). A person diagnosed with mental disabilities was to be detained in prison or psychiatric hospital regardless of whether or not their condition would improve. The South African Constitutional Court held that the provisions limiting the court's options were inconsistent with article 12 of the Constitution which provided for the right to liberty and security of the person as read with article 14 of the CRPD. This resulted in the subsequent amendment of the CPA by the Criminal Procedure Amendment Act,[194] to allow for a wider range of options regarding orders that may be issued against accused persons found incapable of understanding criminal proceedings with the exclusion of detention, which includes hospitalisation as per the decision in *HL v UK*.[195]

According to Barsky and Stein, disposition by way of detention can exacerbate the conditions of persons with psychosocial disabilities, a position that has been acknowledged by several scholars and lawmakers across the globe.[196] Community-based treatment interventions are considered some of the most promising alternatives to existing unfitness detention practices globally and judges and legislators have been at the forefront of signalling this fundamental shift in the criminal justice system.[197] Judge Steve Leifman of Miami in

191 McSherry (n 186) 40.

192 *HL* v *the United Kingdom* (2005) 40 ECtHR 32.

193 BVerfG NJW 2011, 2113; BVerfG NJW 2011, 3571 & *De Vos NO v Minister of Justice and Constitutional Development* (n 72).

194 Criminal Procedure Amendment Act 4 of 2017.

195 *HL v United Kingdom* (2004) ECtHR 2004, para 91.

196 Barsky & Stein (n 190) 16.

197 GA Res 46/119, UN GAOR, 46th Sess, Supp No 49, at 189, UN Doc A/46/49, Principles for the Protection of Persons with Mental Illness and the Improvement of Mental Health Care (1991) (MI Principles).

the US for example, has used his judicial position to spearhead innovative programmes to redirect unfit accused persons with psychosocial disabilities into care and community reintegration.[198] The model emphasises community integration and redirection rather than competency restoration. However, it is only limited to misdemeanours. In New York and California, the Kendra[199] and Laura[200] Laws respectively, have adopted the Assisted Outpatient Treatment (AOT), which is a community-based civil commitment model that is geared towards providing a less restrictive, more holistic, and less expensive alternative to inpatient civil commitment.[201] It is not limited to misdemeanours, which may raise the question of social safety guarantees upon release. According to Morse, such risks should be borne by the society if they want to ensure their liberty and justice.[202]

In Estonia, section 137(1) of the CCRP stipulates that where it becomes evident, as a result of expert assessment, that a person held in custody committed an unlawful act in a state of 'mental incompetence', is 'mentally ill' or 'feeble-minded', or has another severe 'mental disorder', he or she shall be immediately released from custody by an order of the Prosecutor's Office, unless otherwise provided for in section 395 of the CCRP. Under the Singaporean Criminal Justice Reform Act (CJRA),[203] accused persons who are incapable of making their defence or those acquitted by operation of the defence of unsoundness of mind may be released with or without conditions by the minister in charge of prisons, after it is determined by a medical practitioner that they do not pose any danger to themselves or others. Such conditions may include requiring the person to be delivered to the care of a relative or friend.[204]

In England and Wales, the Law Commission has suggested supervision within the community following unfitness declarations. Such community service programmes are useful for three reasons, including continuity of care, expertise in available community services, and non-prison attitude.[205] However, the nature of the supervision order should satisfy concerns about public protection. According to George Szmukler, the supervision order should mandate both regular reviews by persons with special expertise in mental health

198 West (n 71) 282.

199 New York Mental Hygiene Law, para 9.60.

200 California Welfare & Institute Code, paras 5345–5349.5.

201 West (n 71) 280.

202 SJ Morse 'Retaining a modified insanity defense' (1985) 477/1 *The Annals of the American Academy of Political & Social Science* 137–147.

203 No 19 of 2018.

204 ASK Peng 'Implementation of article 12 of the UN Convention on the Rights of Persons with disabilities in Singapore' in M Domański & B Lackoroński (eds) *Models of implementation of article 12 of the Convention on the Rights of Persons with Disabilities (CRPD): private and criminal law aspects* (2023) 441.

205 M Schlanger 'Prisoners with disabilities' in E Luna (ed) *Reforming criminal justice: punishment, incarceration, and release* Phoenix, AZ: Academy for Justice (2017) 319.

matters and mental health assessment from experts if the reviewing officer detects signs of relapse or indicators of a significant risk of reoffending.[206]

Where it is deemed necessary to protect the public from serious harm, such supervision orders may have restrictions attached.[207] Accused persons with psychosocial disability should be liable to recall if they pose a risk to themselves or others as a result of their mental disability as is the case in England and Wales. In the latter jurisdiction, the authorisation of the minister in charge of justice or a mental health tribunal is required before a person with psychosocial disability can be discharged absolutely from hospital or conditionally to the community. The same applies to an absolute discharge from a conditional discharge.

Conditions may be imposed as occurs for non-disabled offenders for example, by prohibiting the individual from attending at a specified place. In other words, supervision should go beyond mere monitoring if it is to be considered constructive for instance by offering support and help for engaging in health care, rehabilitation, education, training, or employment programmes. It is also necessary for the state to ensure that the offender with psychosocial disability has the mental capacity to understand the terms of the supervision order for it to be an option. The suggestions are similar to the proposed supervision orders by the UK Law Commission for those persons found 'unfit to plead'.[208]

Challenges with the targeted approach

The targeted approach is not meant to dismantle the unfitness declarations house, but to reduce any harm to the rights of persons with psychosocial disabilities entering the criminal justice system.[209] The challenge with this type of reform approach is that it may be too slow to happen, rarely holistic and tends to be far too conservative.[210] It also has a pacification effect which, may lead to 'false consciousness'. The latter term has been used to describe the tendency of liberal reforms to 'dupe those at the bottom of the social and economic hierarchy,' including persons with psychosocial disabilities with promises of 'equality, fairness, and neutrality'.[211] Not only may such reforms be ineffective, so the argument goes, they may be harmful and insidious in that they may create the illusion of addressing the challenges of unfitness declarations when in fact they

206 Szmukler (n 135) 43.

207 Mental Health Act 1983, sec 37/41.

208 Law Commission. Unfitness to Plead. Volume 1: Report. 2016 Law Com No 364. http://www.lawcom.gov.uk; Mental health and fair trial: A report by JUSTICE. 2017. www.justice.org.uk.

209 K Kronick 'Intellectual disability, mitigation and punishment' (2024) 65 *Boston College Law Review* 1618.

210 R Darjee & T Marsh 'Arguments for the abolition of the defence of mental impairment' (2023) 30/1 *Psychiatry, Psychology and Law* 92.

211 M Bell 'Abolition: a new paradigm for reform' (2021) 46 *Law & Social Inquiry* 42.

reproduce the systems of inequality, racism, oppression, and injustice that they purport to address.[212] Thus, countries that have ratified the CRPD are advised not to wait for the quiet revolution and incremental journey to obsolescence, which has served the UK and other European jurisdictions well.

The targeted approach operates from the assumption that individual problems in the criminal justice system such as unfitness declarations are fixable with policies that only address particular issues, without confronting deeper systemic ones such as environmental, economic deprivation, or lack of access to health care.[213] It is based on the mythology that the system is fundamentally right and good and capable of achieving justice save for a few wrong areas. They do not shift power, control, and resources out of the criminal justice system. Instead, it keeps power and control within the same institutions and actors that create and sustain the fitness state.

8.1.2 Decolonisation through the power of abolition

The project of abolition may be contextualised as part of the decolonisation process due to its potential and ability to provide a cultural intervention to the colonial unfitness narrative that currently dominates the liberal-progressive paradigm of many criminal justice systems. It concentrates broadly on the impact of mental disability in the formulation of unfitness. It considers the unfitness declarations regime as an obsolete mechanism that cannot be reformed. It is characterised by its challenge to the social, historical, political, and economic sources of coloniality in unfitness declarations. The latter is hidden in institutions and laws that govern psychosocial disability in mental health systems across the globe.

The trend demands much more than surface-level reforms. It is committed to reimagining the possibilities of participation by aiming to shift power from the non-disabled to persons with psychosocial disabilities thus, 'fundamentally transforming their relationship among state and society'.[214] It involves a rejection of the propagated notion that the primary purpose of the unfitness structure is public safety, understanding instead that it exists to sustain and serve the interest of imperialists and identity capitalism. This means changing social structures and institutions rather than simply providing piecemeal reforms.[215]

However, it does not mean that the approach is solely about the total and immediate destruction of the unfitness declaration regime. It may also include steady efforts at reform aimed at dismantling the system thus, inching it closer

212 A Karakatsanis 'The punishment bureaucracy: how to think about criminal justice reform' (2019) 128 *Yale Law Journal Forum* 848–935.

213 Kronick (n 209) 1616.

214 AA Akbar 'Toward a radical imagination of law' (2018) 93 *New York University Law Review* 405–479.

215 Nilsson (n 119) 91.

to total abolition.[216] According to Renée Byrd, the abolitionist perspective is rigorously reflective about the connections between reform and the criminal justice system. It refuses to view the unfitness system as an isolated institution but instead, understands it as a set of relationships that need to be entirely transformed or recreated in order to achieve anything that can actually be called justice.[217]

In the context of unfitness, the abolitionist approach is largely based on the CRPD Committee's guidance to legal capacity. The said body has heavily criticised several nations for non-compliance with the provisions of the CRPD. It has made recommendations for the removal of all declaration of unfitness to stand trial from criminal justice systems in order to allow due process for accused persons with psychosocial disabilities on an equal basis with others.[218] Similar comments have also been made by the CRPD Committee in its concluding observations to Ecuador[219] and Australia.[220] This hardline approach of interpreting the provisions of article 12 of the CRPD requires individuals to always have the right to participate in criminal trials, with or without support.[221] Such directives have remained to be the case even where resulting declarations of unfitness have served to activate procedural safeguards geared towards ensuring the right to fair trial for accused persons with disabilities.[222]

In the Australian case of *Nicholson v Knaggs*,[223] Vickery J observed that article 12 of the CRPD endorsed the concept that people with disabilities, including those with psychosocial disabilities should have the capacity to exercise legal rights on an equal basis with others in all aspects of life. The Peruvian Constitutional Court has likewise, ordered the end of discriminatory identification between disability and incapacity.[224] This trend of reform allows lawmakers to get out from under the constraints of how psychosocial disability is understood within the framework of a majority of criminal justice systems across the globe where non-participation is thought of as an acceptable way to ensure the fair trial rights of persons with psychosocial disability.

216 AA Akbar 'An abolitionist horizon for (police) reform' (2020) 108 *California Law Review* 1787.

217 R Byrd '"Punishment's twin": theorizing prisoner reentry for a politics of abolition' (2016) 43/1 *Social Justice* 1–22.

218 CRPD Committee, Concluding Observations on the Initial Report of the Republic of Korea, 12th sess, UN Doc CRPD/C/KOR/CO/1 (29 October 2014) 5 [28].

219 Committee on the Rights of Persons with Disabilities, Concluding Observations on the Initial Report of Ecuador, CRPD/C/ECU/CO/01 (27 October 2014) 29(b).

220 Committee on the Rights of Persons with Disabilities, Concluding Observations on the Initial Report of Australia, 10th sess, 118th mtg, UN Doc CRPD/C/AUS/CO/1 (21 October 2013) 5 [34].

221 Neuman (n 172) 67.

222 P Brown 'Unfitness to plead in England and Wales: historical development and contemporary dilemmas' (2019) 59 *Medical Science Law* 187.

223 *Julie Ann Nicholson and Others v Timothy Knaggs and Others* (2009) VSC 64.

224 Peruvian Constitutional Court, Exp. 2313–2009-HC/TC, 24 September 2009.

The abolitionist trend challenges traditional legal conceptions of the right to fair trial, which are linked to liberal and progressive narratives of reform that ultimately serve to legitimate, strengthen, and expand unfitness declarations. However, the approach is not popular with legislators across the globe due to several reasons, including on account of fair trial rights.

In *SC v UK*,[225] effective participation was formally recognised as a requirement for a fair trial under article 6 of the European Convention. The Court concluded that effective participation in a trial presupposes several factors, including a broad understanding of the nature of the trial process whether with the assistance of an interpreter, lawyer, social worker, or friend. Criminal defendants must be able to make informed decisions and assist in their defence.[226] In other words, the accused person with psychosocial disabilities must be able to physically and mentally take part in the criminal trial process. The author contends that this definition has failed to protect against the harms of unfitness declarations. First, the definition has stringent preconditions which, may be applied with capacious discretion, and have evolved to incorporate various exceptions such that they do not practically stop the kind of barriers that engenders the problems of unfitness. Second, insofar as these principles focus narrowly on the behaviour of criminal justice actors, they will fail to address the most serious concerns of the rational calculus and oppressive atmosphere, which arise from the foundations of the unfitness declaration system.

Evidently, persons with psychosocial disabilities have a human right to a fair trial by virtue of being human. The latter right may be considered a grounding right which, is distinct from derivative membership rights. The concept of membership rights has been used to advocate for nuanced approaches to resolve the distinct challenges faced by persons with psychosocial disabilities, such as the persistent problem of limited participation in criminal proceedings following unfitness declarations. However, as a grounding right, the right to a fair trial may not include all the entitlements and correlating duties that derivative membership rights involve.

Unfitness declarations deprive persons with psychosocial disabilities of their participation rights on account of their membership status, which in this case is their disability. Simply having a low level of intelligence did not necessarily render an accused unable to follow the course of proceedings.[227] In *R(P) v West London Youth Court* it was held that age and limited intelligence do not necessarily lead to an inability to have a fair trial and adaptations to procedure were suggested to enable participation.[228] However, no detailed test has ever been formulated to define what effective participation means for persons with psychosocial disabilities. To the casual eye, effective participation is

225 *Stanford v UK* (1994) ECtHR.

226 RR Bonnie 'The competence of criminal defendants: a theoretical reformulation' (1992) 10 *Behavioral Science and the Law* 291–316.

227 *JD v R* (2013).

228 *R(P) v West London Youth Court* (2005).

synonymous with fitness to plead. However, the right to participation in itself does not for example, include as its correlative, a duty to provide modifications in criminal proceedings to all right holders. Only those with special circumstances or interests, such as persons with psychosocial disabilities, are entitled to such modifications. Therefore, it can be argued that even though unfitness declarations promote certain grounding rights such as fair trial rights, the same cannot be said for derivative membership rights such as reasonable accommodation thus, the need for reforms.

There are indeed, a few jurisdictions where the disability-based declarations in criminal law have been abolished. Sweden and some states in the United States of America (US) are notable examples.[229] For the US, however, the abolishing of disability-based declarations such as the insanity defence by certain states, was not being done in an attempt to get better outcomes, in terms of justice and equality for persons with psychosocial disabilities. It was done instead, to counter public perception that such orders were being used by people to avoid the goals of the criminal justice system such as punishment and as a way of crime control.[230] As a result, the US legislators and subsequent court decisions[231] that have upheld the elimination of such declarations/defences missed the opportunity to preserve the rights of accused persons with psychosocial disabilities to access of justice.

As for Sweden, although disability-based declarations such as the 'unaccountability due to mental disease or defect' were abolished, the law still allowed for persons with 'severe mental disorders' to be detained indefinitely and compulsorily treated in a forensic facility.[232] This drawing of distinctions based on the intensity or degree of mental disability may be criticised for being arbitrary due to its mandatory nature and because it is imposed against the will of persons with psychosocial disabilities on the pretext of treatment.[233] This book does not seek to argue for a US or Swedish style approach to abolishing unfitness declarations that leaves persons with psychosocial disabilities the mercies of the court and other welfare systems and with limited procedural safeguards. At present, there is a strong movement for reform with several criticisms surrounding the way in which the interests of persons with psychosocial disabilities have been blurred by the need for treatment, principles of criminal responsibility and public protection.[234]

229 Idaho, Utah, Montana, Kansas, and Alaska.

230 Darjee & Marsh (n 207) 89.

231 *Kahler v Kansas* (2020) 140 S. Ct. 1021, 1022.

232 T Bennet 'An integrated model for criminal responsibility in action: how Swedish criminal law operates without an insanity defence' (2024) 35 *Criminal Law Forum* 276.

233 J Breeding 'Practicing Szasz: a psychologist reports on Thomas Szasz's influence on his work' (2014) *Sage Open Journals* 2.

234 P Gooding & T Bennet 'The abolition of the insanity defence in Sweden and the United Nations Convention on the Rights of Persons with Disabilities: human rights brinksmanship or evidence it won't work?' (2018) 21 *New Criminal Law Review* 141–169.

Modern mental health legislation and unfitness concepts are being entirely redrafted, with the specific aim of achieving compliance with the CRPD.[235] For example, Peru and Costa Rica were amongst the first nations to attempt the elimination and replacement of the substitution model of participation with assistive solutions for people with disabilities.[236] In Australia, the Victorian Act similarly, provides among others that persons with psychosocial disabilities are presumed to have capacity and have the rights to dignity, participation in decision-making, preference for voluntary treatment, respect for their views and preferences, tolerance for decisions that involve a degree of risk, and respect, and promotion of their autonomy.[237]

According to Mahomed, Fiala-Butora, and Stein, absolute prohibitions are not ideal especially, when it comes to providing effective solutions to global disability challenges such as, those associated with participation in the criminal justice system.[238] The abolition of unfitness declarations requires careful planning and budgeting to prevent any further violations of human rights. Criticism has centred on the unintended consequences of the absolutist position, especially in the absence of well-conceived and tested alternatives to existing legal models.

For example, it has been argued that abolition of the declarations would severely curtail the provision of expert evidence which could have a retrograde effect not only for accused persons with psychosocial disabilities, but also for the legitimate role of mental health professions in assisting with the administration of justice.[239] That it is accurate, therapeutic, humane, preserving of autonomy, dignity and integrity, and in the public interest for mental health professionals to be involved in judicial processes that focus on mental states.[240] That to treat an unfit person as a fit person under the criminal justice system does not preserve the integrity or justice of the criminal process.[241] Still others have expressed concern that the notion of 100% participation for persons with psychosocial disabilities is a 'legal fiction'.[242] Admittedly, without

235 Victoria, Parliamentary Debates, Legislative Assembly, 12 March 2014, 689–691 (Ted Baillieu).

236 See Peru's Legislative Decree 1384 & Costa Rica's 2016 Law 9379.

237 Victorian Act secs 10(b), 10(d), 11(a), 11(c), 11(d), 11(e), & 70.

238 F Mahomed et al. 'Anna Nilsson, compulsory mental health interventions and the CRPD: minding equality (Hart Studies in Law and Health, 2021) ISBN 9781509931576, 186 pages' (2021) 43/3 *Human Rights Quarterly* 617.

239 ML Perlin & HE Cucolo *Mental disability law: civil and criminal* (3d ed, 2016) para 14–1.2.8.

240 RJ Bonnie 'Fitness for criminal adjudication: the emerging significance of decisional competence in the United States' in R Mackay & W Brookbanks (eds) *Fitness to plead: international and comparative perspectives* 178–179.

241 M Moore 'Intention as a marker of moral culpability and legal punishability' in RA Duff & S Green (eds) *Philosophical foundations of criminal law* (2011).

242 L Harmon 'Falling off the vine: legal fictions and the doctrine of substituted judgment' (1990) 100 *Yale Law Journal* 1.

any established replacement mechanisms to capacity-based approaches to trial participation, nor any broad-based support for abolishing unfitness declarations in the criminal justice system, recommendations for elimination may be impossible to achieve.

The unresolved theoretical and practical difficulties evident in the CRPD Committee's abolitionist approach have meant that some of its more problematic edicts have been politely sidelined in a few major law reform reports concluded since.[243] A number of law reform agencies in the English-speaking world, such as the Law Commission of England and Wales and the ALRC have taken the view that certain accused persons with psychosocial disabilities simply cannot be supported to reach equal standing in conventional trials and hence, require alternative disability-specific procedures.[244] The ALRC, for example, has stated that a failure to allow for special declarations would seemingly violate the right to equal recognition before the law and access to justice under the CRPD.[245] According to the ALRC, the Committee's approach to legal capacity as found in General Comment 1 is provided merely 'by way of guidance' and is not binding on Australia.[246] It also declined to implement certain recommendations by the CRPD Committee for example, withdrawing Australia's interpretive declaration.[247]

The other such criticism is found in the report by the Essex Autonomy Project which, in its advise to the UK Ministry of Justice highlighted on the extreme abolitionist demands of the CRPD Committee in terms of participation of persons with disabilities. According to the report the guidelines under General Comment 1 not binding on the UK and should not be followed because they go beyond what is explicitly stated in the text of the CRPD.[248] While these are valid critiques that may support a quiet reform of unfitness declarations, they do not justify the retention of such court orders as part of fair trial options and the only means of ensuring effective participation of persons with psychosocial disabilities in the criminal justice system. Persons with psychosocial disabilities should not be barred from participation in criminal processes simply because they have a particular diagnosis, a confused thought process, or uncorrectable perceptions about the world. This begs the question whether unfitness declarations are outdated both in terms of language and purpose? To answer the question, it is important to consider another vision of abolition approach, which is the creation of new vocabulary, including the elimination and substitution of certain disability-based terms, such as unfitness.

243 W Martin et al. *Achieving CRPD compliance: is the mental capacity act of England and Wales compatible with the UN Convention on the Rights of Persons with Disabilities? If not, what next?* (Report, Essex Autonomy Project, 22 September 2014).

244 ALRC (n 31) paras 1.21 & 3.45 & Law Commission of England and Wales *Unfitness to plead: an issues paper* (2014), para 2.80.

245 ALRC (n 31), para 7.43.

246 ALRC (n 31) 48, paras 2.55 & 2.56.

247 ALRC (n 31), paras 2.96–2.97.

248 Martin et al. (n 243) 12–13.

Creation of disability-neutral doctrines

The CRPD Committee considers any legislation non-compliant that is based on a mental capacity test, even one using the functional approach.[249] One way of solving this problem is through equal treatment between the disabled and non-disabled people in the criminal justice system. Presently, the declaration is not available to unfit non-disabled persons who may not be able to participate in criminal trials due to external factors affecting the brain such as situational compulsion or social-adversity.[250] The neutrality-approach acknowledges the problematic character of the distinction between fitness and unfitness. The use of such value-based declarations is discriminatory because they mandate differential treatment between persons with psychosocial disabilities and all other persons.[251] On the contrary, value-free terminologies have as their aim the application of similar capacity principles to all persons as opposed only to those with mental health conditions.[252] In other words, they are concerned with the elimination of discrimination in criminal procedures against persons with psychosocial disabilities.[253]

The approach forms part of the decolonial process and what Andrea Broderick has referred to as the transformative approach to equality.[254] The latter obliges states to implement a range of positive measures in order to change stereotypes, customs, and practices that marginalise persons with psychosocial disabilities from enjoying their criminal trial rights.[255] Disability-neutral doctrines may help in this regard by shifting the debate from the legality of unfitness and othering of persons with psychosocial disabilities, to 'the legitimate reach of the law into the autonomy of all citizens'.[256]

This potential of the value-free model to provide accused persons with psychosocial disabilities with procedures available to non-disabled defendants is akin to Slobogin's integrationist approach to criminal law. The latter has as its pivotal element the capacitation of both the disabled and non-disabled persons on an equal basis so as to counter insidious sanist notions of disability-specific declarations, that persons with psychosocial disabilities are unfit.[257] Such a

249 L Series and A Nilsson 'Article 12 CRPD: equal recognition before the law' in I Bantekas et al. (eds) *The UN Convention on the rights of persons with disabilities* (2018) 339–382.

250 N Morris et al. 'Should the insanity defense be abolished-an introduction to the debate' (1985–1987) 1 *Journal of Law & Health* 113–140.

251 S Gurbai 'Beyond the pragmatic definition? The right to non-discrimination of persons with disabilities in the context of coercive interventions' (2020) 22/1 *Health and Human Rights Journal* 280.

252 Neuman (n 172) 59.

253 F Agnes 'Law, ideology and female sexuality: gender neutrality in rape law' (2002) 37/9 *Economic and Political Weekly* 845.

254 A Broderic *The long and winding road to equality and inclusion for persons with disabilities: the United Nations Convention on the Rights of Persons with Disabilities* (2015) 36–37.

255 T Degener 'Disability in a human rights context' (2016) 5 *Laws* 35.

256 P Gooding & E Flynn 'Querying the call to introduce mental capacity testing to mental health law: does the doctrine of necessity provide an alternative?' (2015) 4 *Laws* 266.

257 C Slobogin 'An end to insanity: recasting the role of mental disability in criminal cases' (2000) *Virginia Law Review* 1199–1247.

measure is capable of improving public perception towards criminal justice systems across the globe, which has been plagued by notions of inequality especially towards persons with disabilities.

States are encouraged to apply similar criminal procedures to both non-disabled defendants and accused persons with psychosocial disabilities.[258] To this end, legislators and courts may be forced to confront uncomfortable questions about why laws restricting legal capacity are acceptable if imposed on people with mental disabilities but not the general population. In *Moshoeshoe v Director of Public Prosecutions*[259] for example, the Constitutional Division of the High Court of Lesotho declared section 219 of the Criminal Procedure and Evidence Act,[260] which barred persons with psychosocial disabilities from testifying in court as unconstitutional for violating their rights to freedom from discrimination and equality before the law as enshrined in sections 18 and 19 of the Constitution of Lesotho, respectively.[261] The dehumanising terminology in Gambia's Lunatic Detention Act of 1917 was held to violate the African Charter on Human and People's Rights.[262] Similarly, a domestic constitutional court declared the Zambian Mental Disorders Act[263] unlawful partly due to its discriminatory language.[264] Expressions such as 'feeble-mindedness' and 'abnormality' in section 20 of the German Criminal Code (*Strafgesetzbuch*) have been replaced by the terms 'intelligence impairment' and 'disorder' in relation to a person's lack of criminal responsibility.[265] Likewise, in Chile,[266] Pakistan,[267] Turkey,[268] terms such as 'handicapped', 'faulty', 'mentally retarded', or 'impaired' have been replaced with the phrase 'persons with disabilities' in several laws and decrees in order to abandon derogatory terminology.

258 Barsky & Stein (190) 6.

259 *Koali Moshoeshoe v Director of Public Prosecutions*, CC/14/2017 [2019] LSHC (Lesotho).

260 Criminal Procedure and Evidence Act, 1981 (Act. No. 9/1981) § 219 (Lesotho).

261 Constitution of Lesotho 1993, Chapters 1 and 2.

262 *Purohit and Moore v Gambia* (2003) African Commission on Human and Peoples' Rights.

263 Zambian Mental Disorders Act of 1951.

264 *Mwewa, Kasote and Katontoka v The Attorney General and Zambia Agency for Persons with Disabilities* (2017) ZMHC 77.

265 R Giesen 'Implementation of article 12 of the UN Convention on the Rights of Persons with Disabilities in the Federal Republic of Germany' in M Domański & B Lackoroński (eds) *Models of implementation of article 12 of the Convention on the Rights of Persons with Disabilities (CRPD): private and criminal law aspects* (2023) 253.

266 GL Rivera 'Implementation of article 12 of the UN Convention on the Rights of Persons with Disabilities in the Republic of Chile' in M Domański & B Lackoroński (eds) *Models of implementation of article 12 of the Convention on the Rights of Persons with Disabilities (CRPD): private and criminal law aspects* (2023) 112.

267 *Barrister Asfandyar Khan Tareen, etc. v Government of the Punjab*, W-P No. 29131/2017 (Lahore High Court, 2017).

268 GG Koşar 'Implementation of article 12 of the UN Convention on the Rights of Persons with Disabilities in Turkey' in M Domański & B Lackoroński (eds) *Models of implementation of article 12 of the Convention on the Rights of Persons with Disabilities (CRPD): private and criminal law aspects* (2023) 548.

In the case of unfit defendants, the foregoing decisions imply that competency restoration treatment are impermissible and should be replaced with 'supported decision-making', where the latter is capable of rendering a person with psychosocial disabilities competent as discussed in section two of this chapter.[269] The CRPD envisions a procedure that only applies to trial participation and not unfitness proceedings. If applied properly, the supportive model will eliminate the need for unfitness declarations as it allows for meaningful participation. The latter has countered the argument against the elimination approach to unfitness on account of being anti-therapeutic as the main purpose of support provisions is to ensure the voices of persons with psychosocial disabilities are respected and considered throughout the trial process, which is a fundamental goal of therapeutic jurisprudence.[270] The measures are not being used to coerce defendants with psychosocial disabilities into proceeding with the criminal trial or suppress their right to fair trial as has been argued by certain scholars.[271]

Certain jurisdictions have already begun the process of altering their statutory disability-based terminology to less stigmatising expressions. For example, the insanity defence in Australia has been replaced with the 'mental impairment',[272] 'mental incompetence'[273] and 'mental illness' defences.[274] In Northern Ireland, Canada, and Scotland, the common law expression of 'insanity' was replaced in 1966, 1992, and 2010 respectively, with the phrase 'mental disorder' as a way of defining 'unfitness'.[275] It may be argued that these changes are not entirely consonant with the CRPD since none of them have endorsed the disability-neutral proposals of the CRPD Committee. Moreover, the legal principles on which criminal responsibility is explored in relation to offenders with psychosocial disabilities have remained the same as the M'Naghten-based insanity defence.[276] It is noteworthy, however, that the laws have been amended or reviewed to varying degrees so as to improve compliance with human rights obligations, and particularly the central challenges established by article 12 of the CRPD. Five states and the Australian Capital

269 Slobogin (n 180) 36–42.

270 G Mehgan & ML Perlin '"The pain I rise above": how international human rights can best realize the needs of persons with trauma-related mental disabilities' (2017) 29/3 *Florida Journal of International Law* 290.

271 Perlin (n 182) 505.

272 Criminal Code (Northern Territory) sec 43C, Criminal Code (Western Australia) sec 27, Criminal Code 2002 (Australian Capital Territory) sec 28, & Crimes (Mental Impairment and Unfitness to be Tried) Act 1997 (Victoria), sec 20.

273 Criminal Law Consolidation Act 1935 (South Australia) s 269C.

274 Mental Health (Forensic Provisions) Act 1990 (New South Wales), s 38.

275 Criminal Justice Act (Northern Ireland) 1966, sec 1; Criminal Code (Canada), sec 2; & Criminal Responsibility of Persons with Mental Disorder Criminal Justice and Licensing (Scotland) Act 2010, sec 168.

276 M Wondemaghen 'Testing equality: insanity, treatment refusal and the CRPD' (2018) 25/2 *Psychiatry, Psychology & Law* 182.

Territory have enacted new legislation,[277] and the Chief Psychiatrist of South Australia has recently completed a review of the Mental Health Act.[278]

However, not all derogatory terminologies are being abandoned. The use of such terms in some states is allowed as long as they are easily understood and does not lead to difficulties in practice. In Singapore for instance, the government has endorsed the use of specific derogatory terms in the domain of criminal law, such as unsoundness of mind on account that it has acquired a specific legal meaning that has been developed by the courts over decades.[279] The first danger with such a view, it may be argued, is the potential to create definitional tensions between mental and legal capacity with implications for reform.

The legal nature of the phrase unsoundness of mind it has been argued, is not limited to the mental condition of people and as such, cannot be said to be in conflict with article 12 of the CRPD.[280] This argument is too broad and liberal and without any statutory definition or judicial agreement, it may seem absurd to classify for example, conditions such as psychomotor epilepsy[281] and sleepwalking[282] as unsoundness of mind as has been done by some judicial officers and scholars.[283] It is also not empirically and historically accurate especially, because competency restoration procedures have always been regarded as forms of mental health treatment although, with very little therapeutic value due to their involvement with factors such as involuntary medication and related procedures conducted in a psychiatric hospital.[284] Empirically, unfitness declarations have disproportionately affected accused persons with psychosocial disabilities as evidenced in a study conducted by Latimer and Lawrence in Canada, which revealed that approximately three-quarters of those declared unfit or insane were people who had been diagnosed with psychosocial conditions such as schizophrenia (56%) or an affective disorder (13%) such as bipolar disorder, schizoaffective disorder, or major depression.[285]

277 Mental Health Act 2015 (Australian Capital Territory (ACT)) ('ACT Act'); Mental Health Amendment (Statutory Review) Act 2014 (NSW), amending Mental Health Act 2007 (New South Wales (NSW)) ('NSW Act'); Mental Health Act 2016 (Queensland (Qld)) ('Queensland Act'); Mental Health Act 2013 (Tas) ('Tasmanian Act'); Mental Health Act 2014 (Vic) ('Victorian Act'); Mental Health Act 2014 (WA) ('WA Act').

278 Office of the Chief Psychiatrist 'Review of the Mental Health Act 2009' (Report, Department of Health and Aging (SA), 23 May 2014).

279 Peng (n 204) 440.

280 Wondemaghen (n 276) 181.

281 *R v Sullivan* (1983) 2 All ER 673, 677–678 & *Bratty v Attorney-General for Northern Ireland* (1963) AC 386.

282 *R v Burgess* (1991) 2 WLR 1206.

283 Y Dejchai 'The insanity defence revisited: to retain or abolish? The study from the UK and US regimes' (2019) 8/2 *Nitipat NIDA* 33.

284 M Hale *The history of the pleas of the Crown* (1736) 34–35; W Blackstone *Commentaries on the Laws of England* (1850) 24, vol. 4.

285 J Latimer & A Lawrence *The review board systems in Canada: an overview of results from the mentally disordered accused data collection study* Canada Department of Justice (2006) 20.

Admittedly, physical conditions may limit the participation capacity of an accused as stipulated by the ECtHR,[286] which has also listed mental state,[287] hearing,[288] linguistic and communication ability,[289] intellectual competence,[290] developmental immaturity,[291] age, and social background, as aspects that may also contribute to trial non-participation.[292] These factors affect both disabled and non-disabled persons. However, the presence of the limitations does not automatically result in the non-participation of accused persons. The state has to assess to what extent effective participation has been compromised and the compensatory measures required to remedy the gap such as provision of support.[293] As for the procedure of fitness restoration, the latter is a psycho-legal as opposed to a purely legal measure that disproportionately affects persons with mental disabilities.[294] The High Commissioner for Human Rights affirmed this conclusion when it concluded that considerations of both unfitness and unsoundness of mind are largely based on mental capacity which, negates legal capacity. This is because they are directly and indirectly based on disability.[295] Disability-neutral legislation thus, does not imply a move to ending unfitness declarations, instead, it simply changes the justification for making such orders. The implication of this construct is to open incapacity declaration for use by non-disabled persons with physical illnesses such as hyperglycaemia,[296] arteriosclerosis,[297] and epilepsy,[298] as long as they are sufficiently divorced from disability.[299] It forces us to abandon Descartes theory on the duality between body and mind for monism, the latter of which recognises that a person's behaviour is a product of his or her inseparable, irreducible, and irreplaceable physical and mental properties.[300]

286 *Tarasov v Ukraine* (2013) ECtHR, paras 98–101 (violation regarding a defendant who was unable to walk and sit and had to be brought in on a stretcher and lie there during the entire trial, and who was not able to deliver a closing statement).
287 *Güveç v Turkey* (2009) ECtHR, paras 123–133 (violation involving a minor with psychological problems without counsel).
288 *Grigoryevskikh v Russia* (2009) ECtHR, paras 78–94 & *Timergaliyev v Russia* (2008) ECtHR.
289 *Baytar v Turkey* (2014) ECtHR, paras 46–59.
290 *Vaudelle v France* (2001) ECtHR, paras 50–66 (violation involving a defendant who had been deemed to be unfit to defend himself in earlier civil proceedings).
291 *Blokhin v Russia* (2013) ECtHR, para 157.
292 *Botnik v Ukraine* (2011) ECtHR, para 43.
293 PHPHMC van Kempen 'The right to fair preliminary investigation and trial for vulnerable defendants: The case of the Netherlands' in Mackay R & WJ Brookbanks (eds) *Fitness to plead: international and comparative perspectives* (2018) 239.
294 Brookbanks & Mackay (n 22) 272.
295 UN High Commissioner (n 141) para 45.
296 *R v Hennessy* (1989) 1 WLR 287.
297 *R v Kemp* (1957) 1 QB 399.
298 *R v Sullivan* (1984) 1 AC 156.
299 Bartlett (n 5) 762.
300 Morris, Bonnie, & Finer (n 250) 131.

It means that unsoundness and by extension unfitness cannot be solely attributed to the mind. The latter view, however, may be impossible as the very state that negates participation of persons with psychosocial disabilities in access to justice may in certain cases, be directly linked to the disability.[301] To this end, Wondemaghen has argued that the ultimate move to abandon such declarations because they are not disability-neutral may be insurmountable, especially when they are not replaced with equally extensive alternatives.[302] While this may be true to an extent, it does not mean that issues related to capacity should not be addressed, considering its pivotal position in the relationship between mental disability and other aspects of the law such as criminal defences. It therefore means that the development of non-discriminatory alternative formulations to unfitness declarations should be of paramount importance.

The second risk with Singapore's endorsement of such phrases concerns the debate between language and substance. To members of the public, this may create in them a perception that such terminological reforms are merely symbolic as they seemingly do little to change the existing law. Admittedly, excluding the phrase unfitness from criminal laws is not a panacea to the problem of moral harms that arise from the attitudes of criminal justice actors. It seems not to be concerned with the automatic negation of legal capacity for persons with psychosocial disabilities when declarations such as unfitness are employed.[303] This, however, is not the case because in removing this potent disability-based declaration, the state will reduce the incentives of discrimination and thus mitigate the harms of access to justice that accused persons with psychosocial disabilities face in the criminal justice system.

According to María José Bravo Bosch and Inés Celia Iglesias Canle, moving away from traditional terms such as "incapacity" and "incapacitation" in favor of more respectful and accurate language better reflects the reality that persons with disabilities possess the ability to hold and exercise their human rights, a reality that has long been overlooked.[304] The use of phrases such as 'facilitated', 'supported', or 'assisted' instead of 'special', are well in step with trends in disability policy whose objective is to move away from concepts of vulnerability and 'specialness' towards universal design and acceptance of disability as a norm of human diversity.[305] As such, rethinking terms like 'unfit to stand trial' may assist towards the capacitation of accused persons with psychosocial disabilities in the criminal justice system.

301 Wondemaghen (n 276) 181.

302 As above.

303 Wondemaghen (n 276) 175.

304 MJB Bosch & ICI Canle 'Implementation of article 12 of the UN Convention on the Rights of Persons with Disabilities in Spain' in M Domański & B Lackoroński (eds) *Models of implementation of article 12 of the Convention on the Rights of Persons with Disabilities (CRPD): private and criminal law aspects* (2023) 486.

305 P Gooding et al. 'Unfitness to stand trial and the indefinite detention of persons with cognitive disabilities in Australia: human rights challenges and proposals for change' (2017) 40 *Melbourne University Law Review* 863.

Be that as it may, it is important to note that the mere appearance of disability-neutrality does not negate the existence of discrimination.[306] From an equality perspective, the application of disability-neutral laws may be applied in a manner that indirectly discriminates against persons with psychosocial disabilities.[307] Such an approach for example, might selectively invoke the principle of formal equality to justify ignoring disability-based disadvantages.[308] In other words, it may mask rather than counter the injustices which are inherent in unfitness declarations regime. To remedy this, a thicker as opposed to facial disability-neutral laws should be adopted. The former implies genuine neutrality as opposed to facial neutrality, which may narrowly affect the participation of persons with psychosocial disabilities in the criminal justice system. Thick disability-neutral laws should go beyond the requirement of abolishing disability-based declarations by accounting for differences in the participation of persons with psychosocial disabilities in the criminal justice system.[309] Where this is the case at the national level, article 4(4) of the CRPD will apply and the Convention will not affect such provisions which, may be viewed as being more conducive to the realisation of the rights of accused persons with psychosocial disabilities.

8.2 Conclusion

Decolonisation involves developing forms of autonomy for accused persons with psychosocial disabilities such as, effective involvement in criminal trials. Solutions concerning the active participation of persons with psychosocial disabilities adopted in individual countries vary to a considerable extent. It is not easy to speak of any harmonisation or standardisation of criminal law regulations in this respect. Some of the rules have been developed on the basis of the very generally worded clause under the CRPD. Others are very much rooted in the common law legal tradition, historical experiences, and the general processes of development of given legal systems. For these reasons, a comparative research that is aimed at producing general conclusions is extremely difficult. It is also impossible to develop a one-size-fits-all model for the transposition of CRPD's article 12, into the diverse national legal systems that exists around the globe.

Be that as it may, it is impossible to overlook the profound changes that have been introduced by legislators in countries that have implemented the provisions of the CRPD. Addressing widespread disadvantage in the unfitness declarations system would require comprehensive changes, including in its processes as well as in the detention and release of persons with psychosocial

306 JA Williams 'Reassessing gender neutrality' (2020) 54/1 *Law and Society Review* 23.

307 A Kanter *The development of disability rights under international law: from charity to human rights* (2015).

308 Williams (n 306) 13.

309 R Kayess & P French 'Out of darkness into light? Introducing the Convention on the Rights of Persons with Disabilities' (2008) 8 *Human Rights Law Review* 7.

disabilities. This ambitious task is part of the broader CRPD's objective to ensure respect for differences and acceptance of persons with psychosocial disabilities as part of human diversity and humanity.[310] Some law reform trends across the globe are already heading in the direction of compliance with the CRPD. Although some scholars have pushed for the sort of wholesale reform suggested in the second section of this chapter, none of the nations which have ratified the CRPD have embraced it. Most countries are implementing piecemeal reforms. Typically, the reforms have responded to amending provisions relating to various provisions such as, criteria for determining unfitness, reasonable accommodation, and disposition.

Currently, variations of all two reform approaches can be found among the laws and various court decisions that have considered the unfitness question, and this may continue as long as no institutional changes are implemented to provide for greater coherence in the criminal justice system. So far, states seem to have accepted, albeit sometimes grudgingly, the standard rules of the CRPD, as well as its interpretation and application by the CRPD Committee, in a way that is leading towards reforms of the unfitness declaration regime. In certain jurisdictions, the direction taken is clear in terms of widening the scope of participation of persons with psychosocial disabilities, narrowing the extent of unfitness declarations and treating detention as a measure of last resort. At the same time, the scope of application of reasonable accommodation mechanisms is being widened. In other few jurisdictions, the declaration of unfitness is being abolished as a legal norm. Thus, from the foregoing, it can be argued that the laws relating to unfitness from various jurisdictions contains ingredients of a growing system that links criminal and mental health laws for persons with psychosocial disabilities. In the next chapter, recommendations are provided based on the findings in this chapter and discussions in previous chapters.

References

Agnes F 'Law, ideology and female sexuality: gender neutrality in rape law' (2002) 37/9 *Economic and Political Weekly* 845. https://doi.org/10.2307/4411809.

Akbar AA 'Toward a radical imagination of law' (2018) 93 *New York University Law Review* 405. https://doi.org/10.2139/ssrn.3061917.

Akbar AA 'An abolitionist horizon for (police) reform' (2020) 108 *California Law Review* 1787. https://doi.org/10.2139/ssrn.3670952.

Australian Capital Territory 'New South Wales, Victoria, South Australia, Tasmania and Northern Territory. Crimes Act 1900 (ACT)'.

Australian Human Rights Commission 'Submission No 6 to the Senate Community Affairs References Committee, Inquiry into the Indefinite Detention of People with Cognitive and Psychiatric Impairment in Australia' March 2016.

Australian Law Reform Commission Equality *Capacity and disability in Commonwealth Laws* (Report 124 of 2014).

Baldry E 'Disability at the margins: limits of the law' (2014) 23 *Griffith Law Review* 357, 370–388. https://doi.org/10.1080/10383441.2014.1000218.

310 Art 3(d), CRPD.

Barsky BA & Stein MA 'The United Nations Convention on the Rights of Persons with Disabilities, neuroscience, and criminal legal capacity' (2023) 10/1 *Journal of Law and the Biosciences* 1. https://doi.org/10.1093/jlb/lsad010.
Bartlett P 'The United Nations Convention on the Rights of Persons with Disabilities and mental health law' (2012) 25/5 *Modern Law Review* 752. https://doi.org/10.1016/j.mppsy.2009.09.012.
Bell M 'Abolition: a new paradigm for reform' (2021) 46 *Law and Social Inquiry* 42. https://doi.org/10.1017/lsi.2020.21.
Bennet T 'An integrated model for criminal responsibility in action: how Swedish criminal law operates without an insanity defence' (2024) 35 *Criminal Law Forum* 276. https://doi.org/10.1007/s10609-024-09484-0.
Blackstone W *Commentaries on the laws of England*, Volume 4 (1850).
Blake GA et al. 'Special considerations to the assessment of fitness to stand trial in Australia' (2023) 30/5 *Psychiatry, Psychology and Law* 682. https://doi.org/10.1080/13218719.2022.2100839.
Broderic A *The long and winding road to equality and inclusion for persons with disabilities: the United Nations Convention on the Rights of Persons with disabilities* (2015).
Brown P 'Modernising fitness to plead' (2019a) 59 *Medical Science Law* 131. https://doi.org/10.1177/0025802419863937.
Brown P 'Unfitness to plead in England and Wales: historical development and contemporary dilemmas' (2019b) 59 *Medical Science Law* 187. https://doi.org/10.1177/0025802419856761.
Byrd R '"Punishment's twin": theorizing prisoner reentry for a politics of abolition' (2016) 43/1 *Social Justice* 1.
C v Sevenoaks Youth Court (2010) 1 All ER 735.
Commonwealth of Australia (CoA) *Royal commission into violence, abuse, neglect and exploitation of people with disability*. Final report – Volume 8, Criminal Justice and People with Disability (September 29 2023).
Costa Rica's 2016 Law No. 9379.
Crimes (Mental Impairment and Unfitness to be Tried) Act 1997 (VIC).
Crimes Act 1914 (Cth).
Criminal Code (NT) s 43C; Criminal Code (WA).
Criminal Code 2002 (ACT).
Criminal Code Act 1983 (NT).
Criminal Justice (Mental Impairment) Act 1999 (Tas).
Criminal Law (Mental Impairment) Act 2023.
Criminal Law Consolidation Act 1935 (SA).
Criminal Law Consolidation Act 1935 (SA).
Criminal Procedure (Mentally Impaired Persons) Act 2003 (NZ).
Criminal Procedure Act 51 of 1977.
Criminal Procedure Amendment Act 4 of 2017.
CRPD Committee General Comment 1: article 12: equal recognition before the law (2014) UN Doc CRPD/C/GC/1 dated 19 May 2014.
CRPD Committee *Guidelines on article 14 of the convention on the rights of persons with disabilities: the right to liberty and security of persons with disabilities* UNCRPD (2015).
CRPD Committee 2014c. Concluding observations on the initial report of New Zealand, 31 October CRPD/C/NZL/ CO/1.
CRPD Committee Concluding Observations on the Initial Report of Australia, 10th sess, 118th mtg, UN Doc CRPD/C/AUS/CO/1 (21 October 2013).
CRPD Committee Concluding observations on the initial report of Denmark, 12th sess, 169th mtg, UN Doc CRPD/C/DNK/CO/1 (30 October 2014).
CRPD Committee Concluding observations on the initial report of Ecuador, CRPD/C/ECU/CO/01 (27 October 2014).

CRPD Committee Concluding observations on the initial report of the Republic of Korea, 12th sess, UN Doc CRPD/C/KOR/CO/1 (29 October 2014).

Darjee R & Marsh T 'Arguments for the abolition of the defence of mental impairment' (2023) 30/1 *Psychiatry, Psychology and Law* 89. https://doi.org/10.1080/13218719.2022.2112103.

Davidson L 'From pipe dream to reality: a practical legal approach towards the global abolition of psychiatric coercion' in MA Stein et al. (eds) *Mental health, legal capacity, and human rights* (2021).

Dawson J & Szmukler G 'Fusion of mental health and incapacity legislation' (2006) 188 *British Journal of Psychiatry* 504. https://doi.org/10.1192/bjp.188.6.504.

Dawson J & Szmukler G 'The "fusion law" proposals and the CRPD' in MA Stein et al. (eds) *Mental health, legal capacity, and human rights* (2021). https://doi.org/10.1017/9781108979016.009.

De Vos NO v Minister of Justice and Constitutional Development (2015) SACR 217 (CC).

Degener T 'Disability in a human rights context' (2016) 5 *Laws* 35. https://doi.org/10.3390/laws5030035.

Department of Health 'Social services and public safety (Northern Ireland) and Department of Justice (Northern Ireland)' *Draft Mental Capacity Bill (NI)* Consultation Summary Report (2015).

Devandas-Aguilar C 'Report of Special Rapporteur on the rights of persons with disabilities' UNDoc. A/HRC/37/56, 12 December 2017.

Domański M & Lackoroński B (eds) *Models of Implementation of article 12 of the Convention on the Rights of Persons with Disabilities (CRPD): private and criminal law aspects* (2023).

Dusky v United States (1960) 362 US 402; 80 SCt, 788.

Eagle K & Ellis A 'The widening net of preventative detention and the unfit for trial' (2016) 90 *Australian Law Journal* 172.

Edgar R & Sapire H *African apocalypse: the story of Nontetha Nkwenkwe, a twentieth-century south African Prophet* (2000).

Edwards v Indiana (2008) 554 US 164.

European Convention for the Protection of Human Rights and Fundamental Freedoms (ECHR), 213 UNTS (entered into force on 3/09/1953).

Faretta v California (1975) 422 US 806.

Federal Constitutional Court (2016).

Fernandes de Oliveira v Portugal (2019) ECtHR.

Final Report of the Independent Review of the Mental Health Act 1983 'Modernising the mental health act'.

GAE v Western Australia (2011) EWCA Crim 443.

GAE v Western Australia (2015) WADC 5.

German Statement on the Draft General Comment on Article 12 CRPD. 20 February 2014. http://www.ohchr.org/Documents/HRBodies/CRPD/GC/FederalRepublicOfGermanyArt12.pdf (accessed April 18, 2015).

Gooding P & Bennet T 'The abolition of the insanity defence in Sweden and the United Nations Convention on the Rights of Persons with Disabilities: human rights brinksmanship or evidence it won't work?' (2018) 21 *New Criminal Law Review* 141.

Gooding P & Flynn E 'Querying the call to introduce mental capacity testing to mental health law: does the doctrine of necessity provide an alternative?' (2015) 4 *Laws* 266. https://doi.org/10.3390/laws4020245.

Gooding P & O'Mahony C 'Laws on unfitness to stand trial and the UN Convention on the Rights of Persons with Disabilities: comparing Reform in England, Wales, Northern Ireland and Australia' (2016) 44 *International Journal of Law, Crime and Justice* 122.

Gooding P et al. 'Supporting accused persons with cognitive disabilities to participate in criminal proceedings in Australia: avoiding the pitfalls of unfitness to stand trial laws' (2017a) 35/2 *Law in Context A Socio-Legal Journal* 73.

Gooding P et al. 'Unfitness to stand trial and the indefinite detention of persons with cognitive disabilities in Australia: human rights challenges and proposals for change' (2017b) 40 *Melbourne University Law Review* 863.
Grisso T *Evaluating competencies: forensic assessments and instruments* (2003).
Guidelines on the right to liberty and security of persons with disabilities, adopted September 2015.
Hale M *The history of the pleas of the Crown* (1736).
Harmon L 'Falling off the vine: legal fictions and the doctrine of substituted judgment' (1990) 100 *Yale Law Journal* 1.
Heffernan v The Queen (2005) 194 FLR 370.
Human Rights Committee, General comment 35: article 9 (Liberty and security of person), UN Doc. CCPR/C/GC/35 (2014).
Investigation and Testimony Procedural Act (Accommodations for Persons with Mental or Cognitive Disabilities) (2005).
Julie Ann Nicholson and Others v Timothy Knaggs and Others (2009) VSC 64.
Juma PO & Ngwena C 'Decolonizing African mental health laws: a case for Kenya' (2024) 68 *Journal of African Law* 73. https://doi.org/10.1017/S0021855323000311.
Kanter A *The development of disability rights under international law: from charity to human rights* (2015).
Karakatsanis A 'The punishment bureaucracy: how to think about criminal justice reform' (2019) 128 *Yale Law Journal Forum* 848.
Kessi S et al. 'Decolonizing African studies' (2020) 12 *Critical African Studies* 271. https://doi.org/10.1080/21681392.2020.1813413.
Kronick K 'Intellectual disability, mitigation and punishment' (2024) 65 *Boston College Law Review* 1618.
Law Commission *Unfitness to plead volume 1: report* (Report No 364, January 2016).
Law Commission *Unfitness to plead, vol 2: draft Legislation* (Law Com No 364, London 2016).
Law Commission (England and Wales) *Unfitness to plead* (Report No 364, 2016, vol 1, Law Commission Report).
Law Commission of England and Wales *Unfitness to plead: an issues paper* (2014).
Law Commission of Ontario *Legal capacity decision making and guardianship* (Discussion Paper, 2014).
Laws of Malawi Chapter 34.02, Mental Treatment Act 2005.
Mackay R & Brookbanks WJ (eds) *Fitness to plead: international and comparative perspectives* (2018).
Maher G 'Unfitness for trial in Scots law' in Mackay R & Brookbanks WJ (eds) *Fitness to plead: international and comparative perspectives* (2018).
Marcantonio v R (2016) EWCA Crim 14.
Martin W et al. *Achieving CRPD compliance: is the Mental Capacity Act of England and Wales compatible with the UN Convention on the Rights of Persons with Disabilities? If not, what next?* (Report, Essex Autonomy Project, 22 September 2014).
Mental Capacity Act (Northern Ireland) 2016 (NI Act).
Mental Health (Forensic Provisions) Act 1900 (NSW).
Mental Health (Forensic Provisions) Act 1900 (NSW).
Mental Health Act 2007 (NSW).
Mental Health Act 2013 (Tas).
Mental Health Act 2014 (Vic).
Mental Health Act 2014 (WA).
Mental Health Act 2015 (ACT).
Mental Health Act 2015 (ACT).
Mental Health Act 2016 (Qld).
Mental Health Amendment (Statutory Review) Act 2014 (NSW).
Mwewa, Kasote and Katontoka v The Attorney General and Zambia Agency for Persons with Disabilities (2017) ZMHC 77.

Neuman GL 'Divergent human rights approaches to capacity and consent' in MA Stein et al. (eds) *Mental health, legal capacity, and human rights* (2021) 56.
Nilsson A *Compulsory mental health interventions and the CRPD: minding equality* Hart Publishing (2021).
Office of the Chief Psychiatrist 'Review of the mental health act 2009' (Report, Department of Health and Aging (SA), 23 May 2014).
Owusu-Bempah A & Wortley N 'Unfit to plead or unfit to testify? R v Orr [2016] EWCA Crim 889' (2017) 80/6 *The Journal of Criminal Law* 391. https://doi.org/10.1177/0022018316670081.
Peru's Legislative Decree 1384.
Purohit and Moore v Gambia (2003) 'African Commission on Human and Peoples' Rights'.
R v Cain (2010) QCA 373.
R v Fisher (2011) 210 A Crim R 199.
R v Haines (2013) NSWSC 1609.
R v JG (2014) ACTSC 120.
R v Mathews (2013) QCA 203.
R v Muller (2013) ACTSC 154.
R v Rivkin (2004) 59 NSWLR 284.
Rooman v Belgium (2019) ECtHR.
Series L & Nilsson A 'Article 12 CRPD: equal recognition before the law' in I Bantekas et al. (eds) *The UN convention on the rights of persons with disabilities* (2018) 339.
Slobogin C 'Eliminating mental disability as a legal criterion in deprivation of liberty cases: the impact of the Convention on the Rights of Persons with Disability on the insanity defense, civil commitment, and competency law' (2015) 40 *International Journal of Law & Psychiatry* 36. https://doi.org/10.1016/j.ijlp.2015.04.011.
Stanford v UK (1994) ECtHR.
Szmukler G 'Offenders with a mental impairment under a 'fusion law': non-discrimination, treatment, public protection' (2020) 1 *International Journal of Mental Health and Capacity Law* 41. https://doi.org/10.19164/ijmhcl.26.1093.
UN General Assembly 'Convention on the Rights of Persons with Disabilities: resolution adopted by the General Assembly' 24 January 2007 UN Doc A/RES/61/106 (2007) (CRPD) adopted on 13 December 2006 (entered into force on 3 May 2008).
United Nations High Commissioner for Human Rights (UNHCHR) 'Thematic study on enhancing awareness and understanding of the Convention on the Rights of Persons with Disabilities' (47, U.N. Doc. A/HRC/10/48 (26 January 2009).
Victoria, Parliamentary Debates, Legislative Assembly, 12 March 2014, 689–691 (Ted Baillieu).
Victoria, Parliamentary Debates, Legislative Assembly, 19 September 1997, 185 (Jan Wade, Attorney-General).
Victorian Law Reform Commission Review of the Crimes (Mental Impairment and Unfitness to Be Tried) Act 1997 (Report 28 of 2014).
Weller P 'Legal capacity and access to justice: the right to participation in the CRPD' (2016) 5(1) *Laws* 13. https://doi.org/10.3390/laws5010013.
Westbrook AH "Mental health legislation and involuntary commitment in Nigeria: a call for reform" (2011) 10 *Washington University Global Studies Law Review* 397. https://doi.org/10.5897/IJPC2015.0317.
Williams JA 'Reassessing gender neutrality' (2020) 54/1 *Law and Society Review* 23. https://doi.org/10.1111/lasr.124.

9 Summary, conclusion, and recommendations

9.0 Introduction

This chapter draws conclusions and lessons to be learnt from the various strands of thought expressed in the preceding chapters. The chapter also makes recommendations for the reform of unfitness declarations in Kenya. The mere presence of current or past mental disability or treatment does not necessarily mean that a person is legally unfit. The social model of disability locates disability in the society, which create barriers that prevent disabled persons from fully participating in the community.[1] Although the social model has been a source of empowerment for disabled persons, it has several limitations, including obscuring material reality of impairment and variation in the construction and experience of disability identity. The other criticism is that the social model of disability is based on Euro-American global modernity, which is a form of neo-colonialism because of its emphasis on Western cultural hegemony.[2] In response to the social model's hegemonic understanding of disability which is based on Western values, this book draws from the Foucauldian and decolonial theories, which includes epistemic perspectives of disability from Global South countries. They also direct attention beyond barriers inhibiting the participation of disabled people towards the revelation and disruption of ableist foundations of mainstream institutions and laws.

The CRPD ushered in a paradigm shift towards addressing human rights violations of persons with psychosocial disabilities through the human rights approach. In Kenya, unfitness declarations do not exempt persons with psychosocial disabilities from criminal responsibility. Article 13 of the CRPD on access to justice addresses human rights of disabled persons, including persons with psychosocial disabilities in the courts. This is all the more relevant in light of the fact that the Kenyan judiciary has in recent times embarked on reinforcing the protection of persons with psychosocial disabilities in the criminal

1 TP Dirth & GA Adams 'Decolonial theory and disability studies: on the modernity/coloniality of ability' (2019) 7 *Journal of Social and Political Psychology* 266.
2 Dirth & Adams (n 1) 269.

DOI: 10.4324/9781003647102-9

justice system, thereby suggesting that there is a window of opportunity. In addition to the conclusions of this book, recommendations are made towards the introduction of procedural safeguards and alternative accommodation of persons with psychosocial disabilities who commit crimes under the CRPD. The recommendations seek to inform Kenyan best practice, based on the findings derived from the empirical study on factors of the unfitness declarations laws that lead to the limitation of persons with psychosocial disabilities' right to participation in the context of Kenya's criminal justice system.

9.1 Summary

Currently, it is not possible to enhance the right of participation in access to justice for persons with psychosocial disabilities in criminal proceedings by using the provisions of the Criminal Procedure Code. There is need for meaningful participation of persons with psychosocial disabilities in Kenya's justice sector, which means that they must be capable of understanding the proceedings. Participants stated,

> participation means full involvement in activities of daily living and that involves decision making and having ability to take control and ownership over the decisions that we make that we own the decision whether they make them . . . directly.[3]
>
> Physical presence in court alone . . . is not participation . . . what would be the value of their presence in court? Is it . . . for just ticking . . . that yes the accused was present but in fact the involvement in the process was almost zero. Their participation is just as important as any other person's participation and it has to be constructive participation in the sense that they must have some understanding.[4]

The parliament of Kenya, which has the highest political authority as per the Constitution, has not yet discharged its legislative duty with regard to the issue under consideration. The legislative organ does not also seem to have plans to revise the Code in the foreseeable future. Indeed, it is high time for Kenya to revise its Criminal Procedure Code and incorporate procedural rules that will be instrumental to realise the participation of persons with psychosocial disabilities in Kenya's criminal justice system.

The book examined sections 162 and 167 of Kenya's Criminal Procedure Code and confirmed the need to reform and remove the phenomena of unfitness declarations and put in place safeguards to protect the participation of persons with psychosocial disabilities. The study took an in-depth look at the historical foundations of unfitness declarations in Kenya. It also analysed the

3 FGD with NGO members on 19 April 2022.

4 FGD with defence counsels on 29 March 2022.

provisions of article 13 of the CRPD and found that unfitness declarations against persons with psychosocial disabilities violate the rights of persons with psychosocial disabilities. Persons with psychosocial disabilities are denied their right of access to justice in participation without any periodic review and without any considerations of alternative forms of accommodation.

The study revealed that there are no policy guidelines regarding unfitness declarations. The medical model of disability that is used in health care law has been translated into Kenya's criminal justice system. In practice, persons with psychosocial disabilities who are declared unfit are usually detained either in prison or in Mathare Hospital for care and protection. In *Hassan Hussein Yusuf v Republic*, the High Court held as follows:[5]

> A sick person's place is at the hospital and not in prison. I find section 167 of the Criminal Procedure code discriminative to people with mental illness for prescribing their detention to be in prison instead of a health facility and for the detention to be indeterminate. This offends articles 25 and 29 (f) of the Constitution.

Prison facilities in Kenya are not adequately equipped to offer the highest attainable standard of health to institutionalised persons with psychosocial disabilities. In Mathare Hospital, the conditions are appalling and most persons with psychosocial disabilities live under the constant threat of exploitation, violence, neglect, and abuse.[6] Further, Mathare Hospital houses persons with psychosocial disabilities who have been committed through both the civil and criminal process without any distinction. Equal measures are taken in respect of all persons with psychosocial disabilities and they all receive as much, or as little, treatment as any other, irrespective of their individual conditions.

The right to participation for persons with psychosocial disabilities will be better protected if reasonable accommodation is provided. The CRPD, Foucauldian, and decolonial legal scholars have accumulated a fund of knowledge on how persons with psychosocial disabilities right to participation can be protected. The nature of accommodations will differ depending on an individual's needs. The failure of the law to differentiate between the circumstances of different persons with psychosocial disabilities means that there are no special accommodations for their different needs.

Under Kenyan law it is mandatory for the trial to be postponed when a trial court makes an order that a person with psychosocial disability is unfit.[7] When a trial is postponed it means that persons with psychosocial disabilities will either be detained indefinitely until further orders from the president or

5 *Hussan Hussein Yusuf v Republic* [2016] eKLR.

6 F Kamundia 'Choice, support and inclusion: implementing article 19 of the CRPD in Kenya' (2013) 1 *Africa Disability Rights Yearbook* 55.

7 Criminal Procedure Code, secs 162.

released after depositing sufficient security.[8] The postponement of the trial is indefinite and subject only to a report which is prepared by the representative of the mental hospital or place where the person with psychosocial disability is being detained. While on the surface continuing proceedings against an accused person with psychosocial disability may seem categorically unfair, in reality a sound basis exists for allowing proceedings to continue, when they can, with appropriate safeguards.

According to Mégret, the concept of reasonable accommodation lies at the 'intersection of desirable and feasible' which combines an absolute and relative approach to ensure the realisation of participation rights of persons with psychosocial disabilities.[9] The absolute and relative approaches are meant to discourage states from eternally pushing reasonable accommodation under the guise of progressive realisation or making it conditional on the limits of the state's economic capacity.[10] Unfitness declaration laws do not provide safeguards and alternatives to ensure the participation of persons with psychosocial disabilities. To this extent, unfitness declaration laws in Kenya contribute to societal barriers for persons with psychosocial disabilities.

The inclusion of the president in Kenya's unfitness procedures defeats the separation of powers and the independence of the judiciary.[11] Article 160(1) of the Constitution provides that in the exercise of judicial authority, the judiciary shall only be subject to the Constitution and the law and not subject to the control or direction of any person or authority. Furthermore, there is no procedure to apply for the continuance of the trial in case the trial court or the president fails to make any further orders involving a detained person with psychosocial disabilities. The vesting of such discretionary powers to the president is counter-productive since it could lead to abuse, not to mention the lack of the necessary qualifications in dealing with mental health issues. The operation of section 162 and 167 is clearly archaic, cumbersome, and bureaucratic.[12] This was affirmed in *Nyawa Mwajowa v Republic*[13] as follows:

> [W]hile we understand the basis of the practice of sidestepping the legal requirement involving the Cabinet Secretary and the President to be a desire to speed up the trial or conclusion of the issue of the accused persons

8 As above.

9 F Mégret 'The disabilities convention: towards a holistic concept of rights' (2008) 12 *International Journal of Human Rights* 270.

10 S Raha & S Sengupta 'Rights of women with disabilities under Indian legislations' (2018) 14 *Socio-Legal Review* 196.

11 Article 48 Initiative (A48), Arthur's Dream Autism Trust (ADAT) & Southern Africa Litigation Centre 'An exploratory study of the interaction between the criminal justice system and persons with intellectual and psychosocial disabilities in Nairobi, Kenya' September 2021, 57.

12 African Policing Civilian Oversight Forum (APCOF) and the National Gender and Equality Commission (NGEC) *Pre-trial detention for persons with disabilities in correctional institutions* African Policing Civilian Oversight Forum (2017) 19.

13 *Nyawa Mwajowa v Republic* (2016) eKLR.

> mental status which is otherwise delayed by the bureaucracy of the two offices, we must emphasize that these are requirement of the law in respect of which no office can claim to be too busy. The situation in our opinion lies not in short-circuiting the requirements of the law but in insisting that the concerned offices discharge their legal duties with due dispatch as expected under the Constitution and the Criminal Procedure Code.

Sections 162 and 167 of the Criminal Procedure Code offer no alternative forms of accommodation to ensure the participation of persons with psychosocial disabilities. Further, there is no periodic re-evaluation for persons with psychosocial disabilities whose trials have been postponed.

9.2 Recommendation

In view of the difficulties in ensuring the participation in access to justice of persons with psychosocial disabilities, this section provides recommendations drawn from the issues discussed and from the findings of the empirical component of this study. The reform agenda for Kenya's unfitness declaration laws involves two intersecting theories, Foucauldian and decolonial, whose aim is to strengthen the social model's concept of reasonable accommodation. The recommendations emphasise the need for legislative enactment and reform not only to promote the participation in access to justice of persons with psychosocial disabilities but also to remove the barriers inhibiting the agency of persons with psychosocial disabilities.

9.2.1 Reforms relating to the procedure of unfitness declaration in Kenya

Participation under sections 162 and 167 is based on the accused persons' rudimentary understanding of the trial process. The sections do not stipulate at what stage unfitness should be raised. Once an accused person with psychosocial disability is declared unfit, the courts have no option but to stop the proceedings. If the disability is permanent, a finding of unfitness means that the accused person with psychosocial disability can never be brought to trial. Often, the accused person with psychosocial disability is confined for life. Proceedings are adjourned even without the consent of the accused person with psychosocial disability. Furthermore, the threshold for unfitness is a low one thus resulting in limiting the participation of disabled persons in Kenya. There is no statutory requirement that the accused's capacity to participate effectively in the criminal proceedings be tested as part of the test for unfitness to stand trial. It is not also clear who should diagnose for unfitness to plead. A literal reading suggests that the trier of fact is to diagnose and form an opinion. In practice, doctors conduct mental assessments tests to determine the decisional capacity of the accused person with disability to stand trial. Generally, the doctor's role in this process is to provide the court with a summary of an accused person's skills, abilities, and deficits that may relate to their overall mental capacity.[14] The court would then consider the doctor's evidence along with other relevant information before deciding on the accused person with disability's competency

The criteria doctors use to determine whether an accused person with psychosocial disability is fit to plead is not stipulated in the law and this was made clear during the empirical research.[15] Generally, doctors adopt a mixture of functional and status approach, which presumes that persons with psychosocial disabilities are unfit and cannot effectively make decisions based on the appreciation of choices and weighing of subsequent consequences. The fact that a person has a psychosocial disability is not synonymous to being incapable of following a trial or giving evidence or instructing counsel or generally participating effectively in a trial.[16] Psychosocial disability does not necessarily affect basic cognitive functions such as understanding evidence or entering a plea in the same way as learning disability.[17] Legal capacity should not be determined by mental capacity.

Medical evidence on assessments is rarely contested suggesting a medico-legal approach to unfitness, where judicial officers simply rubber-stamp psychiatric opinions without exercising independent judicial decision-making. The opinions should be scrutinised for undue influence or improper considerations such as equating unfitness with characteristics of the accused person or diagnoses of mental disability, instead of considering the degree of participation, which is the main thing the legal profession is really concerned about.[18] When assessing the mental capacity of an accused person with psychosocial disability, just like an age assessment, a holistic approach needs to be undertaken, factoring in a wide range of information, including not just medical opinion but a variety of other information and circumstances.[19] This is not the case in Kenya. For instance, in *Republic v SE*[20] where SE was facing a charge of murder, the mental assessment report merely stated that he was not mentally fit to plead and required treatment.[21] In a similar fashion, the subsequent report, which was filed into court by Mathare Mental Hospital simply stated that the accused

14 D Miller 'Dementia and competency in United States courtrooms: a case law review' https://academicworks.cuny.edu/cgi/viewcontent.cgi?article=1157&context=jj_etds (accessed 10 September 2021) 13.

15 Chapter 7.

16 P Brown 'Unfitness to plead in England and Wales: historical development and contemporary dilemmas' (2019) 59 *Medicine, Science and the Law* 197.

17 As above.

18 G Ferguson 'Unfit to stand trial: Canadian law and practice' in R Mackay & WJ Brookbanks (eds) *Fitness to plead: international and comparative perspectives* Oxford: Oxford University Press (2018) 119.

19 *Kevin Kiprotich Amos alias Rotich v Republic* (2016) eKLR.

20 *Republic v SE* (2017) eKLR.

21 *Republic v SE*, the mental assessment report provided as follows: S was accompanied to hospital by a police officer for mental assessment. He is wearing torn and dirty civilian clothes. He is able to respond to most question asked, though some responses are inappropriate. His mood

had become capable of making a defence.[22] The effect of mental assessment reports is to deprive persons with psychosocial disabilities of their right to participation and instead detain them at the president's pleasure indefinitely. Weller has also argued that mental assessment tests offend the principle of indirect discrimination because they have a disproportionate impact on persons with psychosocial disabilities.[23]

Further tensions also exist between the CRPD and unfitness declarations. Sections 162 and 167 do not mirror the CRPD's expectations. Rather than being excluded on the basis of a lack of mental capacity, the CRPD recommends for the provision of appropriate information and support.[24] The CRPD Committee has stated that

> [D]eclarations of unfitness to stand trial and the detention of persons based on that declaration [are] contrary to article 14 of the Convention since it deprives the person of his or her right to due process and safeguards that are applicable to every defendant.[25]

The CRPD Committee implies that separate processes for disabled persons in criminal law is prohibited.[26] Although such policy pronouncements by UN treaty bodies, in the form of General Comments or recommendations are not binding international law, they aid in the interpretations of treaties and guide national policies in a rights-affirming direction.[27]

Nevertheless, the CRPD Committees' views on the violations of the rights of disabled persons to due process following unfitness declarations and subsequent detentions have been criticised as wrongheaded and potentially destructive.[28] Critics have argued that the CRPD Committee's Comments violate the dignity of persons with psychosocial disabilities by forcing them to trial even when they are not competent to consult with counsel or understand the

---

is low. He has been having auditory hallucinations. He lacks insight. He is not fit to stand trial. He will benefit from treatment (antipsychotics) as he is mentally unstable.

22 *Republic v SE*.

23 P Weller 'Legal capacity and access to justice: the right to participation in the CRPD' (2026) 5 *Laws* 18.

24 Weller (n 23) 44.

25 CRPD Committee, Report of the Committee on the Rights of Persons with Disabilities on Its Twelfth Session, 12th sess, UN Doc CRPD/C/12/2 (5 November 2014) annex IV 15.

26 P Gooding & T Bennet 'The abolition of the insanity defense in Sweden and the United Nations Convention on the Rights of Persons with Disabilities: human rights brinksmanship or evidence it does not work?' (2017) (Forthcoming) *New Criminal Law Review* 6.

27 A Wolman 'Abortion in Korea: a human rights perspective on the current debate over enforcement of the laws prohibiting abortion' (2010) 9 *Journal of International Business & Law* 163.

28 M Perlin 'God said to Abraham/kill me a son: why the insanity defense and the incompetency status are compatible with and required by the Convention on the Rights of Persons with Disabilities and basic principles of therapeutic jurisprudence' (2017) 54 *Criminal Law Review* 480.

proceedings against them.[29] Trials of persons who have been declared unfit violates every basic tenet of due process and any reform that makes it more likely that there will be an increase in such trials should be rejected.[30] Instead of abolishing unfitness declarations, some legal commentators have called for reforms that are geared towards promoting 'a more distinctly relational approach to the practice of law . . . which emphasises psychological wellness over adversarial triumphalism'.[31]

Institutional structures and processes should be altered to accommodate persons with psychosocial disability.[32] Sections 162 and 167 are based on the medical model of disability which views disability as an antiphony of everyday life which must be pensioned off and relegated to medical institutions.[33] The sections portray persons with psychosocial disabilities as being incapable of performing tasks which are considered 'normal and hold that disability can be used as an excuse to restrict or deny someone's rights and that disabled people are incapable of making important decisions about their lives'.[34] The social model of disability emphasises inclusion and participation.[35] However, it has very little to say about mental disability since its main focus is on physical disabilities and the removal of barriers created by mainstream society in order to ensure effective participation of disabled persons in the society.[36]

9.2.2 Reforms relating to agency

The Foucauldian theory plays an important role in enabling agency and participation of persons with psychosocial disabilities in access to justice. Unfitness declaration structures in Kenya are built upon assumptions that persons with psychosocial disabilities are not normal. However, Foucault, seeks to enable a person with psychosocial disabilities to have agency despite their possession of differing characteristics, which, in interaction with the justice system, might hinder and prevent participation in access to justice. Unfitness declarations are based on ableist's notion of ability according to Foucault's theory. The system of ableism is made up of expectations about ability, which includes stereotypes, prejudice, and discrimination towards disabled persons.[37] The

29 Perlin (n 28) 487.

30 Perlin (n 28) 489.

31 W Brookbanks 'Therapeutic jurisprudence: conceiving an ethical framework' (2001) 8 *Journal of Law & Medicine* 329–330.

32 As above.

33 P Juma 'Right to self-representation for people with mental disabilities in Kenya's courts' (2019) 7 *African Disability Rights Yearbook* 86.

34 DARU 'Understanding models of disability' https://www.daru.org.au/wp/wp-content/uploads/2019/03/Human-rights-info-sheet-for-website.pdf (accessed 13 August 2021).

35 Weller (n 23) 45.

36 DARU (n 34).

37 JRR Freer 'The tripartite intervention: breaking down attitudinal barriers in education' (2021) *Journal of Disability Studies in Education* 2.

expectations are usually very low and if acted upon often impact negatively on the experiences that disabled persons have in society, including within the justice sector. Unfitness declarations are a product of the medicalised conception of disability and contradicts the guarantees provided under article 12 of the CRPD, which recognises the ability of all persons, without distinction, to exercise legal capacity.[38]Accordingly, unfitness declaration laws should be reformed to mirror article 12 of the CRPD which indicates a departure from capacity-based declarations, which distinguishes between persons with capacity and those without thus limiting the participation of persons with psychosocial disabilities in the criminal process.[39]

Reforms ensuring the agency of persons with psychosocial disabilities can take multiple forms. They can occur either at the individual, institutional, or cultural levels. At the individual and cultural level, unfitness declarations are characterised by poor attitudes towards disability, which can present barriers for disabled persons, including persons with psychosocial disabilities.[40] Unfitness declaration proceedings are based on ableists negative perceptions of disability which frames all persons with psychosocial disabilities as abject victims of a 'personal tragedy' that need protection.[41] In Foucault's words, unfitness declaration laws subjects persons with psychosocial disabilities to control and dependence.[42] As part of ableist laws, unfitness declarations reify and codify mental disability in terms of dependency and victimhood. They give persons with psychosocial disabilities an identity of social injury.[43] To remedy these barriers at the individual and cultural level, unfitness declaration reforms should aim at ensuring that the law recognises the agency and interdependence between persons with psychosocial disabilities and justice system actors. At the institutional level, unfitness declaration reforms should urge for prohibition of discrimination and acceptance of diversity by justice system actors.

9.2.3 Reforms relating to the persistence of coloniality in Kenya's unfitness declaration laws

The system of unfitness declarations is also a form of coloniality that continues to influence and oppress persons with psychosocial disabilities long after

38 DM McNamara 'The insanity defence, indefinite detention and the UN Convention on the Rights of Persons with Disabilities' https://www.researchgate.net/publication/341264966_The_Insanity_Defence_Indefinite_Detention_and_the_UN_Convention_on_the_Rights_of_Persons_with_Disabilities (accessed 20 August 2021) 9.

39 McNamara (n 38) 9.

40 As above.

41 A Anders 'Foucault and "the right to life": from technologies of normalisation to societies of control' https://dsq-sds.org/article/view/3340/3268 (accessed 8 August 2021).

42 M Foucault 'The subject and power' in P Rainbow & N Rose (eds) *The Essential Foucault* (1994) 130.

43 As above.

colonialism ended.[44] Unfitness declarations are symbols of exclusion, which have been affirmed as sad necessities of signification.[45] For a long time, persons with psychosocial disabilities have internalised this form oppression and have become part of it.[46] The coloniality of being is what has led to persons with psychosocial disabilities being labelled unfit.[47] The coloniality of knowledge is perpetuated by Kenya's criminal justice system in its reliance of the colonial doctrine of unfitness declaration, which create a separate and lesser form of justice for people with psychosocial disabilities.[48] This knowledge is connected to the power relations that define and maintain unfitness systems and to the grid of power that created and legitimised them, forming a regime of truth.[49] Prior to colonialism, the day-to-day activities of native Africans were governed by cultural norms as opposed to state laws.[50] Since Africans did not identify with any legal system, social order was maintained through informal sources.

The advent of the colonialists transformed the way social order was being maintained by Africans. Colonialists imposed the common law system which as Oliver Wendell Holmes said, was not a reduction of the dictates of nature and logic into words but merely a means of achieving certain ends, designed, and implemented by men according to their desires.[51] Unfitness declarations and the non-participation of persons with psychosocial disabilities were imposed on Kenya by the colonialists on the paternalistic notions of protection. At worst, persons with psychosocial disabilities who are declared unfit to stand trial are subject to indefinite detention, including being detained for longer than if they had been convicted and sentenced in the first place.[52]

Decolonial work in Kenya requires justice actors to cease from replicating unfitness declaration power that exclude persons with psychosocial disabilities from the criminal process. The reforms suggested by participants during the empirical study were aligned with the decolonial theory which aims to empower persons with psychosocial disabilities. Majority of the respondents agreed that persons with psychosocial disabilities have the ability to participate

44 S Ndlovu 'Obstacles and opportunities for students with disabilities in entering and in preparation to graduate into professions in higher learning: the case of a university in South Africa' PhD Thesis, University of South Africa, 2016, 136.

45 R McRuer 'Composing bodies; or, de-composition: queer theory, disability studies, and alternative corporealities' (2004) 24 *JAC* 57.

46 Ndlovu (n 44) 137.

47 Ndlovu (n 44) 138.

48 Ndlovu (n 44) 141.

49 M Dubois 'The governance of the third world: a Foucauldian perspective on power relations in development' (1991) 16 *Alternatives: Global, Local, Political* 7.

50 MA Edwards 'The alignment of law and norms: of mirrors, bulwarks, and pressure valves' (2015) 10 *Faculty Scholarship* 22.

51 Edwards (n 50) 24.

52 P Gooding et al. 'Unfitness to stand trial and the indefinite detention of persons with cognitive disabilities in Australia: human rights challenges and proposals for change' (2017) 40 *Melbourne University Law Review* 819.

effectively in access to justice through the use of accommodations.[53] To emphasise the need for accommodations, one participant stated as follows:

> if accommodations are given . . . provisions of legal representation and the various accommodations . . . the use of intermediary for example the constitution provides for use of intermediaries . . . . And with the necessary aids, with necessary accommodations . . . in courts and outside they are able to communicate they are able to . . . answer questions sometimes and it's so just a matter of how we treat them.[54]

Most of the respondents emphasised legal aid, diversion, ADR, procedural accommodations, and assistive technology as some of the methods that may be used to facilitate the participation of persons with psychosocial disabilities in Kenya's justice sector. Participants in the FGD session also agreed that legal aid and interpreters enhance the participation of persons with psychosocial disabilities in Kenya's criminal courts. Moreover, ADR, diversionary and traditional mechanisms with enhanced emphasis on agency and human rights allows accused persons with psychosocial disabilities to have an alternative mode of dispute resolution and enables them to be active participants in the proceedings because they are oriented towards their needs.

However, the law should not restrict itself to only a little set of accommodations, but rather allow court discretion on an individual basis. The fact that a psychosocial disability is severe does not excuse the state from its obligation to provide reasonable accommodation. Apart from reasonable accommodation the state also has the duty to investigate alternative models that will ensure the participation in access to justice for persons with severe psychosocial disabilities as discussed in Chapter 5. The decision as to which accommodations should be provided to a person with psychosocial disability during criminal proceedings should be predetermined at the beginning of the trial. In determining which accommodations are appropriate, a judicial officer should give primary consideration to the accommodation requested by the person with psychosocial disability. However, the court should not be limited to the requested accommodation. The court's decision to this effect may also be based on expert witness testimony or advocacy groups that can offer guidance as to the reasonableness and availability of accommodations for a particular person with psychosocial disability in all cases, including in situation where the accused person is unable to make a request due to the severity of the psychosocial disability.

9.2.4 Reforms relating to abolition of unfitness declarations

This reform method focuses largely on replacing the current unfitness declaration system with participatory procedures that apply to everyone. Accused

53 See Chapter 6, Table 7.11.
54 FGD with prosecutors on 24 March 2022.

persons with psychosocial disabilities should be subjected to the usual adjournment rules for reasonable cause under section 205 of the Criminal Procedure Code, that apply to non-disabled persons but on account of limited degree of participation. The test thus, should be one of meaningful participation rather than disability or decision-making capacity. This will help reduce the level of stigmatisation against accused persons with psychosocial disabilities since it is not disability-based. The adjournment should be for 15 to 30 days depending on whether the defendant is in custody or out on bail respectively. However, the accused person with psychosocial disability and the prosecutor should be allowed to consent to a longer period where there are compelling circumstances warranting an extension of time.

The period will allow the state to conduct a needs assessment. The latter can be done by either a psychiatrist, clinical psychologist, registered medical practitioner, or a panel of mental health professionals for offence involving serious violence such as murder or rape. The state and the accused person with psychosocial disabilities will be required to identify any obstacle to effective participation and appropriate support measures that may assist in ensuring trial participation. The accused person, however, should not be compelled to cooperate with the assessment team especially, if he or she chooses to remain silent. Where an accused person with psychosocial disability is found to be able to participate if given access to reasonable or procedural adjustments such as, the use of interpreters, intermediaries, lawyers, social workers, or friends, the trial should proceed. If not, the criminal jurisdiction of the court should come to an end with the court making an order either quashing the charges or dismissing the indictment without deciding on the guilt of the accused person with psychosocial disability.

A trial of the facts or disposition hearing should then be conducted by a court or review board for purposes of making a disposition order and of satisfying itself as to what *actus reus*,[55] if any, an accused committed, as opposed to making a finding of guilt. During this hearing, regard should be had to, a) the strength of the evidence against the accused, b) the nature of the alleged offence and the alleged circumstances of its commission, c) the accused person's needs, d) possibility of reintegration into the society, and e) self/public safety. The burden of proof for this inquiry should be on a balance of probabilities. Three possible disposition options should be available, namely, 1) an absolute discharge, 2) a supervision order either through support programmes or in a safe, therapeutic environment, rather than detention, or 3) a custody order, with or without restrictions. Where conditions are imposed, procedures should be put in place so as to address instances of breach and, where appropriate, impose sanctions. However, the accused person with psychosocial disability should not be required to submit to any treatment unless the court orders otherwise.

55 Guilty act.

As for custody orders, they should only apply where it is shown by the state, on a balance of probabilities, that there are reasonable grounds that the accused persons with psychosocial disabilities if released, will pose a threat to themselves or others. Such detention orders, however, should not act as automatic orders for treatment. Medication should only be imposed with the consent of the accused person with psychosocial disability or with the court's permission. As regards the period of detention, the proposal is that it should not exceed the period which the court determines the person would have been detained if convicted of the offence charged or two years as per *R v SOM*, whichever is shorter. As for offences punishable by life, the cap should be life. Both periods should, however, be subject to periodic reviews by a review board, composed of a lawyer, a psychiatrist, and a community member such as a social worker within a specified period of time, in accordance with the decision in *R v SOM*. The review should be thorough and include a hearing, with availability of provisions permitting the institutionalised person to challenge orders for commitment between automatic reviews. Subject to some limitations, it is recommended that hearings before a review board should be open to the public, be inquisitorial rather than adversarial, and operate somewhat more informally than courts. Their decisions should be recorded, must be supported by reasons, and appealable directly to the Court of Appeal.

References

African Policing Civilian Oversight Forum (APCOF) and the National Gender and Equality Commission (NGEC) *Pre-trial detention for persons with disabilities in correctional institutions* African Policing Civilian Oversight Forum (2017).

Anders A 'Foucault and "the right to life": from technologies of normalisation to societies of control' https://dsq-sds.org/article/view/3340/3268 (accessed 8 August 2021).

Article 48 Initiative (A48), Arthur's Dream Autism Trust (ADAT) and Southern Africa Litigation Centre 'An exploratory study of the interaction between the criminal justice system and persons with intellectual and psychosocial disabilities in Nairobi, Kenya' September 2021.

Brookbanks W 'Therapeutic jurisprudence: conceiving an ethical framework' (2001) 8 *Journal of Law & Medicine* 329.

Brown P 'Unfitness to plead in England and Wales: historical development and contemporary dilemmas' (2019) 59 *Medicine, Science and the Law* 197. https://doi.org/10.1177/0025802419856761.

Criminal Procedure Code, Chapter 75 of 1930.

CRPD Committee 'Report of the Committee on the Rights of Persons with Disabilities on its twelfth session, 12th sess' UN Doc CRPD/C/12/2 (5 November 2014) annex IV 15.

DARU 'Understanding models of disability' https://www.daru.org.au/wp/wp-content/uploads/2019/03/Human-rights-info-sheet-for-website.pdf (accessed 13 August 2021).

Dirth TP & Adams GA 'Decolonial theory and disability studies: on the modernity/coloniality of ability' (2019) 7 *Journal of Social and Political Psychology* 266. https://doi.org/10.5964/jspp.v7i1.762.

Dubois M 'The governance of the third world: a Foucauldian perspective on power relations in development' (1991) 16 *Alternatives: Global, Local, Political* 7.

Edwards MA 'The alignment of law and norms: of mirrors, bulwarks, and pressure valves' (2015) 10 *Faculty Scholarship* 22.

Foucault M 'The subject and power' in Rainbow P & Rose N (eds) *The essential Foucault* (1994).

Freer JRR 'The tripartite intervention: breaking down attitudinal barriers in education' (2021) *Journal of Disability Studies in Education* 2. https://doi.org/10.1163/25888803-bja10006

Gooding P & Bennet T 'The abolition of the insanity defense in Sweden and the United Nations Convention on the Rights of Persons with Disabilities: human rights brinksmanship or evidence it does not work?' (2017) 21/1 *New Criminal Law Review: An International and Interdisciplinary Journal* 6. https://doi.org/10.1525/nclr.2018.21.1.141.

Gooding P et al. 'Unfitness to stand trial and the indefinite detention of persons with cognitive disabilities in Australia: human rights challenges and proposals for change' (2017) 40 *Melbourne University Law Review* 819.

Hussan Hussein Yusuf v Republic (2016) eKLR.

Juma P 'Right to self-representation for people with mental disabilities in Kenya's courts' (2019) 7 *African Disability Rights Yearbook* 86. https://doi.org/10.29053/2413–7138/2019/v7a4.

Kamundia E 'Choice, support and inclusion: implementing article 19 of the CRPD in Kenya' (2013) 1 *Africa Disability Rights Yearbook* 55.

Kevin Kiprotich Amos alias Rotich v Republic (2016) eKLR.

McNamara DM 'The insanity defence, indefinite detention and the UN Convention on the Rights of Persons with Disabilities' https://www.researchgate.net/publication/341264966_The_Insanity_Defence_Indefinite_Detention_and_the_UN_Convention_on_the_Rights_of_Persons_with_Disabilities (accessed 20 August 2021).

McRuer R 'Composing bodies; or, de-composition: queer theory, disability studies, and alternative corporealities' (2004) 24 *JAC* 57.

Mégret F 'The disabilities convention: towards a holistic concept of rights' (2008) 12 *International Journal of Human Rights* 270. https://doi.org/10.1080/13642980801954363.

Miller D 'Dementia and competency in United States courtrooms: a case law review' https://academicworks.cuny.edu/cgi/viewcontent.cgi?article=1157&context=jj_etds (accessed 10 September 2021) 13.

Ndlovu S 'Obstacles and opportunities for students with disabilities in entering and in preparation to graduate into professions in higher learning: the case of a university in South Africa' PhD Thesis, University of South Africa, 2016.

Nyawa Mwajowa v Republic (2016) eKLR.

Perlin M 'God said to Abraham/kill me a son: why the insanity defense and the incompetency status are compatible with and required by the Convention on the Rights of Persons with Disabilities and basic principles of therapeutic jurisprudence' (2017) 54 *Criminal Law Review* 480. https://doi.org/10.2139/ssrn.2683480.

Raha S & Sengupta S 'Rights of women with disabilities under Indian legislations' (2018) 14 *Socio-Legal Review* 196. https://doi.org/10.55496/LVON2936.

Republic v SE (2017) eKLR.

Weller P 'Legal capacity and access to justice: the right to participation in the CRPD' (2026) 5 *Laws* 18. https://doi.org/10.3390/laws5010013.

Wolman A 'Abortion in Korea: a human rights perspective on the current debate over enforcement of the laws prohibiting abortion' (2010) 9 *Journal of International Business & Law* 163.

Index

Note: Page numbers in *italics* indicate a figure, page numbers in **bold** indicate a table, and page numbers followed by an 'n' indicate a note on the corresponding page.

Made in the USA
Las Vegas, NV
19 September 2026

918ca71b-745a-4556-9454-8fb292aa6d65R02